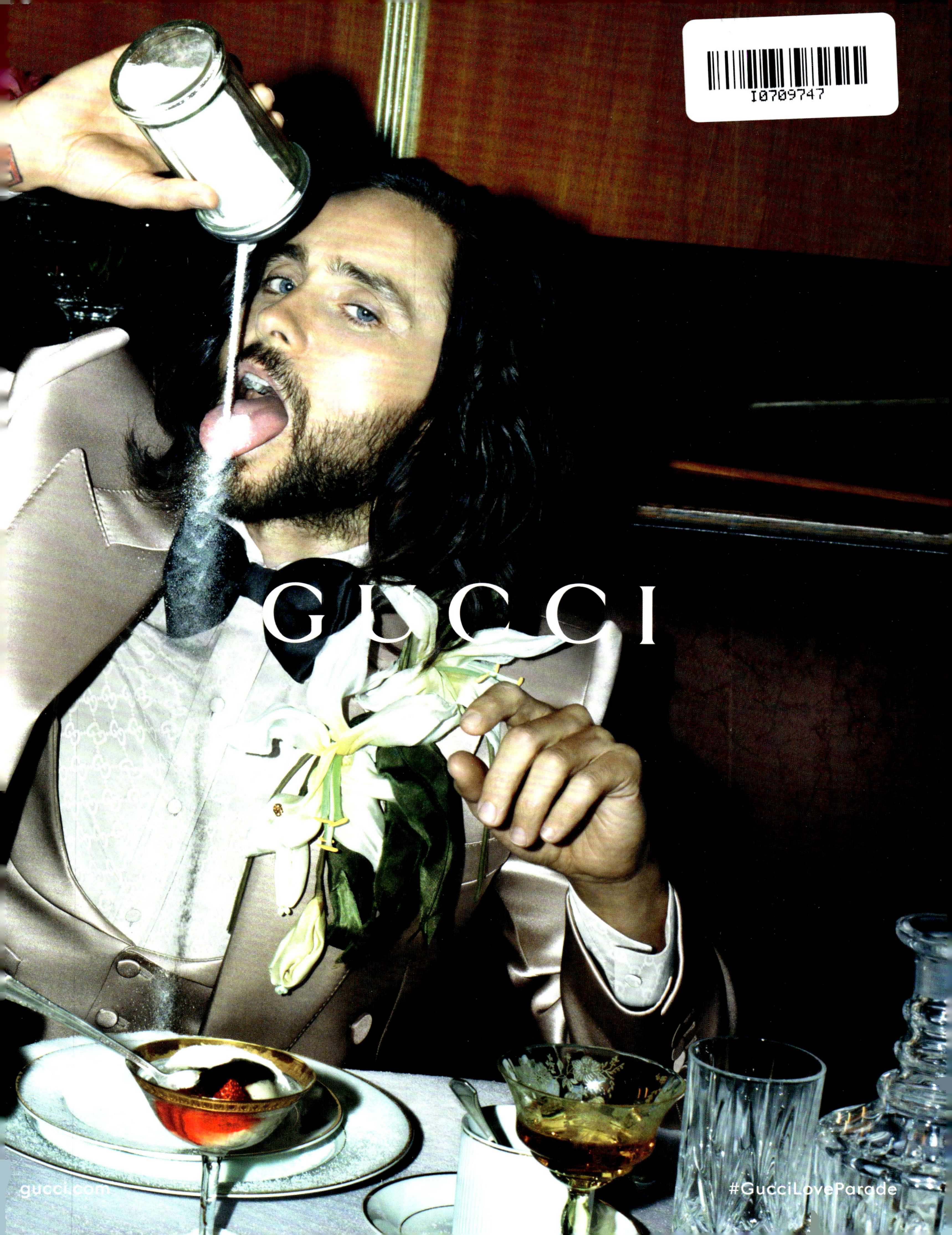
I0709747
GUCCI
gucci.com
#GucciLoveParade

Summer 2022
Sleepwalking

Front cover:
**Emila Medková, *Vodopád
vlasů* (Hair waterfall),
from the series *Stínohry*
(Shadowplays) (detail),
1949–50**
© Eva Kosáková Medková
(See page 48)

**Opposite:
Maja Daniels, *Lorena,
Mervelier*, 2021**
Courtesy the artist
(See page 90)

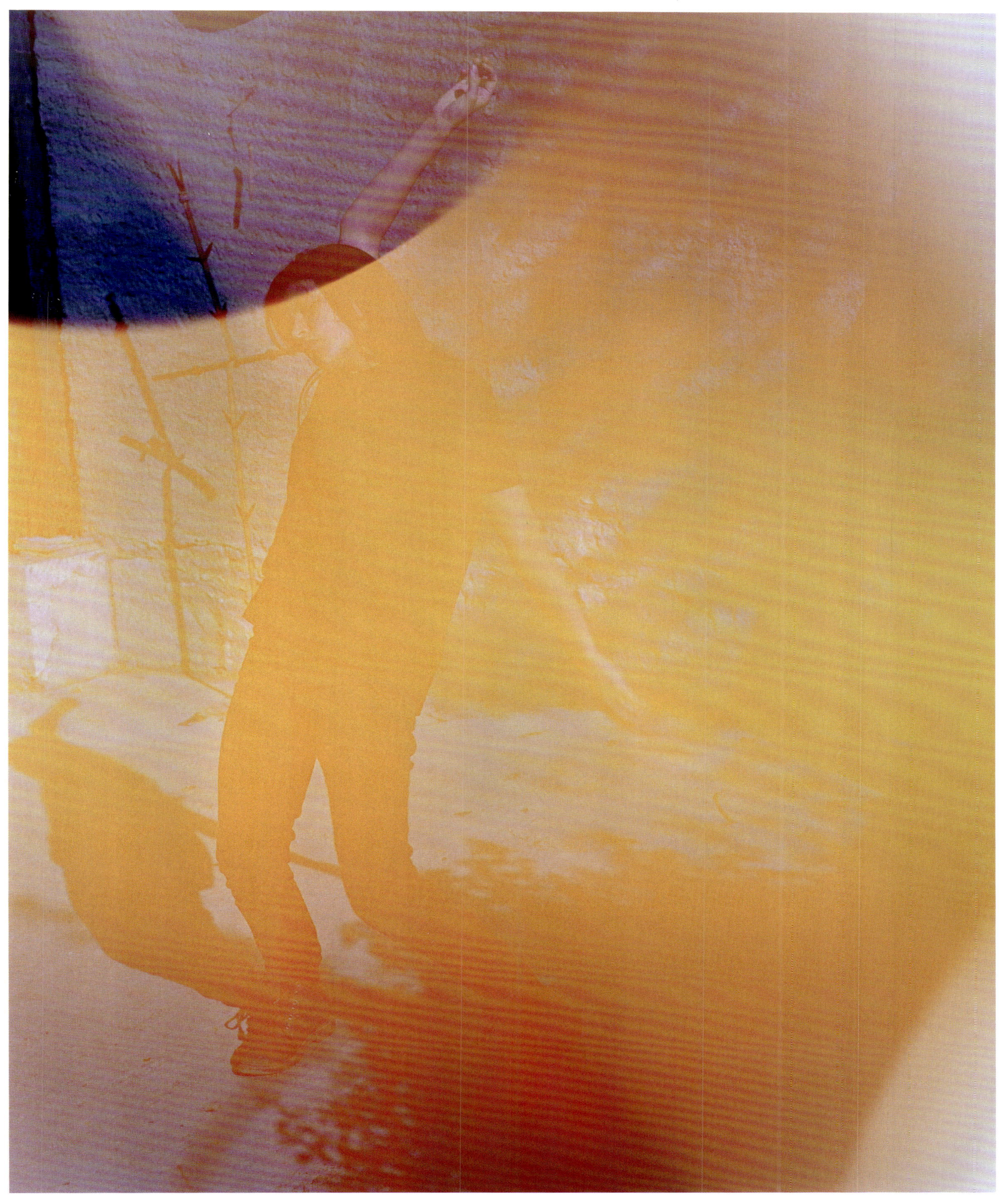

aperture

The Magazine of Photography and Ideas

Aperture, a not-for-profit foundation, connects the photo community and its audiences with the most inspiring work, the sharpest ideas, and with each other—in print, in person, and online.

Aperture (ISSN 0003-6420) is published quarterly, in spring, summer, fall, and winter, at 548 West 28th Street, 4th Floor, New York, N.Y. 10001. In the United States, a one-year subscription (four issues) is $75; a two-year subscription (eight issues) is $124. In Canada, a one-year subscription is $95. All other international subscriptions are $105 per year. Visit aperture.org to subscribe. Single copies may be purchased at $24.95 for most issues. Subscribe to the *Aperture Digital Archive* at aperture.org/archive. Periodicals postage paid at New York and additional offices. Postmaster: Send address changes to *Aperture*, P.O. Box 3000, Denville, N.J. 07834. Address queries regarding subscriptions, renewals, or gifts to: *Aperture* Subscription Service, 866-457-4603 (U.S. and Canada), or email custsvc_aperture@fulcoinc.com.

Newsstand distribution in the U.S. is handled by CMG. For international distribution, contact Central Books, centralbooks.com. Other inquiries, email orders@aperture.org or call 212-505-5555.

Become a Member of Aperture to take your interest in and knowledge of photography further. With an annual tax-deductible gift of $250, membership includes a complimentary subscription to *Aperture* magazine, discounts on Aperture's award-winning publications, a special limited-edition gift, and more. To join, visit aperture.org/join, or contact membership@aperture.org.

Library of Congress Catalog Card No: 58-30845.

ISBN 978-1-59711-525-4

Printed in Turkey by Ofset Yapimevi

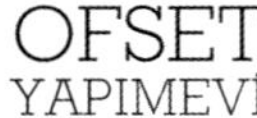

Support has been provided by members of *Aperture*'s Magazine Council: The Kanakia Foundation, Jon Stryker and Slobodan Randjelović, Susan and Thomas Dunn, and Michael W. Sonnenfeldt, MUUS Collection. Additional support is provided in part by the New York City Department of Cultural Affairs in partnership with the City Council.

Aperture Foundation's programs are made possible in part by the New York State Council on the Arts with the support of the Office of the Governor and the New York State Legislature.

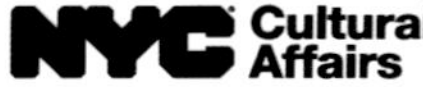 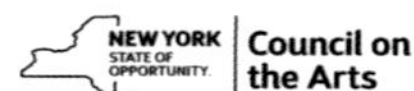

Editor
Michael Famighetti

Guest Editor
Alec Soth

Senior Managing Editor
Brendan Embser

Assistant Editor
Eli Cohen

**Contributing Editors,
The PhotoBook Review**
Samantha Marlow, Lesley A. Martin

Copy Editors
Hilary Becker, Donna Ghelerter

Production Director
Minjee Cho

Production Manager
Andrea Chlad

Press Supervisor
Ali Taptık

Art Direction, Design & Typefaces
A2/SW/HK, London

Chief Operating Officer
Dana Triwush
magazine@aperture.org

Director of Corporate Partnerships
Isabelle Friedrich McTwigan
212-946-7118
imctwigan@aperture.org

Advertising
Elizabeth Morina
917-691-2608
emorina@aperture.org

**Executive Director,
Aperture Foundation**
Sarah Meister

Minor White, Editor (1952–1974)

Michael E. Hoffman, Publisher and Executive Director (1964–2001)

aperture.org

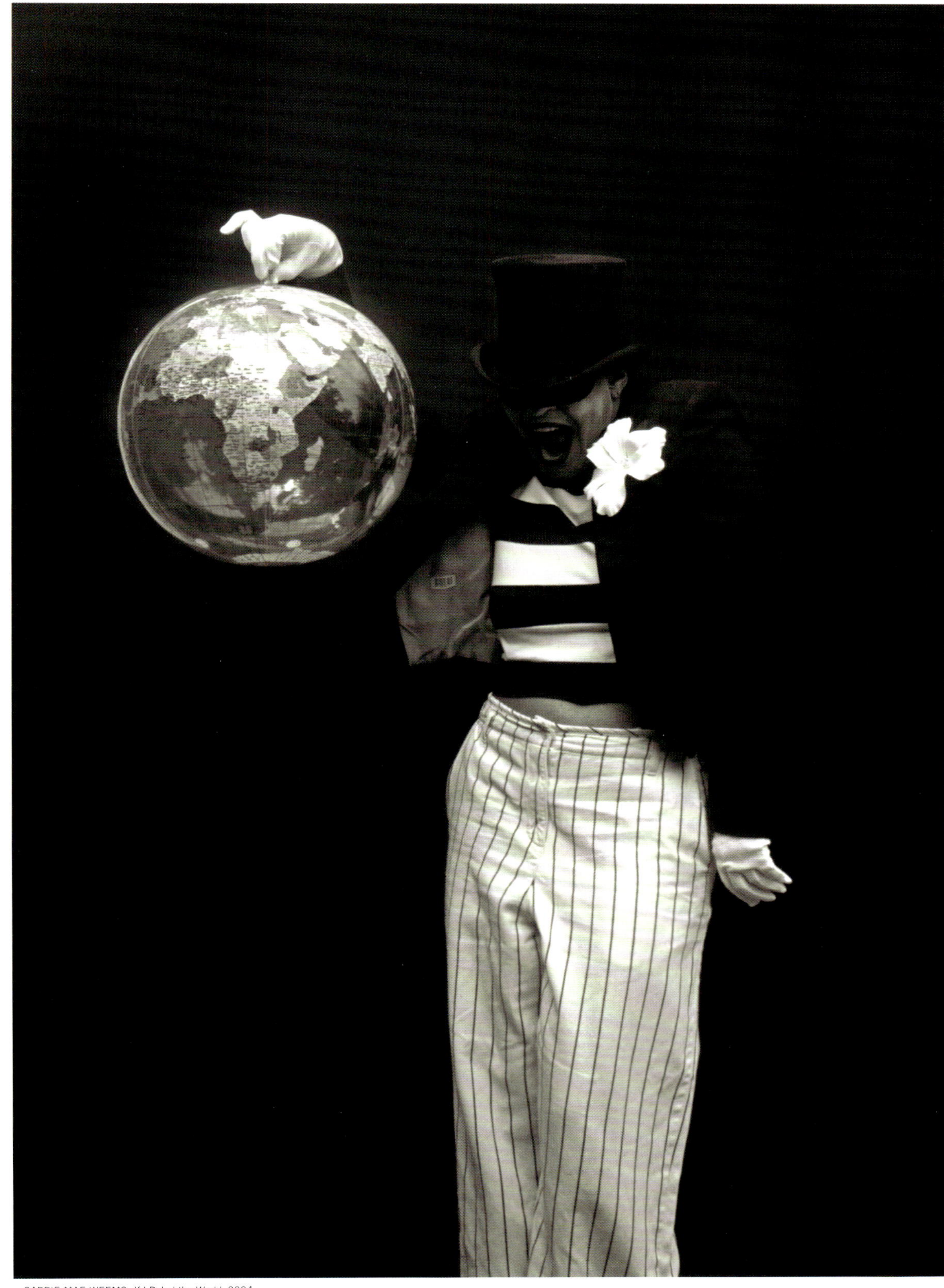

CARRIE MAE WEEMS, *If I Ruled the World*, 2004

CREATE
NEXT
with LAS FOTOS PROJECT
Members of Las Fotos Project
CONVERSE
Photographed by Thalia Gochez

Agenda
Exhibitions to See

Charlotte March

Celebrated for her mid-century fashion photographs in *Vogue* and *Vanity Fair*—and for her portraits of the Black supermodel Donyale Luna in the West German magazine *Twen*—Charlotte March also extensively captured the streets and daily life of postwar Hamburg. As part of the city's 8th Triennial of Photography, *Currency*, which considers themes of circulation and knowledge, March's work is being presented at the Falckenberg Collection. This retrospective focuses on March's sensitive portrayals of Hamburg, where she lived throughout her life, and Ischia, Italy, where she traveled in the 1950s and 1960s. "In their depiction of forms of simple work and social life that were already disappearing at the time they were taken," say the curators Goesta Diercks and Dirk Luckow, March's images "can be read as a reference to the humanist photography of the time."

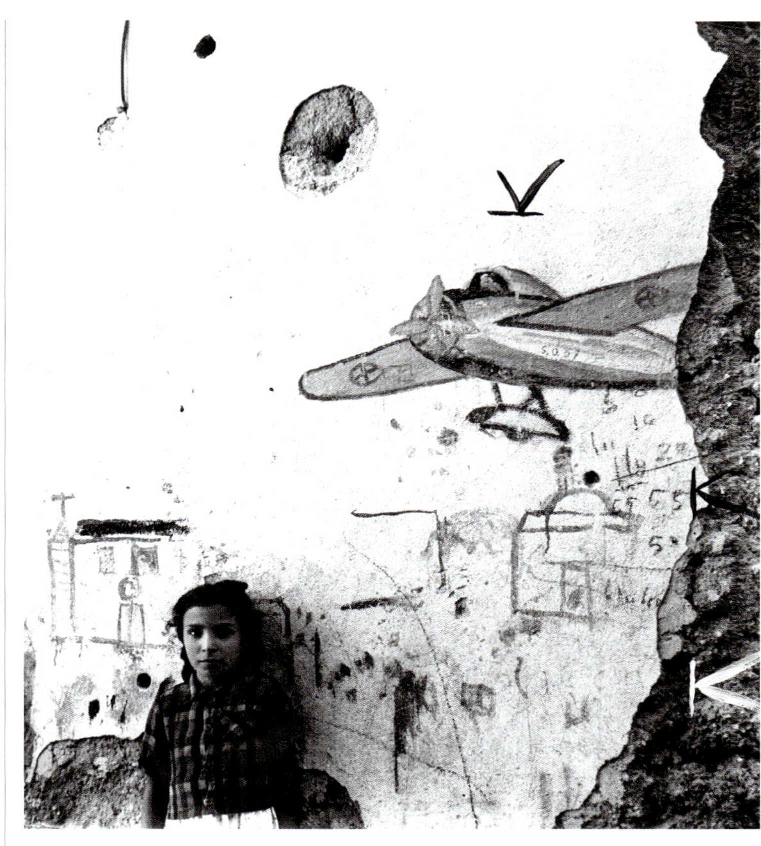

Charlotte March, *Untitled (Ischia)*, 1953
© the artist and courtesy Deichtorhallen Hamburg/Falckenberg Collection

Charlotte March **at the Triennial of Photography Hamburg, through August 21, 2022**

Pao Houa Her

Pao Houa Her was born in Laos and grew up in Saint Paul, Minnesota, where a community of Hmong refugees formed after the Vietnam War. But Her rejects the chronological path from prewar Laos to present-day Minnesota: "One challenge of my photography," she has said, "is to create a narrative that does not require a beginning or an end." A solo exhibition at the Walker Art Center, in Minneapolis, features portraits of familial moments mixed with staged, performative scenes and still lifes full of florals and greenery. The artist's photography can also be seen in this year's Whitney Biennial. Throughout her work, history—of Laos, of the United States, of Her's family and community—emerges as a question without an answer.

Pao Houa Her, *Untitled*, 2019
Courtesy the artist and the Walker Art Center

Pao Houa Her **at the Walker Art Center, Minneapolis, July 28, 2022–January 22, 2023**

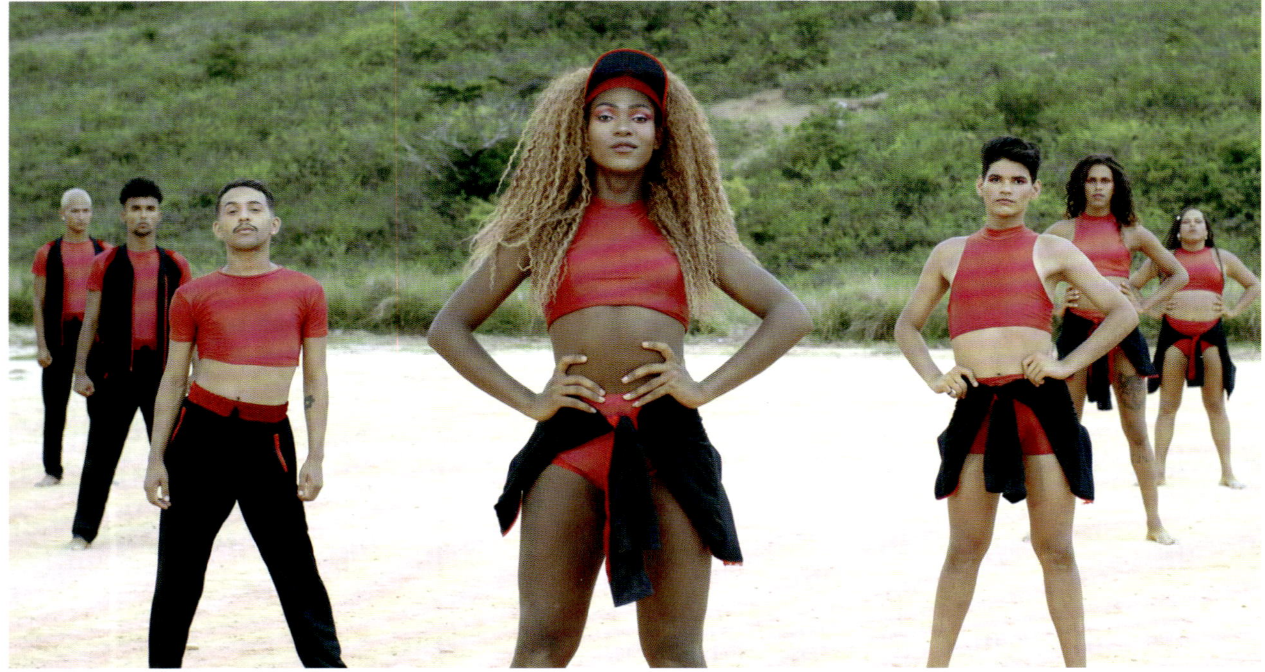

Bárbara Wagner and Benjamin de Burca, Still from *Swinguerra*, 2019.
Two-channel video, color, sound; 21 minutes, 16 seconds
Courtesy the artists and Fortes D'Aloia & Gabriel, São Paulo and Rio de Janeiro

Bárbara Wagner & Benjamin de Burca

Music video or war dance? Rehearsal or showdown? Bárbara Wagner and Benjamin de Burca's electrifying "documentary musical" *Swinguerra* (2019) draws on a three-year collaboration with dance groups from the Brazilian city of Recife and stars Black, queer, and nonbinary performers staging routines and competitions. As a photographer, Wagner has long been captivated by Brazil's music cultures. *Swinguerra*, which premiered at the 2019 Venice Biennale, is about "looking and being seen," says Anni Pullagura, a curatorial assistant at the ICA, Boston, where the two-channel video is on view in a dynamic exhibition. With their athletic grace and fierce costumes, the dancers, Pullagura adds, provoke a dialogue about contemporary politics in Brazil, as dance becomes a way to "make the periphery an active, elusive site of joy."

Bárbara Wagner & Benjamin de Burca: Swinguerra at the ICA, Boston, through September 5, 2022

Our Selves

"What is a feminist picture?" asks Roxana Marcoci, curator of *Our Selves: Photographs by Women Artists from Helen Kornblum* at the Museum of Modern Art, New York. From this starting point, the show navigates deftly throughout the history of photography, from the early botanical cyanotypes of Anna Atkins to the critical intersections of Black and Indigenous artists such as Carrie Mae Weems and Hulleah J. Tsinhnahjinnie. Though *Our Selves* may not provide an explicit answer to its leading question, the photographs speak for themselves and, as a collective, make the case for an alternate history of the medium, one that posits an inclusive and politically active vocabulary. As Marcoci notes, "These stories—who tells them, about whom, through what lens—are relevant for our political futures, and to our creative ones."

Our Selves: Photographs by Women Artists from Helen Kornblum at the Museum of Modern Art, New York, through October 2, 2022

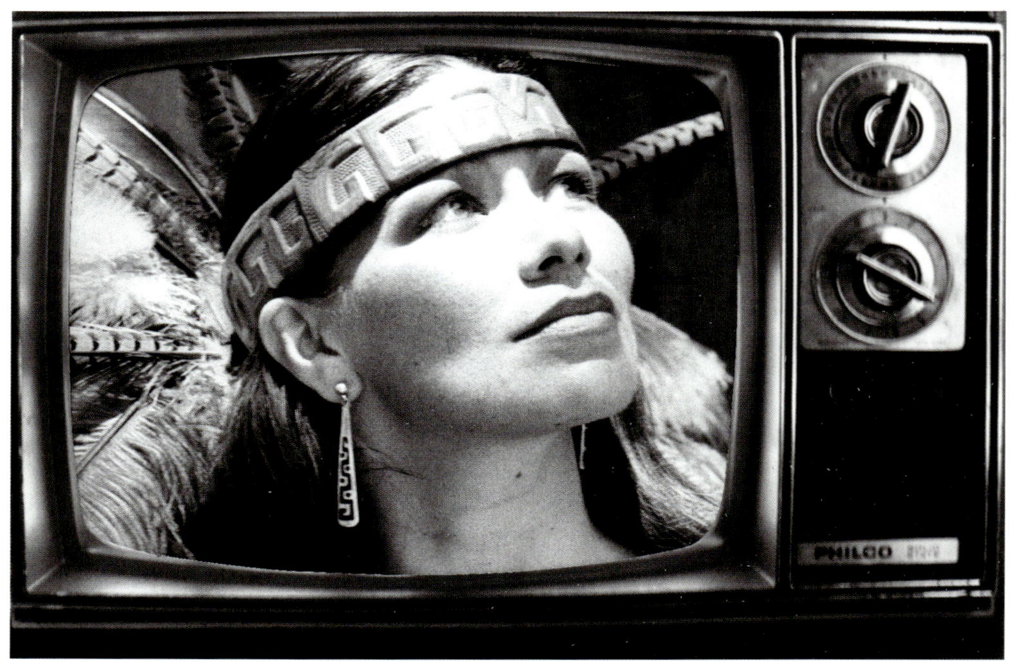

Hulleah J. Tsinhnahjinnie, *Vanna Brown, Azteca Style*, 1990
© the artist and courtesy the Museum of Modern Art, New York

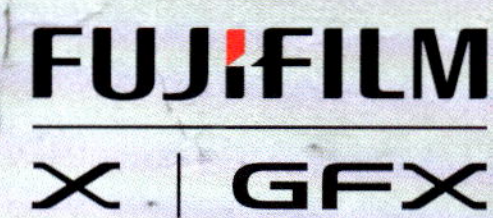

FUJIFILM
X | GFX

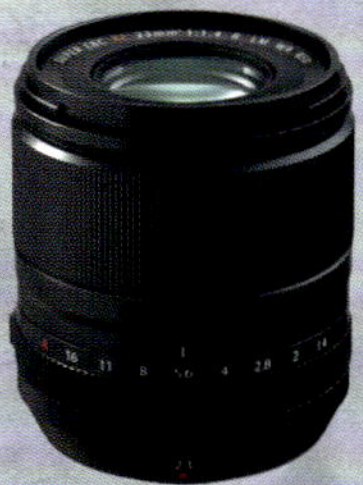

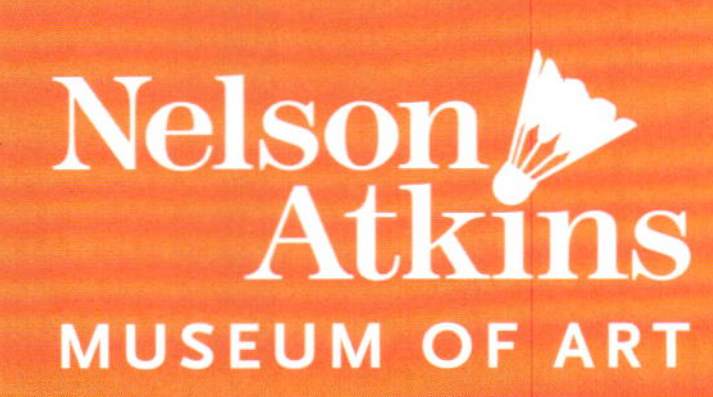

816.751.1278 | nelson-atkins.org
45th & Oak, Kansas City, Missouri

May 7–October 9, 2022

SIGNS

PHOTOGRAPHS BY JIM DOW

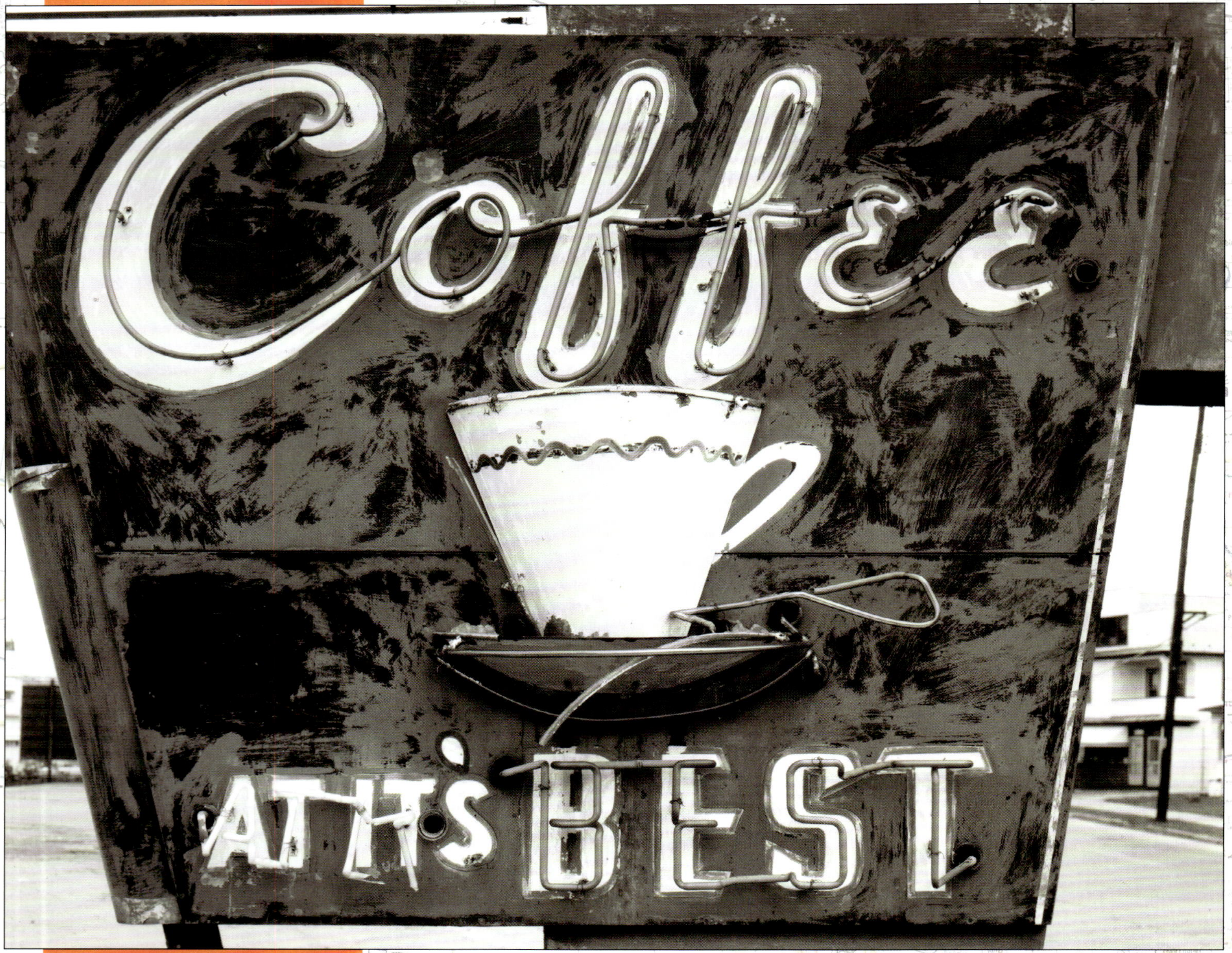

Jim Dow, American (born 1942). *"Coffee At It's Best" Sign. US 11, Pittston, Pennsylvania,* 1973. Gelatin silver print, 8 x 9 15/16 inches. Gift of the Hall Family Foundation, 2018.56.1.

Jim Dow's early black-and-white photographs are vivid, clear-sighted images of American vernacular subjects that celebrate individual agency and creativity amidst the changing social landscape of the 1960s and 1970s.

Day Jobs

Janet Delaney's fascination with workers began with her father, a beauty supply salesman.

Glen Helfand

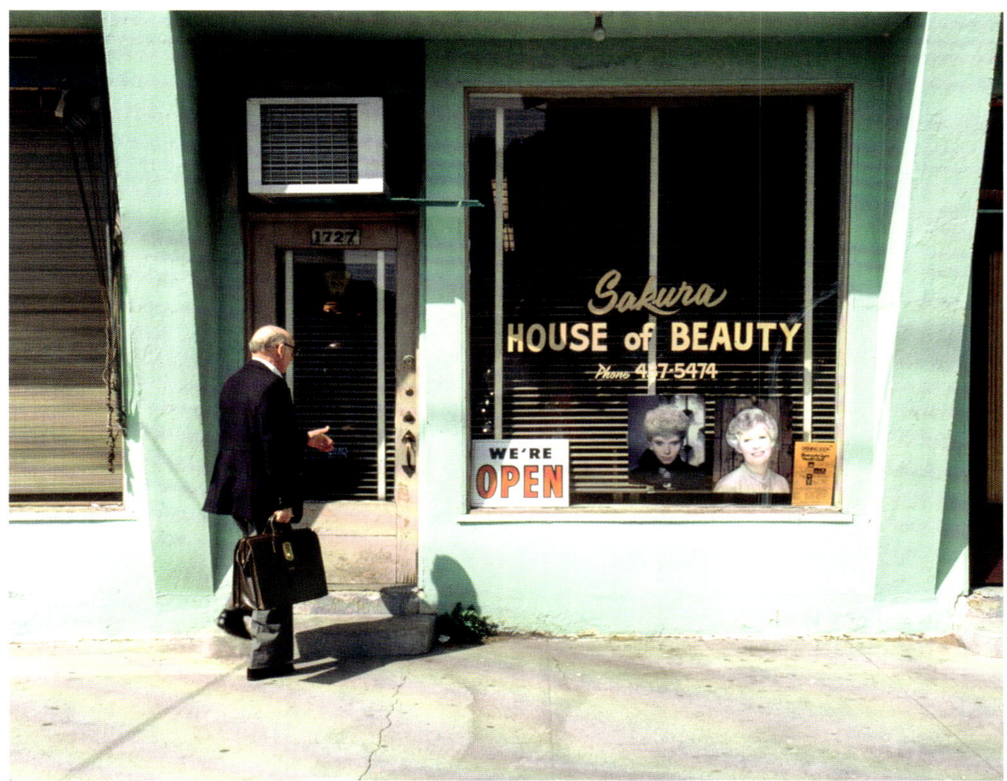

Janet Delaney's work experience started early. "As soon as I learned to write, I took orders for my dad on the phone, his clients knew me," Delaney said recently. "Shirley would call and say, 'Hey, Janet, can you tell your dad that I need a case of perms?'"

Bill Delaney, her father, was a beauty supply salesman, 1960s, LA region, servicing shops in prosaic places such as San Pedro and Wilmington. His inventory was stored in the garage—and in the Plymouth Valiant required to cover his territory. "You'd have to push the rollers and cases of lipstick over so you could sit in the back," Delaney recalls. "It's probably why I'm so fascinated with photographing work. I lived in it."

The theme has persisted in Delaney's art at this foundational human level. She started photographing workers, workplaces, and urban environments in the late 1970s, with pictures of people taking pride in their vocations (or lack thereof), and continued that practice for decades. Those 1970s and '80s images, which still resonate today, have been collected in *South of Market* (2013), a book showing San Francisco's formerly industrial, working-class neighborhood, and in the recently released *Red Eye to New York* (2021), which includes street scenes of hot dog vendors, truck drivers, businessmen, and hotel workers on strike.

"My dad was interested in providing for his family and was a good salesman. He devoted himself to getting up and going out, making cold calls, talking to regulars to find out how many permanents they needed and offering them deals," explains Delaney. As a teen, however, she took rebellious issue with his wares: "I had a tacit disdain for his job, even though I loved him dearly. Coming of age during the Summer of Love, beauty products were not my thing." Delaney had a few teen job stints—babysitting, a short-lived Kentucky Fried Chicken gig, and later, after moving to the Bay Area, documenting social services for a non-profit advocacy group.

By 1980, when Delaney entered graduate school at the San Francisco Art Institute, she looked at her father with fresh eyes. He became the subject of her first MFA project: a slideshow, with sound, and a self-published book. In the slideshow, which now also exists as a video, you hear Bill's sales philosophy, his easy rapport and playful haggling with shop owners. There is an ambient soundtrack of pop hits that played in rooms where women sat under dryers in bare-bones salons. The images flow like a successful sales day—though in the end, as Bill has a barbed conversation with a client, you sense some weariness and his impending retirement.

"I really would have been a filmmaker," Delaney says. "Growing up in LA, that was the language. I only didn't do it because someone told me that you had to have a family member in the union, and I didn't have that."

Delaney proudly works from home, as did her husband for many years, a contractor who built her a spacious studio on the second floor of their Berkeley house. "I always had my studio at home," Delaney says, noting that she's currently busy there on a Guggenheim Foundation–funded photo and interview-based project about tech offices and their employees. "I can't imagine not having that kind of seamlessness. To be with the people I love the most—and to work."

Janet Delaney, *Salesman Bill Delaney arriving at the Sakura House of Beauty*, Los Angeles, 1980
Courtesy the artist and Euqinom Gallery, San Francisco

Glen Helfand is a writer and curator based in Oakland, California.

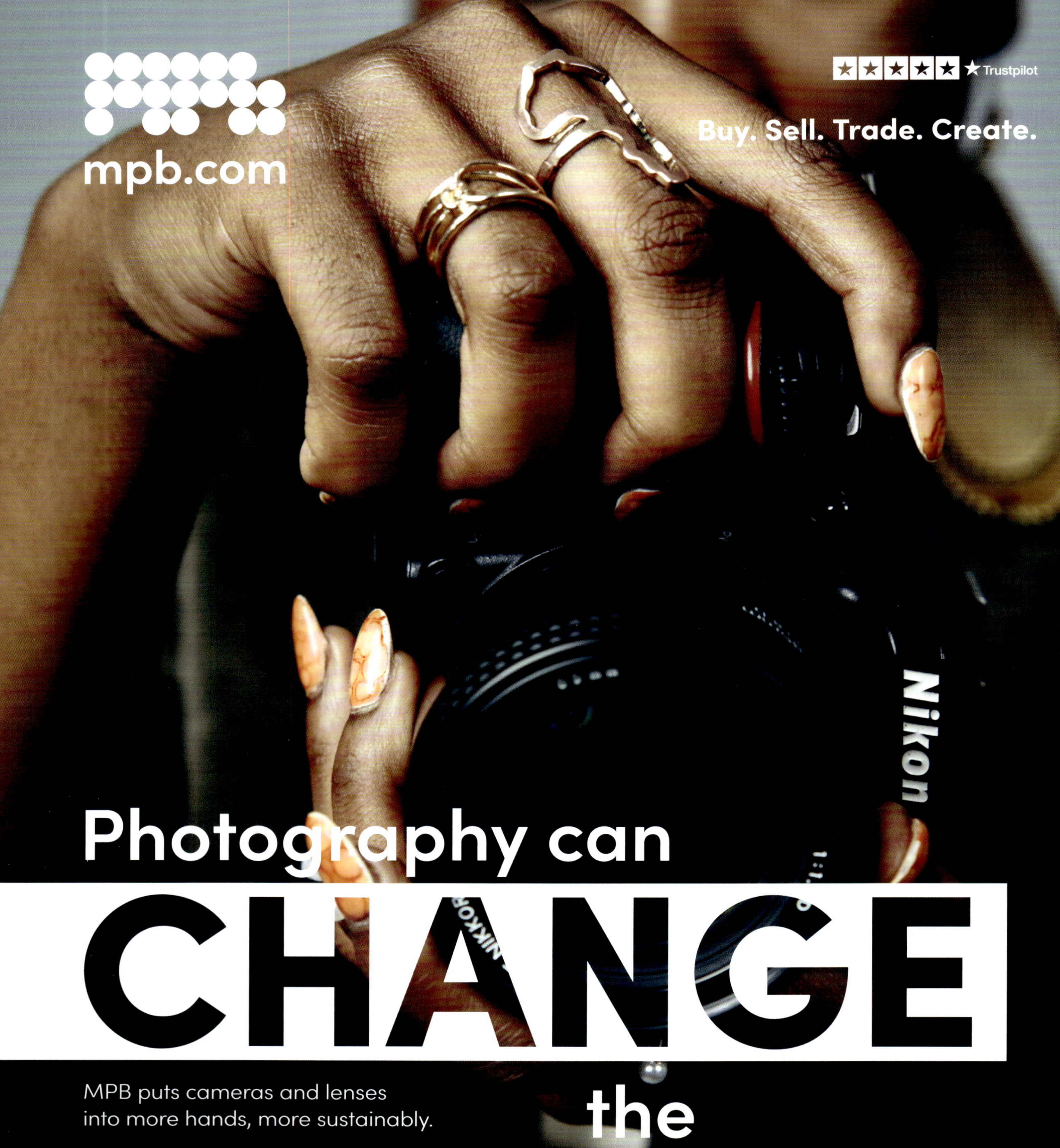

mpb.com
Buy. Sell. Trade. Create.
Trustpilot
Nikon
Photography can
CHANGE
the
bigger
picture.
MPB puts cameras and lenses
into more hands, more sustainably.
MPB. The platform to buy and
sell used photo and video kit.
mpb.com #ChangeGear

Viewfinder

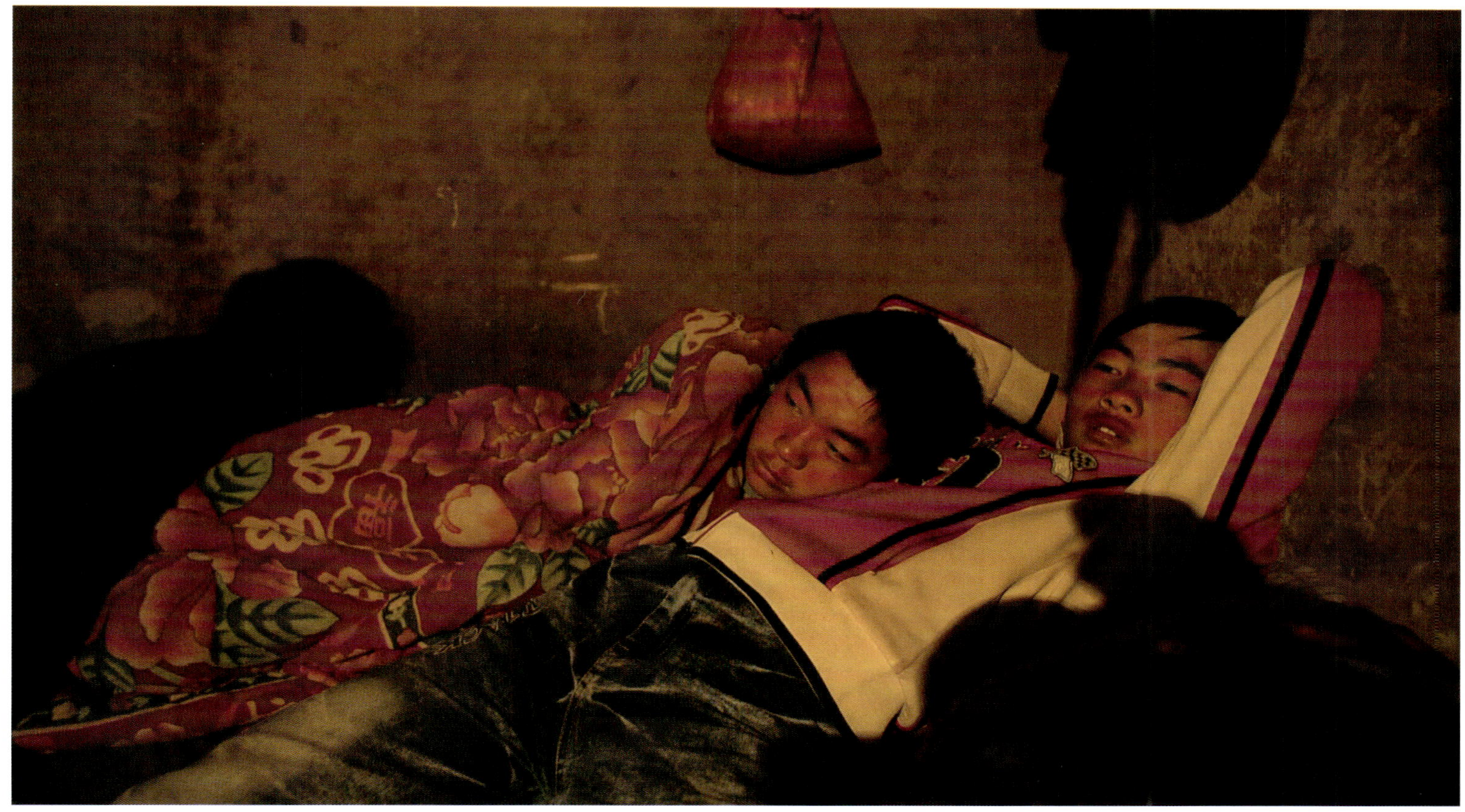

**In his immense documentaries, Wang Bing depicts the lives
of Chinese people with intricate and unsparing detail.**

Phoebe Chen

In 2003, the Chinese filmmaker Wang Bing, then an unknown graduate of the Beijing Film Academy, debuted a durational colossus: *West of the Tracks*, a nine-hour document of industrial decline in the Tiexi factory district of Shenyang Province. Amassed over four years with little more than an amateur video camera and faith in the instructive texture of reality, *West of the Tracks* found a new form for the chasmic infrastructural changes of post-Socialist China.

Immense run times and handheld spontaneity have come to define most of Wang's subsequent films, each teeming with the minutiae of daily subsistence in various pockets of regional China. Although Wang is attuned to the present, his work is always marked by a broader intuition of historical process and state-led economic restructuring. His subjects have spanned the extractive labor of oil-field workers on the Tibetan plateau in *Crude Oil* (2008), the carceral optics of a psychiatric institution in Yunnan Province with *'Til Madness Do Us Part* (2013), and, in *15 Hours* (2017), the conditions of migrant workers at a children's garment factory in Zhejiang Province.

Last fall, these latter two films, along with *West of the Tracks*; *Man with No Name* (2010); *Father and Sons* (2014), which follows the solitary days of a migrant worker's unsupervised children; and a shorter piece, *Traces* (2014), were screened as multichannel video installations at Le Bal, a photography space in Paris, in a solo exhibition titled *The Walking Eye*. For a filmmaker who seems so steadfast in his outward orientation to the world, it's striking how often he has invoked a vivid subjectivity to describe his output. As Wang recalls about the early days of making *West of the Tracks*: "I wondered how I could create . . . something singular, something personal."

Across a two-decade oeuvre laden with the heterogeneous rhythms of life in contemporary China, what is "personal" in Wang's work is not its proximity to his own biography but to a deeply embodied experience of discovery made possible by his filming. Wang seems prone to self-effacement—no on-screen appearance;

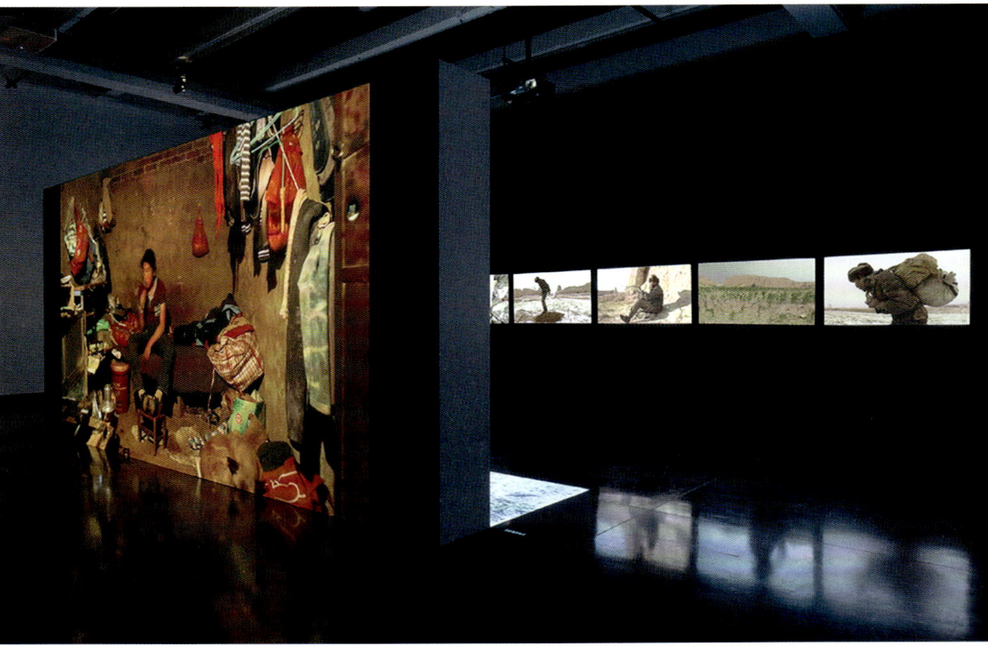

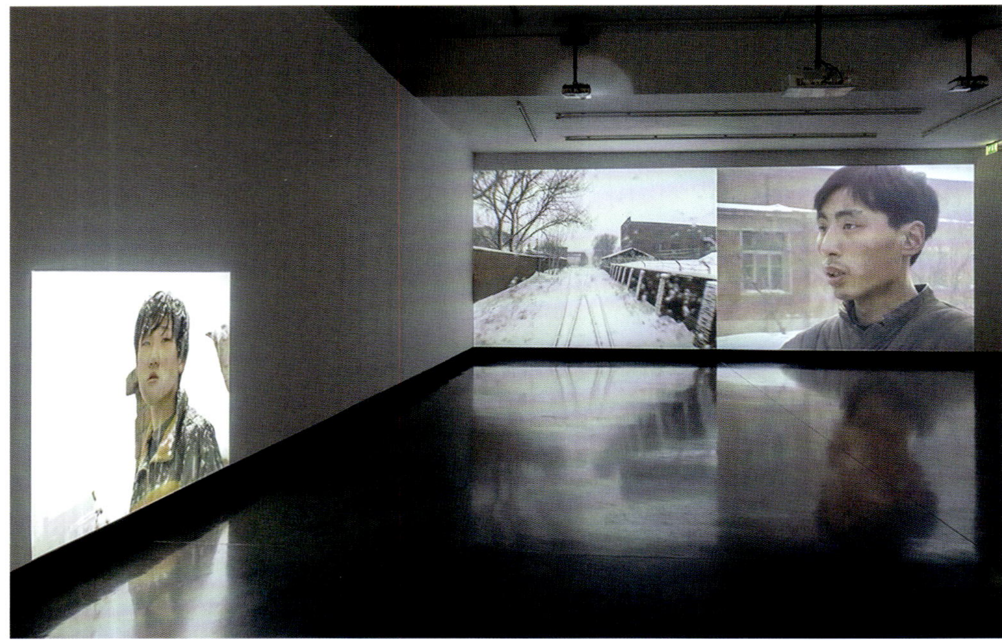

only the rarest flashes of his voice as interlocutor—but his physical presence is both anchor to and genesis of every film. Even as he enlists a stray assistant here and there, Wang is the very force that walks the camera's unblinking eye.

Against his categorization as a maker of documentaries, Wang has stressed a different impetus: "The most important thing for me is to film people and to understand why and how I film them. Whatever story and whatever kind of cinema that may produce." Wang's films exceed the mere accrual of information. We learn, for instance, that the metal-workers in *West of the Tracks* undergo mandatory hospitalization to treat the lead that has leeched into their bodies. Where another filmmaker might briefly limn this as a sobering medical fact, Wang lingers on the eventless days of the workers' confinement, as they sing karaoke together in scantly furnished rooms, lounge and rove listlessly through hospital halls awaiting their release.

In the usual context of their single-screen display in cinemas, the audience is asked to move through factories and fields, following a figure from behind or stuck to whichever lone purview Wang has framed. But the multiscreen installation of *The Walking Eye* alters the experience. Of the five films in the exhibition at Le Bal, only *Father and Sons* was screened in its entirety; the others were presented as curated sequences approved by Wang himself, split across two or more screens. If the theatrical presentation of Wang's filmmaking invites a kind of temporal immersion into one monumental trajectory, their multiplied projection in the gallery seems to pull apart their layered rhythms, as if to unveil all the dense strata that comprise any given moment in history.

There is a similar effect in *The Walking Eye*, the eponymous book published by Roma Publications for the exhibition. Of its over eight hundred pages, more than seven hundred display stills and translated text from eight of Wang's films. Most of these are single images that bleed across two pages, sandwiched like centerfolds, or vertically stacked, two stills to a page. Some are further miniaturized and arrayed as four—maybe six, maybe eight—frames in quick succession, trained on the unfolding of a specific scene. Any print-based documentation of moving-image work is fated to stasis, but the unusual heft of *The Walking Eye* is, admittedly, confusing. Why freeze and compile thousands of images from a filmmaker who has said, in an interview closing this very book, "I conceive of the camera as the instrument of movement"?

These arrested frames risk turning real-time discovery into fixed curios of an ethnographic other. Wang knows that the "movement" of a world as it becomes known—as it draws us into its opening—cannot be pinned down and collected. If anything, *The Walking Eye* in book form shows us the limits of fixing moving-image art on the printed page and, in the end, the power of Wang's films in motion.

**Phoebe Chen is a writer
based in New York.**

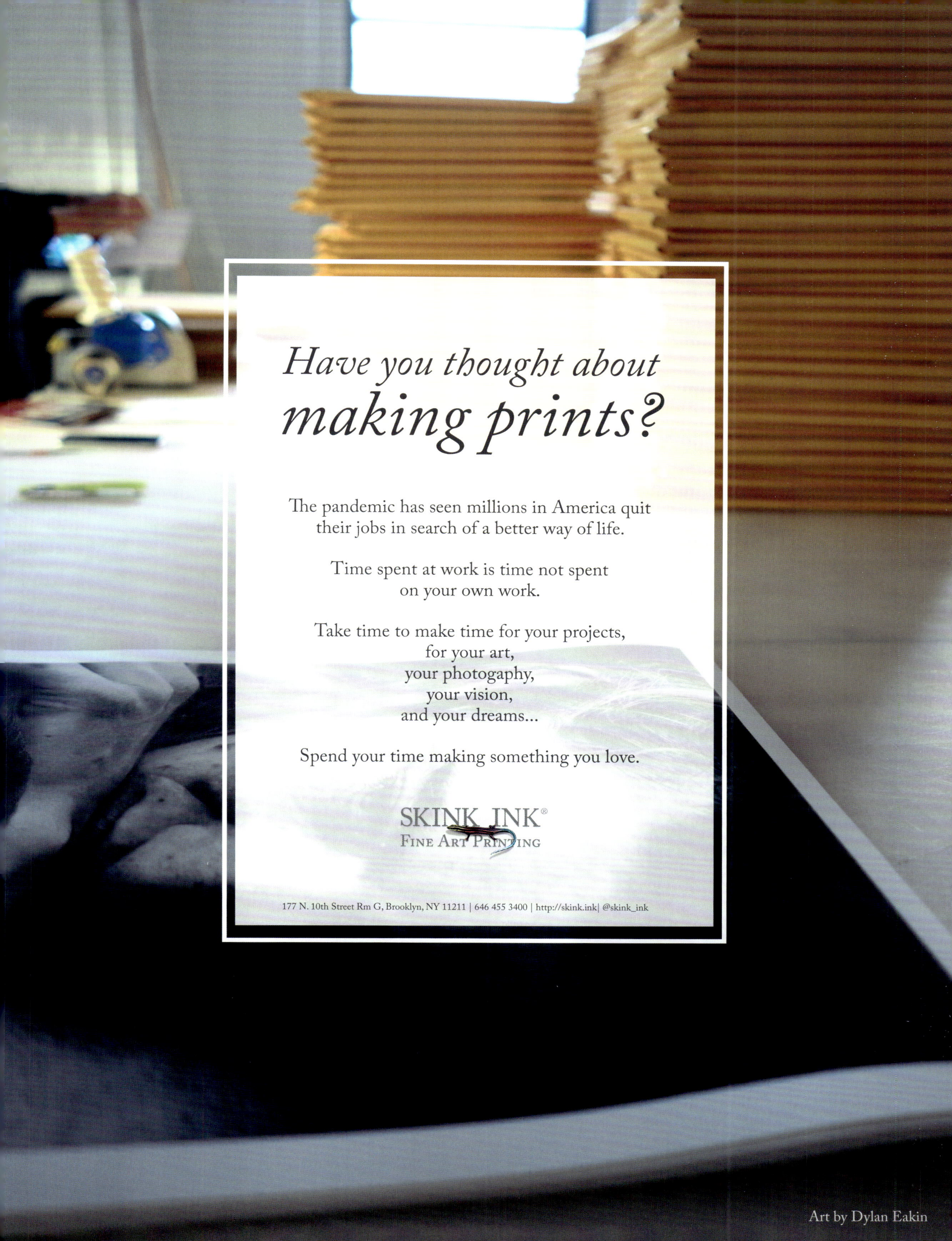

Have you thought about
making prints?

The pandemic has seen millions in America quit
their jobs in search of a better way of life.

Time spent at work is time not spent
on your own work.

Take time to make time for your projects,
for your art,
your photogaphy,
your vision,
and your dreams...

Spend your time making something you love.

SKINK INK®
FINE ART PRINTING

177 N. 10th Street Rm G, Brooklyn, NY 11211 | 646 455 3400 | http://skink.ink| @skink_ink

Art by Dylan Eakin

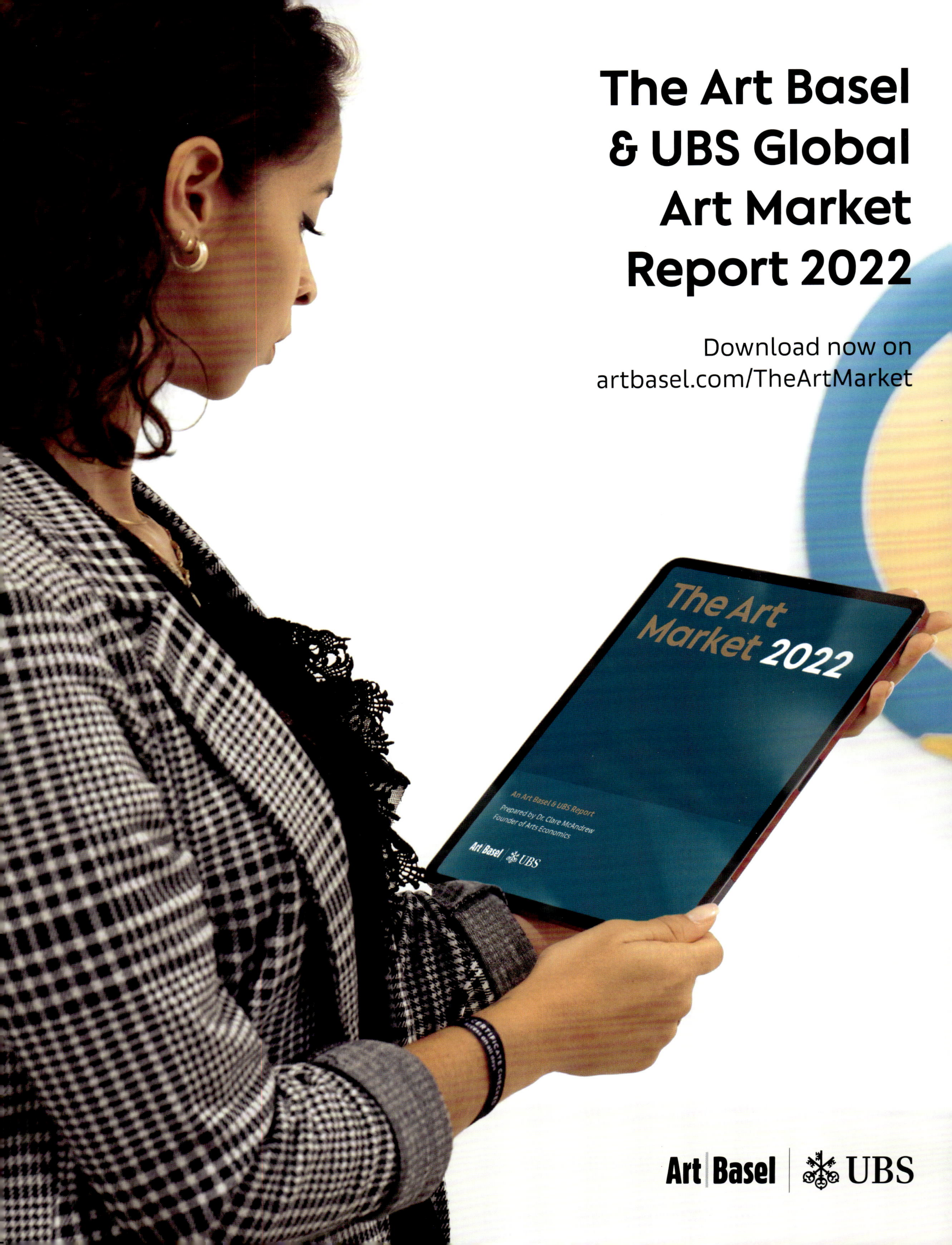
The Art Basel
& UBS Global
Art Market
Report 2022

Download now on
artbasel.com/TheArtMarket

The Art
Market 2022

An Art Basel & UBS Report

Prepared by Dr. Clare McAndrew
Founder of Arts Economics

Art Basel ✣ UBS

Art Basel ✣ UBS

**How Anthony Hernandez
heightens the textures of a
changing urban landscape.**
Juliana Halpert

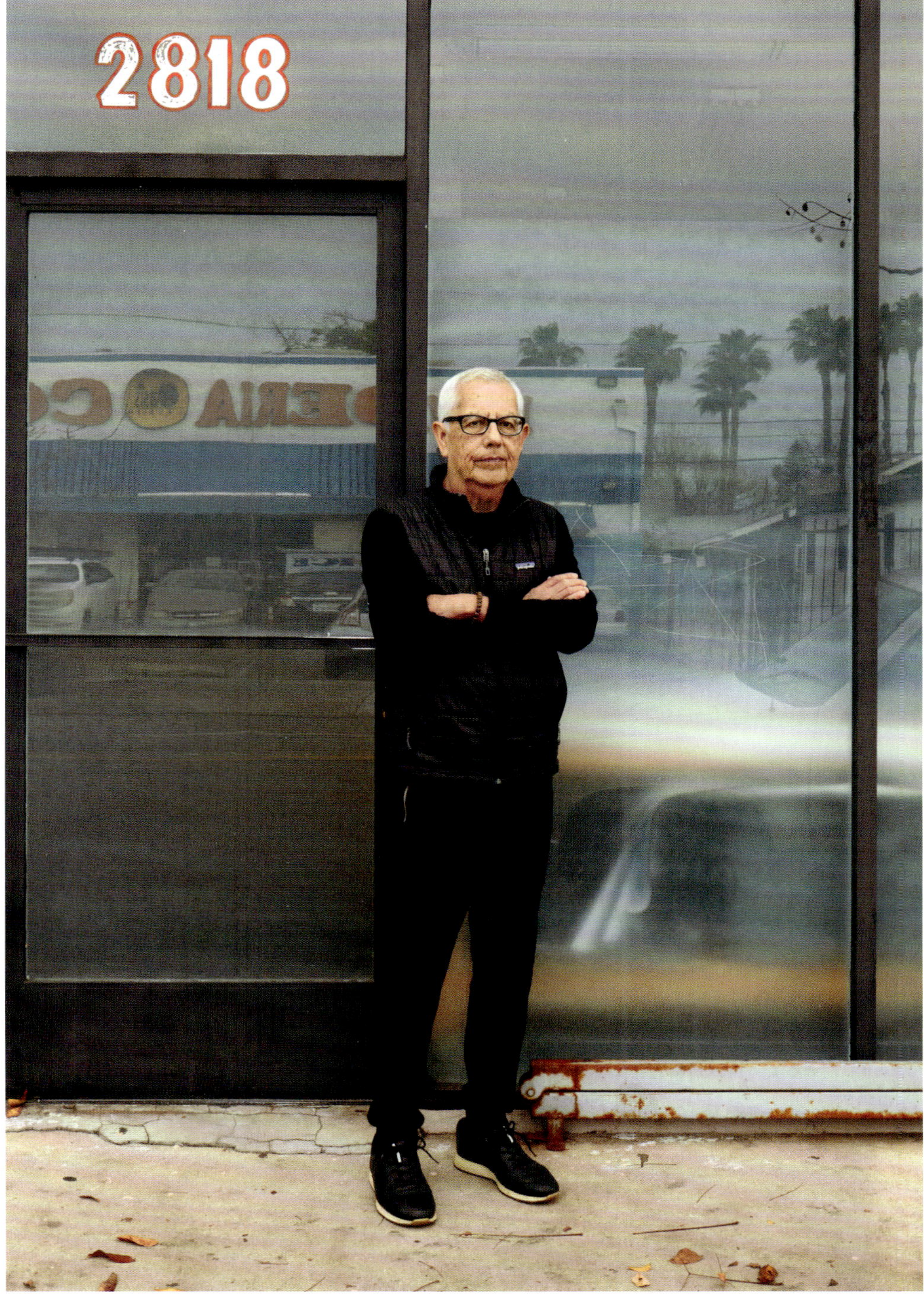

On West Jefferson Boulevard, a four-lane thoroughfare that cuts east-west through South Central Los Angeles, the din of the city is loud as cars and trucks streak down the blocks. Anthony Hernandez's studio occupies a small storefront right on West Jefferson, in a brief commercial district squeezed between the more residential, "historic" neighborhoods of Jefferson Park and West Adams. On a sunny Saturday morning in mid-February, its painted-pink facade seemed to bask in the heavy sunlight and sound, soaking them both in. Across the street, a clothes boutique blasted reggaeton from speakers stationed by its open doors.

Once inside, the street seemed to fall away. As I walked into his studio, I felt the air cool and the light brighten to a crisp white. The clamor of the city quickly deadened, and the voice of the opera singer Maria Callas quietly trilled out of a small stereo system on a low table. A few dozen CDs—mostly jazz—are stacked on the side. A black leather Eames lounge chair and a large, modern desk sit at the room's back corners. Pinned to the gallery's immaculate walls are giant prints of hazy, pale streetscapes, a silhouetted figure sometimes traipsing through. Flat files and boxes of photographs are arranged neatly on the under shelf of a wide, industrial table. Privacy film covers the wide windows, diffusing the daylight.

Hernandez, a photographer for the past fifty years, has been here for eight. It's his first and only studio. The sparse, clean space operates more like a showroom than a work area since his practice takes place *out there*, most often on and around streets similar to this one, preserving glimpses of LA not likely to receive historic designations anytime soon. Two of his best-known series, *Landscapes for the Homeless* (1988–2007) and *Forever* (2007–12), studied the stuff of the city's most transient populations. Hernandez fixed his eye on cardboard shelters and strung-up bed sheets, initials carved into tree trunks and piles of cigarette butts strewn in the dirt. Rarely, if ever, do these images feature any human subjects. It's clear that the inhabitants of these sites are more ephemeral than the tiny traces they leave behind.

Hernandez remains attuned to this fact, and to its reality just outside his studio door. He was concerned about whether I was able to find nearby parking—a very Angeleno courtesy—and said that it's gotten worse. "There are dead cars everywhere around here now," he explains. "And a lot of people living in their vehicles. There was a guy living in his car right here, and another one camped on the sidewalk just out front." I asked where they were now. "They died," he replies, as if stating the obvious.

Hernandez was born in 1947 in Aliso Village, a housing project built in the

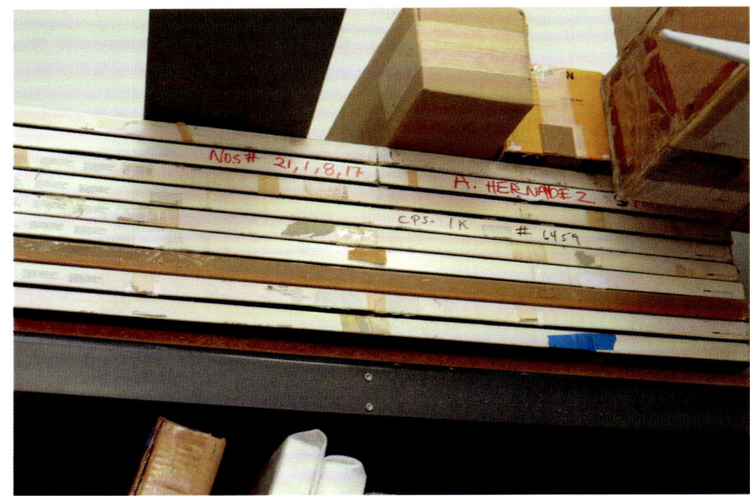

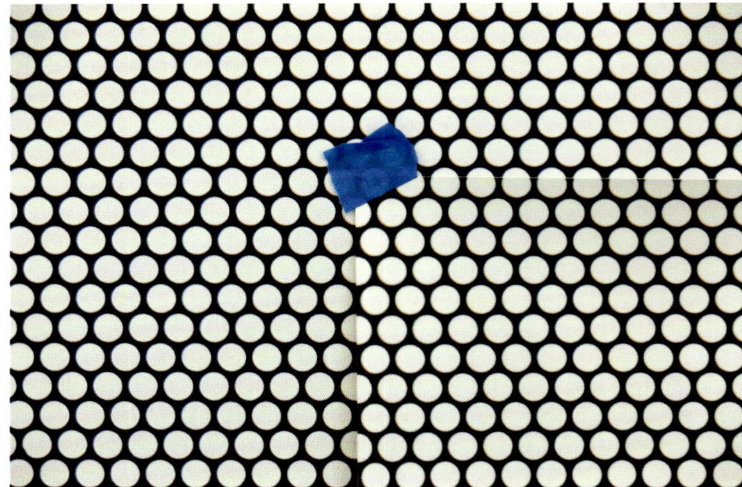

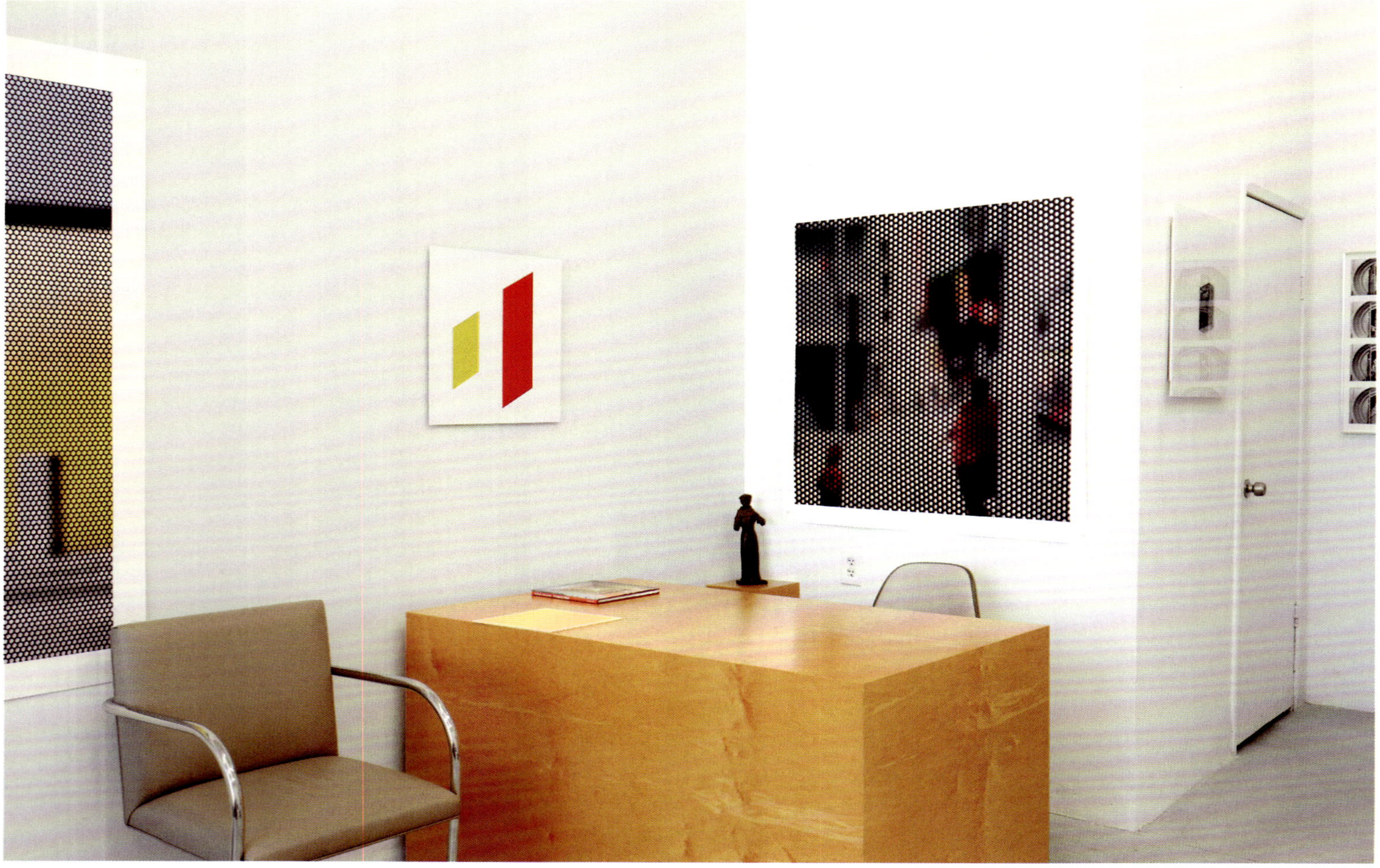

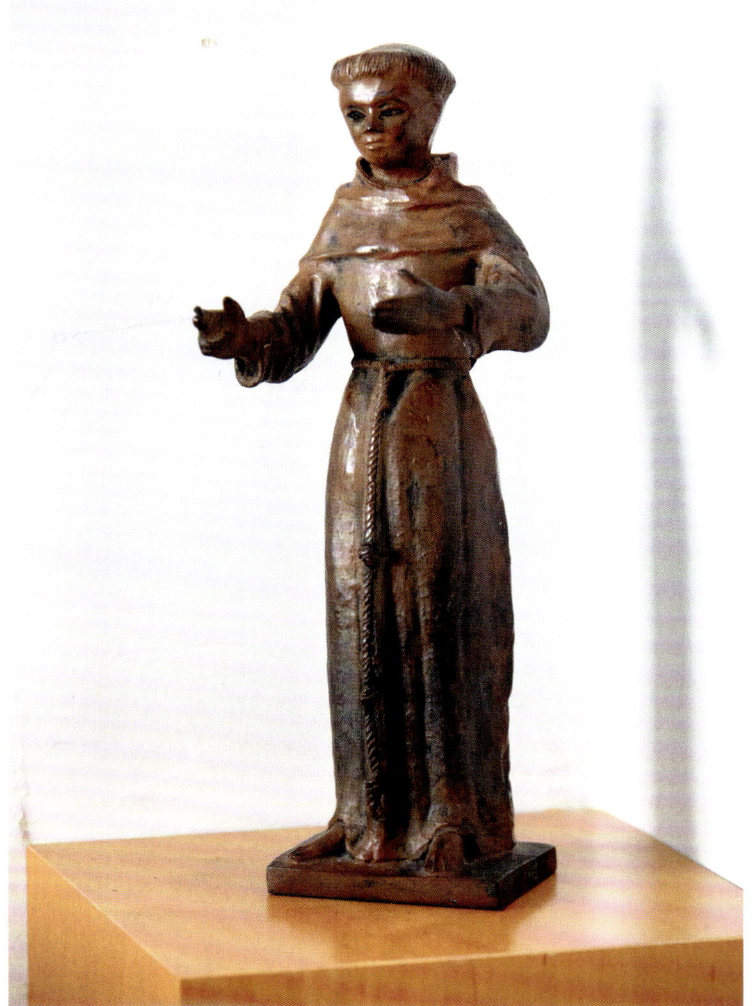

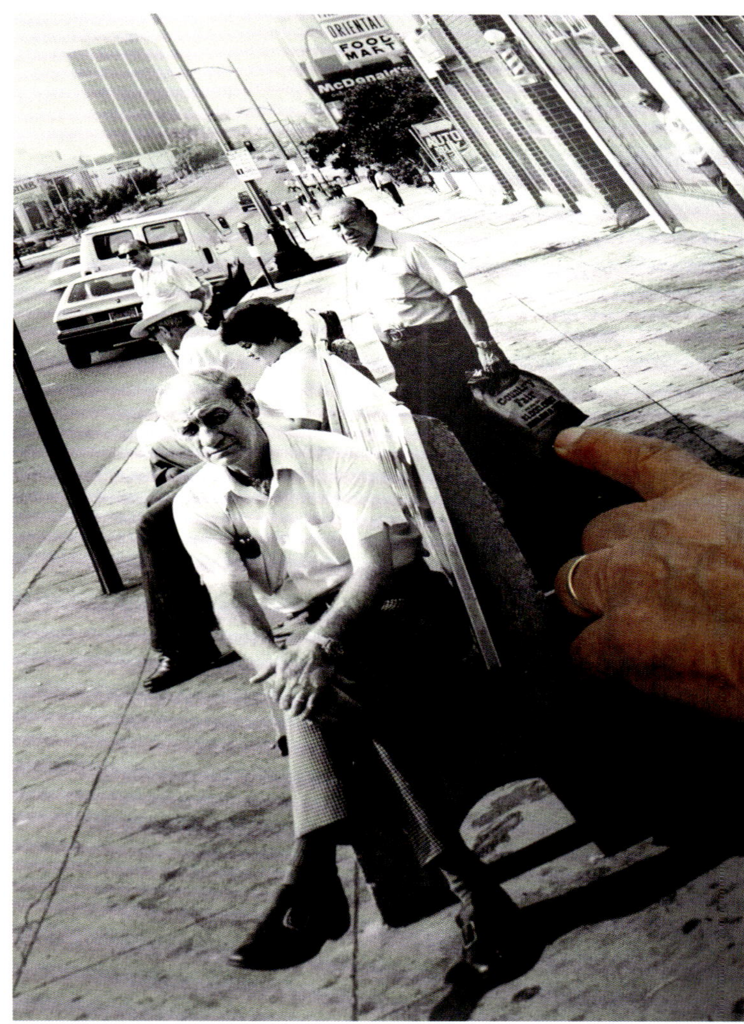

Taking pictures became a natural extension of Hernandez's love of roving the streets of East LA.

1940s after its predecessor, the Flats—identified by Jacob Riis in the early twentieth century as one of the worst slums in the country—was demolished. His family's house was two blocks from the Los Angeles River. "Back then, there were no fences anywhere," he explains, with a touch of excitement. "My friends and I would just explore the river and tunnels and streets all day." Hernandez loved walking and was uniquely adept at navigating the area's complex network of streets. "My first day at school, they let us out for recess," he says, grinning, "and I thought that meant school was over, so I walked home. It was over a mile. My dad had to drive me back—he was amazed that I had found my way to the house."

Taking pictures became a natural extension of Hernandez's love of roving and surveying the streets of East LA. We stood at the large table and looked through prints of a project, *Screened Pictures* (2017–18), originally intended for a two-person exhibition with David Lynch. Visions of brightly colored walls, renovated storefronts, old housing developments, expansive graffiti, and people—yes, people—are pictured through a tight, black mesh pattern, seemingly right on the image's surface.

Everything behind it blurs into hazy shapes and swathes of color. Hernandez first discovered this technique when photographing a man through the metal scrim of a bus-stop structure; he since had his own screen fabricated to reproduce the effect. Human figures, often captured while simply walking or loitering in the frame, become shadowy and anonymous. Graffiti tags start to resemble abstract expressionist paintings. The perfect geometry of a recent modernist storefront is further reduced. It looks like an architectural rendering.

Why this newfound remove from the city Hernandez has always known so well? "LA keeps building so many walls and fences," he bemoans, "just to keep certain people out of certain places." *Screened Pictures* embodies that lament, accentuating the erasure of a city's coarser textures. Yet as the morning turned to afternoon, I was relieved to walk back into the strong light and blaring noise, the boutique now playing Wisin & Yandel at full volume, a few boys on the sidewalk smoking a blunt. All signs of a city still very much there.

Juliana Halpert is an artist and writer based in Los Angeles.

Curriculum
Vasantha Yogananthan

The French photographer Vasantha Yogananthan grew up reading a comic-book version of the Ramayana, the epic Indian poem about Rama, a legendary prince and deity. In 2013, while traveling in India, Yogananthan began work on his own retelling of the Ramayana, a seven-volume photobook called *A Myth of Two Souls* (2013–21), which incorporates spectacular pastel-hued staged photographs, often rendered with delicate hand-painting techniques, along with intimate accounts of nighttime festivals, where he had to find each flash-lit image in complete darkness. The idea of connecting contemporary India to ancient narrative, of "traveling through time and space," is at the center of the project, Yogananthan has said. "It's something photography is really good at."

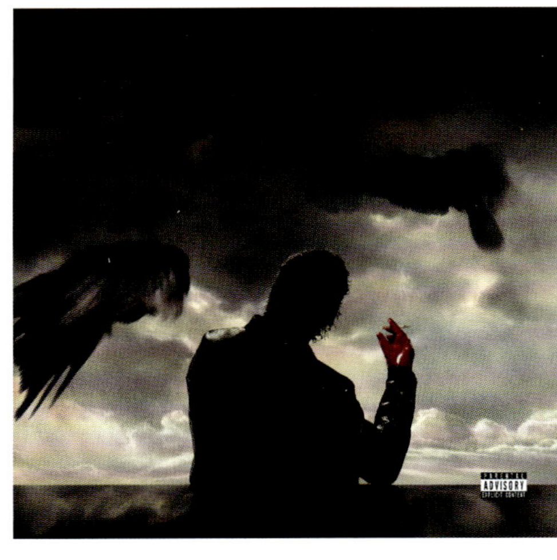

Laylow, *L'Étrange Histoire de Mr. Anderson*, 2021

The rapper Laylow and his alter ego Mr. Anderson—a name taken from Neo's alias in *The Matrix*—are the narrators of last year's standout French hip-hop album. Their meandering thoughts oscillate from materialistic desires to chilly storytelling about domestic abuse on the track "HELP!!!" or police violence on "LOST FOREST." Laylow/Anderson live in a world where, as the featured guest Damso puts it bluntly on "R9R-LINE," "giving birth to a Black child is a crime." Often skipping rhymes or any coercing hip-hop-writing rules, they sound like friends, or enemies, having conversations on top-notch productions. Their two selves merge to create an unlikely character, at once an individualist, a preacher, and a dreamer. Pay close attention and you'll hear—in the midst of Lamborghini engine noises—moments of grace such as on the last song of the LP: "If you stop running just for a minute / You'll see your own star in the sky."

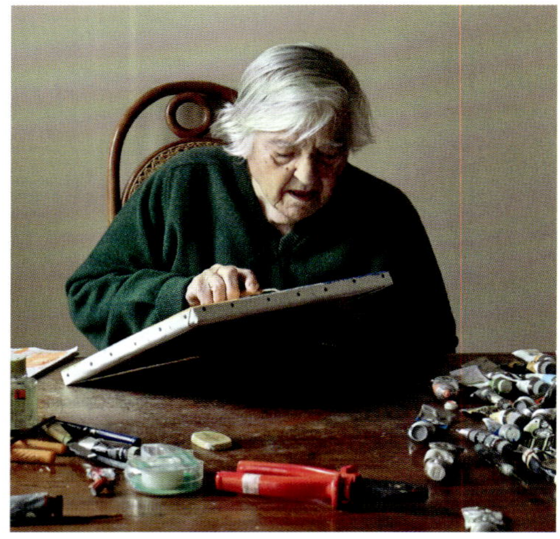

Etel Adnan

I wonder if immediacy plays a part in Etel Adnan's unique color combinations. She completed her small paintings in single sittings of two to three hours. If we were to trace her work to one artist, it would certainly be Paul Klee. Their paintings share the same existential quality. Adnan may have found her true self while repeatedly and obsessively painting Mount Tamalpais, just north of San Francisco, as Cézanne, another painter she admired, did with Montagne Sainte-Victoire. Adnan, who was born in 1925 and died last year, was also a writer of poems and texts in Arabic (she was raised in Beirut), English (she lived in California), and French (she had frequent stints in Paris). The way she wrote about our world—from politics to philosophy, from culture to identity, from life to art—is at once accessible and thoughtful. I'm reminded daily of her observation: "Every one of us is a radio transmitter."

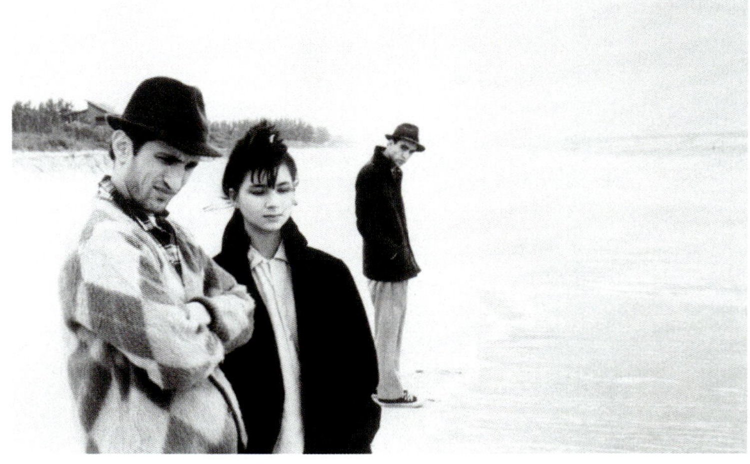

Jim Jarmusch, *Stranger Than Paradise*, 1984

Stranger Than Paradise is the film I have watched the most in my life. The story is divided into three chapters. First up is the New World: Eva arrives from Hungary to New York, where she is hosted by her cousin Willie. One year later, Willie and his friend Eddie set out on a road trip to visit Eva in Ohio. The three friends will eventually end up in "paradise" (aka Florida). As the film moves from New York's nondescript neighborhoods to Cleveland's desolate factories to Florida's run-down motels, the landscape dissolves all hopes of a new life in the land of dreams. Over ninety minutes, Eva, Willie, and Eddie don't do much but smoke Chesterfields in cramped spaces, but they miraculously make you feel like hitting the road to experience for yourself the grayish and melancholic America they left the Old World to find.

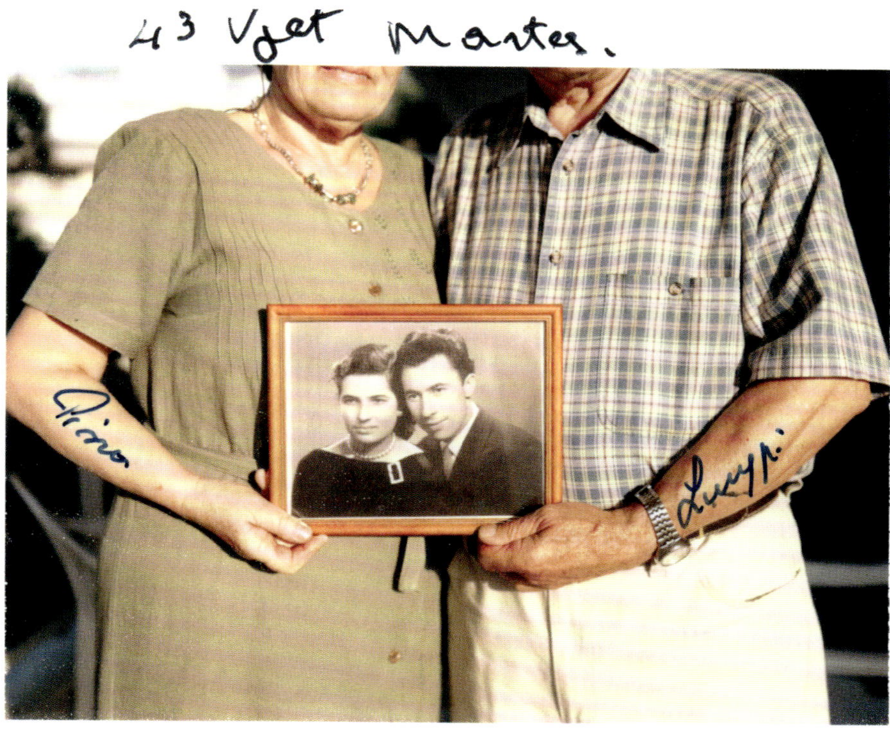

This spread, left to right:
James Mollison, Etel
Adnan, Paris, 2014;
Jim Jarmusch, Still from
Stranger Than Paradise,
1984; Album cover of
Laylow's *L'Étrange Histoire
de Mr. Anderson*, 2021;
Jim Goldberg, *Athens,
Greece (Married 43 Years)*,
2003; Patrick Faigenbaum,
Raphaël, Piazza San Pietro,
2008; Lubaina Himid,
The Operating Table, 2019

Jim Goldberg, *Open See*, 2009

In 2017, Jim Goldberg was asked during an interview, "The people you photographed for *Open See*, do you know anything . . . about how life has panned out for them since?" To which Goldberg answered, "Most of the people I photographed were seeking asylum. . . . Their lives were incredibly fragile, unpredictable, and transitory. . . . Out of the hundreds . . . I met and photographed, there is only one person that I'm still in touch with." It certainly is a delicate matter for a stranger who shares neither the culture nor the fate of the people he photographs to tell the lives of those strangers. But by asking people to add texts and draw over his Polaroids, Goldberg opened up a new space within the field of documentary photography. He willingly lost control over the final work in order to let their voices in. The resulting collaborative photographs are hybrid objects embodied with personal stories that mark history.

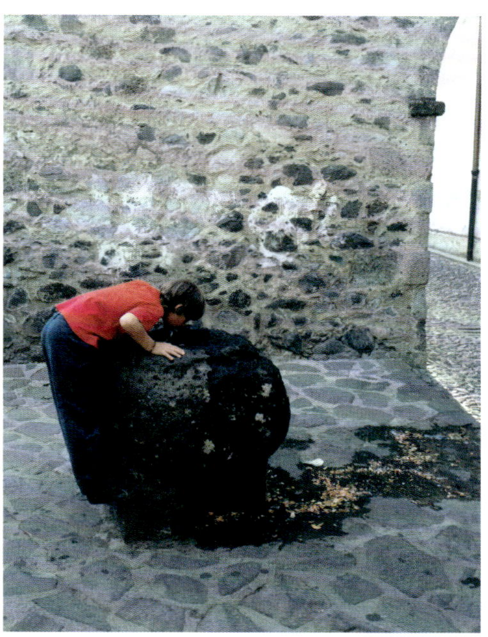

Patrick Faigenbaum, *Santulussurgiu*, 2008

Leafing through the pages of *Santulussurgiu*, one is reminded of Paul Strand and Cesare Zavattini's *Un Paese* (1955). Both Strand and Patrick Faigenbaum are outsiders who are granted an insider's view of a small Italian village. While Strand photographs Zavattini's hometown, Faigenbaum photographs his wife's. Is it the ideal position a photographer might find himself in—close but not too close? Faigenbaum's sense of sequencing is effortless. He mixes landscapes, portraits, and still lifes, using an unparalleled range of colors and a subdued black and white. With great intensity, Faigenbaum portrays his family and the village, the interior and the exterior, the local and the country.

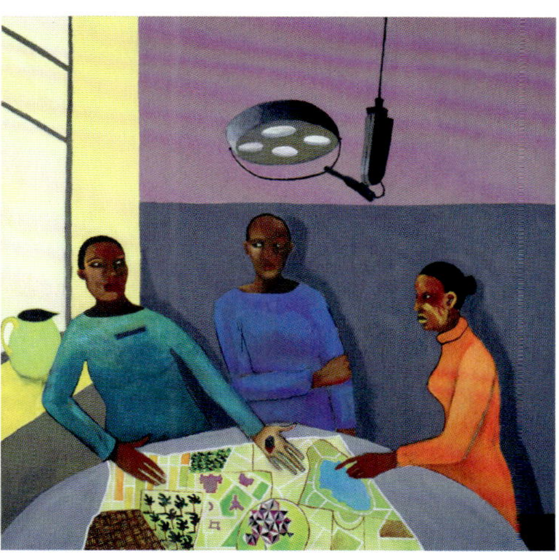

Lubaina Himid: Work from Underneath, 2019

Lubaina Himid, a British painter born in Tanzania who has dedicated her career to uncovering marginalized and silenced figures, histories, and cultural expressions, does not restrict herself to the canvas. For Himid, form always follows function. For example, she has overpainted ephemera such as newspapers from the archives of the *Guardian*. Redacting and adding new elements to the *Guardian*'s pages, Himid questions the words and pictures used by mainstream medias to produce the news. The intimate palette Himid developed over the years flows like life itself—sometimes bright, sometimes muted. She has a playful aesthetic that makes us look, read, and think about our past in intriguing ways.

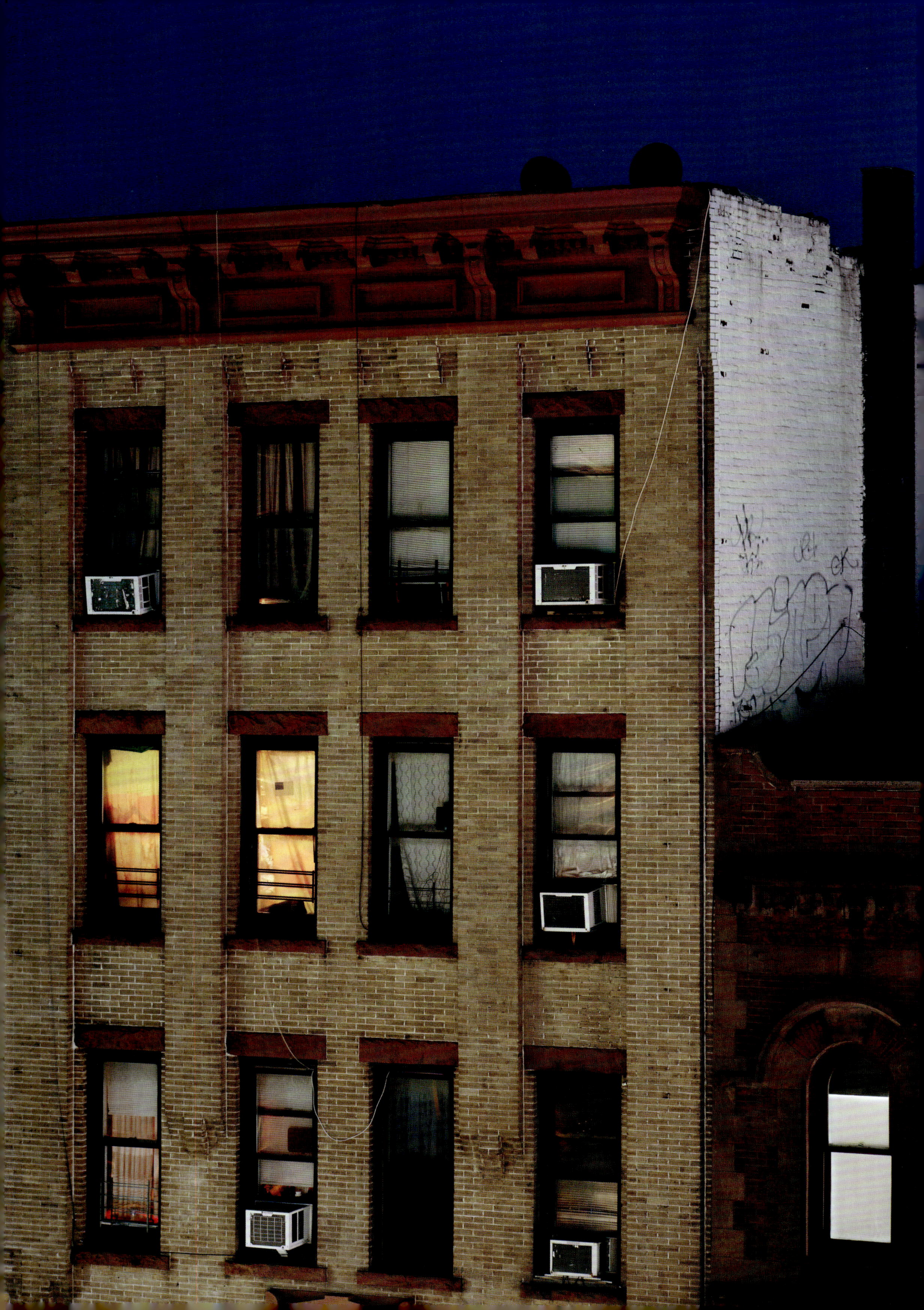

Sleepwalking

Guest edited by Alec Soth

It is easy to imagine Alec Soth daydreaming in pictures. As an acclaimed photographer, teacher, publisher, YouTuber, and one-time blogger, he is as dedicated to thinking about what pictures mean as he is to making them. Since his acclaimed 2004 debut, *Sleeping by the Mississippi*, a series he described not as a chronicle of place but an excuse to wander, Soth has made lyrical bodies of work—modest meditations on consciousness—that parse the surfaces of the everyday. "In my projects, I allow myself to change course and follow my nose," he notes of his process, which is decidedly driven by a search for serendipity.

As guest editor, Soth pursued a theme that wouldn't constrain him. "This 'Sleepwalking' issue," he says, "is one in which I'm always surprised on turning the page, where good old descriptive photographs of the real world tap into the logic of dreams. I want the reader to feel like they *are* sleepwalking." We hope you enjoy the journey with eyes wide open, or shut. **—The Editors**

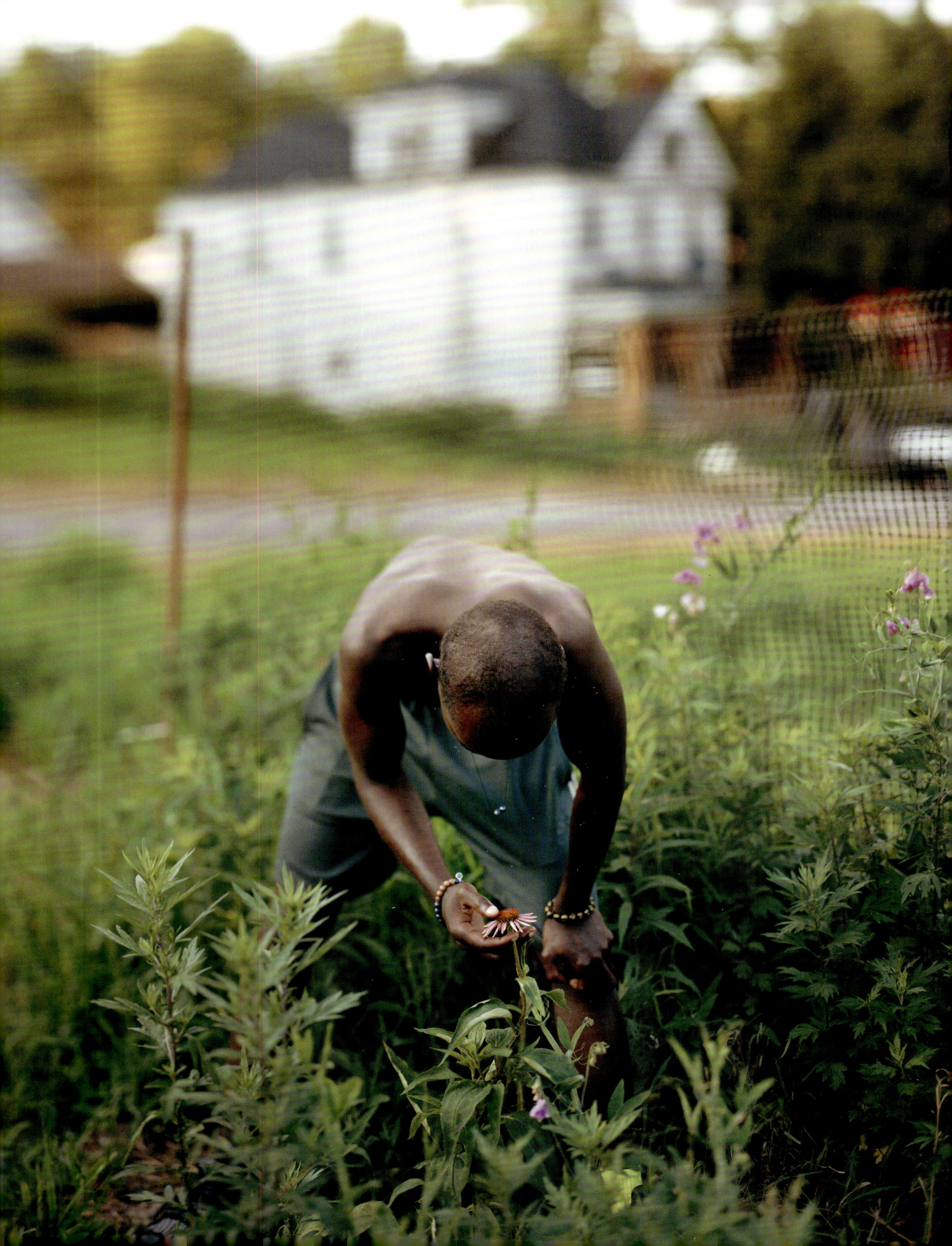

Alec Soth
Song of the Open Road

A Conversation with Siri Hustvedt

For his latest book, *A Pound of Pictures*, Alec Soth originally set out by car to follow the route of Abraham Lincoln's 1865 funeral train, hoping to consider America's current political division through the prism of a past historical crisis. When that idea felt forced, he let it go. But he kept driving. In Los Angeles, he encountered a woman who, to his astonishment, sold photographs by the pound. This discovery yielded compelling images of images and gave Soth a leitmotif: the weight of photography's own history. For Soth, this weight was not a burden but rather a wellspring of connections and associations found in the surfaces of his surroundings and in his travels to cemeteries, darkrooms, and bedrooms that reference Walker Evans, Robert Frank, and Nan Goldin, to name just a few touchstones that appear in the book.

In January, as yet another new COVID variant sent people back indoors, Soth spoke from his home in Minneapolis, via Zoom, with the writer Siri Hustvedt about the rhythms of narrative, Walt Whitman, and the democratic possibilities of sleep.

Siri Hustvedt: **I thought we should focus on your most recent book, *A Pound of Pictures* (2022), in order to rein in our conversation a bit.**

Alec Soth: What's good about that is, it has a retrospective quality where I'm thinking about the medium.

SH: **There is a real narrative pulse to this book. Even before opening it, the viewer-reader encounters a fairly long Whitmanian list on the cover. You establish a rhythm for what we're going to see—an introduction to what I think is a crucial aspect of narrative: rhythm.**

AS: Absolutely.

SH: **Do you know this quote from Virginia Woolf? She was writing to Vita Sackville-West about literary style: "As for the *mot juste*, you are quite wrong. Style is a very simple matter; it is all rhythm."**

AS: That's beautiful.

SH: **I think the rhythmic foundations of narrative are corporeal and prelinguistic, but the way we imagine time in space is connected to literacy. The way we read images has a spatial component that acts as a metaphor for time. English speakers imagine time as a horizontal line moving from left to right. Arabic speakers imagine time going in the other direction. I read the other day that Mandarin speakers often imagine time as vertical. The cars in your pictures allude to a narrative journey, and they're all going backward, that is, into the past.**

AS: That's an amazing way of looking at it.

SH: **Every single car, except one. In the memorial image with the flowers on a street corner, there's a parked car that's headed into the future in terms of the spatial metaphor. And there's the car with the bust of Lincoln, which is a quasi-comic image because it looks like he's driving, and he's headed for the past. I know from the book that Lincoln's funeral was the original inspiration for taking the journey across the country and making these photographs.**

AS: You are treating this as a book, which is beautiful. The book is, for me, the ultimate form for my work. But 99 percent of the people who see these pictures will see them in a different context, without that

narrative. That's part of my apprehension of investing too much in the narrative. So, I have to try to make it function on different levels—for the ideal reader like you, who's willing to look through the book in that sequential way versus the person who's going to see one picture on a wall somewhere. That narrative functions differently when it's internal to a photograph.

SH: **But any image of a road implies motion, moving into the future or the past.**

AS: The thing about the road, and the road trip, is it's such a cliché, and I kind of hate it, yet I keep returning to it—process-wise it just works for me so well. But also, it's a way to suggest narrative. So whether it be driving along the Mississippi River, or this imagined Lincoln funeral procession, that idea of a line moving in a direction helps.

SH: **Another recurring image is of telephone lines. They extend beyond the frame of the photograph, so you're led out of the picture, which also has narrative implications. And that can happen in a single picture.**

AS: The thing that I always say about photography—and I think it's true—is that it mostly just suggests narrative rather than gives you a story.

SH: **Right, it's not explicit. The meaning is made between the particular viewer and your photograph, but all viewers also carry larger cultural narratives, depending on where we come from and what we do. This is outside of *A Pound of Pictures*, but that image from *Broken Manual* (2010) with the school bus and the horse took me instantly back to the orange school bus I rode every day as a child in Minnesota. It's an empty school bus. It's not going anywhere. I didn't ride horses, but my sisters competed in rodeos and Western games. The combination, horse plus school bus, produced a plethora of personal meanings in me. But the photo also has the abstract, bizarre quality of some hypnagogic imagery. Do you see images before you go to sleep?**

AS: Definitely in a napping situation, I have that. But with photography, it's so utterly specific. That school bus and that horse and that place are so specific.

SH: **The horse was really wandering by? You didn't bring the horse over there?**

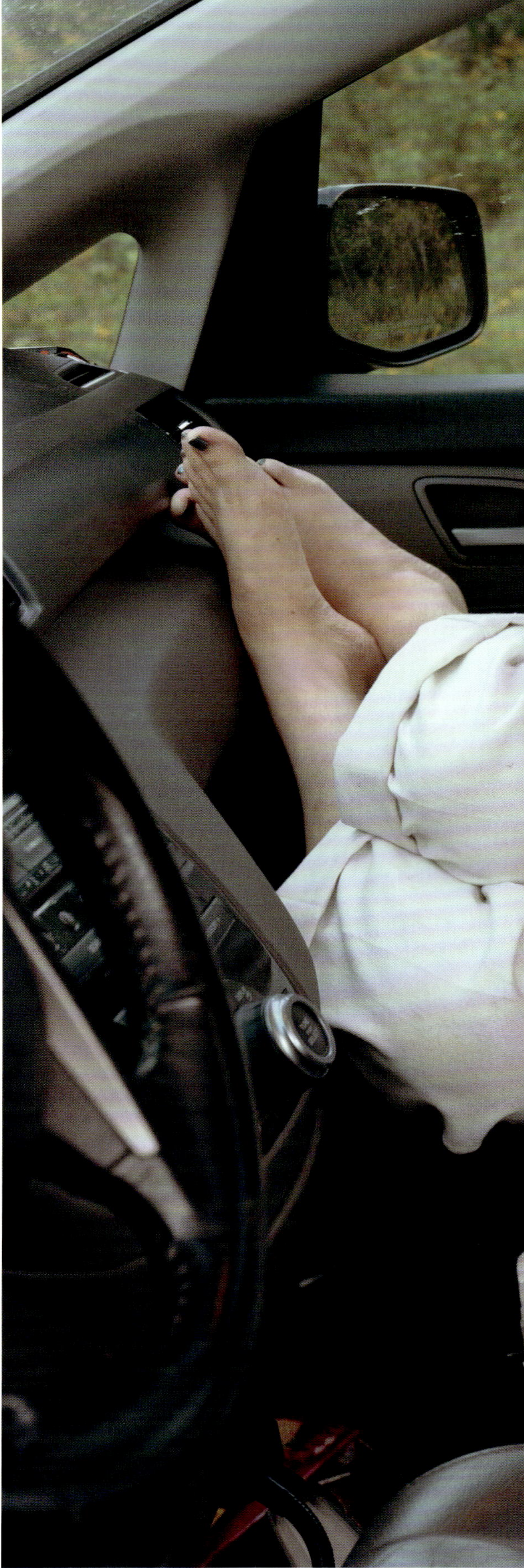

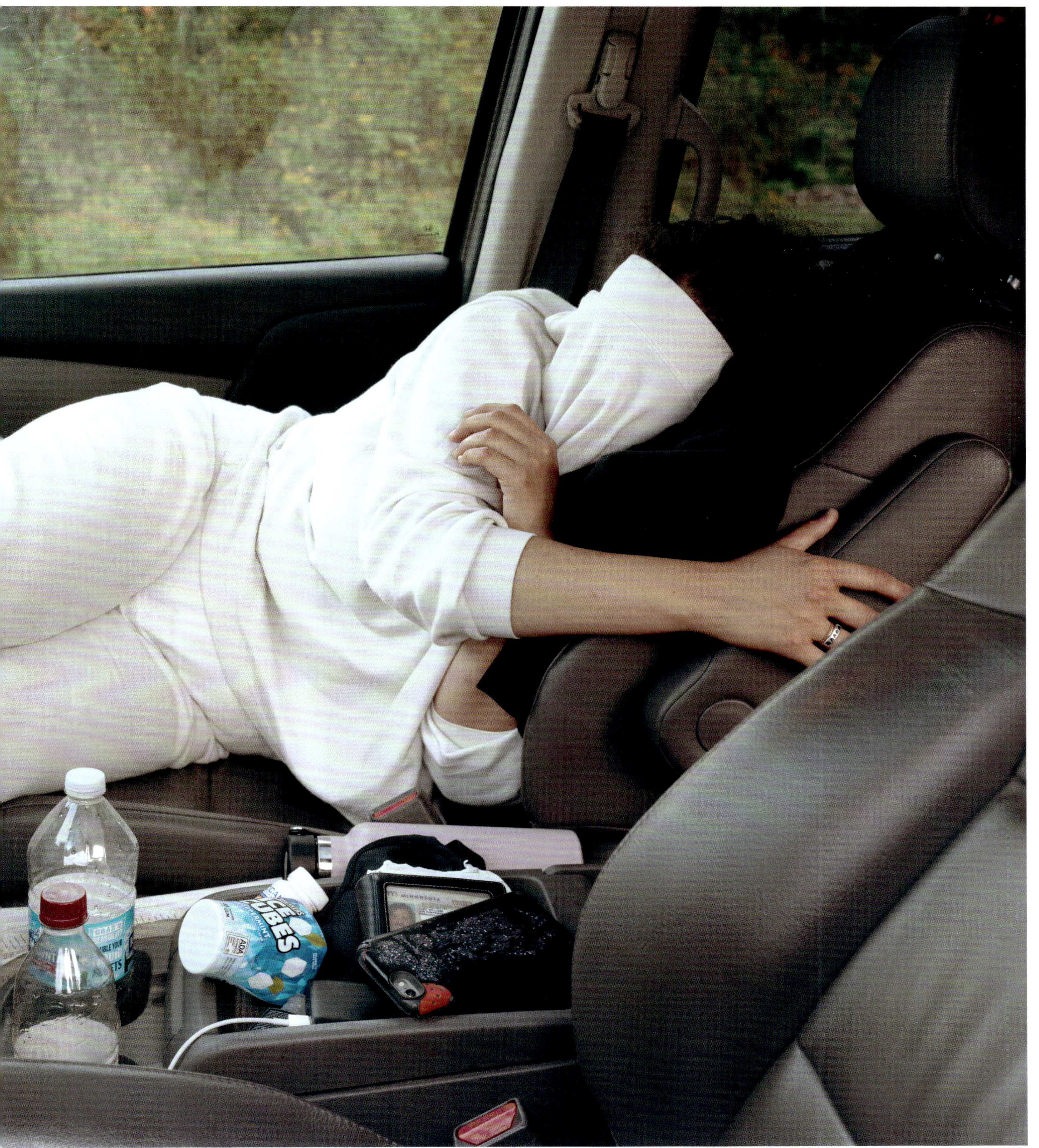

Page 24:
*Stuart. Pittsburgh,
Pennsylvania, 2021*

This spread:
*Molly napping in the
Odyssey. Watersmeet,
Michigan, 2019*

AS: Oh, no. I absolutely didn't bring the horse over there. My sense is it used the bus to protect itself from the wind or something. The hope is that someone will make that spark and launch off into some sort of imaginary space, or it could be from your own experience. I sometimes think of photographs as a diving board into a pool of imagination.

Let me ask you this. Would you agree with me that between the novel and the poem this difference in narrative is somewhat like the difference between a photograph and a film?

SH: **Yes, although there are many possibilities. There are narrative poems, too. This book struck me as an elegy related to Whitman's "When Lilacs Last in the Dooryard Bloom'd," which you quote in the book. There's a repetition, a motion you establish of blooming flowers, especially yellow flowers, coming back.**

AS: You got it! I found my audience.

SH: **The famous lines—"Lilac and star and bird twined with the chant of my soul, / There in the fragrant pines and the cedars dusk and dim"—could be an epigraph for the book. There's a lot of verdant foliage, but there are also, near the end, those desiccated individual blooms—stalks standing in front of the overgrown railroad tracks, which made me think of Lincoln's funeral trip again.**

AS: I'm just so happy that you get the book.

SH: **The short Whitmanian list—lilac, bird, star—in an elegy for a dead man. At the same time, the poem counters dying. Despite the death of the one he loved (he says, "for him I love"), there is burgeoning and blooming going on, and that snapping of the lilac branch. Whitman really is our great poet of democracy. He is continually leveling. My most beloved poem of his is "The Sleepers."**

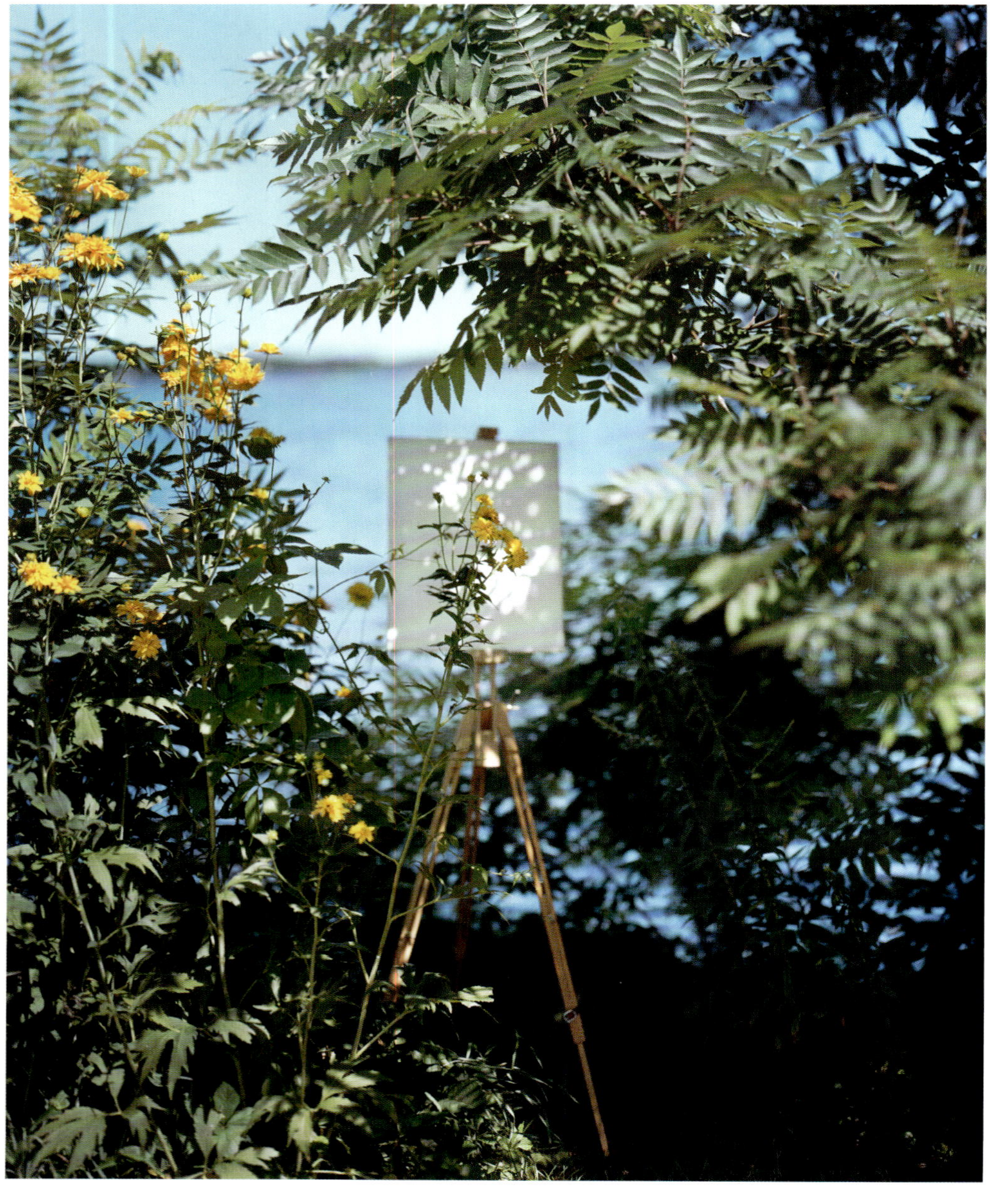

I sometimes think of photographs as a diving board into a pool of imagination.

AS: Perfect.

SH: **There sleep becomes the democratic force. That force is in "Crossing Brooklyn Ferry" too. But in this moment of pain and strife, the evocation of Whitman's elegy for Lincoln is particularly poignant.**

AS: I like what you say about sleepers. It makes me imagine a photography project in which, with all this political divisiveness, if you could just watch everyone sleeping . . .

SH: **You do have sleeping people. Lots of sleepers and beds.**

AS: There's a lot of it. There is something about that state that does feel more forgiving or something.

SH: **I think Whitman understood that deeply. As the poem goes on, it mounts to embrace all of humanity in this ideally American way with its promise of democracy, a promise that has never been fulfilled. But there's another push in your book to represent representation itself. You make that clear right from the beginning. First, we see a cemetery with a photographer. Second, a blank easel. I looked very closely. I can't find anything on the easel.**

AS: Just the shadow.

SH: **Just the shadow and the trees. The idea of representation and the presence of the photographer, whether it's you or not, runs through the book. And we literally see piles of pictures. Other times mounted photos of really old pictures that are fading. I love the picture of a grave with a photograph. You can't read the inscription, but the photograph is so clear. It's a nineteenth-century photograph that nevertheless seems to have survived or been replaced . . .**

AS: Stronger than stone. I don't think it's been replaced.

SH: **And then, the little white flowers. It's beautiful, and it's framed by the foliage.**

AS: At a certain point, I made this connection between flowers and photographs. In photography, in my world, there's this feeling that there are just way too many pictures, and we're overwhelmed with them. Then I suddenly had this thought of, like, someone complaining about there being too many flowers. A flower is beautiful

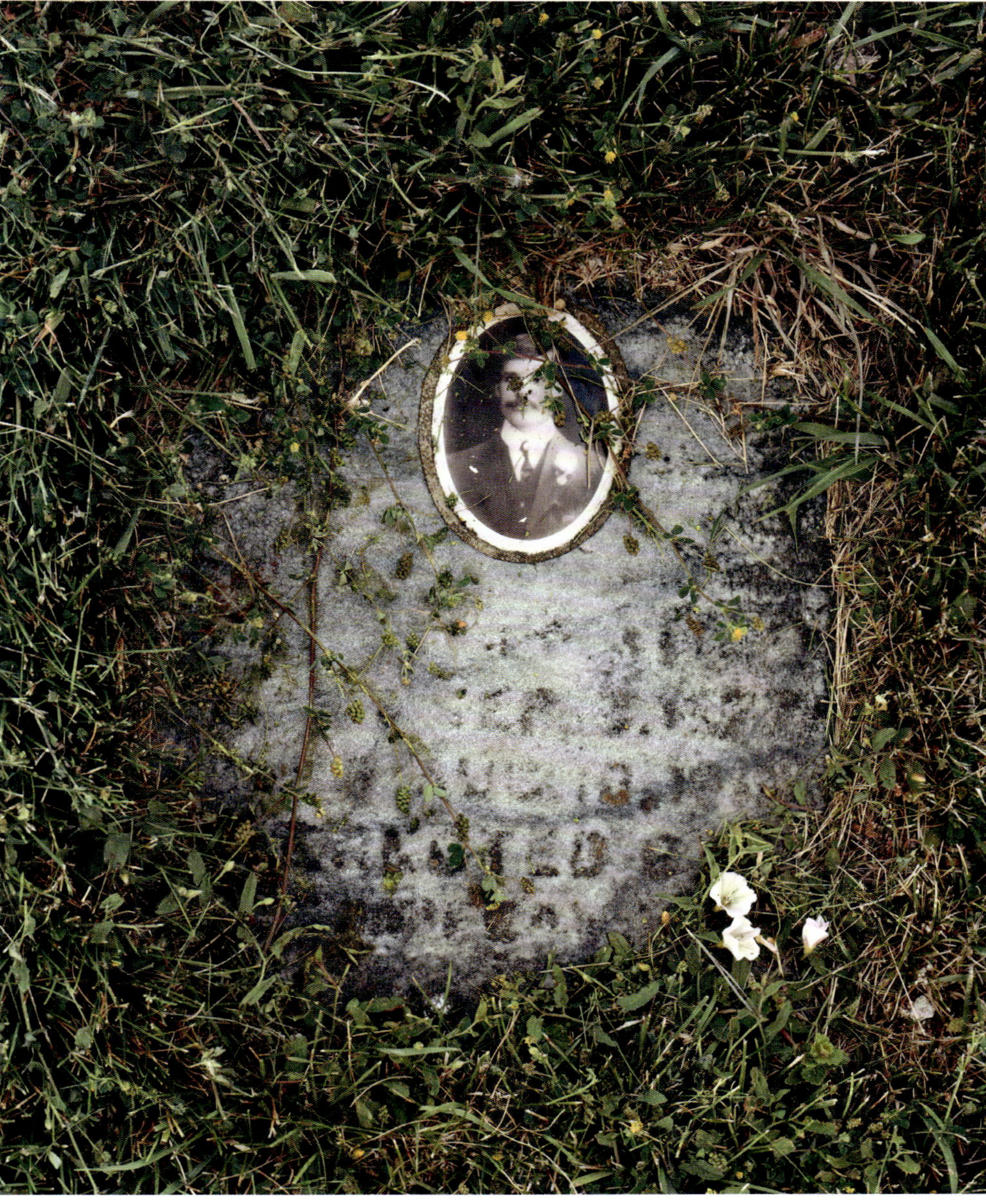

because it's going to die. We think we take a photograph because it's not going to die. It's going to keep something alive. But it never works. And the photograph itself fades. But this connection with photographs and death, and then flowers and death too—that you would want to put a photograph on a grave. There's something in that connection. One of my favorite pictures in the book is that woman with flowers on a street in Tulsa, and she's got the tattoo.

SH: **The picture is fascinating. You focus on the woman even though she's far away. There's a tenderness about the way she's handling the flowers, a kind of reverence that recurs throughout the book. There's another picture of a young shirtless boy bending over a pink daisy-like flower. His gesture is so delicate and evokes what you're saying— the transience of blooming—which is also in Whitman's poem. And then winter arrives in your book.**

AS: Maybe I should give you a little backstory in terms of the evolution of this book. As we've said, it started with the funeral train project. But then I had this idea that it was going to be a diary, hundreds of pictures intermixed with text, which is something I've never done. What happened was the pandemic hit, and so much happened in the world. It just felt impossible to then, a year later, pick up again with that diary format. During the pandemic, I forgot how to approach people and also got so in my head about: Oh, is it right for me to approach someone? What are the ethics of this? The political ramifications?

SH: **You've talked about this before, and I think it's important. You're sensitive to the power dynamics involved in taking a photograph. I've had my picture taken for my work for over thirty years now. I've gone from pretty young thing to old lady. Especially when I was younger, but sometimes even now,**

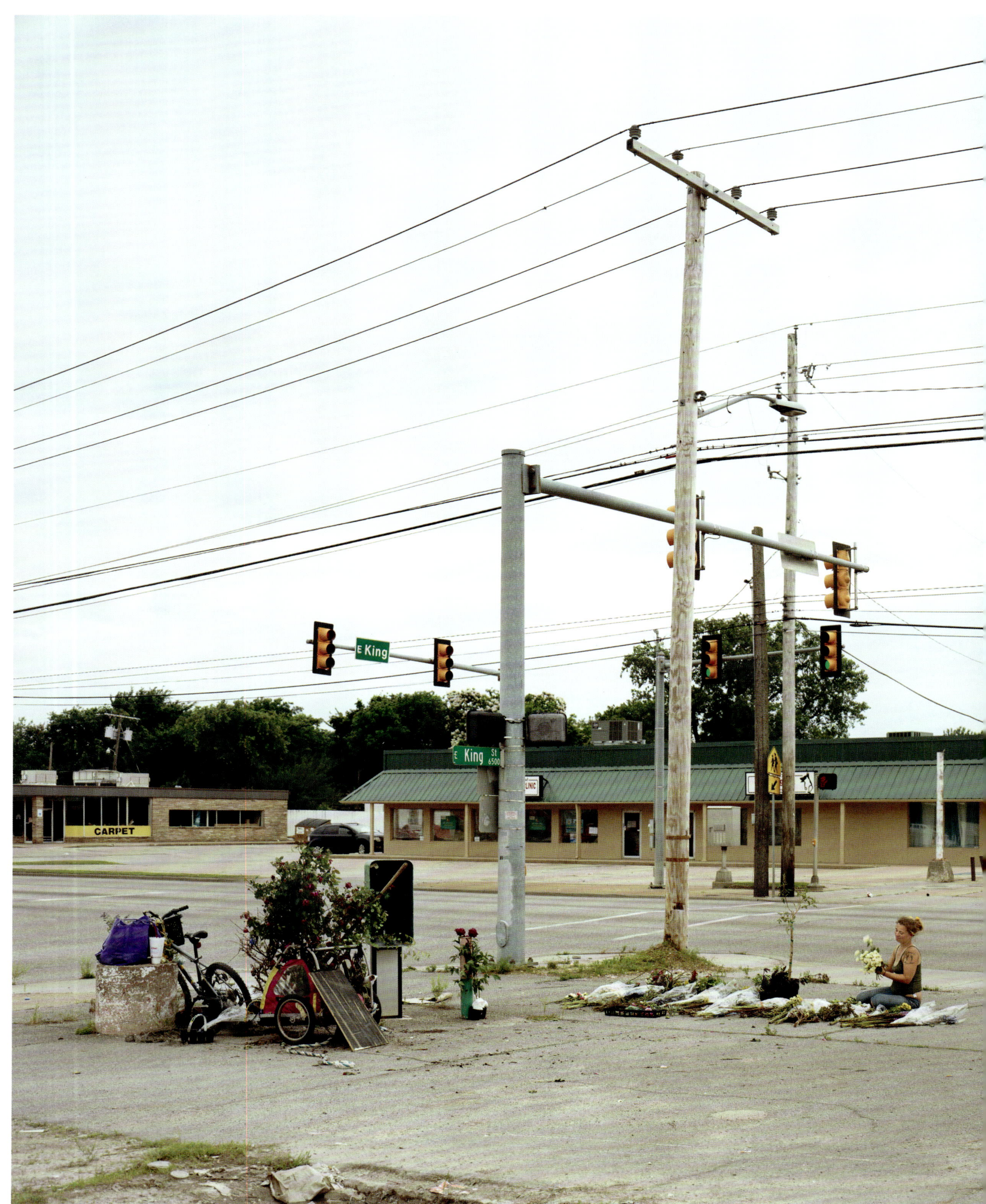

E King
E King St 6500
CARPET
CLINIC

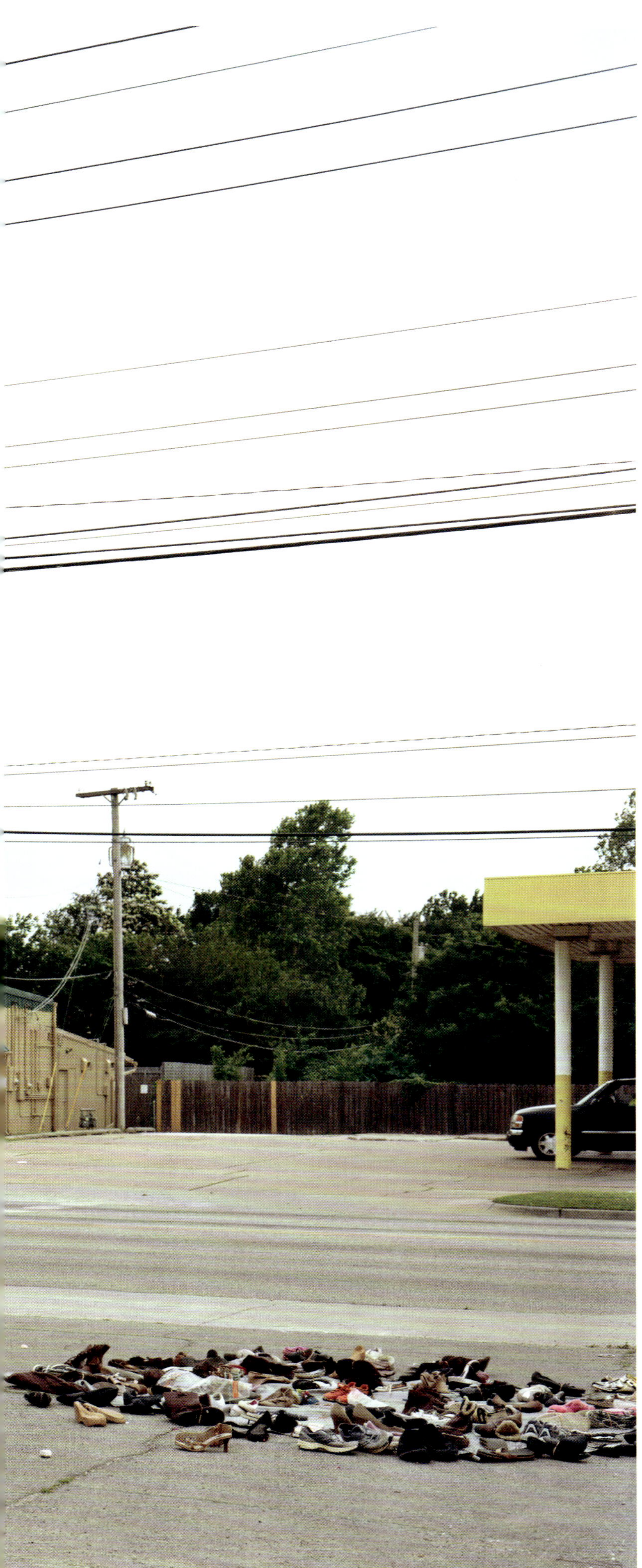

King & Sheridan, Tulsa, Oklahoma, 2021

I have felt emotionally and psychically assaulted by photographers. Photographs have a potential for cruelty that is real.

AS: Absolutely. For me, there're two parts to it. There's the taking of the picture, which nowadays is almost always a positive experience for me, and I think it is for the other person. I really try to have full consent, and I want them to be engaged and not afraid. And more often than not, they feel good about the experience. The problem comes in putting it on the wall and selling it for a bunch of money and putting it out in the world.

SH: **I do feel that your work in general has a dialogical quality. The image of— I think her name is Bonnie—she's holding up a picture of a cloud angel. There's integrity in her posture. She's confronting you with this image. It's almost as if the exchange between you two is present in the image. How is that visibly present?**

AS: I definitely don't have an answer for that. I am aware that people project onto these pictures a kind of intimacy that didn't exist. Because I'm always told: "You're so close with the people you photograph"—and I'm not. I know photographers who work that way, but I'm not that person. So, it's this other kind of intimacy, hopefully.

SH: **Writing about his work as a pediatrician, D. W. Winnicott said, "People need to be seen."**

AS: Oh, yeah. So true.

SH: **This relates to your interest in connectivity. You have that nice John Berger quote about the constellations, which also relates to narrative—the only way we can see the bears in the sky is if we draw the lines.**

AS: Yes. There aren't bears in the sky.

SH: **No. We make them there.**

AS: They have meanings through the stories of the bears in the sky.

SH: **You have talked about this publicly, but you had a transcendent experience in Finland?**

AS: Yes.

SH: **I have migraines with aura and have had a number of ecstatic experiences. We are hardly alone. Many people in**

I thought of this project as my ars poetica in photography. Trying to do something about the medium but in a lyrical way.

these states feel boundaries dissolve and have a powerful sense that all things are connected.

AS: What do you do with that knowledge in your art?

SH: In my novel *The Blazing World*, I have a character named Sweet Autumn. She began as a comic character, a New Age kind of idiot. As I was writing her and listening to her, she became bigger and bigger. She's not the main character, but she's given the last word because her ecstatic insights, which are very nonintellectual, are finally the most profound. She has synesthesia. I have mirror-touch synesthesia.

AS: It's funny because I'm sitting here, looking right at you through Zoom— and you're over there, actually at this enormous distance away, and we're exchanging these words back and forth, trying to figure it out, to navigate this space between us. Which is exactly the way I think of my photography. What happened in that ecstatic moment was that that all kind of just fell away. It felt like there wasn't that separation, and all these atoms, with my atoms mixed in, were all one thing. I found that problematic as a photographer, that photography was promoting separation in a funny way. But, of course, we don't live in that ecstatic state.

SH: We all have to retreat to pedestrian reality and the boundaries that are part of it. John Dupré, a philosopher of biology, repeatedly stresses in his work that organisms are not things but processes. I would extrapolate— even in death, if you think about time as cyclical, there's return—which is in your book. The graveyards, the earth, the dirt, the blooms returning in spring.

AS: I do think it's that moment when you feel the thingness sort of start to

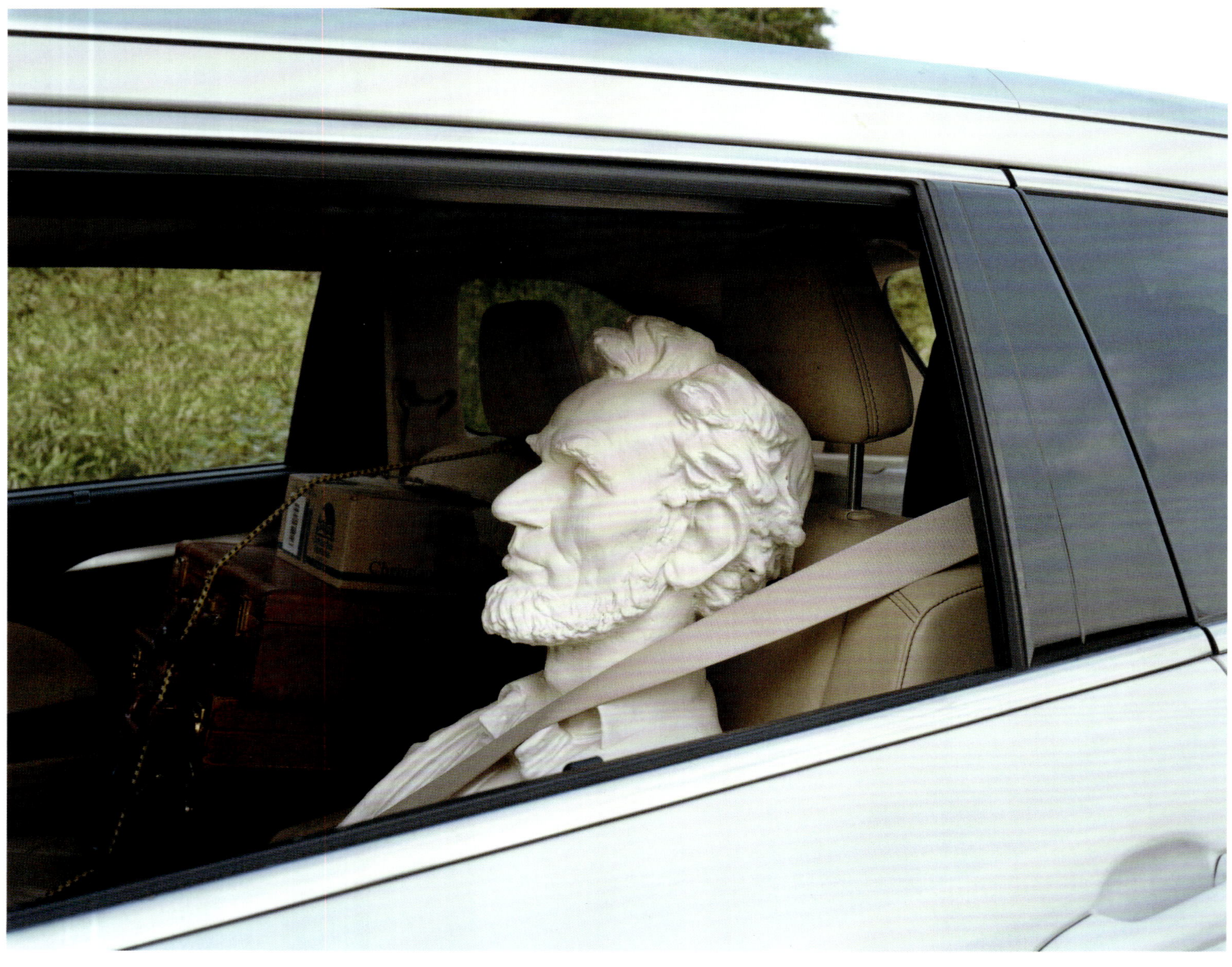

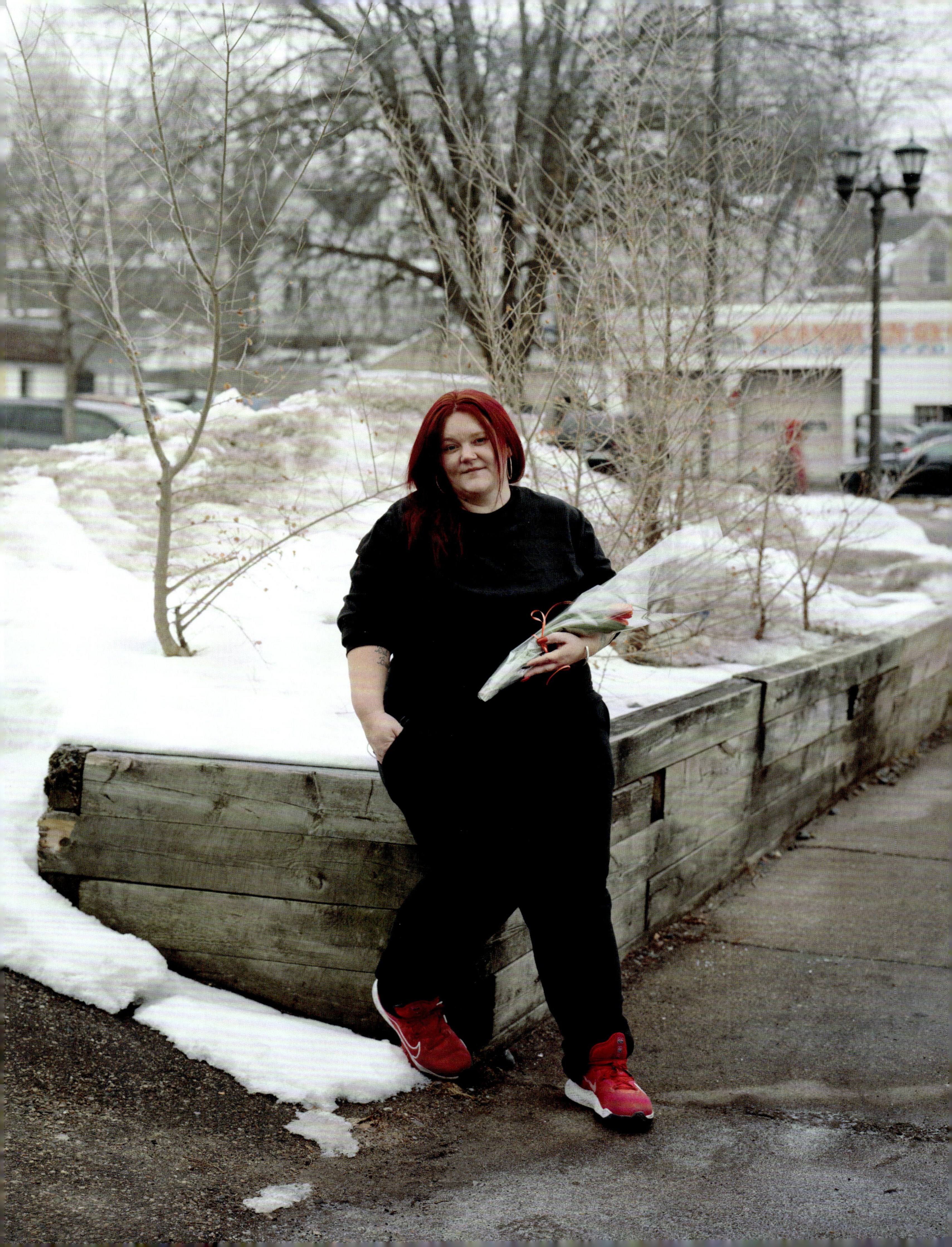

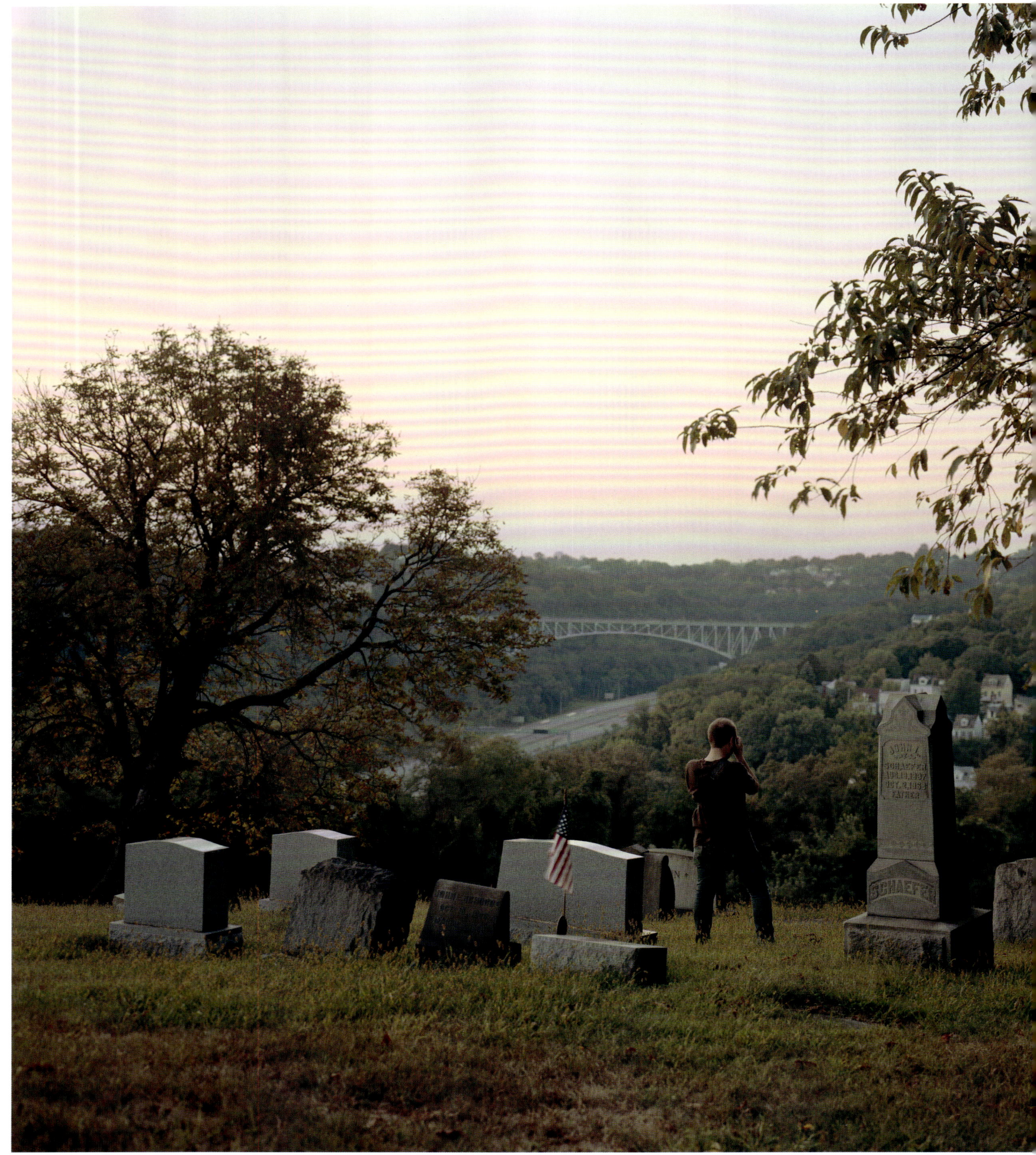

*Ed Panar. Pittsburgh,
Pennsylvania, 2019*

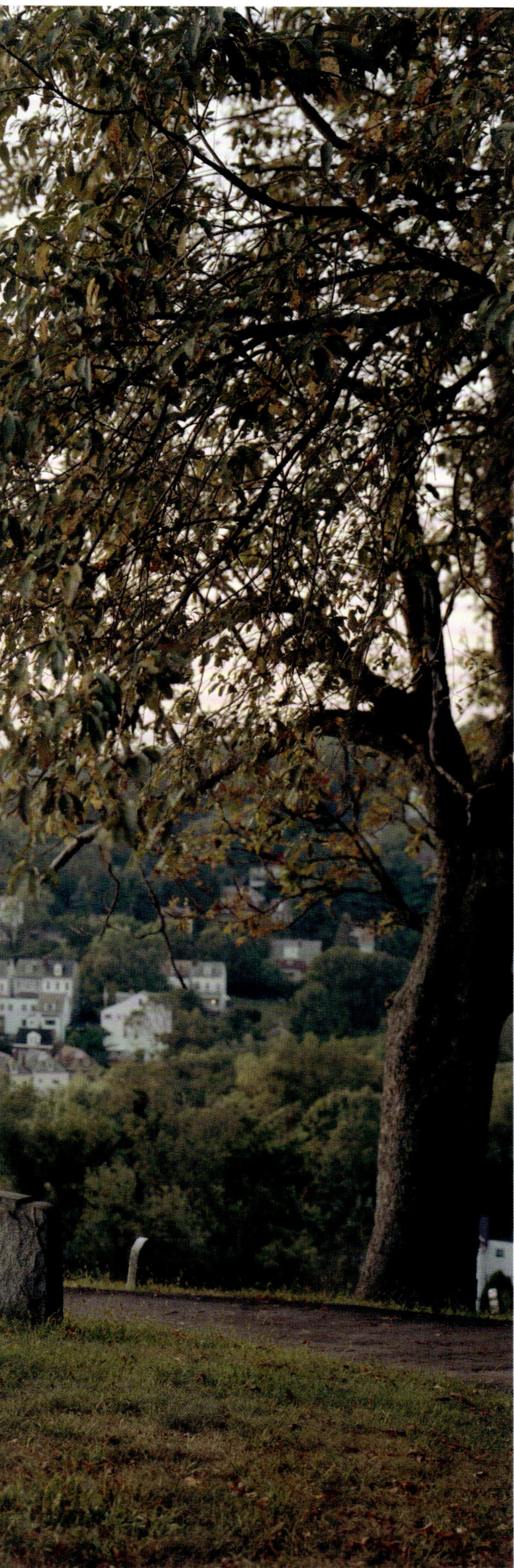

dissolve, and the lines becoming blurry—
a hypnagogic state.

SH: **It's like the weirdest kind of cinema
entertainment.**

AS: And there's something about when
I am immersed in my work that has a similar
quality, where it's a kind of hyperfocus to
the point of things beginning to dissolve
a little bit. Not in that ecstatic sort of way
but a nice little version.

SH: **I've been thinking that what is vital to
artistic work is a state of physical relaxation
accompanied by concentration.**

AS: Well, that's interesting.

SH: **With relaxation you become open,
and that openness allows both the world
and unconscious presences and memories
to act, to become available in ways that
they're not if you're tense.**

AS: The photographic act is really not
relaxed for me. It's quite tense.

SH: **I guess you have to be arranging
everything, don't you?**

AS: And I'm super tense when I'm doing
it. But then there's the other side, the
daydreaming about what is this going to be
about, what am I looking for, all of that—
which is that relaxed state.

SH: **Even though there are technical
aspects that have to be fulfilled, none
of that could happen if you weren't
in a state of openness to what you're
seeing.**

AS: Right. And it's achieving that state of
openness. The thing about that list at the
beginning of the book, it's a way to say,
hopefully, that this is open, that this is not
a documentary about X.

SH: **Exactly. And of course there's that
quote from Wallace Stevens's poem
"Of Modern Poetry" that you included
there too . . .**

AS: Oh, my gosh. You found that.

SH: **Yeah, I love Stevens. When I was
really young and writing, I used to have
Wallace Stevens and Emily Dickinson
and a few other people open on my desk
because I thought they could send me
signals and make me a better writer.**

AS: I thought of this project as my version
of an ars poetica in photography. Trying

to do something about the medium but in
a lyrical way. And that poem is such a great
example of that. He is always this poet
of consciousness. That's a funny thing
to want to aspire to in this clunky medium
of photography, but I think there is a
way to use it to address consciousness in
some way.

SH: **This is a great question. The mind-
body problem.**

AS: It's so crazy.

SH: **Consciousness is an unsolved problem.
In your writing at the end of the book,
you point out that a great deal of sensual
information is missing from a photograph.
You don't hear birdsong, for example. No
smells. This is true of all the arts. Even in
film, the screen is flat.**

AS: Right. But I think that lack of other
information, or the peculiarity of just
having a flat image, is what allows us to
reflect on it.

SH: **Oh, but that's what's so beautiful
about it! And the fact that it's silent.
Photographs and paintings have this
in common. You can stand in front of
them, and you need time to take in what's
there, even though it's there all at once.
You can't take something out or put
something in once it's done.**
　　**Lastly, I do feel there's underground
politics in the book, in that it's related to
what now appears to be the failing dream
of democratic equality.**

AS: I don't know if that was my intention.
That's where I started—in that mindset.
Then I felt like I was illustrating some idea
about America. And once I broke free of
that, I once again found positive, affirmative
things out there. Because during the
lockdown period, I thought, Wow,
everything that I ever said about America
is totally wrong. The whole thing is
broken. And then, going out into the
world and having some of these encounters
made me think, Oh, it's more complicated
than that. That's where I'm happy for
other people to read into the pictures
as they wish. How any of my work is
interpreted about America tends to be
highly charged in that way. That's not how
I think about it, but, of course, everything
is political.

SH: **Interpretation is a complex
business. Agitprop and fierce rhetoric
have their place in the world, but
they're not going to give you the
complexity, richness, and ambiguity**

I like to feel from all the arts. And yet,
the country is in desperate straits at
the moment.

AS: That goes without saying.

**SH: Ideology can create wooden, dead
art. It has also inspired some stirring
manifestos and extraordinary poetry.**

AS: What I do love about Whitman, just
to go back to where it all started, was that
I found comfort in reading him at that
moment. I was thinking about the Civil
War and the assassination of Lincoln, and,
like this moment, it was a pretty bad time.
And then you have this guy who's able to
find all this beauty while still acknowledging
everything that's broken.

SH: He was a nurse, after all.

AS: Yeah, absolutely. He gave me a little
bit of hope. He always does. And certainly,
in terms of aspiring for more openness,
he's pretty good for that.

**SH: Oh yes, he's positively disinhibited,
I would say. And the list. The list. It's
the most democratic form you can find.**

AS: Absolutely.

SH: Everything has equal value in a list.

AS: Walker Evans was a great list maker,
and we think of his work as having that
democratic quality as well. And photography
is often called this democratic medium, in
that it's almost like list making in its visual
representation—here's a car, here's
a street.

**SH: Unlike a painting, a novel, or a movie,
a photograph is of the world. Or that is
what the viewer feels, right? There really
was an orange school bus.**

AS: There really was.

Siri Hustvedt is a novelist and scholar. Her
most recent book is a collection of essays,
Mothers, Fathers, and Others (2021).

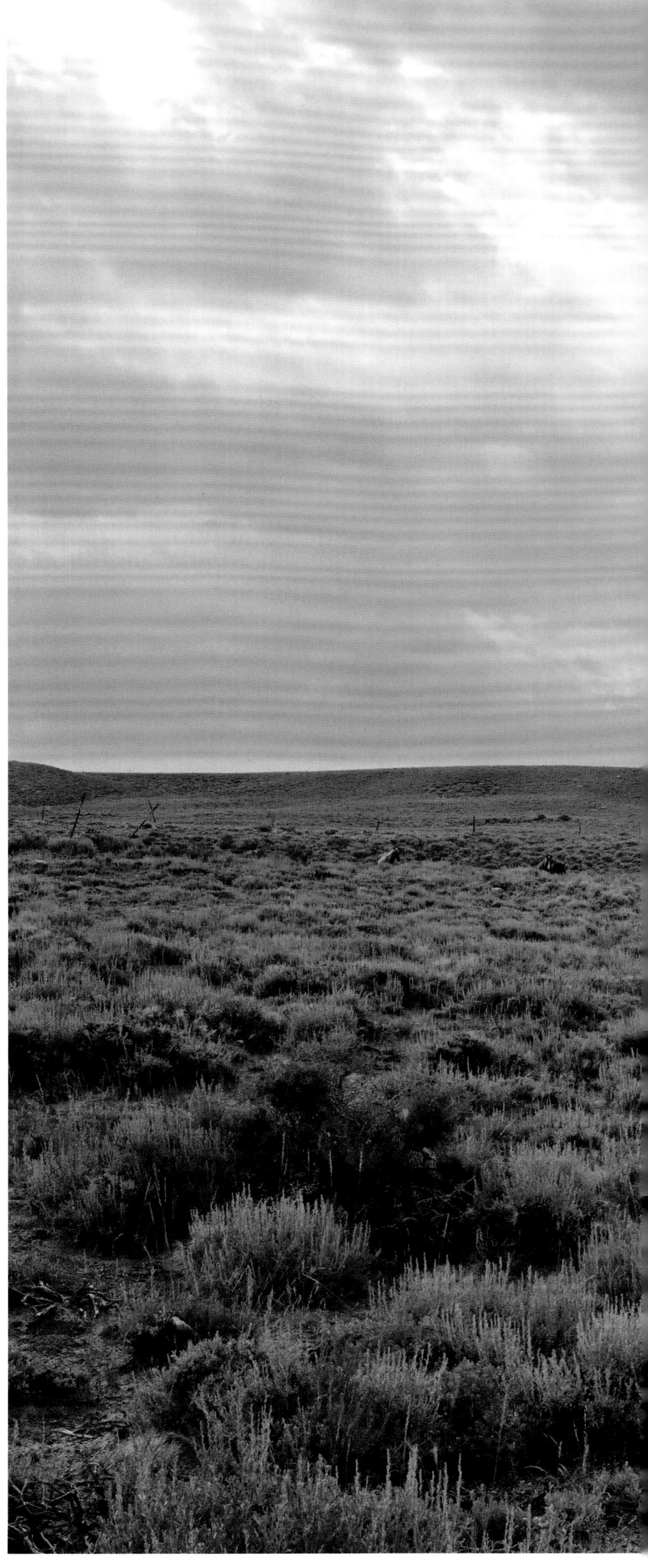

2008_08zL0047, 2008
All photographs courtesy
the artist; Sean Kelly, New
York; Fraenkel Gallery,
San Francisco; and
Weinstein Hammons Gallery,
Minneapolis

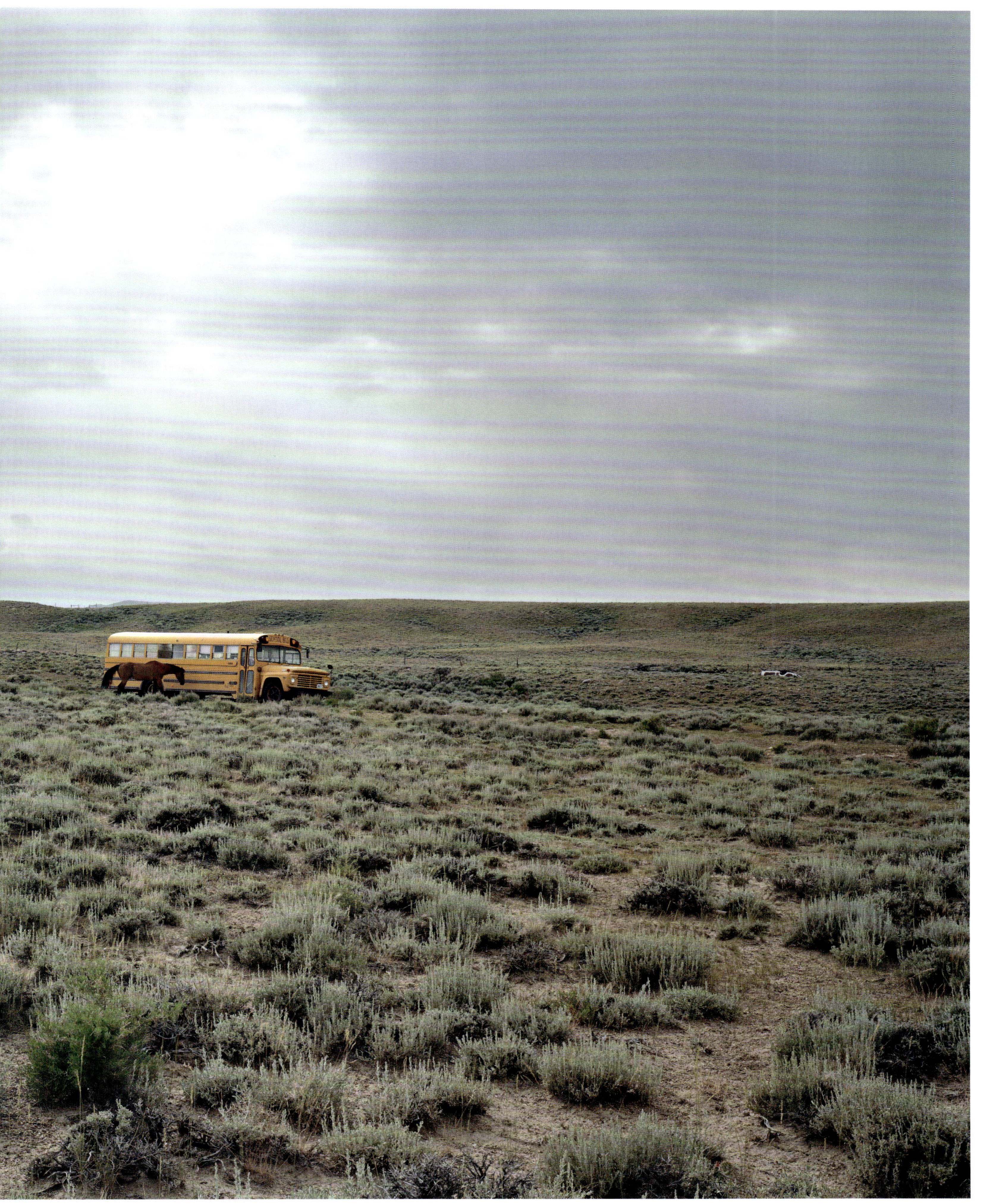

Alec Soth

Pictures for Dreaming

The artists and images that have inspired, haunted, and provoked me.

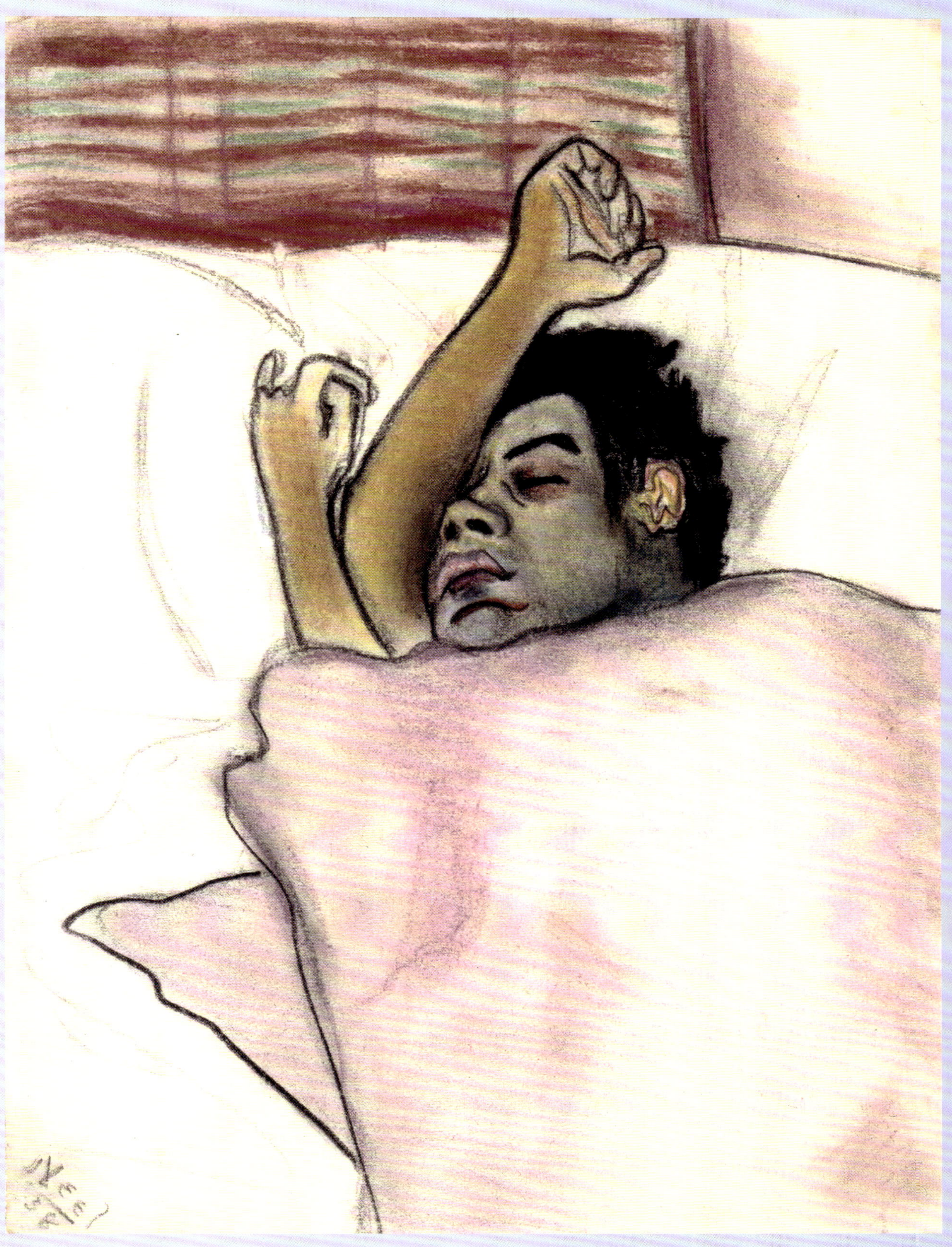

Alice Neel, *José Asleep*, 1938
Courtesy the Estate of Alice Neel and David Zwirner

Alice Neel
I came to art via painting. I made sloppy abstract paintings because it was all I could do. At the time, I was focused on the Abstract Expressionists and didn't even know the work of figurative painters such as Alice Neel. If I'd discovered her portraits back then, maybe I would've continued painting. The mix of intimacy and intensity in her canvases is a constant source of inspiration.

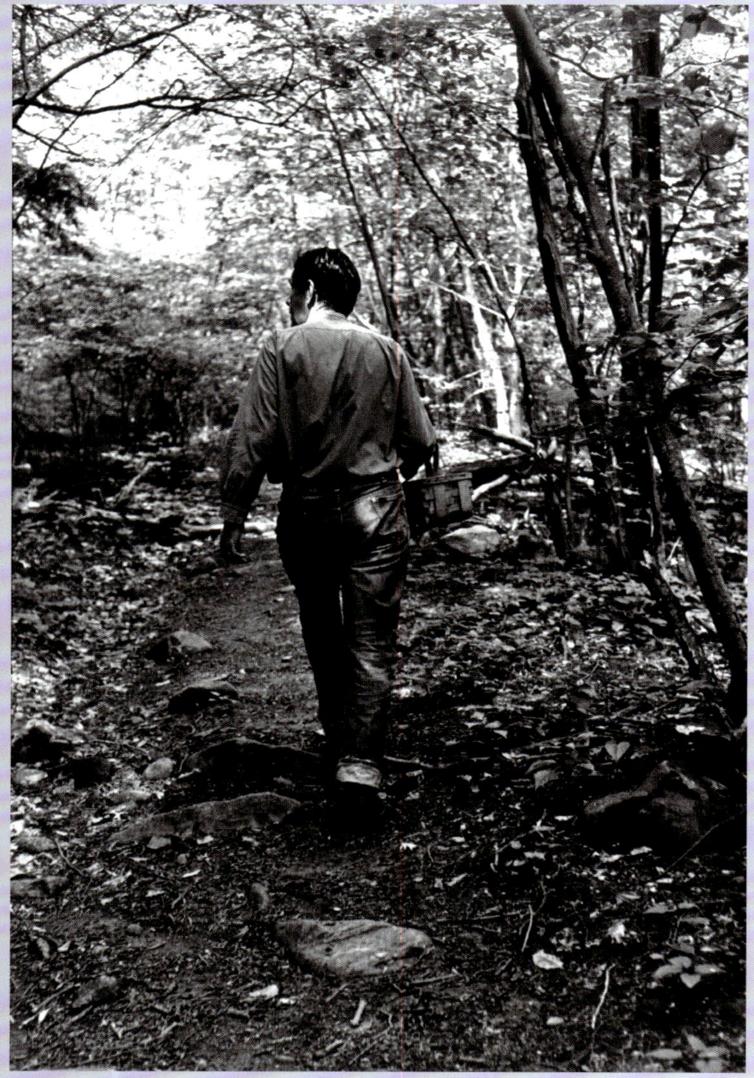

Richard Long, *A Line Made by Walking*, 1967
Courtesy DACS, London/
Artists Rights Society (ARS),
New York/Tate

William Gedney, John
Cage walking in the woods,
carrying basket, 1967
Courtesy the David M.
Rubenstein Rare Book &
Manuscript Library, Duke
University

John Cage and Richard Long
When I was in high school, I had a recurring dream
about meeting John Cage. While I never did meet
him and no longer have those dreams, Cage is still
present in my life. In 2013, I even published a book
of his writings. Another of my teenage creative
crushes was Richard Long. He taught me that
something as simple as a walk could be a work of art.
A few years ago, I gave a lecture in Bristol, England,
and was told that Long would be in the audience.
I went on a walk and picked up a stone in his honor.

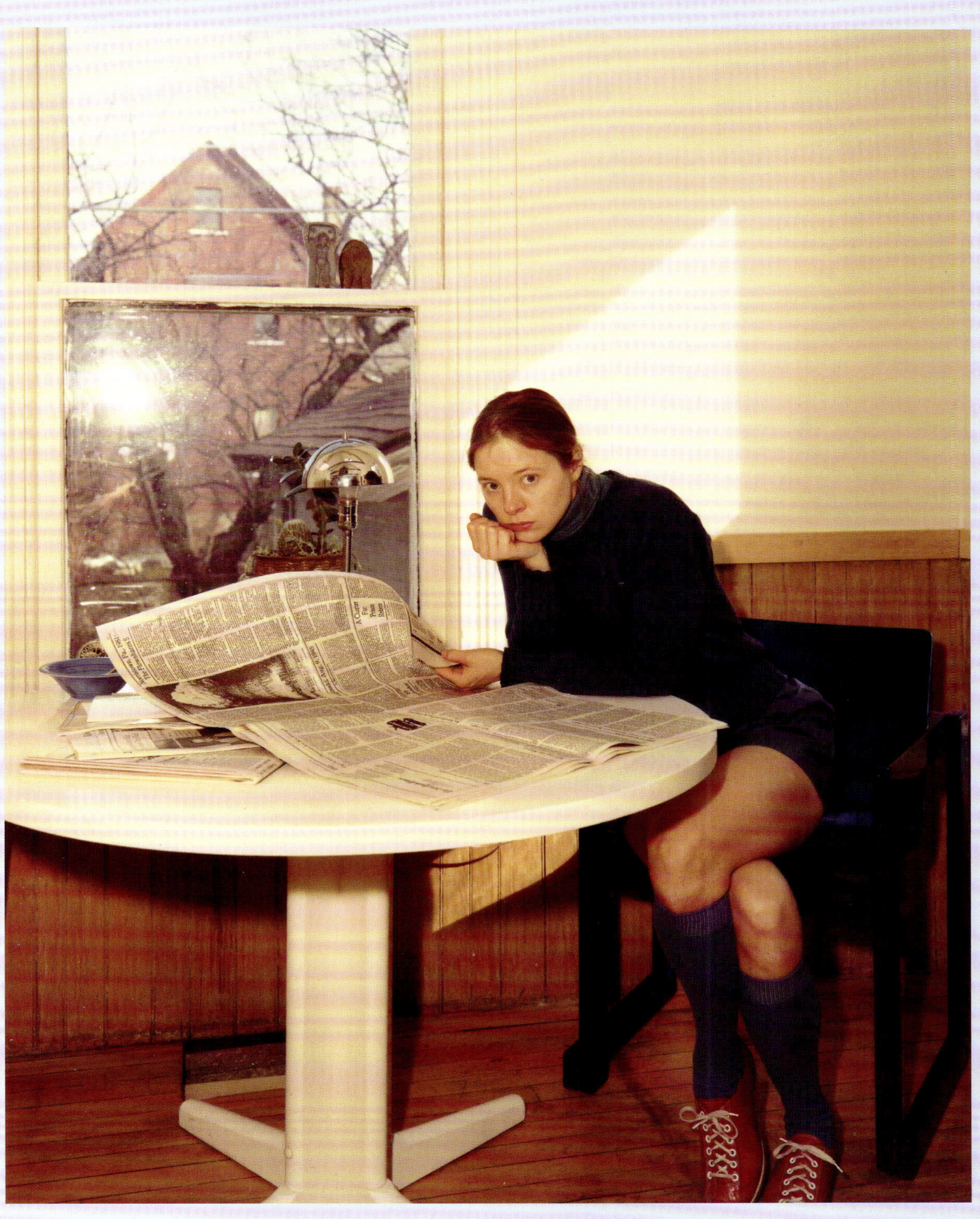

Roger Mertin, *Michaela Allan Murphy, Rochester, New York*, 1981
© and courtesy George Eastman Museum

Roger Mertin
The book *New Color/New Work: Eighteen Photographic Essays* (1984) had a huge impact on my photography. It included now-legendary photographers like Stephen Shore and William Eggleston, and the lesser-known Roger Mertin, whose work has continued to inspire me.

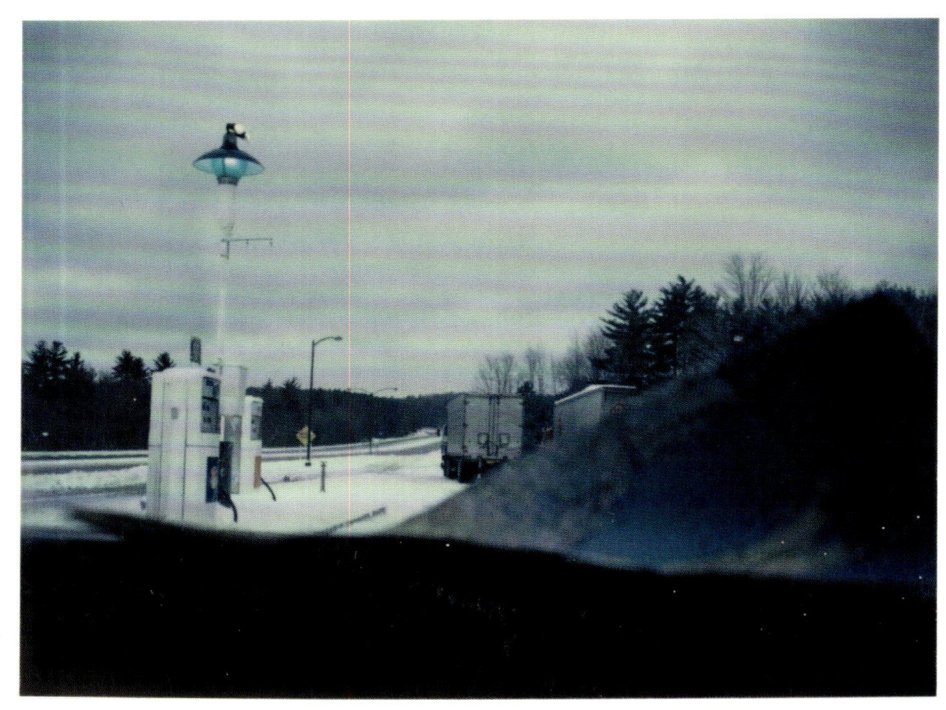

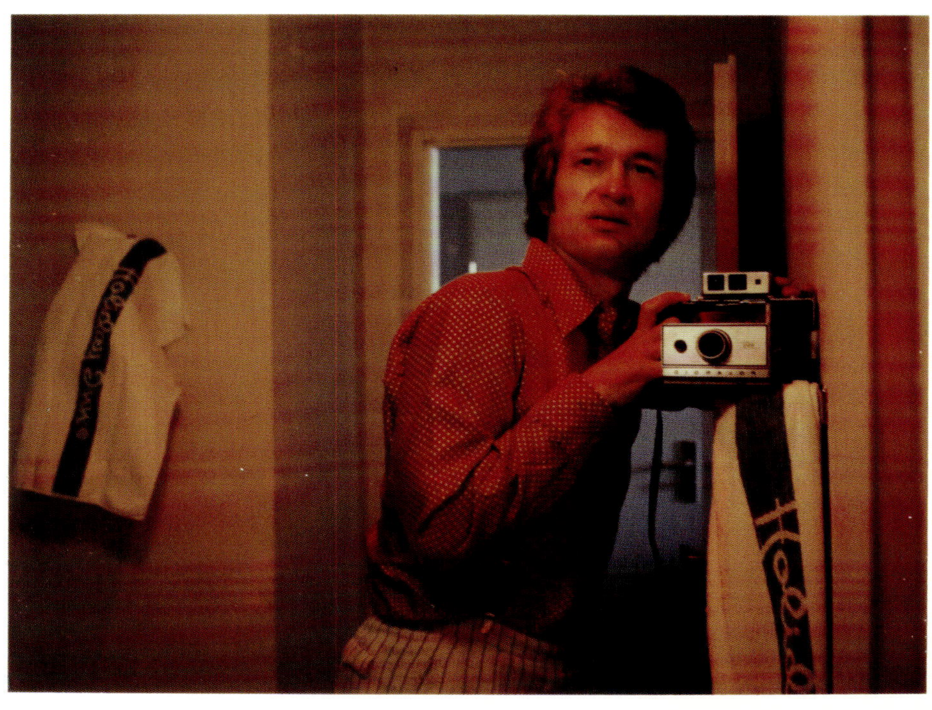

Wim Wenders
Like countless photographers, I had a desire to
make cross-country road trips. But this passion
wasn't ignited by Walker Evans, Robert Frank,
or even Stephen Shore. In fact, it didn't even come
from a photographer. It was the films of the great
German director Wim Wenders that made me
want to hit the road.

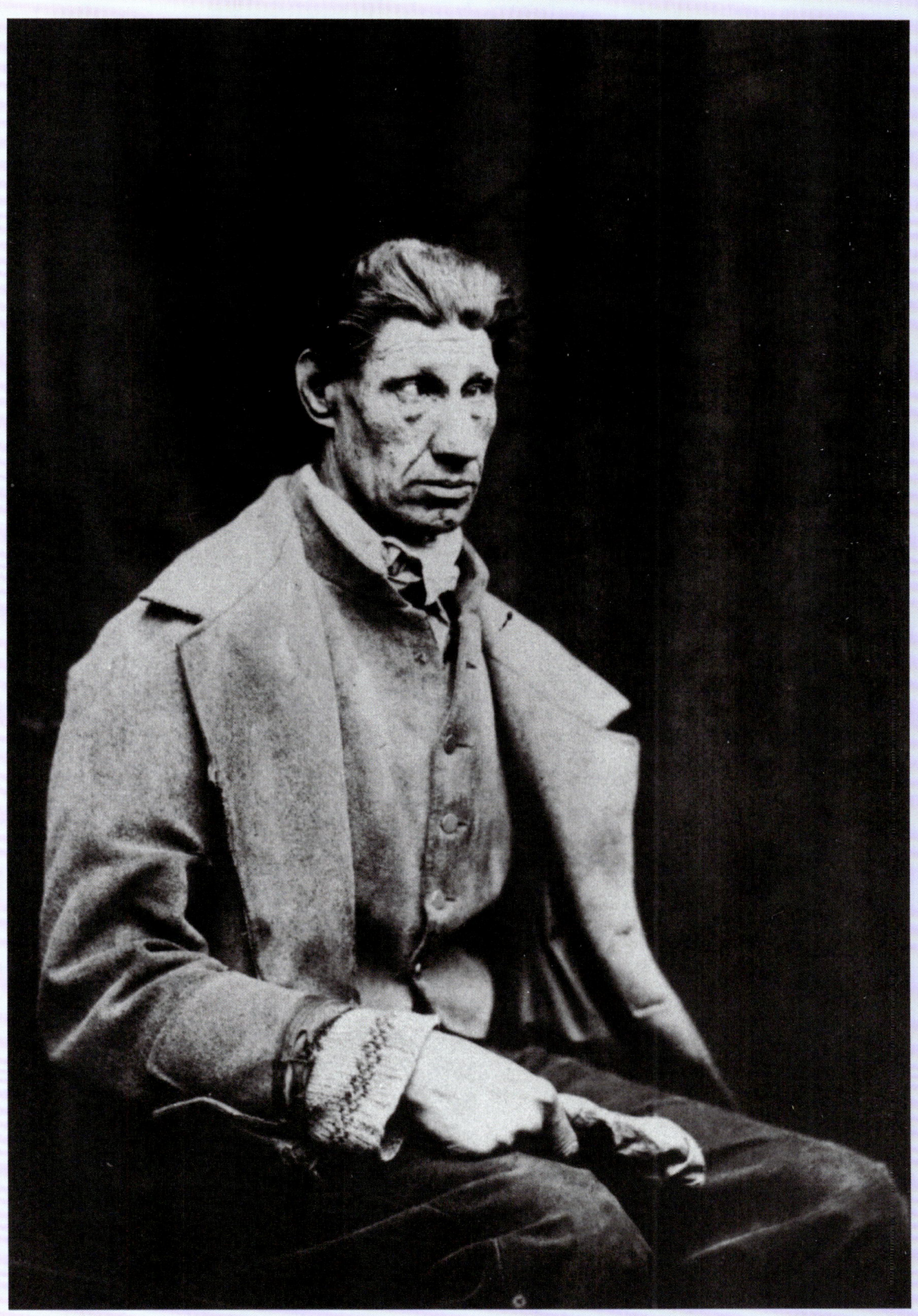

Hugh Welch Diamond,
Male Mental Patient,
ca. 1850s
Courtesy the Royal Society
of Medicine, London

Hugh Welch Diamond
Before I ever heard about August Sander or
Diane Arbus, I came across photographs by this
British psychiatrist that haunt me to this day.

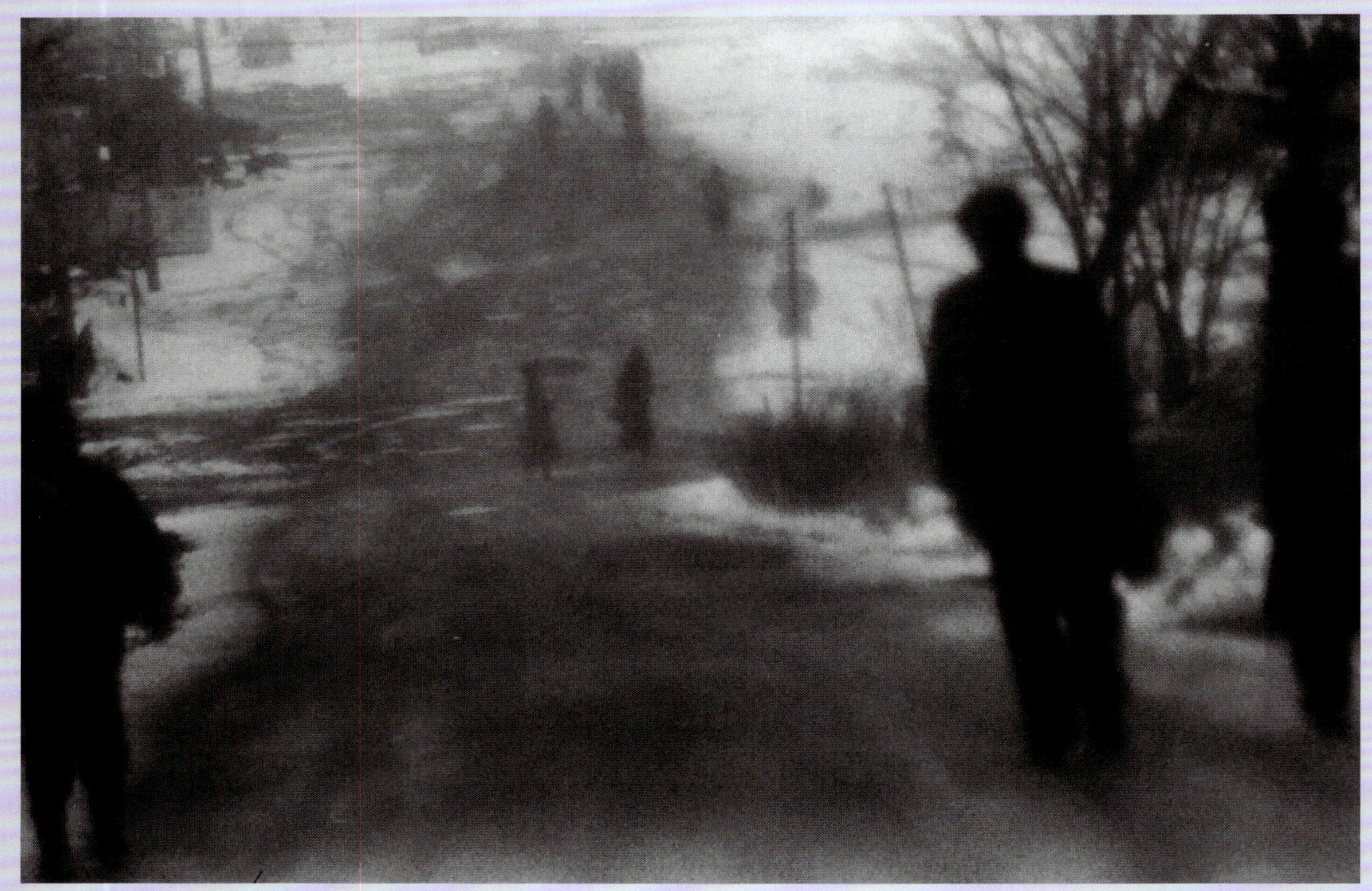

Masahisa Fukase
While I've always been drawn to "straight photography" (such an awful term), my eye has always traveled to the moody side of its documentary spectrum.

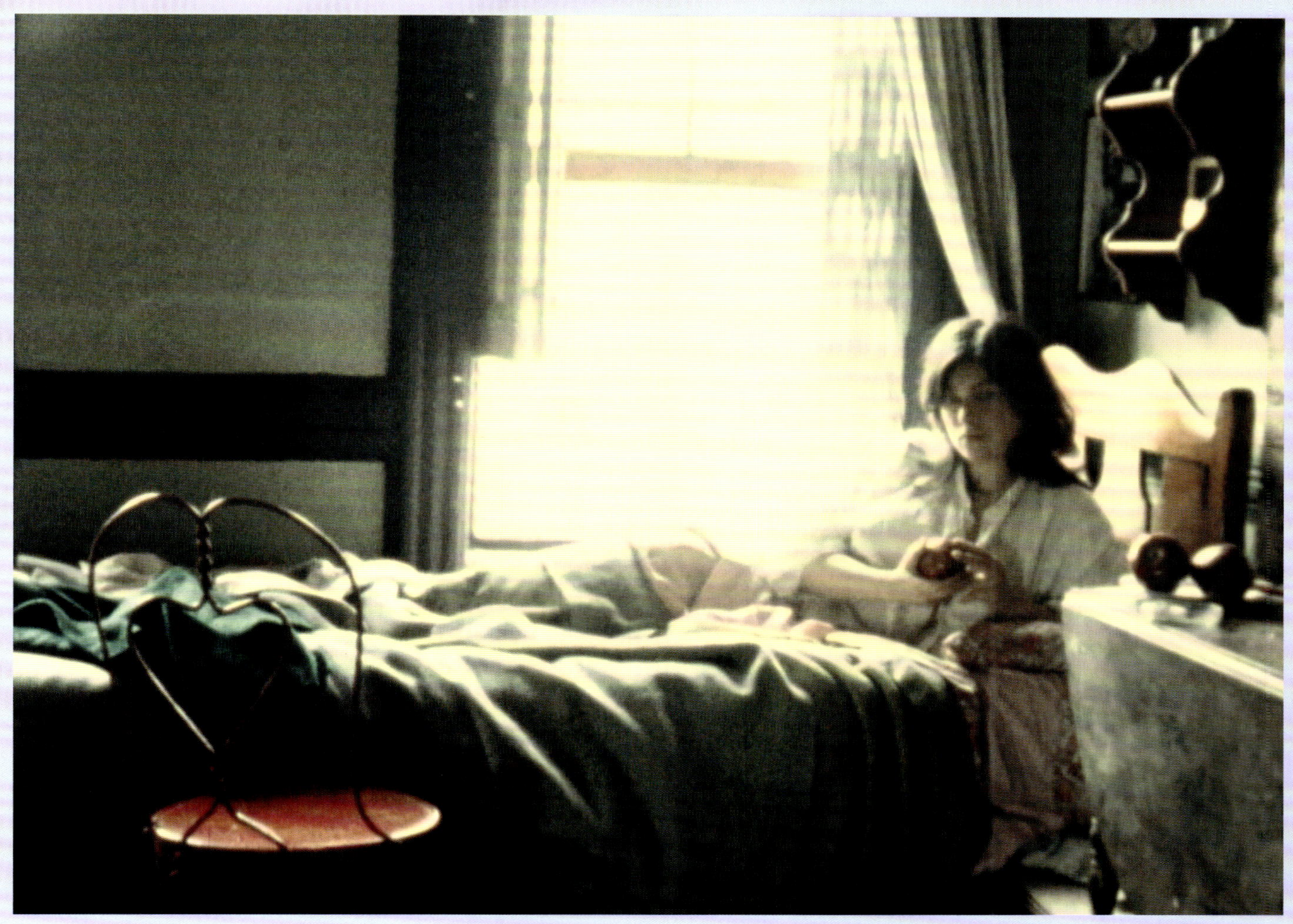

Chantal Akerman, Still from *La chambre*, 1972
© Chantal Akerman Foundation and courtesy Collections Cinematek, Belgium

Chantal Akerman
I became a fan of Chantal Akerman when I saw a museum installation of her film *D'Est* in the early 1990s. Recently, I've been revisiting this filmmaker's incredible oeuvre. Whether it is her early fictional masterpiece *Jeanne Dielman, 23, quai du Commerce, 1080 Bruxelles*, from 1975, or her final autobiographical documentary, *No Home Movie*, from 2015, Akerman consistently paired clarity with psychological introspection.

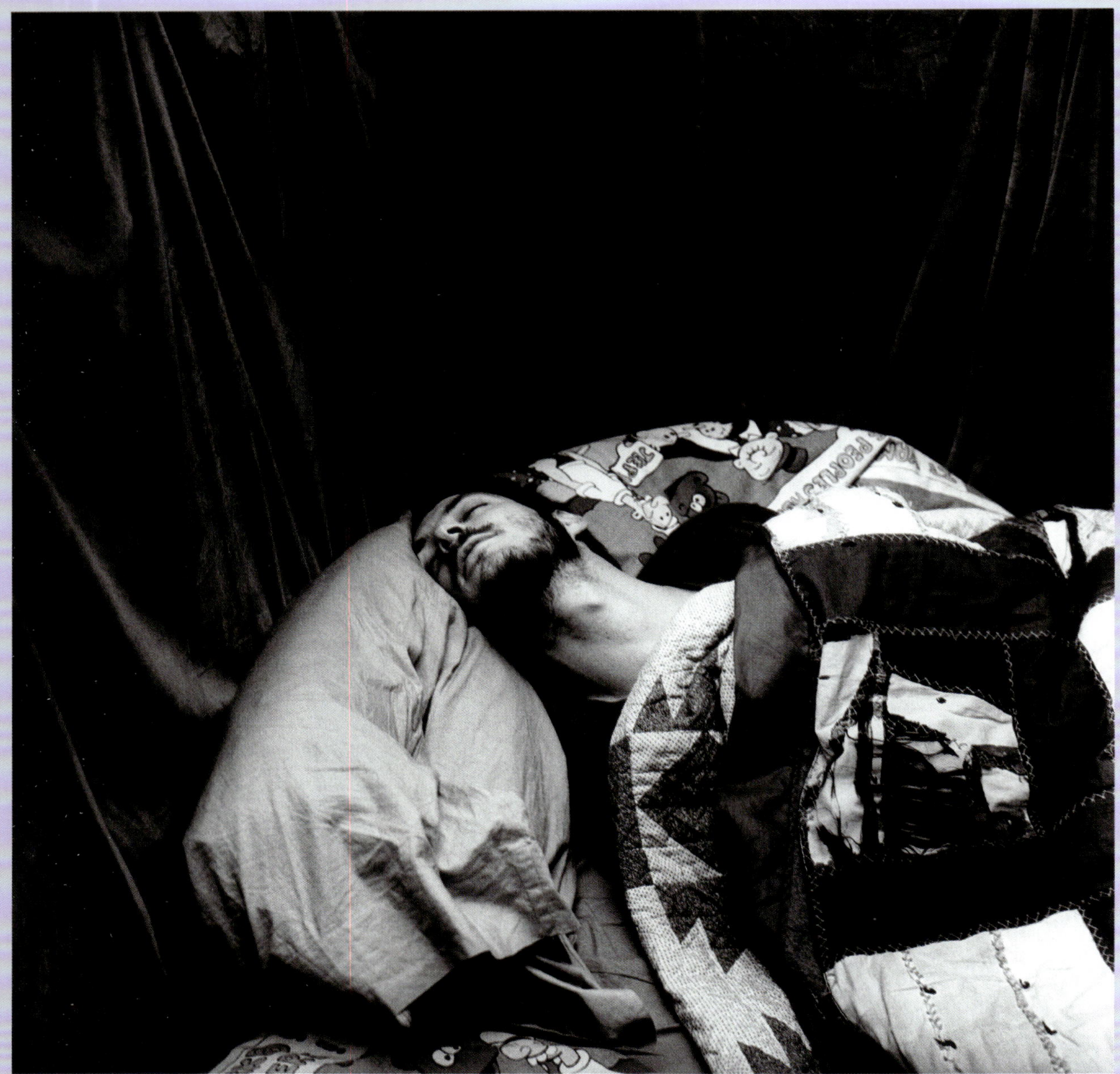

Peter Hujar, *Bill Elliott*, 1974
© The Peter Hujar Archive/ Artists Rights Society (ARS), New York

Peter Hujar
Once I learned how to approach strangers, I wanted my images to have more energy. I admired Diane Arbus, but rather than her confrontational ardor I was looking for a depth of intimacy. Peter Hujar's portraits became my guide.

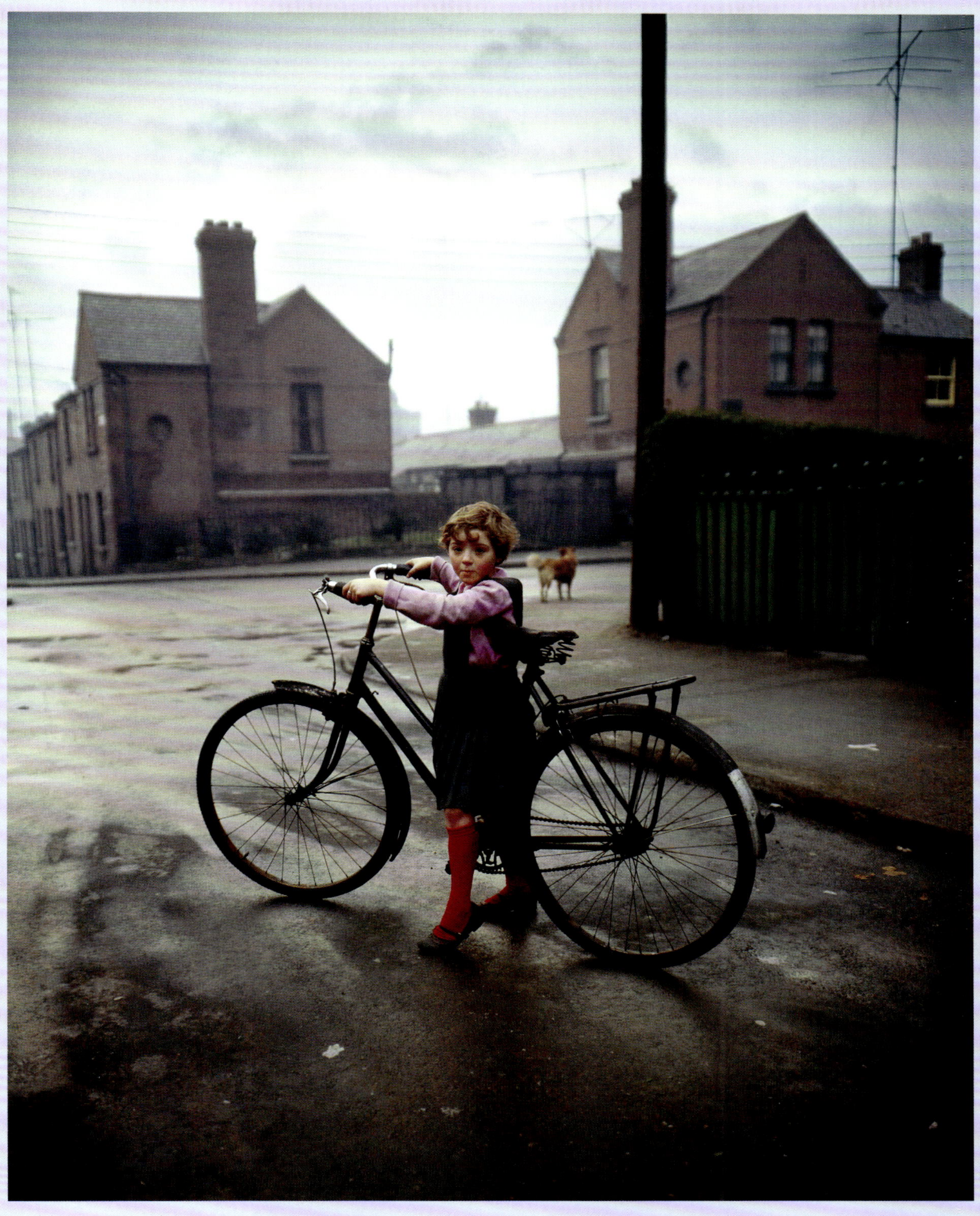

Evelyn Hofer, *Girl with Bicycle*, Dublin, 1966
© Estate of Evelyn Hofer

Evelyn Hofer
One of the first large-format photographers to produce exceptional portraits in color, Evelyn Hofer made straight editorial pictures that, nonetheless, feel otherworldly.

Emila Medková

The potent visions of a Czech Surrealist.
Olivia Laing

Sideways Logic

Untitled, from the series
Stínohry (Shadowplays),
1949

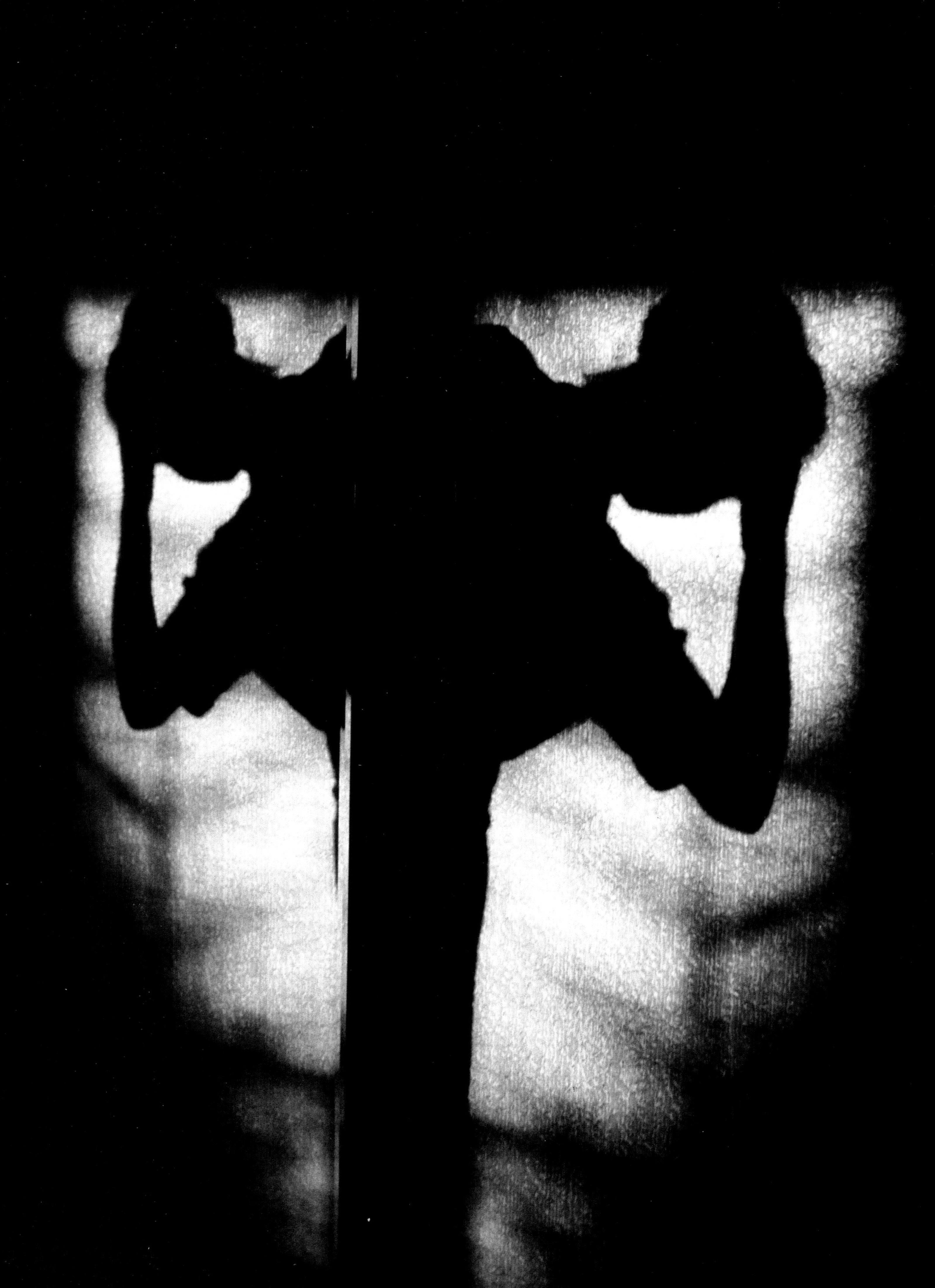

Dream logic is essentially sideways logic: similarities or kinships that work not by means of sense but along other avenues of relationship. Puns, for example, exhibit dream logic. What kind of socks do bears wear? None. They usually have bare feet.

Visual puns likewise find resemblances between objects not otherwise the same. Since human eyes are self-interested, the similarities they tend to discover are to human faces, from the composite vegetative figures of the sixteenth-century painter Giuseppe Arcimboldo to those comic staples of today's social media, the carrot that seems to smirk or the leering face in a tree.

Back up eighty years, and here's the Czech Surrealist photographer Emila Medková, carrying out an austere version of the same absurdist project. Her work spans four decades, from the end of World War II to her death in 1985. With the exception of the brief liberalization in 1968 around the Prague Spring, Medková operated in the dark of totalitarian rule. Her work was rarely exhibited. Censorship was rife and resistance necessarily coded and covert. Her photographs were made as an act of subversion and bitter humor for a close circle of Czech Surrealists.

She started out in a fairly conventional, if virtuosic Surrealist mode. In the *Shadowplay* series of the 1940s, real objects are twinned with their shadow selves, the exception being a female figure in *Lukostřelec* (Archer) (1949), who exists solely in the domain of shadow. With an arrow, she pursues what looks like a flotilla of fish, made perhaps from knots in wood. In another scene, she gazes at a mysterious assemblage, which includes a tap gushing hair and an eggcup that appears to be capped with an eyeball, cheery as the cherry on an ice cream sundae.

These images have a definite power, but are in some ways reliant on a readymade Surrealist language, which centers on the objectification and estrangement of the female body. In her later work, Medková excised the human form altogether, finding far stranger and more potent bodily resonances by way of objects.

I've got four of her found forms in front of me. The first, *Zavřená hlava* (Closed head), from her long-running series *Closed* (1960–61), shows the middle region of two wooden doors, their surfaces riven and pockmarked. Each has a square black aperture near the top. Underneath, there's a metal hasp, yoking the two doors together, which has been padlocked shut. It's irresistible to read this image as a cartoon face, with doleful eyes and flat mouth. In fact, it looks exactly like the emoji for *shhh* or *zip it*, the ideal affective icon for the Stalinist government under which Medková worked.

The face is above all a conveyer of expression, while the object is intrinsically speechless and inert. That's the weird bathos, the lol of the face-in-object. In Medková's faces, this tension is heightened by the way they're so often further encumbered by having their mouths locked, filled, choked, or otherwise impeded. Everywhere, these faces that can't speak are having their capacity for speech emphatically denied.

In *Křik* (The scream, 1971), we're seeing another virtuosic surface, every crater and crevice crisply rendered. Is it a road in close-up? Much of the photograph appears dark, surrounding a pale region shaped like a cartoon face in profile—like the "Kilroy was here" face ubiquitous in 1940s graffiti. Kilroy's hair is grass and his mouth is enormously wide. It looks as if he's vomiting the darker matter, or, on the other hand, as if it's being forced down his open gullet, choking the apparatus from which language is produced.

There's more uncanniness afoot in an untitled 1951 photograph from the series *Inkvizitoři* (Inquisitors). The face is made of bark, with a hank of hair, and another single eyeball, maybe a marble, though it looks a lot like what my godson calls "googly eyes" (a natural-born Surrealist, he often sticks them on

unsuspecting fruit and eggs). But this face is lying on a table, as food tends to do. It has a fork shoved in its mouth, which pushes it toward the status of face, and a knife skewered through its cheek, which converts it back into food. Object or subject? Who's doing the eating, and who is being consumed?

One more, this time not a face at all. This image, wittily titled *Arcimboldo* (1978), shows a crumple of machinery, with intestinal spokes and ribs and teeth. It looks like a torso, the damaged interior of a body. The French Surrealists, well-fed, enjoyed imagining women's bodies emerging from inanimate objects in ways that were alternately nightmarish and exposing. Medková's take is more skeptical and scathing.

Perhaps this is all a person is, she seems to say, a bundle of disarticulated parts, functional until it's not. But what could seem like a dutiful totalitarian statement is undermined by the cool, displacing irony of Medková's gaze. The oddness of the composition makes it impossible not to sense the presence behind the camera. The shadow is no longer necessary. What she's actually managed to document is a person in the forbidden act of looking, thinking, dreaming freely. Maybe this particular rebellious object wasn't so silent after all.

Olivia Laing is the author, most recently, of *Everybody: A Book About Freedom* (2021).

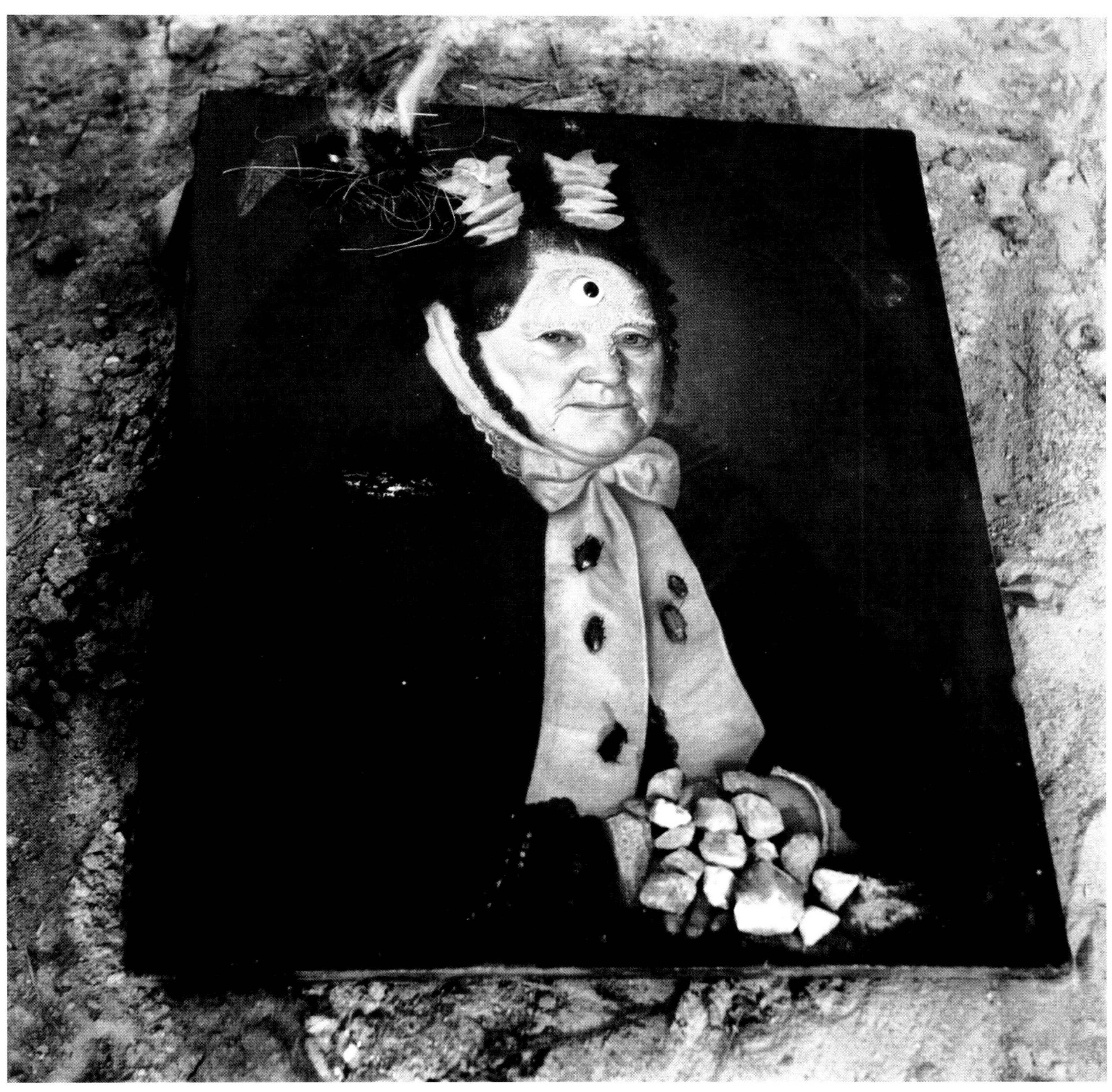

Konec obrazu (The end of the painting), 1948

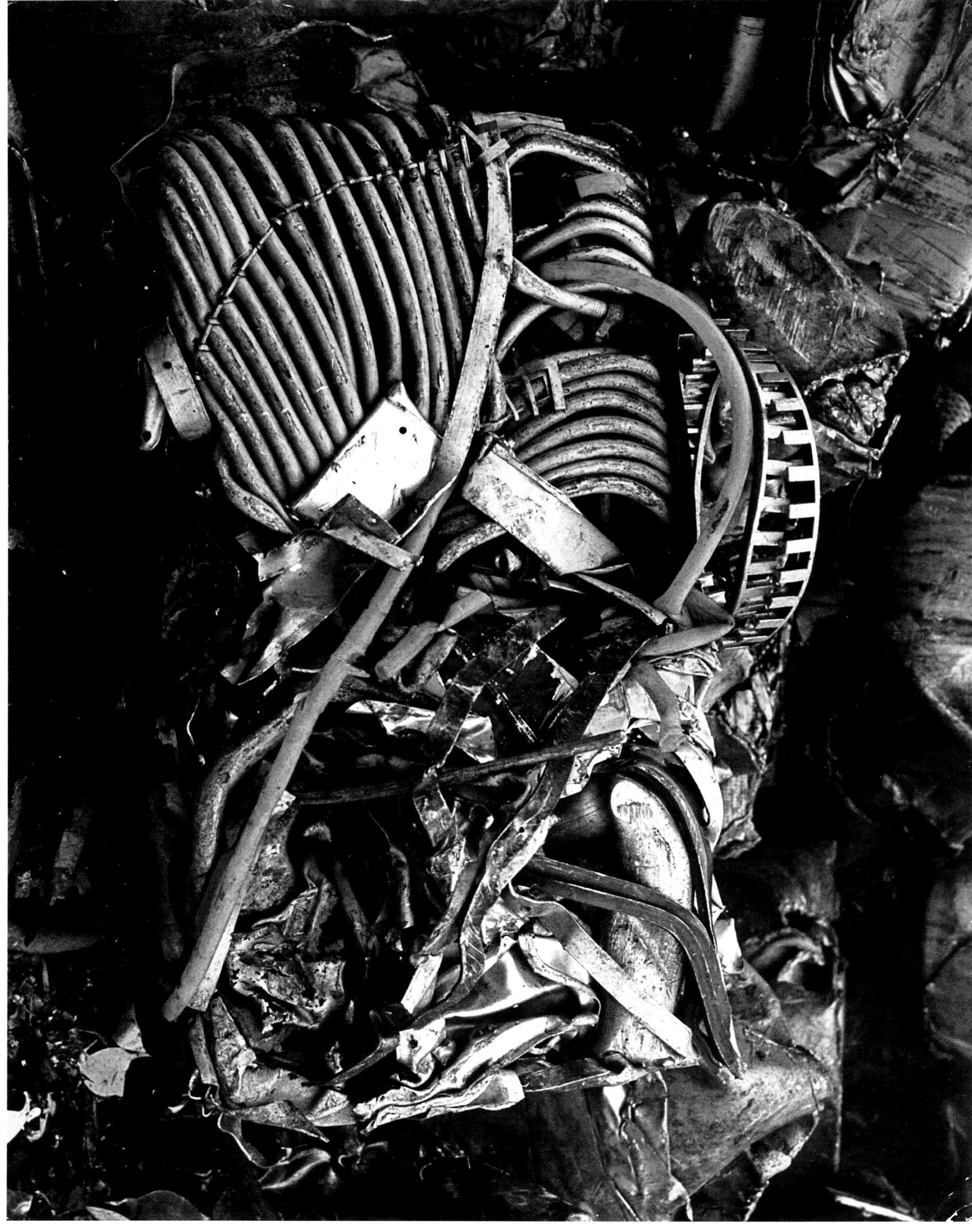

Arcimboldo, 1978

Untitled, from the series
Inkvizitoři (Inquisitors),
1951

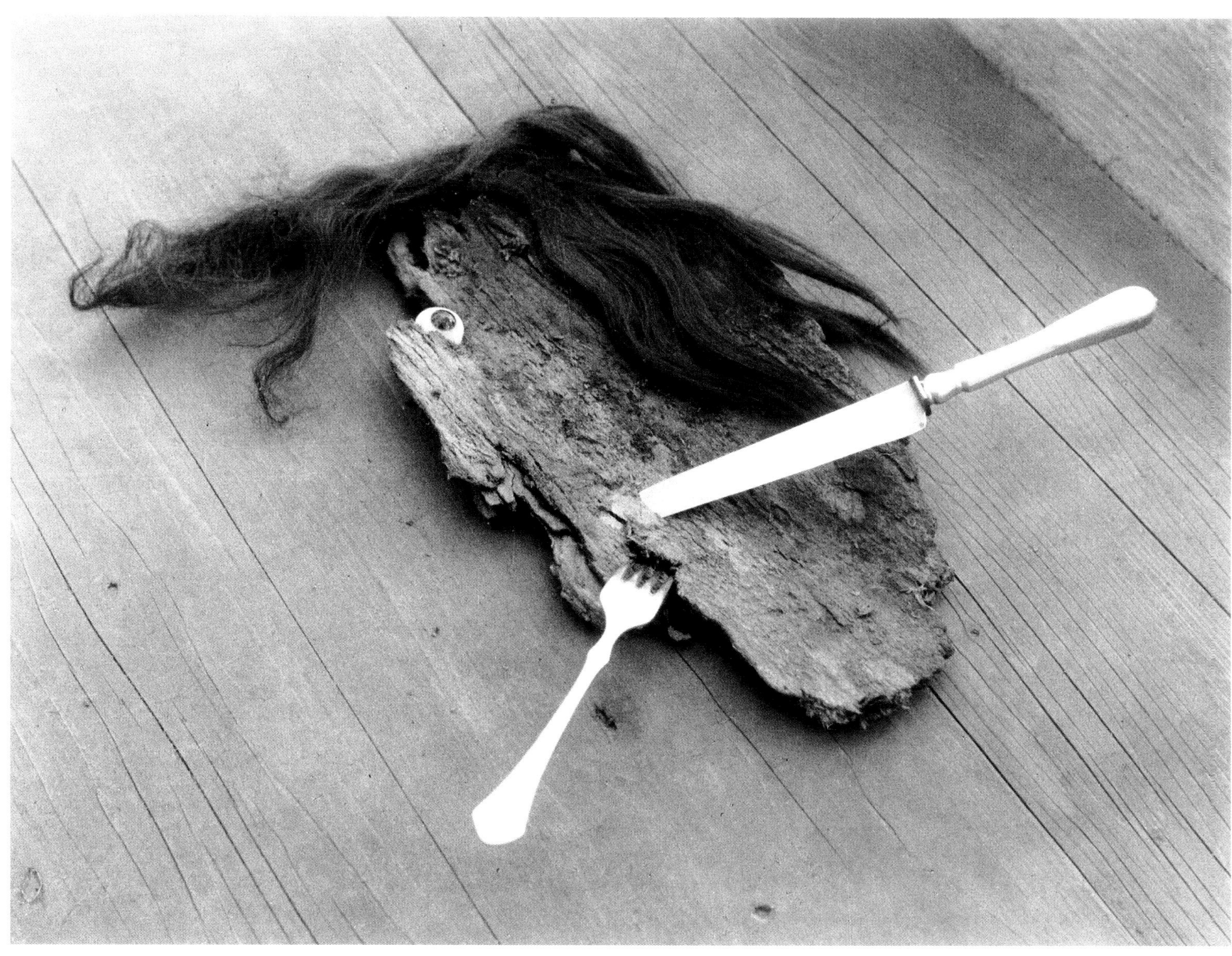

Left:
Křik (The scream), 1971;
right: *Zavřená hlava*
(Closed head), from the
series *Zavřeno* (Closed),
1960–61

Opposite:
Lukostřelec (Archer),
from the series *Stínohry*
(Shadowplays), 1949
All photographs © Eva
Kosáková Medková

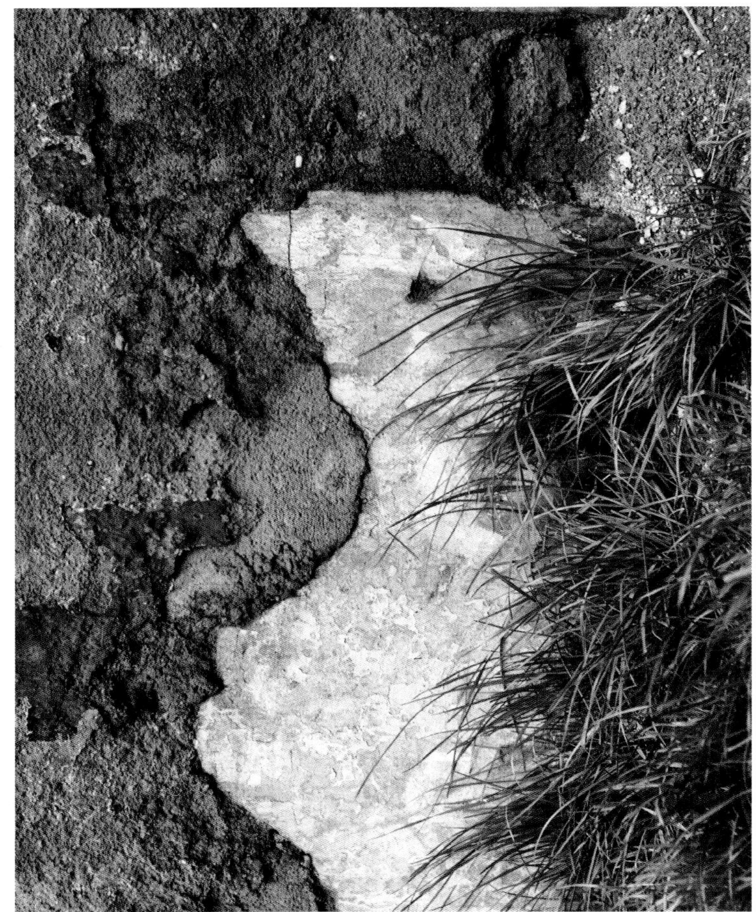

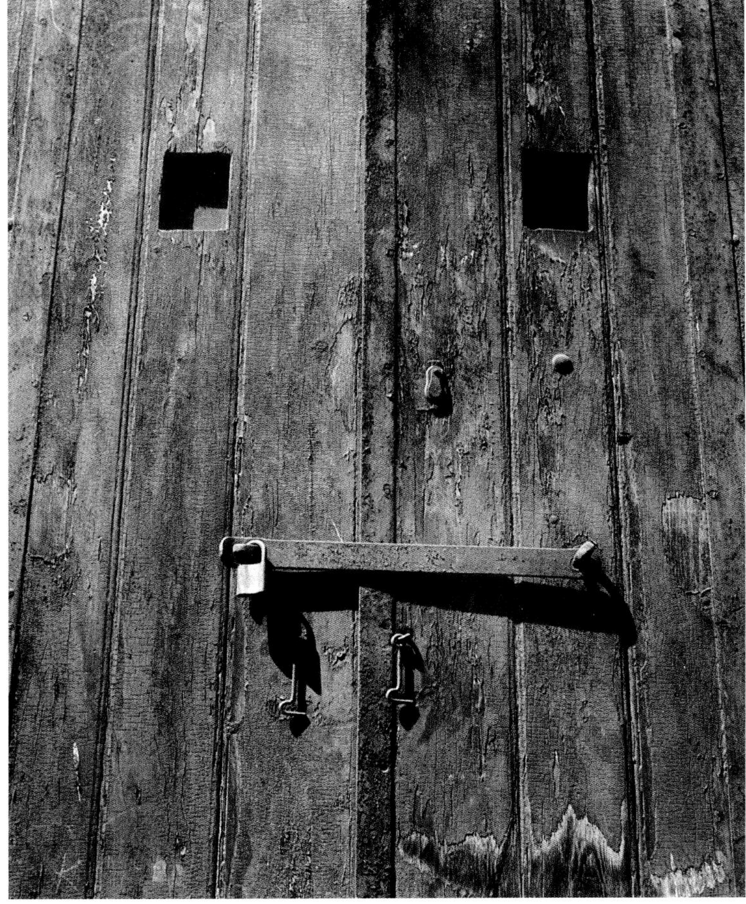

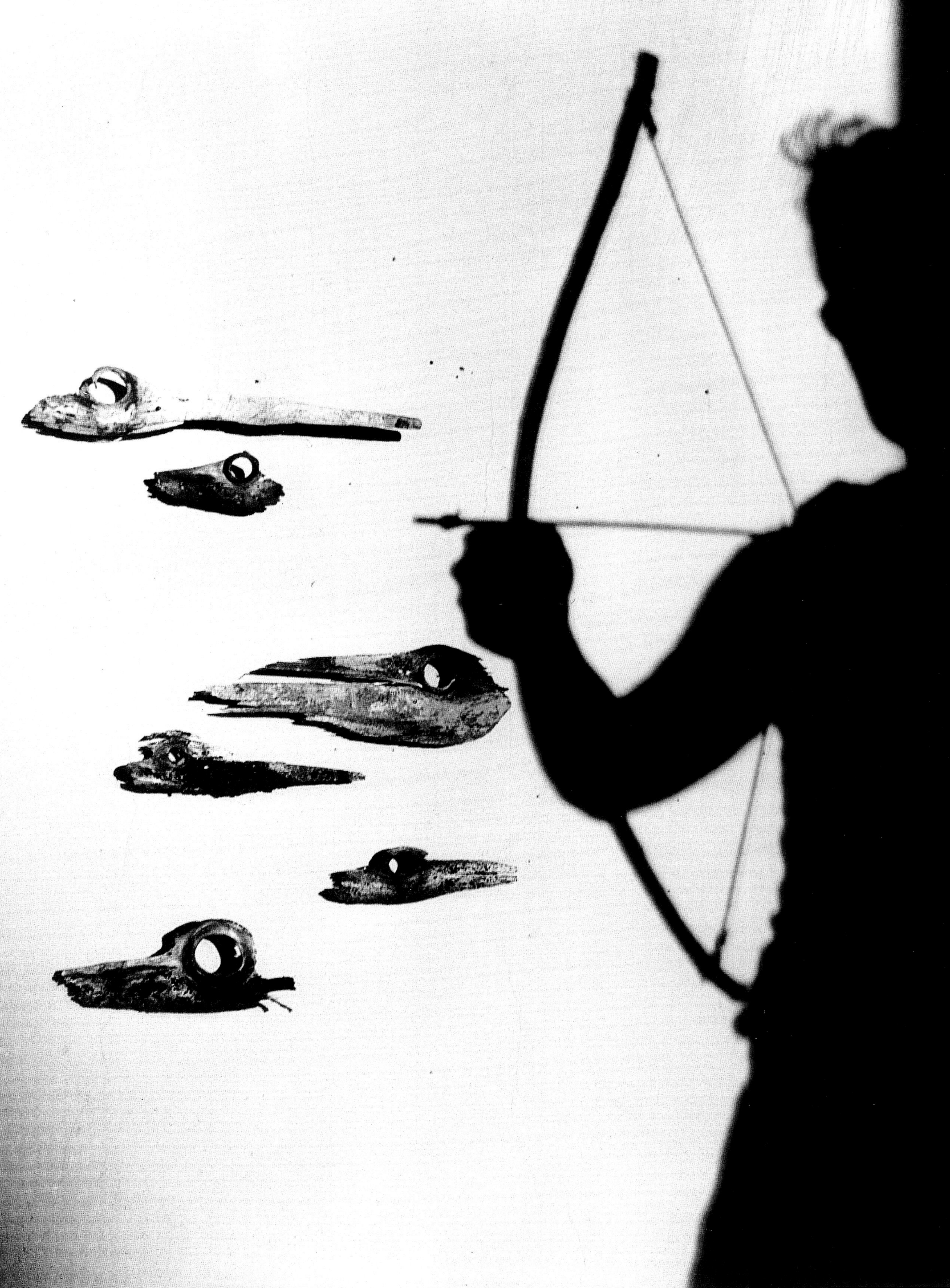

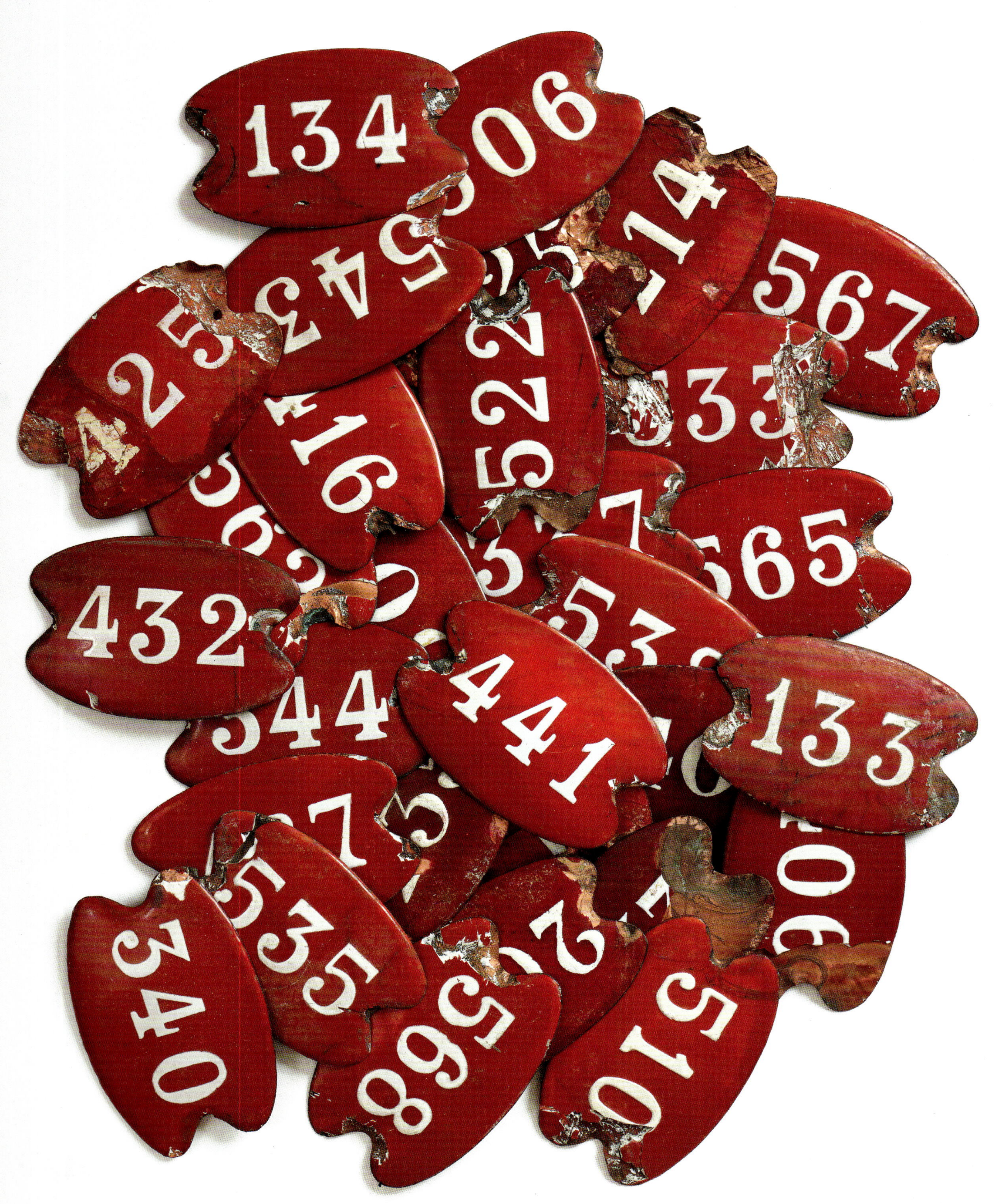

Sophie Calle has squatted in an abandoned Parisian hotel, worked as a nosy chambermaid, and followed an unsuspecting stranger across Venice—all to create uncanny works with the pulse of detective stories.

The Narrative Artist
Aaron Peck

Her artistic career began with a kind of sleepwalking. In 1978, Sophie Calle spent her days strolling Paris. She had just returned to France after seven years of travel. Like so many artists and writers before her, she walked the French capital. On one of her ambles, she noticed a door ajar. It opened into an abandoned hotel connected to the former Orsay train station. It was as if she had drifted into a dream. She wandered the empty building and then left, taking note to come back. That year, Calle started making the work that she would become known for: following people, inviting them to sleep in her bed while she photographed them, taking on personas. A year later, she returned to Orsay. The building had remained abandoned. Calle took pictures, found discarded objects and documents. She even settled into a room on the fifth floor, 501. Nearly forty years later, Calle found herself at a dinner party where she was seated across the table from Donatien Grau, the head of contemporary programs at the Musée d'Orsay. She let slip something that no one at the museum knew: that Calle had squatted in the building, when it was abandoned, before it became the site of a museum. She told Grau that she had also kept a number of items from the old hotel and station.

Calle is the daughter of a well-known art collector and a journalist. A one-time student of the theorist Jean Baudrillard, who helped her get her first book published in 1983, Calle tells stories that question the relationship between self and other, the stories we tell about ourselves, or the traces that others leave. From her early to most recent books, such as *The Hotel* in 1984 to this year's *The Elevator Resides in 501*, she mixes a variety of formats and mediums simultaneously. More than many other artists of her stature, though, the name Sophie Calle conjures different things to different people. The art historian Yve-Alain Bois claims her "favorite mode of display" is "intertwining text and photo,"

Calle's narratives are a precursor to contemporary autofiction, while also fitting in a longer twentieth-century literary tradition that juxtaposes text with image.

while others, such as the writer Heidi Julavits, in a conversation with the artist for *Interview* magazine, focus on describing the performance elements of her output. The novelist Paul Auster, Calle's longtime friend and erstwhile collaborator, made the fascinating claim that she is "essentially a writer." If so, perhaps she is among the first to write in an "expanded field," to borrow a phrase from the art critic Rosalind Krauss, for the ways in which her stories rely on not only photography but also exhibitions, which many others have since followed. Discussing her significance, Grau remarks: "She has explored at once literature and the visual arts, and assembled them with many other methodologies, while unearthing and inventing new narrative forms that are simultaneously deeply personal and universal." She herself apparently likes the phrase "narrative artist."

After that dinner party, Grau informed Laurence des Cars, then director of the Musée d'Orsay and Musée de l'Orangerie, who set up a meeting with Calle. Now, decades after she squatted in the building, the museum has exhibited *The Ghosts of Orsay*, an installation consisting of her photographs and detritus collected from the former train station and its hotel. The exhibition also coincides with the book *The Elevator Resides in 501*, published in both French and English editions by the Arles-based publishing house Actes Sud. For this book, Calle invited the celebrated French archaeologist Jean-Paul Demoule to write fictional ethnographic notes about the material. A short autobiographical text by Calle and the pieces by Demoule thread through her images of dilapidated rooms, exposed pipes, ledgers, empty hallways, abandoned mattresses, former room keys. The material has an oneiric quality, as if the museum were now manifesting a dream of its forgotten past.

This exhibition and book further add to a wider reconsideration of Calle's early work, particularly, as seen in her publications, how she blends writing with quasi-documentary photography—that is,

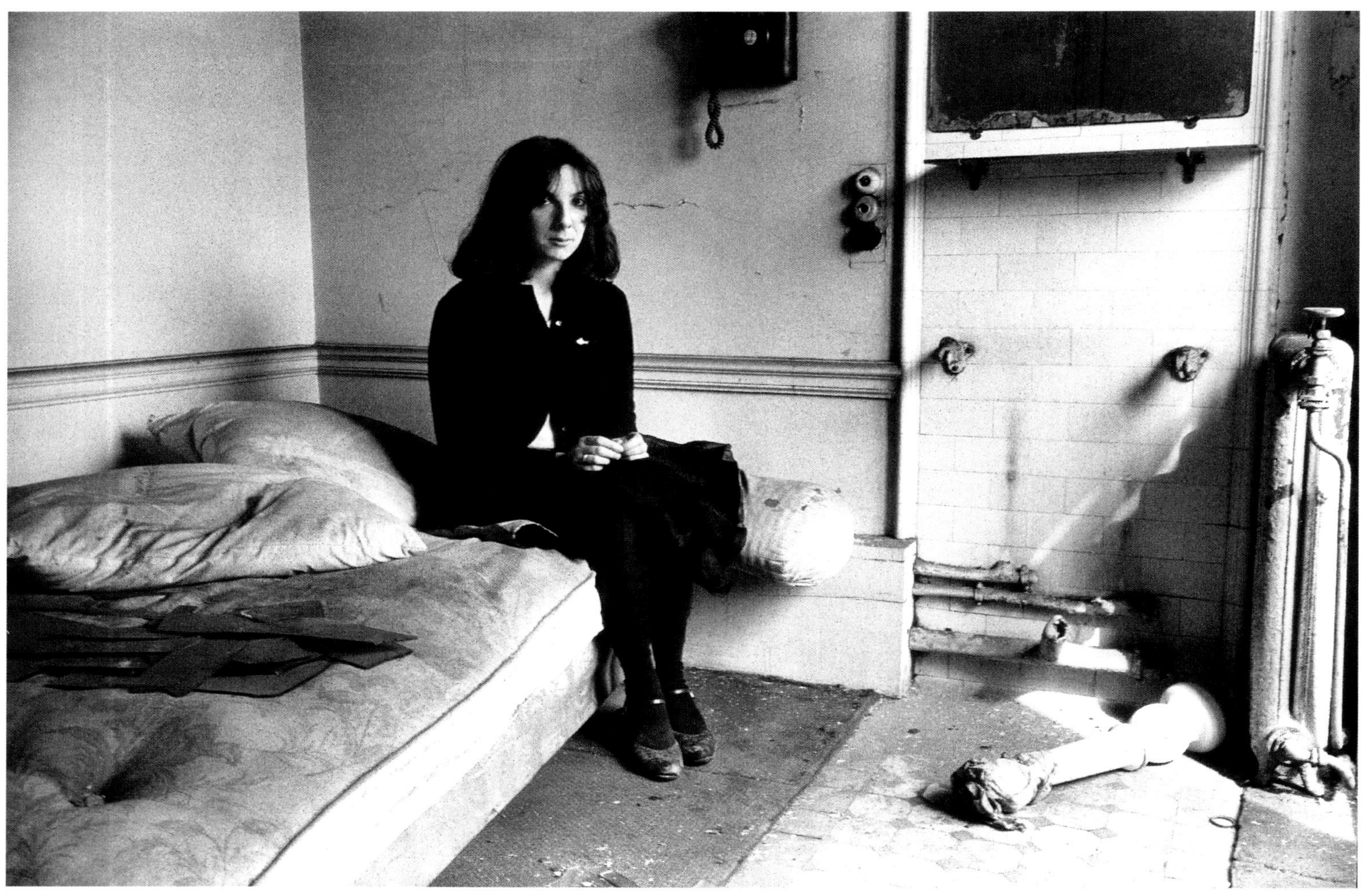

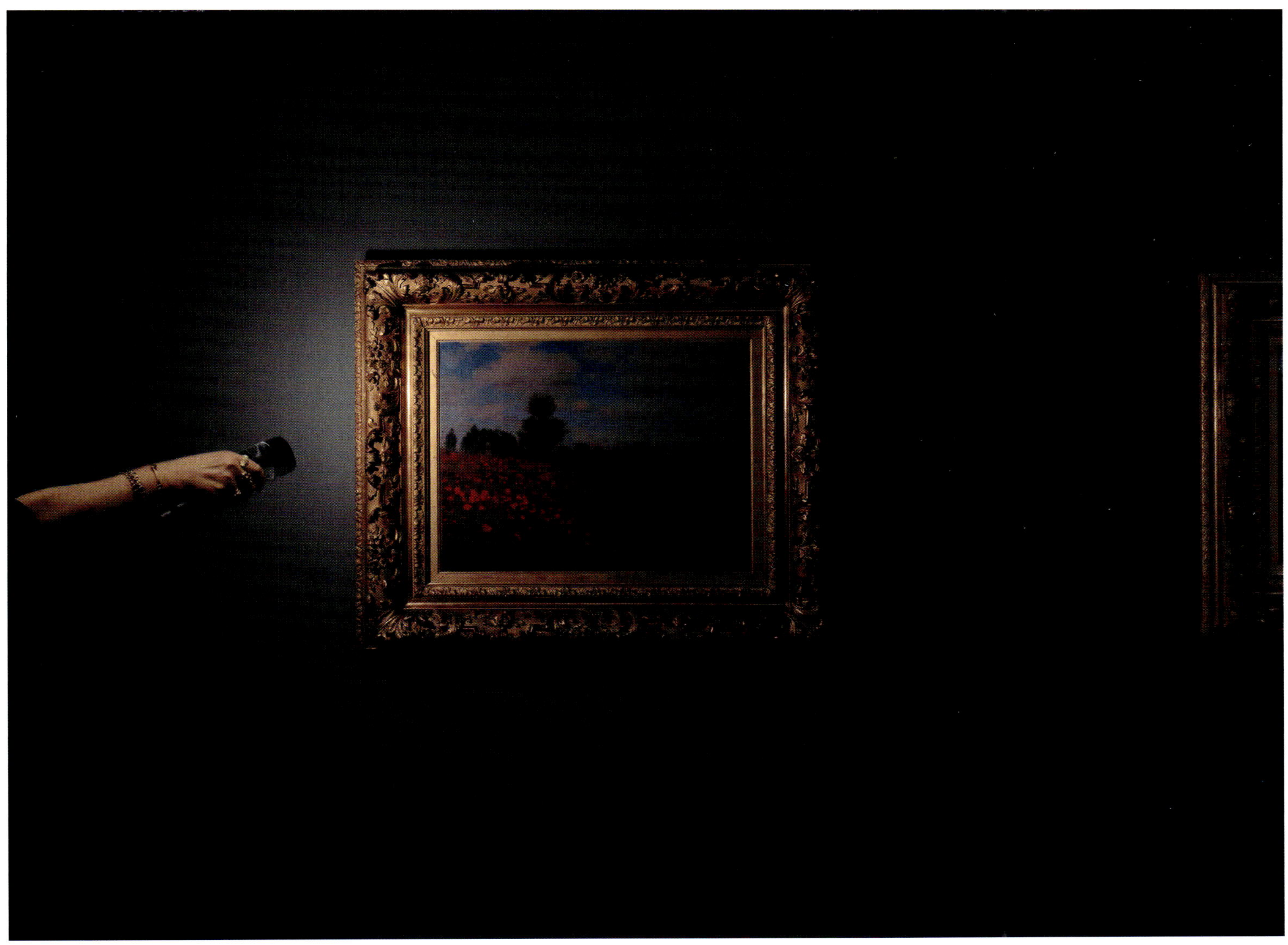

a kind of documentary photography that may not quite aspire to truthfulness. Her narratives are, in some senses, a precursor to contemporary autofiction, writers such as Chris Kraus and Sheila Heti, while also fitting in a much longer twentieth-century literary tradition that juxtaposes text with image, from its Surrealistic origins in André Breton's 1928 *Nadja* (about, indeed, a man who follows a woman around Paris) to the 1990s books by W. G. Sebald. In the United States, over the past decade, Siglio Press has been reprinting elegant editions of Calle's early pieces, most recently *The Hotel* (reprint 2021; first published 1984, work from 1981), but also *Venetian Suite* (reprint 2015; first published 1983, work from 1980) and *Address Book* (reprint 2009; first published 1983 in the newspaper *Libération*, work from 1983).

In *Address Book*, Calle found a misplaced address book. Before returning it, she photocopied its contents and began contacting all of the people listed to render a portrait of its owner; her written notes of the meetings were published in *Libération*, presented alongside photographs. *Venetian Suite* chronicles her surveillance of a man in Venice. One afternoon in Paris, Calle had been following a random man only to lose him in a crowd. A few hours later, by chance, she was introduced to him at an art opening. He mentioned to her that he was going to Venice the next day. So, she, too, left for Venice, to continue shadowing him while taking clandestine photographs of his activities, like a private investigator. In 1981, Calle returned to Venice for the project that became *The Hotel*. Securing a job as a chambermaid, she photographed the sundry belongings of the hotel guests, while she made their beds, in order to attempt to reconstruct who they were. *The Hotel*, which includes her written observations and photographs, appeared as a book in 1984 after being exhibited the previous year at Galerie Chantal Crousel in Paris. Her seemingly matter-of-fact photographs are uncanny next to the narrative account of cleaning rooms and snapping pictures.

While photography is central to Calle's art, there was for decades a long-standing truism that she was not particularly good at it. Her friend, the French writer and photographer Hervé Guibert, who wrote an essay on her at her invitation, "Panégyrique d'une faiseuse d'histoire" (1991), claimed that she "can't even manage to take a proper photograph." Her New York gallerist, Paula Cooper, once admitted that her photographs are not what people think about when they think of her art. She is not the sort of person who carries a camera with her; she only takes pictures when they are part of the rules of a project. (In a 2010 interview with Michel Guerrin in *Foam* magazine, the same year she received the Hasselblad Award, Calle stated that only with *Take Care of Yourself*, in 2007, did she begin to take more interest in the craft of photography.) But the loose compositions of her early work—the "bad" quality of the pictures, the poor or unbalanced framing, the out-of-focus subjects—have powerful effects. They provide the texts with an awkward intimacy, even in *The Hotel* where there are no human figures. Feeling as if they were taken quickly before a guest may return and interrupt her clandestine project, they also have the effect of disrupting the flow of reading. Her use of photographs is, in this way, less about documentation than it is about editing.

Throughout her pieces, inconsistencies in detail further emerge that give them a surreal quality. A number of the photographs

Photograph from *The Hotel*
(Siglio, 2021)

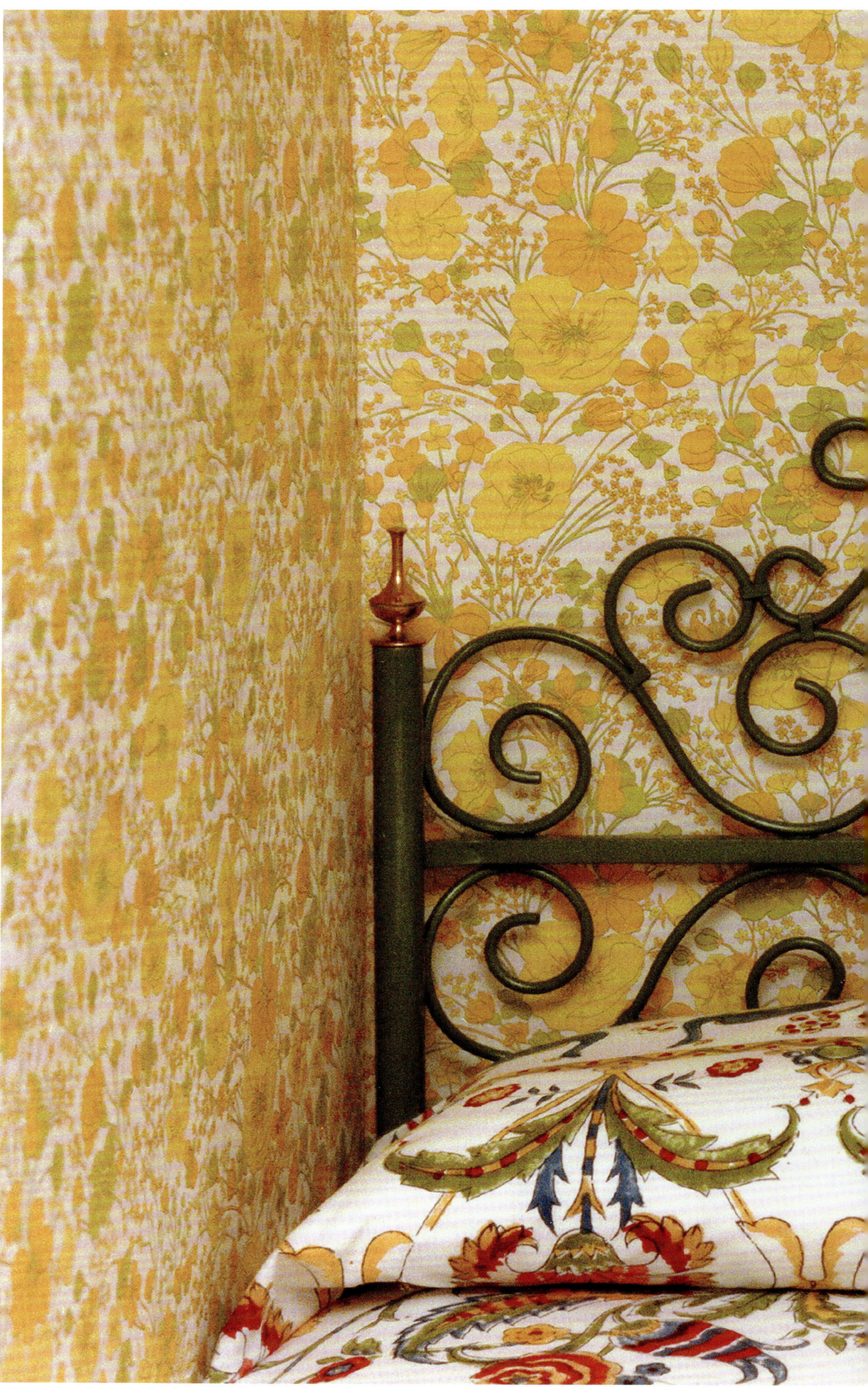

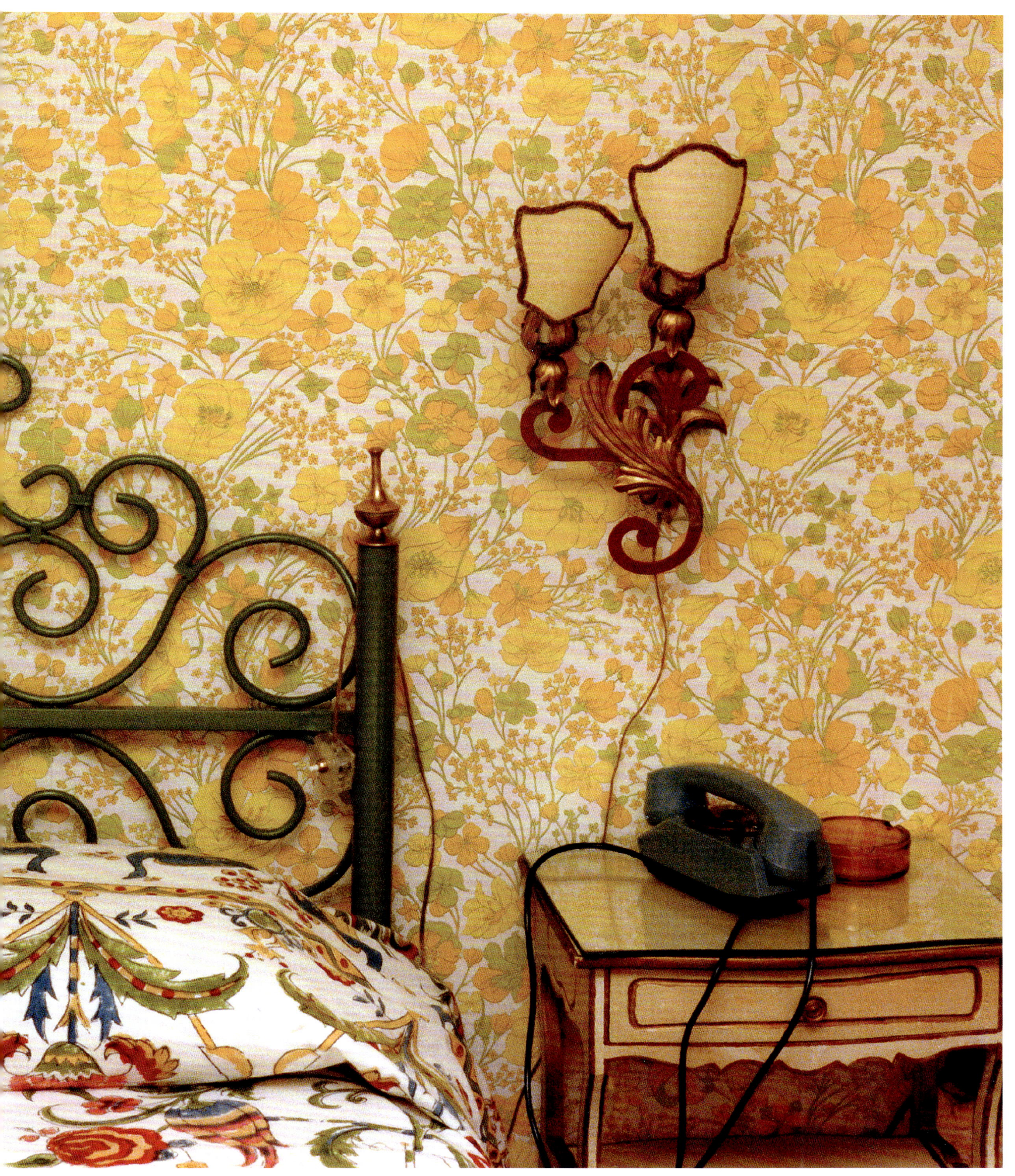

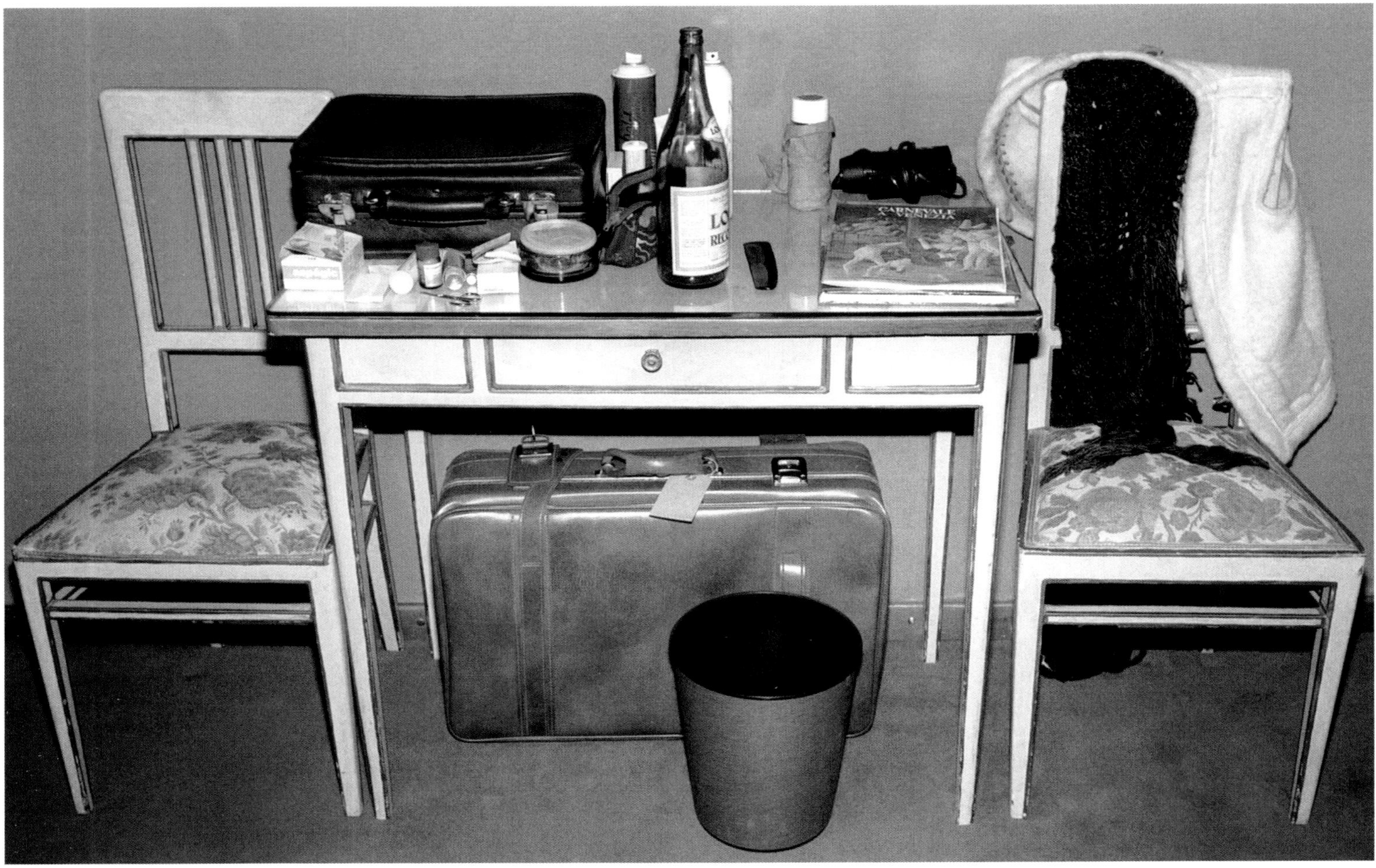

This page:
Photograph from *The Hotel*
(Siglio, 2021)

Opposite:
Photograph from *Suite
Vénitienne* (Siglio, 2015)
Courtesy the artist and Siglio

of abandoned rooms seen in *The Elevator Resides in 501*, for example, were also used in *Address Book*. In 1993, Calle confessed to the art historian Bice Curiger that everything in *The Hotel* was truthful except the contents of one room, which she staged. In *The Hotel*, after days of being unable to enter room 45, she gains access, feeling "a certain lack of interest," she writes. She claimed that she had only ten minutes. "I content myself with taking a few photographs: the carnival masks hung on the sconces, the Pierrot costume, the iron I noticed in the suitcase, two pairs of slippers waiting at the foot of each bed. In the folds of the sheets, I find a lobster claw."

All of this feels like it comes out of a dream, the waking dream of a young woman who opens the door to an abandoned building, or an occupied hotel room. Over the past forty years, Calle has, in many ways, invented her own genre, somewhere between the traditional photobook and a literary piece. The juxtaposition of autobiographical writing with her particular style of quasi-documentary photography is her major aesthetic contribution, the skeleton key to her practice. Just as her photographs defamiliarize her texts, Calle's work reflects on the relationship between self and other, how each of us remains a stranger to ourself. From 1980s books such as *The Hotel* up to her latest (based on material from those early years), she mixes writing and photography in ways that result in disrupting the absorptive experience of reading, as if jarring a sleeper out of a dream, or stepping into an even deeper one. "The dread of doors that won't close," states the cultural critic Walter Benjamin, "is something that everyone knows from dreams." Her pictures are like the unclosed doors of her narratives.

Aaron Peck is a writer based in Paris and currently a contributing editor at *Frieze*. He has written for *Artforum*, the *Los Angeles Review of Books*, and *The Happy Reader*.

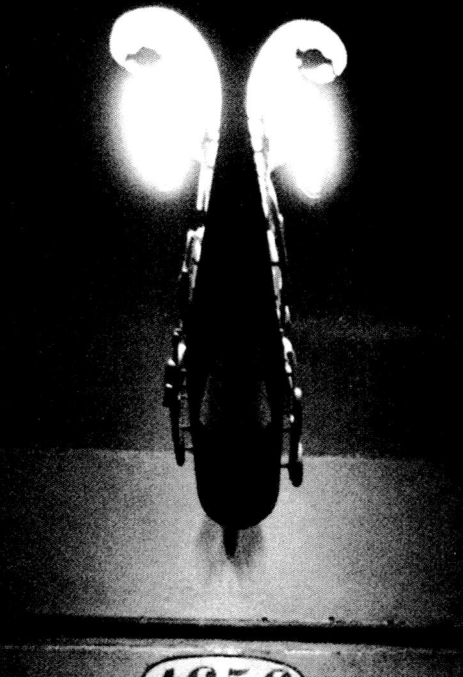
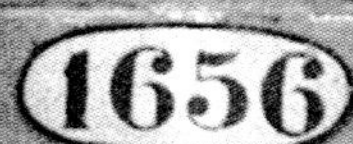

1656

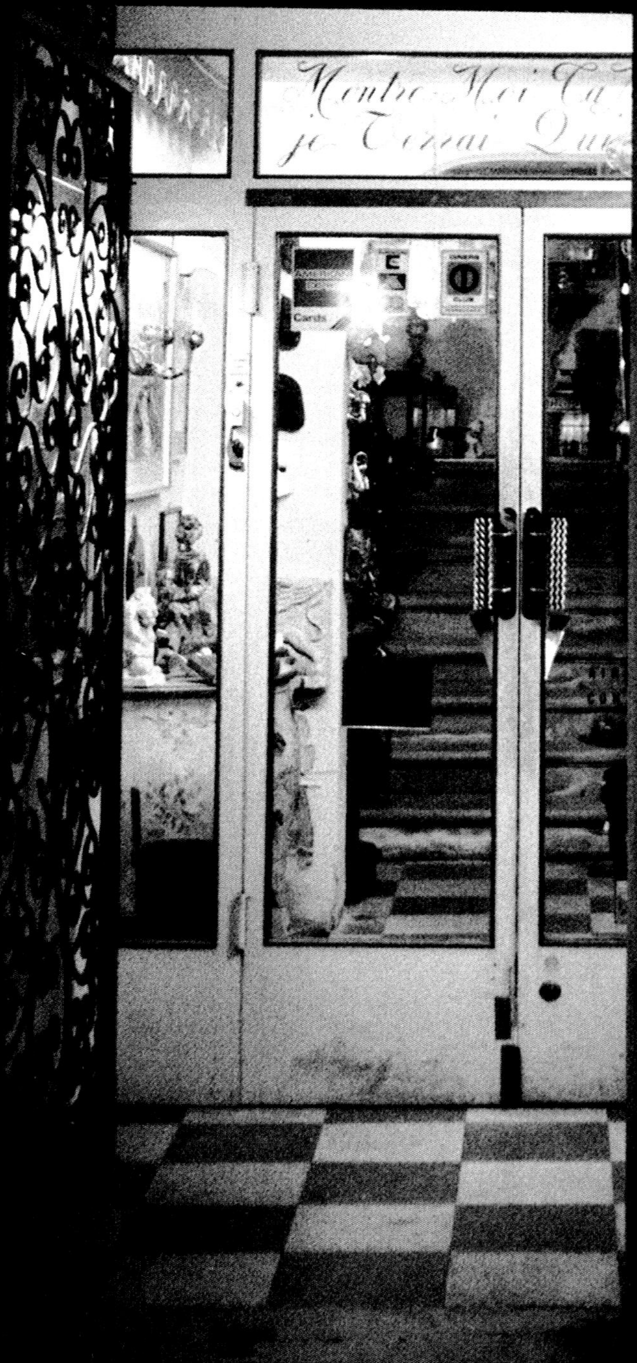

Cards

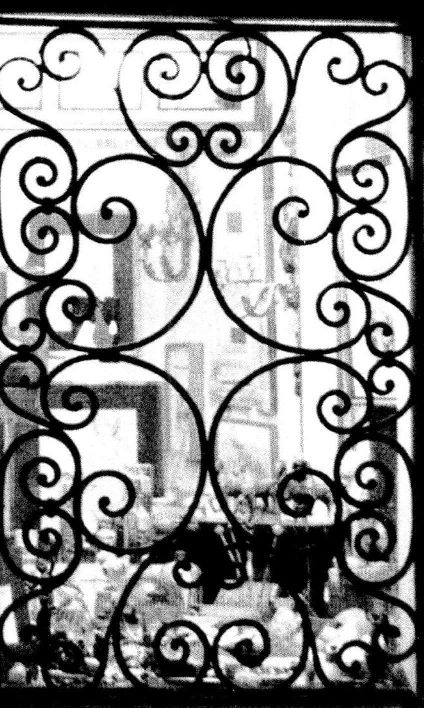

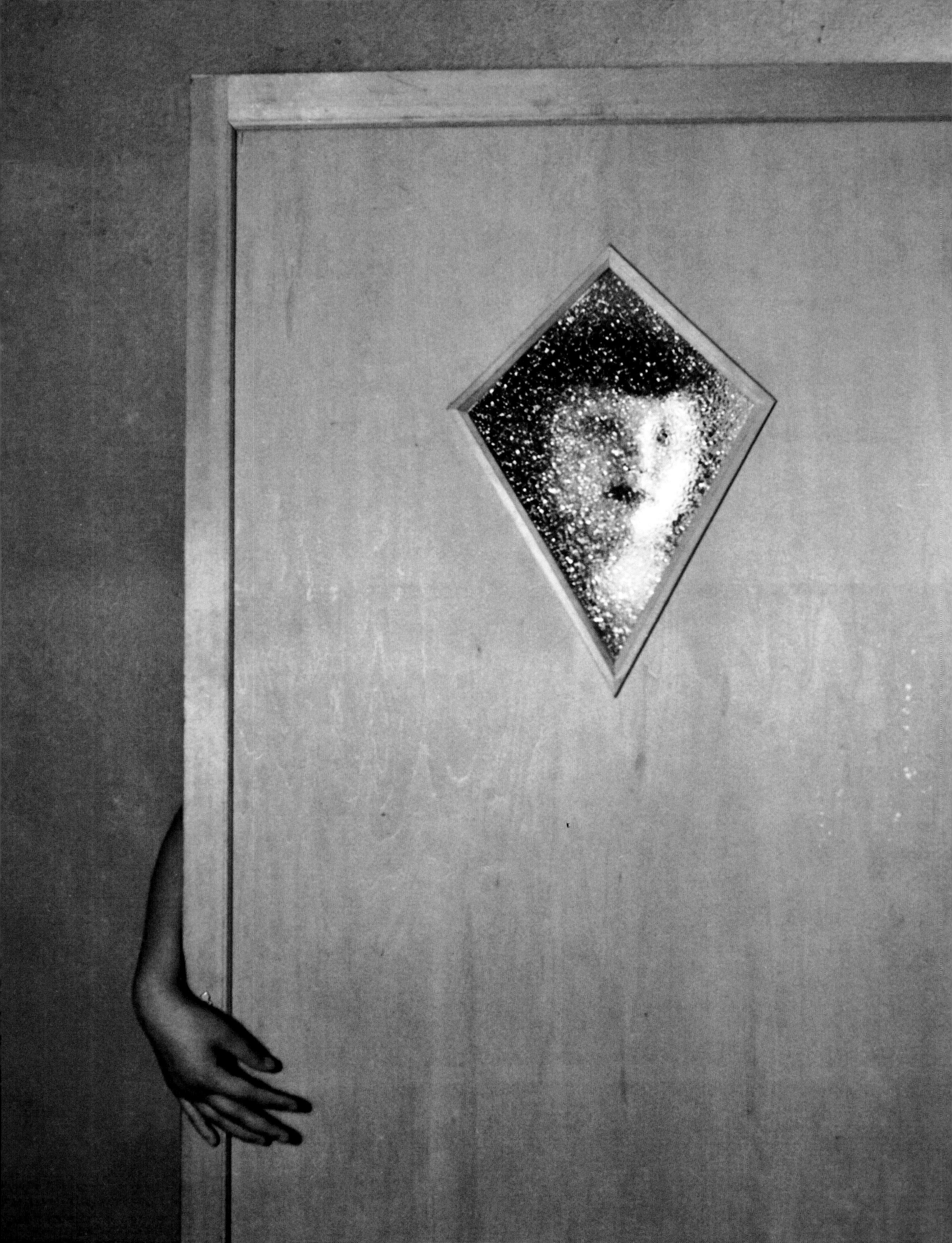

Apparitional Automaton

For centuries, the image of the sleepwalker has fascinated artists and writers. How might this premonitory figure make visible our hidden thoughts and desires?
Marina Warner

Doctor: You see her eyes are open.
Gentlewoman: Ay, but their sense are shut. —*Macbeth*, act 5, scene 1

Unlike a dreamer or someone under hypnosis, a sleepwalker looks awake; they will leave their bed and move and even speak as if conscious. Their altered state may cause them to reveal their innermost thoughts, as does Lady Macbeth, who's haunted by the deaths she and Macbeth have wrought, and every night gets up, paces, and rubs at the blood she imagines still stains her hands, indelible and stinking: "All the perfumes of Arabia will not sweeten this little hand." Witnessing someone under the spell is an eerie experience, like eavesdropping on their secrets; it feels voyeuristic, since the sleepwalker does not know you are there. "You have known what you should not," the Doctor says to Lady Macbeth's Gentlewoman.

Lady Macbeth's nightmares return us to the scenes of the couple's crimes, and what is past becomes present, over and over again—not only for her but for the audience as well. Her torments also foreshadow her imminent death: a sleepwalker is a living phantom, not risen from the dead but on the threshold. A proleptic ghost. Lady Macbeth walks at a certain time of the night, as does Hamlet's father's ghost, disappearing at cockcrow. The temporality of the experience chimes with the condition of dead souls: in Dante's *Inferno* and in Samuel Beckett's responses to Dante (*Happy Days*, *Endgame*), the dead are shut off in their memories, condemned to endless repetition. A sleepwalker, unresponsive to all else but their inner world, is similarly closed off.

Photography as a medium, with its capture of a moment, and film, with its flashbacks and looping recapitulation, would prove a wonderfully hospitable vehicle to what the philosopher Gilles Deleuze calls, "*l'image-temps* (image-time), communicating the undecidable alternatives between layers of the past."

The somnambulist's state doesn't always betray inner turmoil and secret guilt; as terror of the devil faded in modernity and philosophers, doctors, psychologists, and artists began to probe the mind, sleepwalking became one of a range of unconscious activities that inspired wonder and even envy. André Breton and the Surrealists were committed to exploring the potential of dream states, and sleepwalking presented a pure form of automatism, which they valued, as they willed themselves to lose conscious control of their faculties in order to write and make art.

Automatism used to gather up under its rubric many different varieties of experiences, which the Surrealists and the members of the Society for Psychical Research both relished and examined: the ecstasy of visionaries, the trances of mediums, out-of-body dream voyages, catatonia, narcolepsy, levitation, glossolalia, déjà vu. The American gothic writer Charles Brockden Brown, a keen investigator into paranormal topics, commented that sleepwalking was "one of the most common and most wonderful diseases or affections of the human frame." It offered him, he felt, a proper American theme for his tumultuous, ferocious novel *Edgar Huntly; or, Memoirs of a Sleep-Walker*. Set in the uncharted wilderness of newly settled territory, with Native Americans ever concealed in the margins, he could explore its psychological correlative, the wonderful mind of a sleepwalker.

The book came out in 1799, an era of high Romanticism, when it was part of a male hero's charisma that he was subject to altered states, and might roam far and wide by night and teeter over terrifying chasms in his sleep. But Edgar Huntly, an adult man, is an exception among sleepwalkers. Over the course of the nineteenth century, many psychological phenomena, from hysteria to somnambulism, were more and more identified with the female psyche. Girls and women figure far more prominently in stories of trance phenomena than men: Saint Bernadette, who was pricked by witnesses as she knelt before her vision of the Virgin Mary to test if she would twitch or flinch (she didn't); the majority of the "hysterics" whom Jean-Martin Charcot exhibited; mediums such as Eva Carrière and Eusapia Paladino; and the *filles de joie* whom Brassaï

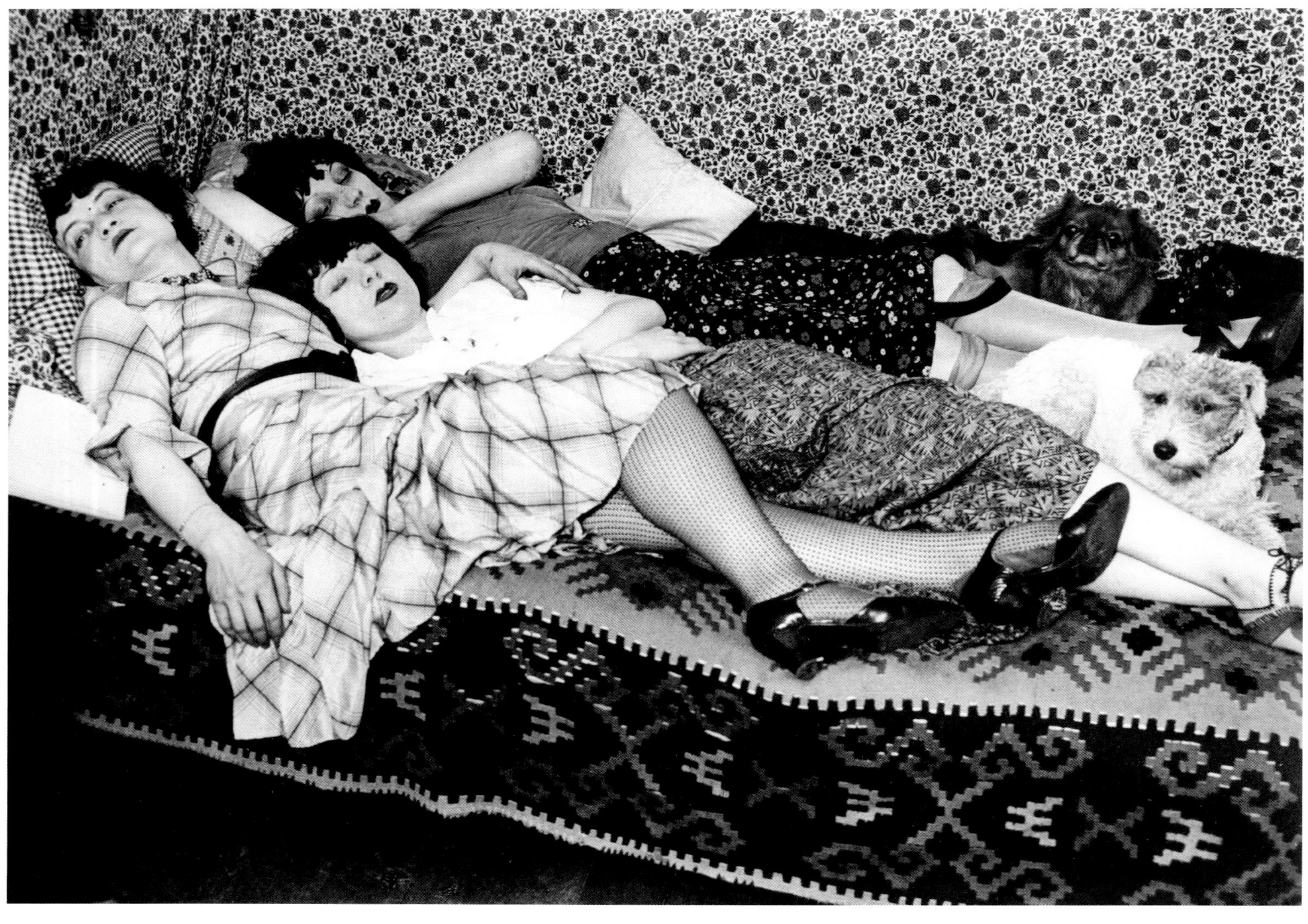

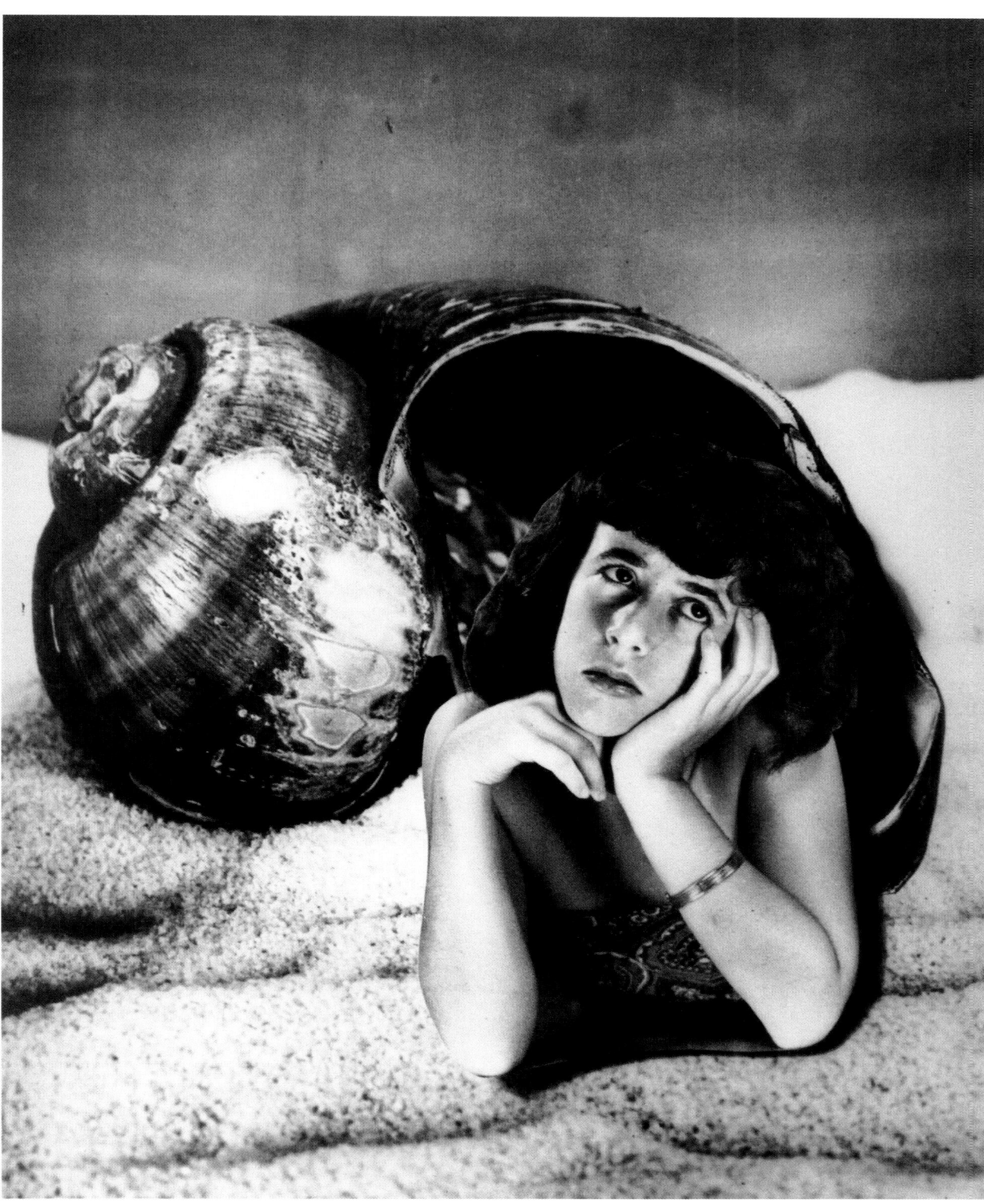

photographed in one another's arms, fully dressed and drowsing, dominate nineteenth- and early twentieth-century inquiries into the mysterious human mind. Sleepwalking is also saturated with the continually changing politics of gender.

The all-male group in jackets and ties in a famous Surrealist photomontage of 1929 have also closed their eyes and aren't undressed for bed: Magritte's nude in the center stands, rebuslike, for "woman," as the image is captioned, "Je ne vois pas la [femme] cachée dans la forêt" (I don't see the [woman] hidden in the forest). She invites us to imagine her rising before them in their mind's eye as the prime catalyst of their undirected dreams. They are posing as mind-voyagers, aspiring visionaries, seeking to lose themselves and drift on automatic images—to see with eyes shut, the inverse of the somnambulist. The naked figure embodies the Surrealist adage, "La femme est l'être qui projette la plus grande ombre ou la plus grande lumière dans nos rêves. . . . Elle vit spirituellement dans les imaginations qu'elle hante et qu'elle féconde" (Woman is the being who projects the greatest shadow or the greatest light into our dreams. . . . She lives spiritually in the imaginations she haunts and fertilizes), a quintessentially male line from Charles Baudelaire that Breton included in the *Dictionnaire abrégé du Surréalisme* under the entry "Femme." By contrast to those subjects' threshold state, a sleepwalker isn't recumbent but kinetic and acts under a compulsion that can't be thwarted. Indeed, the phenomenon trails a sense of endangered innocence. Automatism places the somnambulist at risk: it's accepted lore that you must never shake or try to wake a sleepwalker but let them be and find their way back to bed. But you must be watchful. When I was told as a child that my auntie Beatrice would go up onto the roof and walk along the edge in her nightgown while her sisters, my mother included,

The sleepwalker, a real-life phantom, moves through life wrapped in a dream.

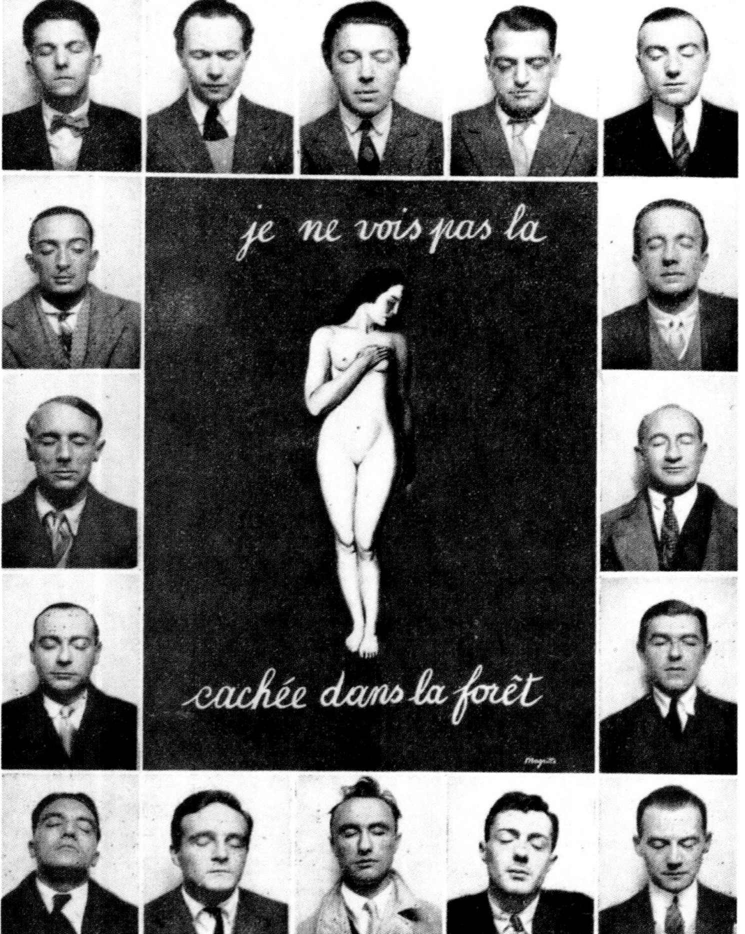

would stand by, heart in mouth, knowing they must not disturb her, I felt the uncanny vulnerability of the sleepwalker.

In *La Sonnambula* (1831), an opera by Vincenzo Bellini, when the heroine Amina has been seen in the bedroom of the count, her fiancé instantly assumes she's unfaithful and rejects her. But at the end, she's seen again, walking along the parapet of a high bridge and in this way proves her nocturnal wanderings are entirely blameless. It's surprising—and rather reassuring—that sleepwalking itself has not on the whole been stigmatized, though in Bram Stoker's 1897 novel, *Dracula*, Lucy Westenra, who is prone to sleepwalking, returns from the dead as a vampire.

In 1946, George Balanchine created a ballet inspired by Bellini's opera. His Amina, simply known as the Sleepwalker, materializes out of the darkness in her white nightgown with a lit candle and, eyes wide open and unfocused, glides diagonally across the stage *en pointe* at extraordinary speed, as if preternaturally possessed by inner forces. The Poet is delighted but soon baffled by her unresponsiveness as he begins to play with her, to spin her and bend her, a puppet master enjoying the enigma of her absence in presence. But she eludes his touch or caress at every move: theirs is a duet of shadows. The story ends in bloodshed (unlike the opera), but the lovely vision of the Sleepwalker reappears, lifts the dead body of the Poet, and together they float away. She figures here as a walker between worlds, a spirit from the afterlife.

When Balanchine was planning the ballet, he was introduced to Dorothea Tanning, and Mr. B., ever quick to sense talent (and respond to a young woman's beauty), immediately asked Tanning to design the set and the costumes for *Night Shadow*, as it was then called (it was later renamed *La Sonnambula*). Tanning's unsettling and powerful paintings of dream states in *Eine Kleine Nachtmusik* (1943) and *Birthday* (1942) feature young girl visionaries, their hair on fire, and doors opening on to another room where another door stands ajar. Her designs for *Night Shadow*, fanciful and ethereal, convey the web of affinities of a sleepwalker with a femme-enfant, a fairy child, a rapt visionary, a wraith who can walk between worlds—and an automaton.

In the years of World War II and its aftermath, European artists and writers fanned out across the globe, and many found safe haven in Latin America, especially Mexico and Argentina. Tapping into the unconscious no longer reveled in experimental creativity for its own sake but reflected the inexplicable incoherence of what was happening and what had happened. Within that context, the figure of the sleepwalker became emblematic of the disorientation and dislocation experienced by so many; somnambulism embodied shared powerlessness for numerous exiles and refugees as they were tossed at the mercy of forces beyond their control.

The German Argentine photographer Grete Stern, when making her series of photographic collages *Sueños* (Dreams) in Buenos Aires, was also working on designs for the magazine *Sur*, where, in 1940, a defining fable of contemporary consciousness first appeared: Jorge Luis Borges's short story "The Circular Ruins." The narrator describes how an unnamed sorcerer, who believes himself to be autonomous, alive, and indeed real, labors to dream a man into being, only to discover at the end that he is himself being dreamed—he's a figment in another's consciousness. (The story, inspired by *Through the Looking-Glass* by Lewis Carroll, in turn, underlies the plot of *The Matrix*.) Another contributor to *Sur* was the writer Adolfo Bioy Casares, Borges's "secret master," or so Borges said, crediting him with supplying many of his phantasmic plots. Bioy's *The Invention of Morel* (1940) is a wonderfully suggestive, enigmatic novella and lifts the Borgesian vision of life as a waking sleep out of Borges's own preferred haunts (archives, libraries) and into the contemporary sphere of photographic media. The narrator here is hiding out on an uninhabited tropical island, but he begins to realize that every day, in a certain place, people appear and talk,

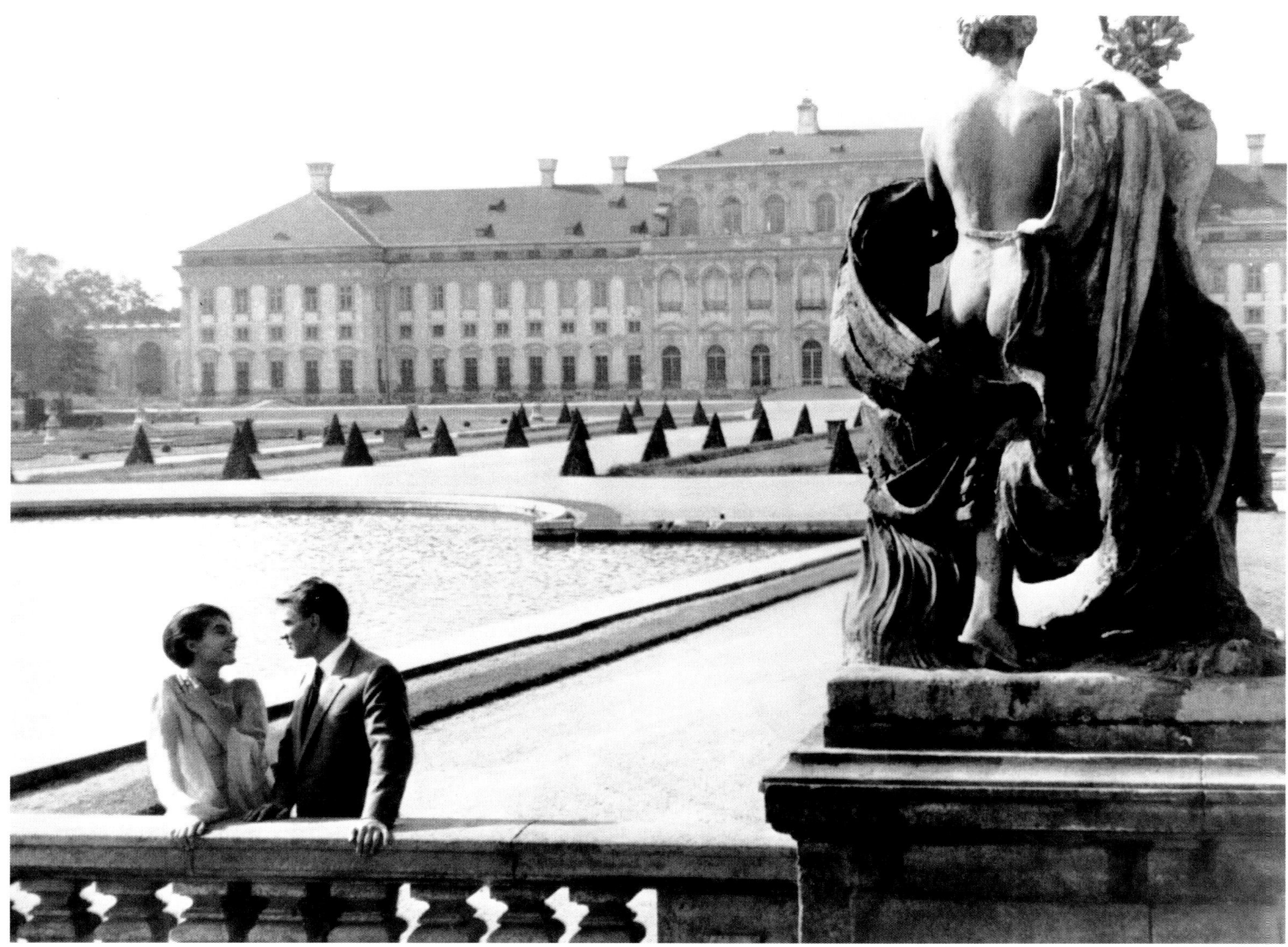

yet when he approaches them, he can't make them see or hear him; they repeat the same words, the same motions and exchanges. They are like sleepwalkers—their eyes are open, but their senses are shut. With these qualities, they are also cinematic revenants: they live in the eternity of unchanging images, like our film idols in stills and on-screen. He falls intensely in love with the woman, Faustine, and to join her in the dematerialized dimensions of space-time she occupies, he gradually wills himself to dissolve into film-flesh, like her.

Alain Robbe-Grillet acknowledges Bioy's novella as a source of his script for the cult film *L'Année dernière à Marienbad* (Last Year at Marienbad, 1961), and its director, Alain Resnais, filmed Delphine Seyrig and the rest of the cast haunting a magnificent rococo hotel, drifting down its infinite corridors, past innumerable doors and mirrors in hallucinatory recession. The characters are "metaphysical mannequins" writes Jean-Louis Leutrat in his study of the film; its overall effect is hypnotic, involving the spectator in the enigmatic state of cinematic reality and its affinity with dreams.

Robbe-Grillet recognized the prescience of Bioy's scenario, the way the novella had foreseen photography's interaction with memory, fixing the past archivally, halting time, repeating events and images. Now, with the coming of virtual and augmented reality, media encounters can eclipse individual empirical experience and crowd the mind with presences that are figments. "What are these images, actually?" asks Robbe-Grillet. "They are *imaginings*: an imagining. If it is vivid enough, is always in the present. The memories one 'sees again,' the remote places, the future meetings, or even the episodes of the past . . . are something like an interior film continually projected in our own mind." In *Last Year at Marienbad*, we are invited to look past the love triangle's rigid automatonlike exterior into the tumult of their interior passions, as if they are all sleepwalking in one another's dreams, which for us, as we watch, coincides with our own consciousness and dreams. This bewildering, eerie film gives us "the feeling of watching an apparition," writes Leutrat.

The figure of the sleepwalker, a premonitory, real-life phantom, moving through life wrapped in a dream, marvelously embodies the apparitional aspects of today's reality, in which photography plays such a dominant part, not only filling our minds with images but also making visible thoughts and desires and allowing us to eavesdrop on that private movie in the mind that is consciousness.

Marina Warner is a contributing editor to the *London Review of Books*. Her latest book is *Esmond and Ilia: An Unreliable Memoir* (2022).

Gregor Schneider's spaces make you feel like you're being swallowed up by your own fears, your own memories. At the 2001 Venice Biennale, he transplanted the inner world of his parents' house to the Giardini: inside the Nazi-era German Pavilion, visitors entered a nightmare of West German stuffiness—cramped, stifling, psychotic—extensions and replicas of the original rooms. It earned Schneider the Golden Lion award. People queued for six hours. "They could have visited the same house in Rheydt, back in the Rhineland," Schneider told me recently. Today, he lives across from *Haus u r* (as the original project is called), which he has been working on since 1985, when he was just sixteen. Still fully in its grip, the artist has warehoused the countless copies of those rooms (Schneider calls them "repetitions") he has created since then.

Duplication is the core principle of his work, after all. In 2004, he carried it to its extreme: *Die Familie Schneider* (The Schneider Family) consisted of two semidetached houses—at 14 and 16 Walden Street in London's East End—which the artist took great pains to match, inside and out, to a hair's breadth. These perfectly English spaces were entirely indistinguishable, from the carpet to the fireplace, down to every single stain on the wall. Visitors (only two per appointment) had to pick up the keys in an office and were allowed to spend ten minutes in each house.

Visiting the first one was spooky enough, the oppressive atmosphere of its hallway, kitchen, living room, children's room, bathroom—all dimly lit and mustily furnished—making it hard to breathe. The proportions seemed off somehow, and you got the strange sense that there was someone breathing right behind you. And, in fact, you weren't alone: in the kitchen, a woman was silently washing dishes, and in the bathroom, a man stood under the shower, hunched and facing the wall as he jacked off. The whole experience was as chilling as it was fascinating, you couldn't wait to leave, yet something made you want to stay and immerse yourself in this psychological drama pitched somewhere between a ghost story and a conjugal thriller.

But what was truly uncanny was the second house: the same yellowish light, the same crampedness, the same sticky residue covering everything. And the same *people*—Schneider had hired pairs of twins to perform identical acts in each house. Experiencing exactly the same thing twice not only doubled the creeping claustrophobia, the slow delirium, it also killed off any conviction of an *individual* experience. "The impression that a unique event could actually repeat itself was perceived as horrifying," Schneider says. "This exposes deficiencies in our perceptual apparatus; our inability to see any differences," which, of course, were minimal. You started to question your *own* perceptions. "Observing yourself observing spaces," suggests the artist.

This feeling is also found in the films and photographs of the work. Schneider transfers his spatial research to another medium in order to better understand the effects these spaces have on us. The images are not just documentations, but compressions, expansions. "The photographs show the conceptual side of the work. They convey a certain distance. It's impossible to tell that they depict rooms *within* rooms. They seem transported into an elsewhere; they do not compete with the real experience," Schneider states. Some images are from a central perspective; others appear more like snapshots. And, of course, there are two of each subject. This enables side-by-side comparison, but they could also depict just one walk through one house.

Yet, however much they capture the rooms' ghostly atmosphere, the photographs do not reflect their physical sensation. Like zombies locked into repetitive motions, the mute residents have been associated with the alienation, isolation, and loneliness of characters in a Samuel Beckett play—but they would have been just as at home in 1970s horror movies. The nuclear family as a nucleus of horror, the home as both tomb and prison: if Schneider's aesthetics didn't tend toward gloomy German romanticism, his proximity to Mike Kelley, Paul McCarthy, or Robert Gober would be even more obvious. The photographs in *Die Familie Schneider* are like any pictures in a family album: nothing's what it seems.

Gregor Schneider
The Family

Gesine Borcherdt

All photographs from the series *Die Familie Schneider*, London, 2004
© the artist and courtesy Konrad Fischer Galerie, Berlin

Gesine Borcherdt is an art journalist and curator based in Berlin. Translated from the German by Florian Duijsens.

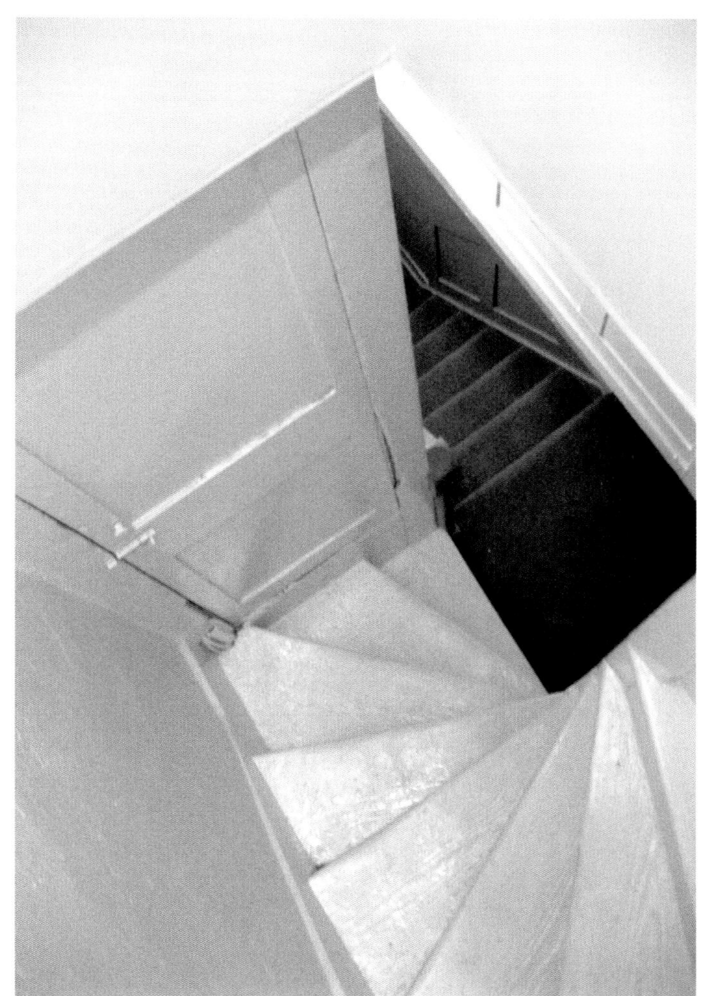
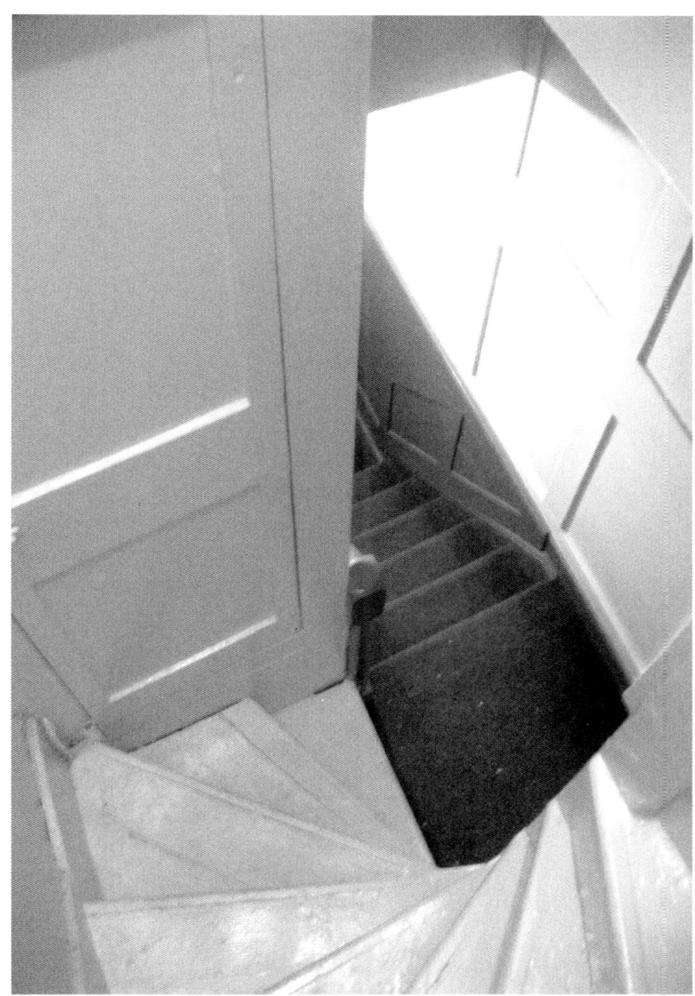
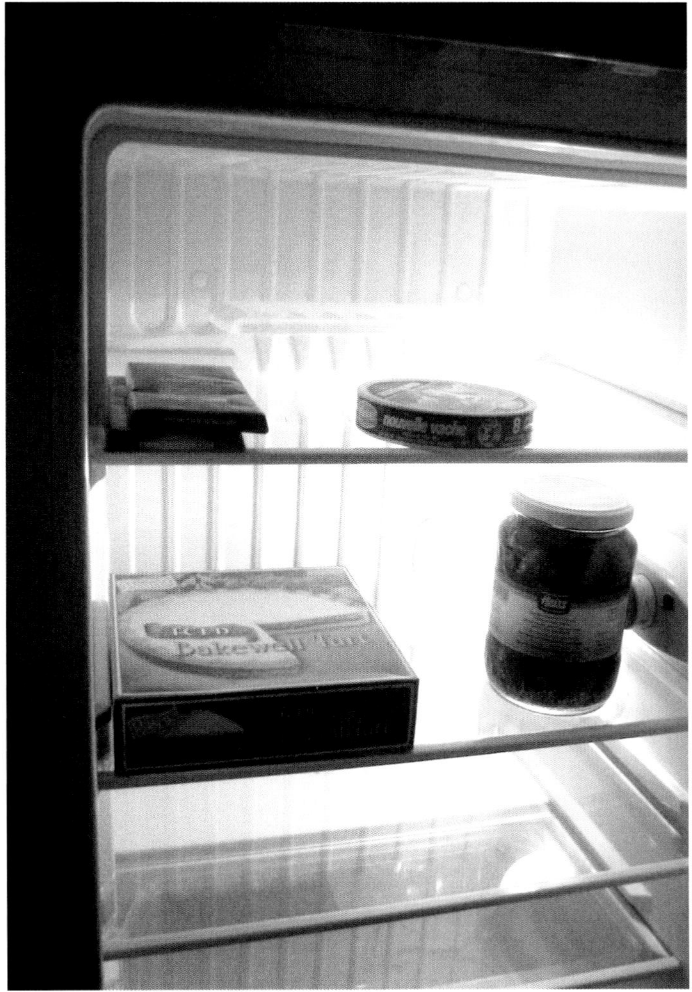
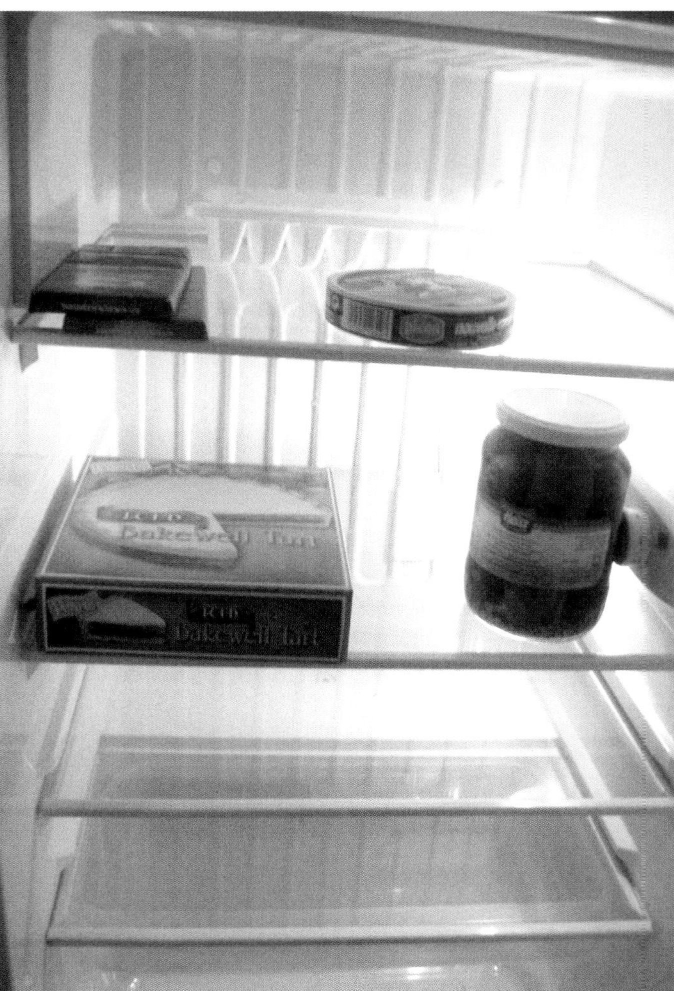

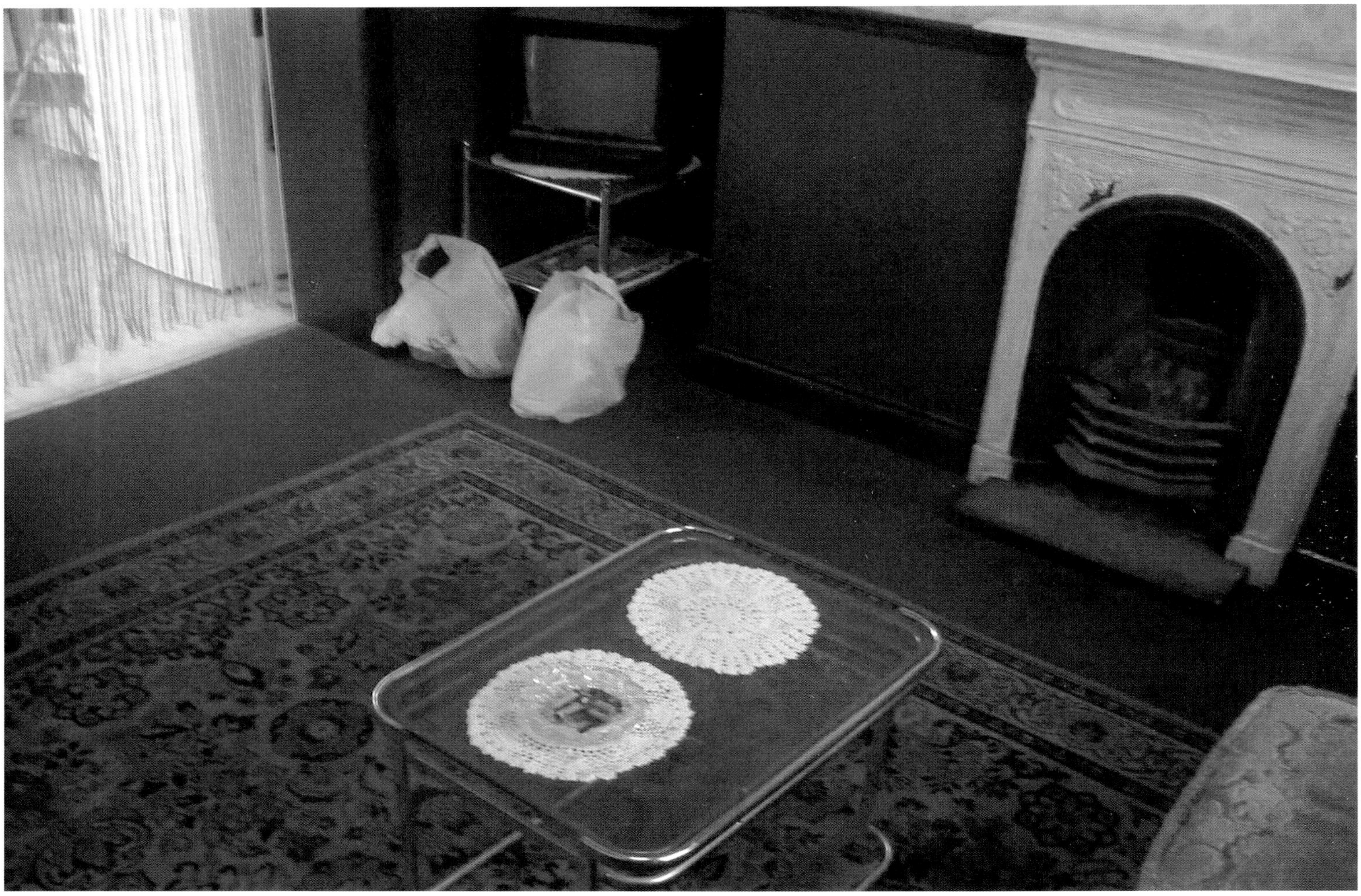

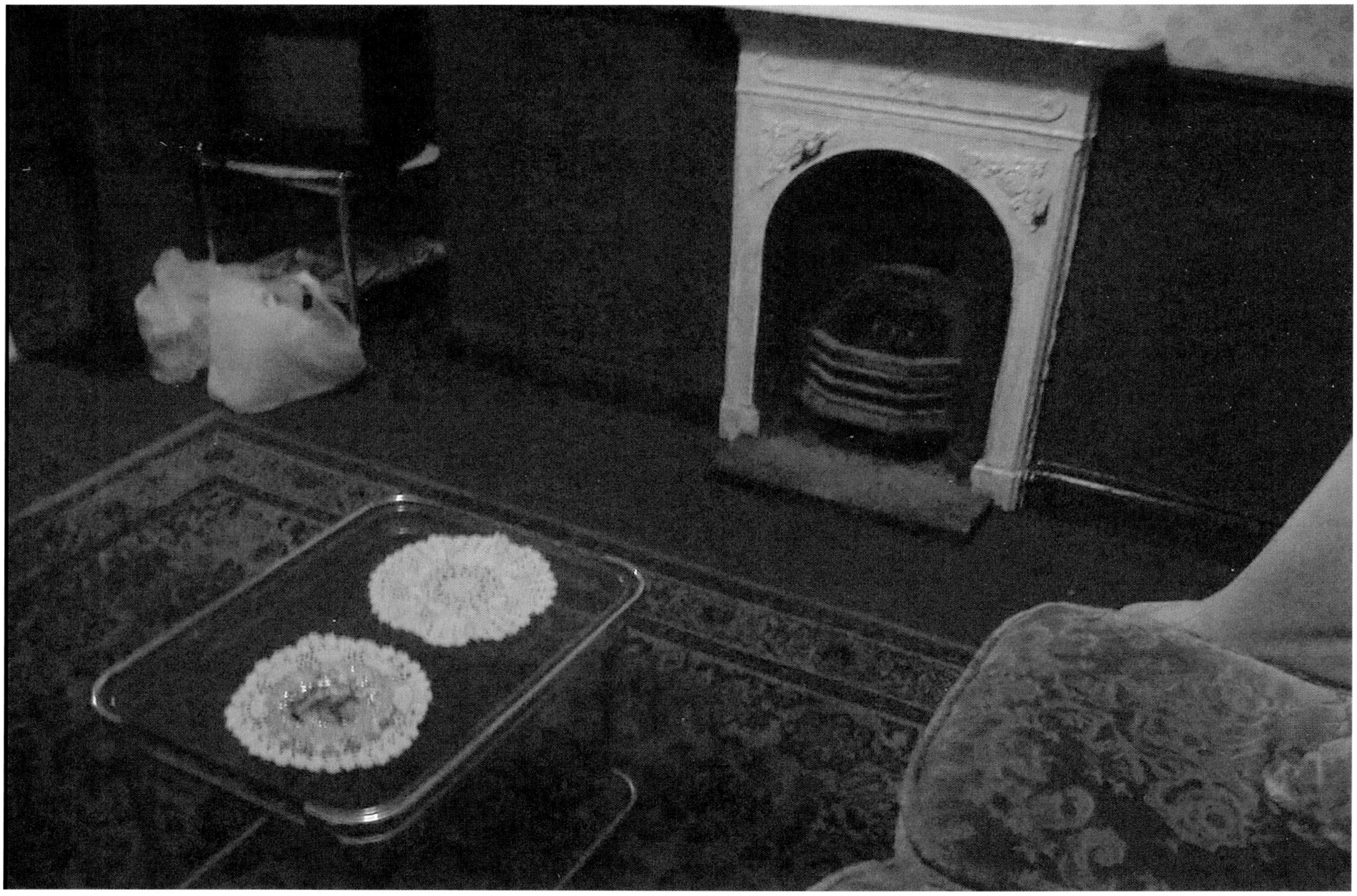

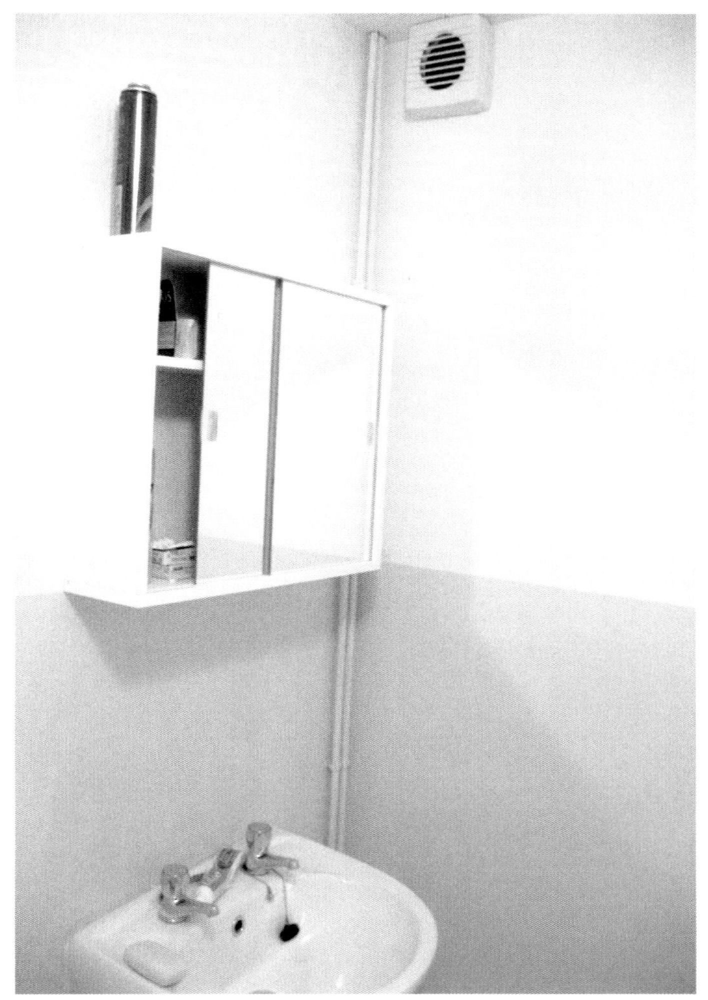
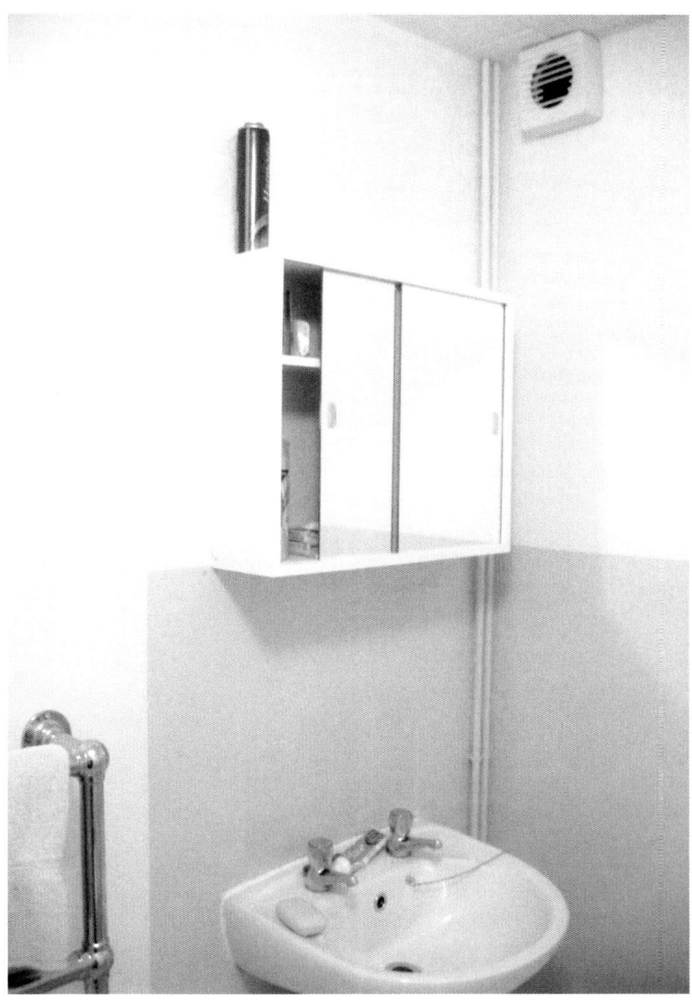
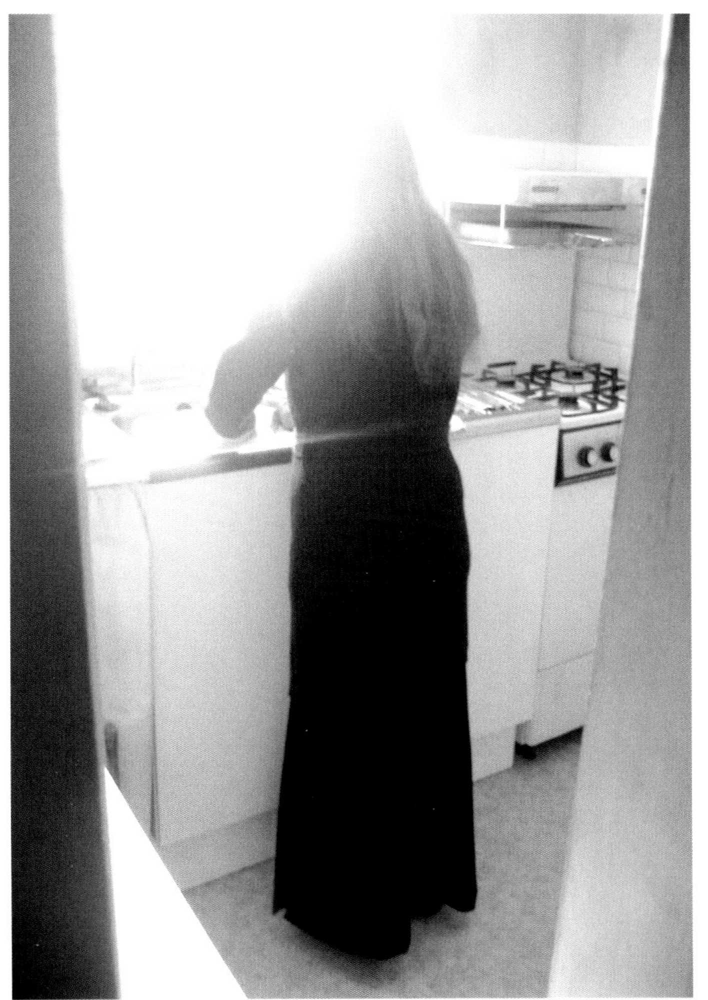
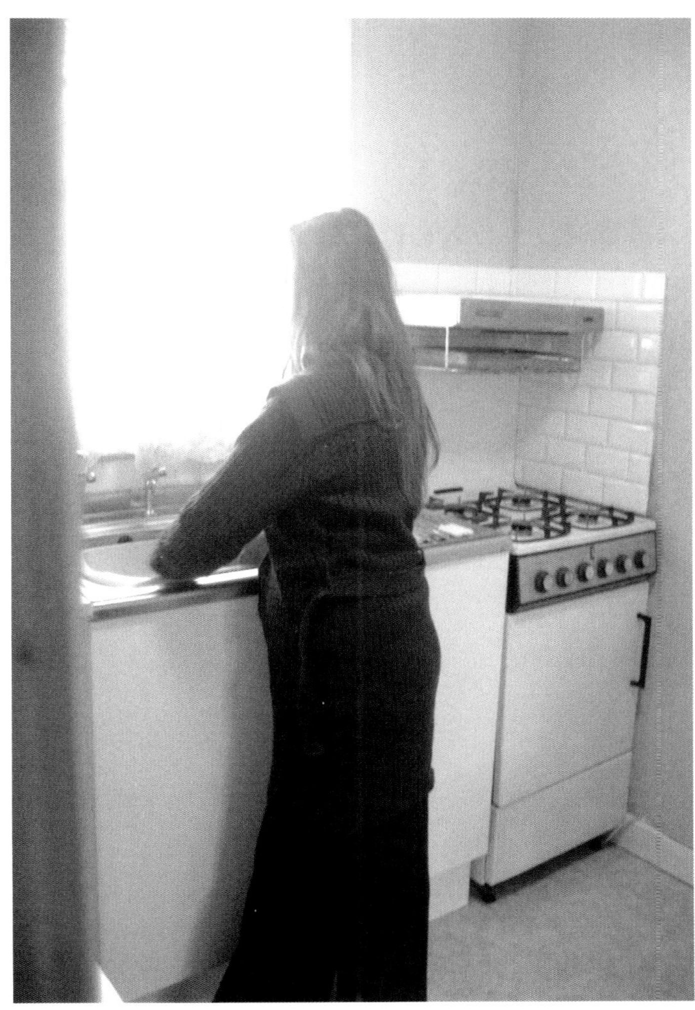

Etienne Courtois
Things Out of Place

Sara Knelman

As the Belgian artist Etienne Courtois and I chat over Zoom, a strange thing happens: someone crawls into a corner of the frame, a blonde head advancing and retreating in and out of the lamplight at intervals over the course of our conversation. I don't mention it, but note to myself that it's just the kind of curious detail Courtois has been chasing, then creating, for over a decade.

Courtois, a civil engineer turned investment banker, became obsessed with photography around the turn of the twenty-first century, looking and reading voraciously. In 2010, the bank he worked for collapsed in the wake of the financial crisis, and Courtois quit his day job. In the same year, he made an image of his young daughter as a response to a prompt to photograph "sleeping children," part of a Flickr workshop led by Alec Soth. Under a pile of too many hair clips in the day's dwindling light, her eyes are heavy but open, and looking straight at us. Is she sleepwalking? Daydreaming? Wide-awake? It's a question his images all seem to ask.

Inspired by the work of William Eggleston, Paul Outerbridge, and John Baldessari, among others, Courtois scavenged the landscape for things out of place, or waited for something to happen. After a while, he began intervening, keeping props in the trunk of his car and deploying them instinctually, creating the event he was hoping to find. Courtois was hunting images that already existed, seeking out dreams in the conscious world. A futile exercise, of course. Unable to find them, Courtois brought the practice home and started making them himself. In his studio, what was an odd detail within a larger landscape became the central subject, as Courtois began making abstract sculptures out of everyday objects.

Though the possibilities of image making in the digital realm inspire some of his techniques (cutting and pasting and layering), Courtois still uses analog film and natural light, old-fashioned glue and paint. His works can be laborious, often involving complicated masking or double exposures to frame or reframe the objects he appropriates; some are made three-dimensional and solidly unique with the addition of handmade frames, vinyl, or paint.

As images, though, they are lighter, recalling the joy of Surrealist invention and Pop art, the discarded things of modern life remixed, and celebrated. A Ping-Pong paddle smiles back, a disembodied ear listens closely to the sound of a fan unfurling, perforated insoles dance. It's as though Courtois has zoomed in on the strangeness he once discovered and conveyed in his earlier black-and-white landscapes, and turned a light on it, flooding it with color and energy. Even titles are part of the game: Courtois keeps long lists of words and phrases as they occur to him in the course of reading, watching, and dreaming, matching them to images only when they're displayed in exhibitions.

Though abstract, there's a wonderful sense of storytelling in Courtois's works. He likens the feeling they might evoke to a literary conceit: the uncanny presentiment when we're made aware of our position outside of the narrative; the jarring understanding that we're making all of this up, that we might decide to tell it all, or see it all, differently. "Sometimes," Courtois thinks, "a picture can do that."

Sara Knelman is a regular contributor to *Aperture*.

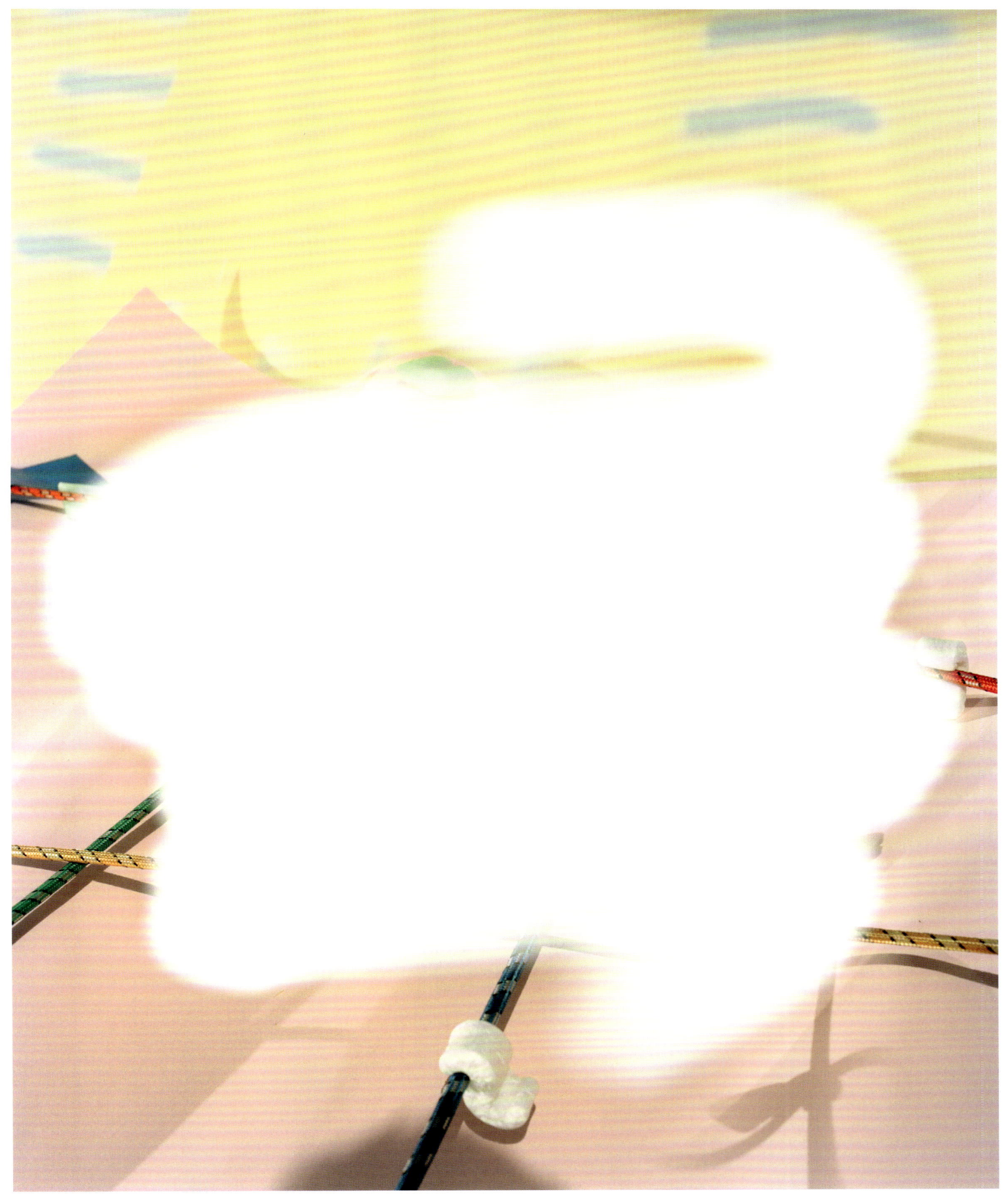

Slip Trap, 2014

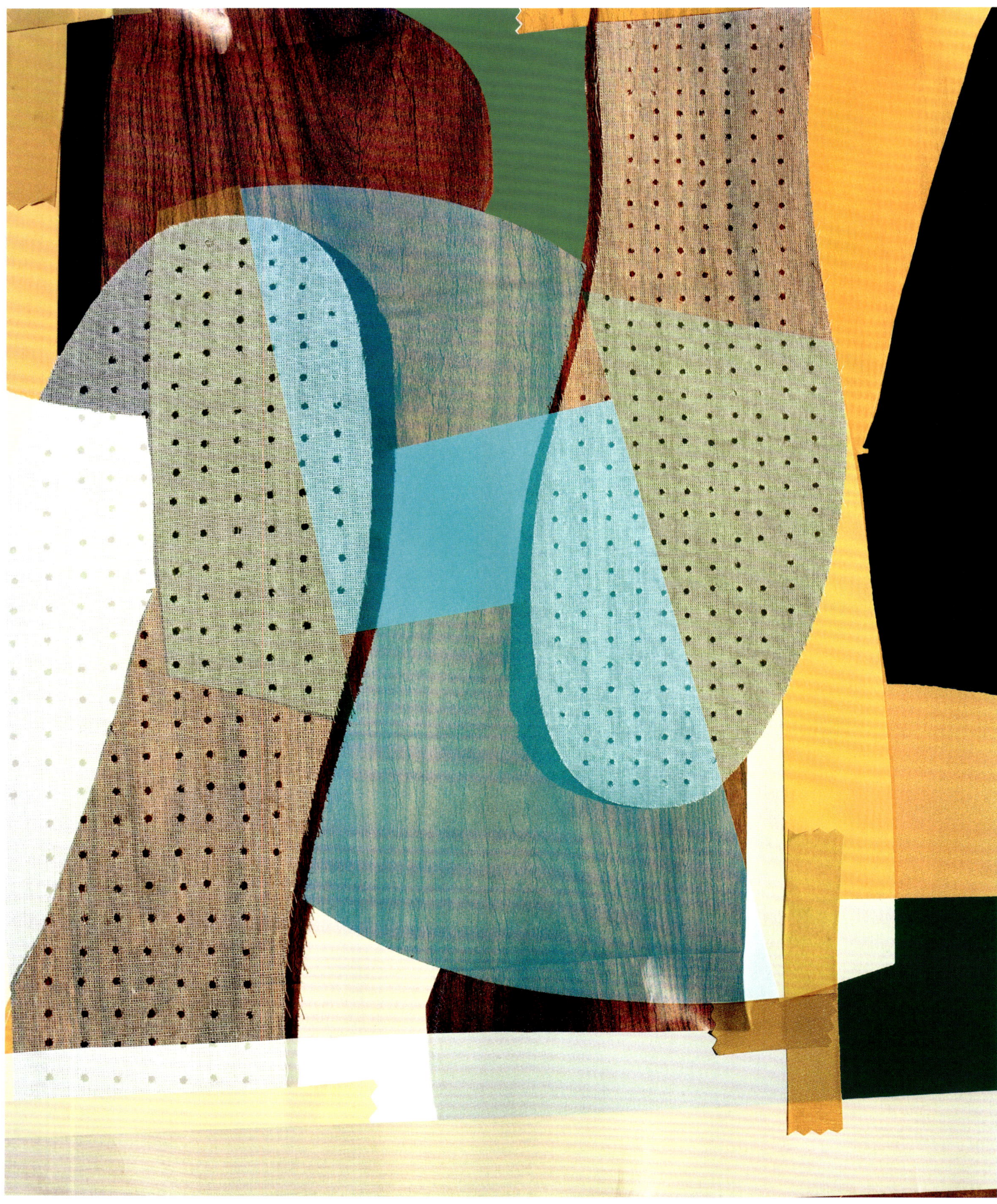

L'autre Confident, 2015

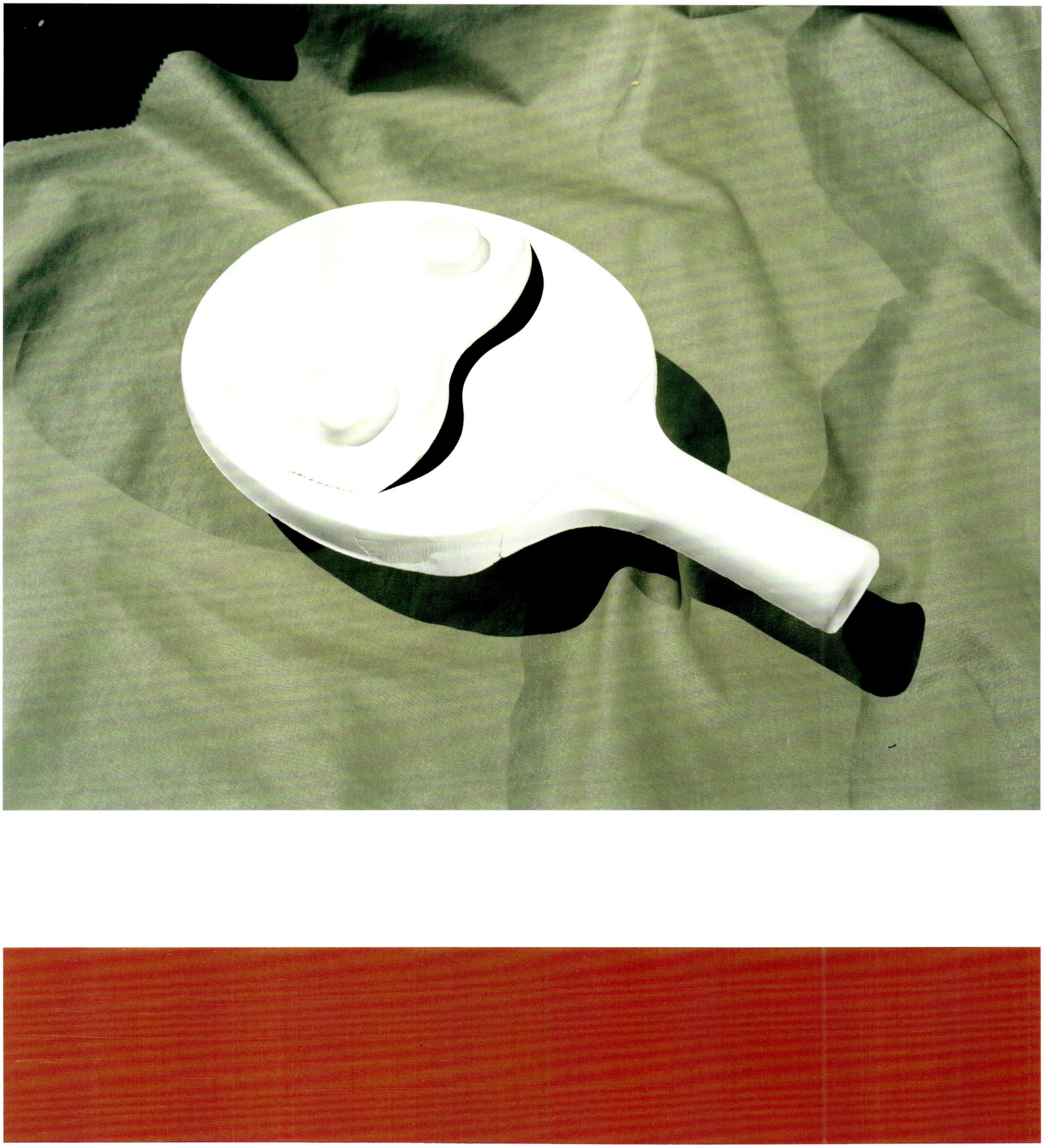

Playtime Playtime, 2018

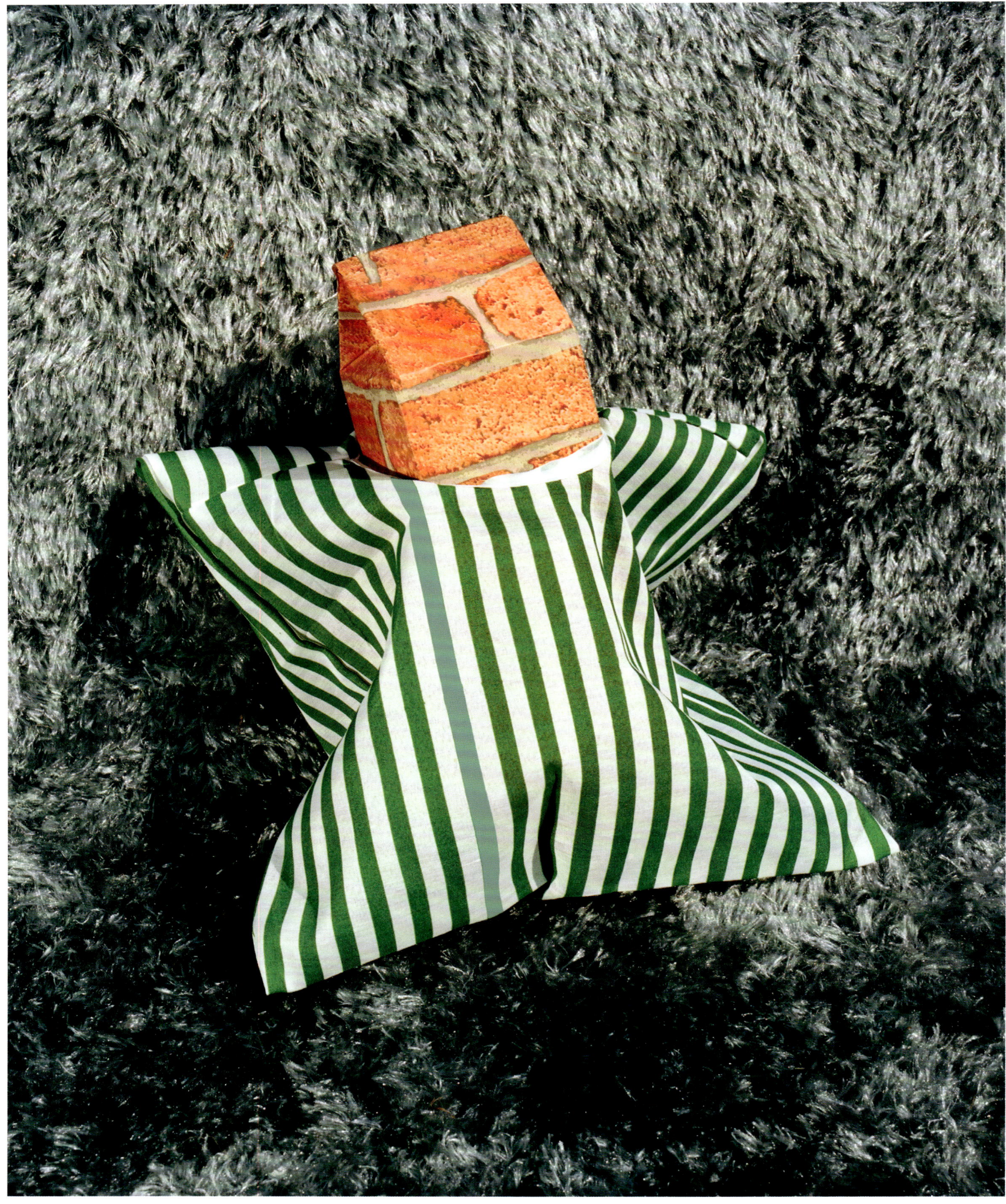

Meta Brik, 2016

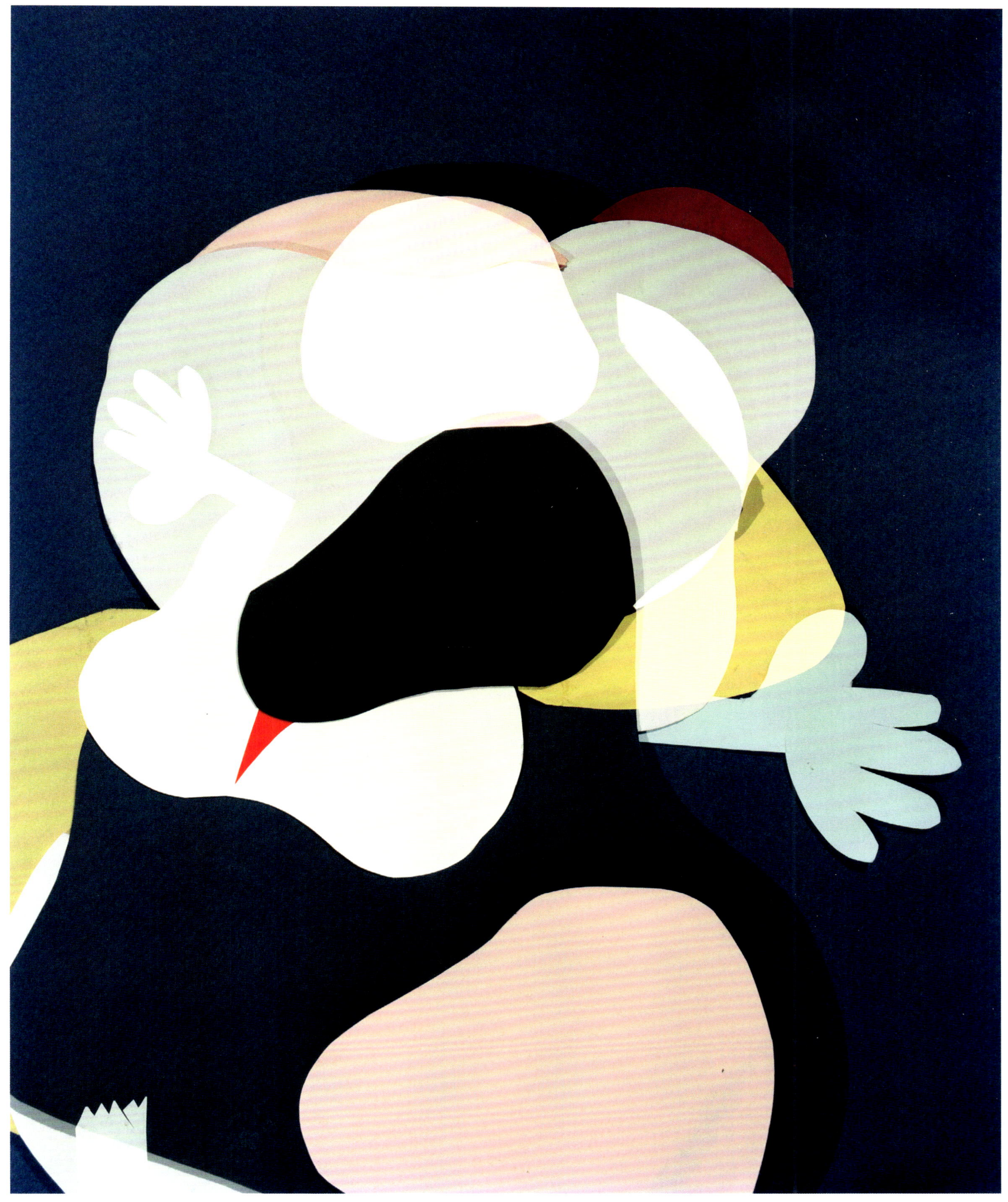

Au cirque la chamade II,
2015

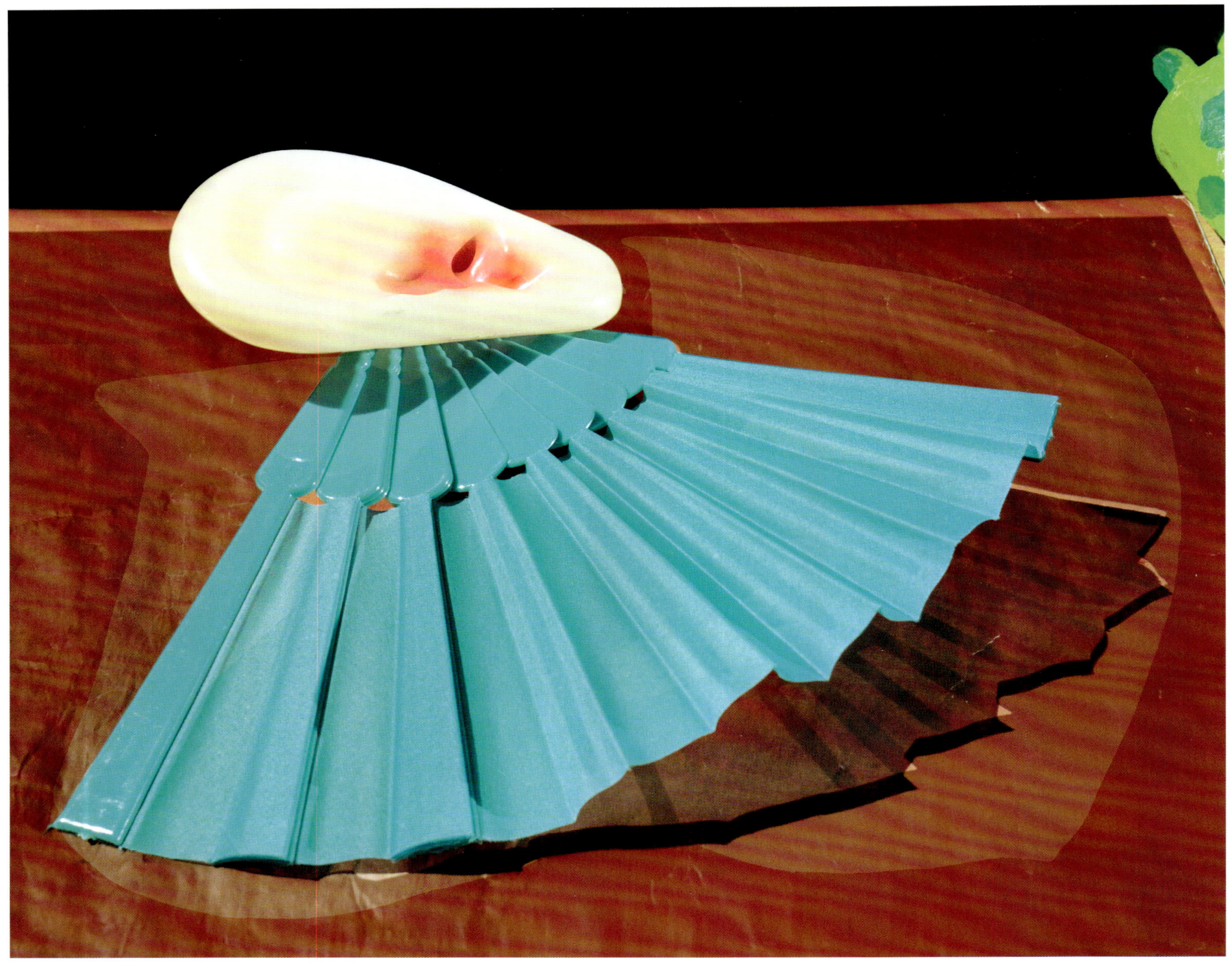

Potentiel évoqué, 2019

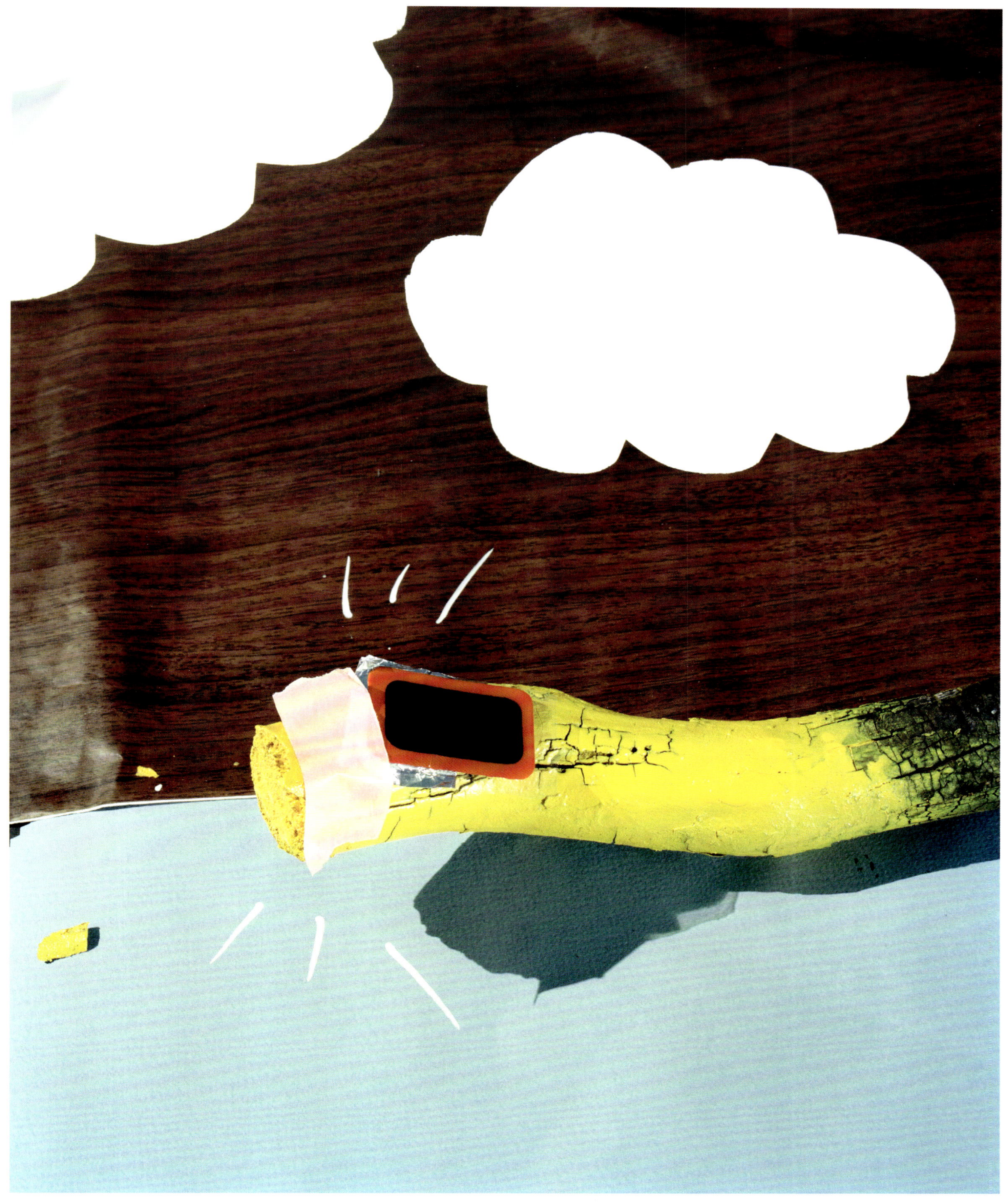

Flagrant délit, 2015

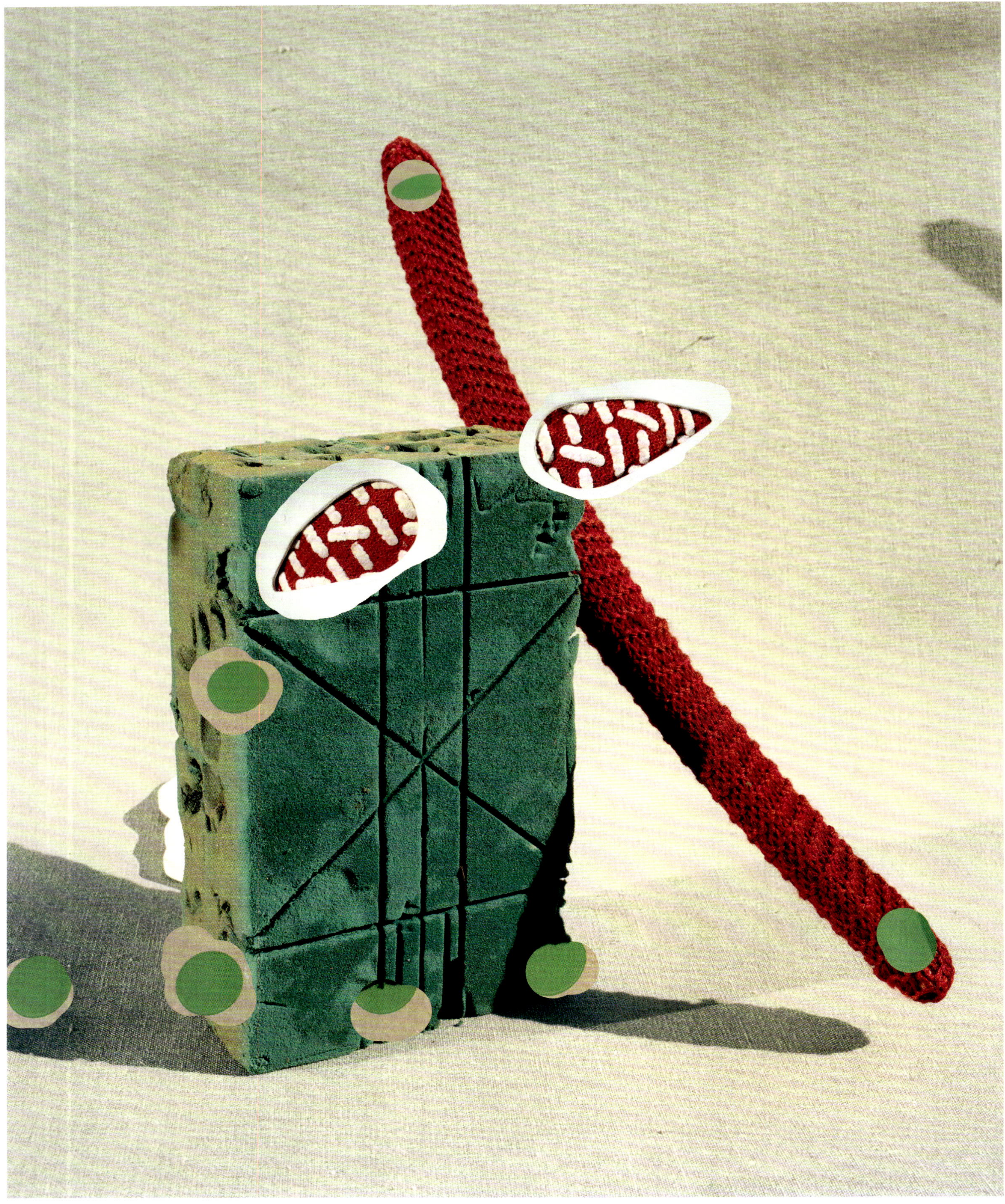

Bandit manchot, 2018

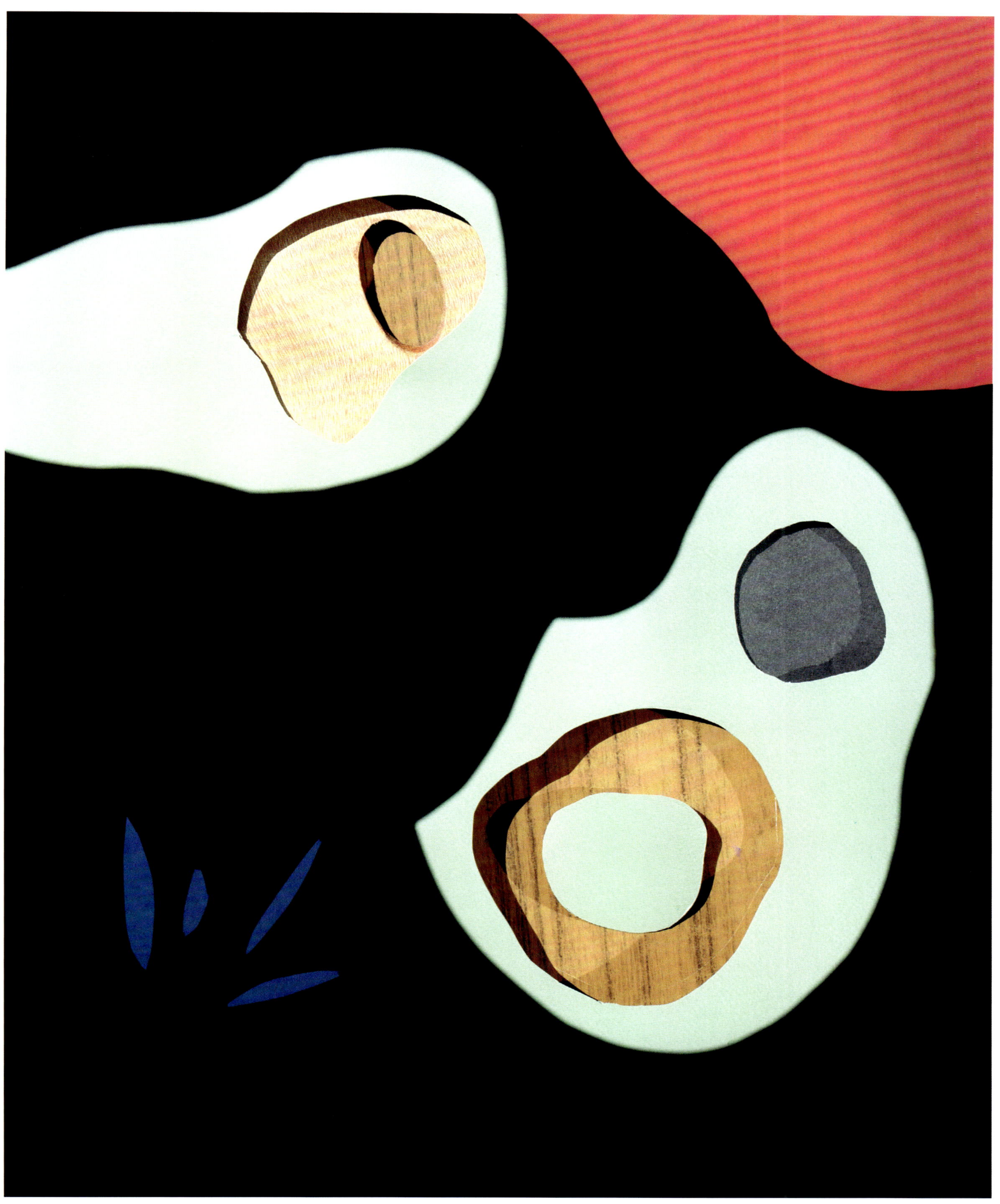

Pied de Grue, **2015**
All works courtesy the artist

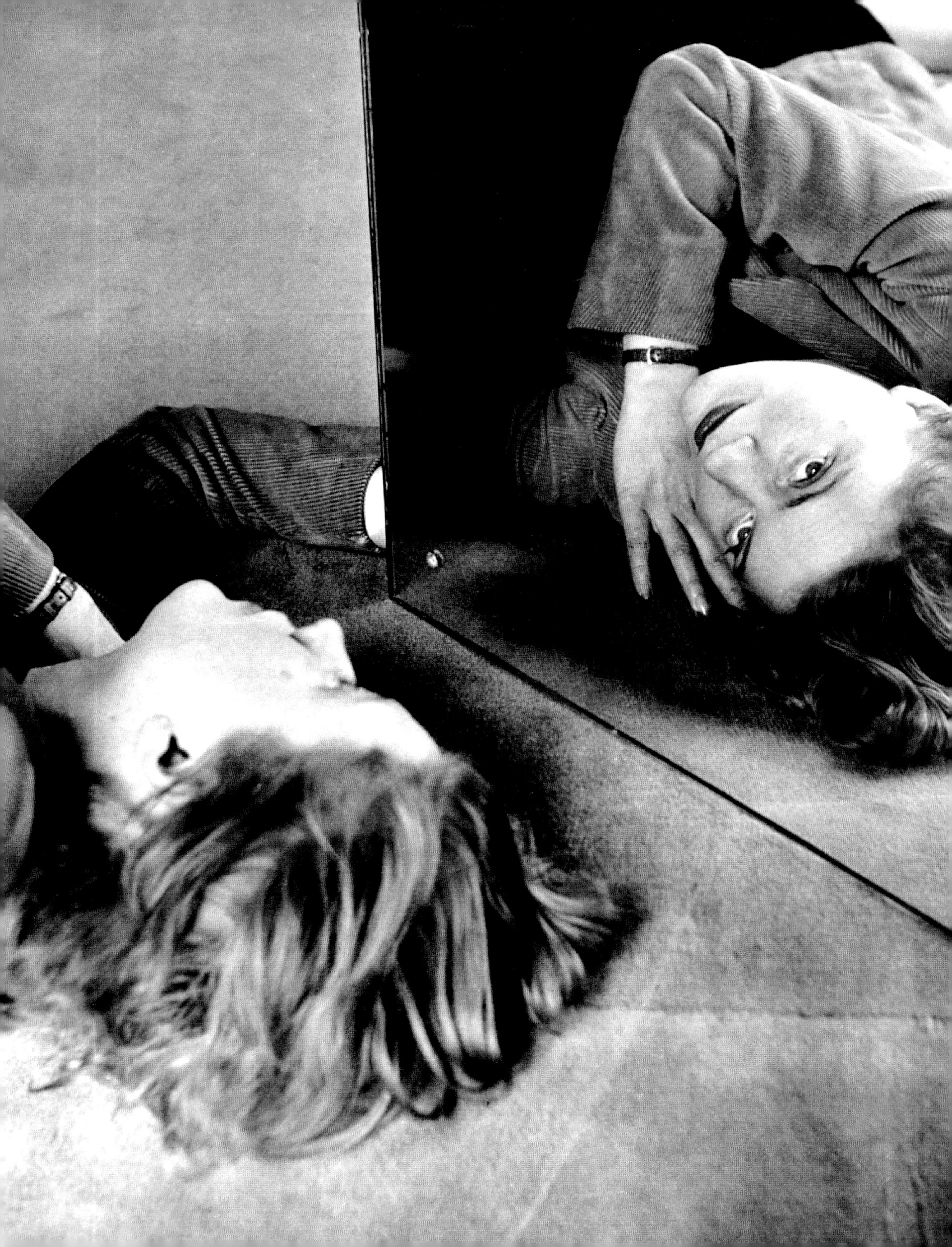

An artist and muse, fearless war correspondent and professional chef, Lee Miller looked at the world with a flair for drama.

Angel, Fiend, Surrealist

Lauren Elkin

David E. Scherman,
Lee Miller (Mirror Series),
Downshire Hill, Hampstead,
London, 1946

"One could say that Lee's feel for the incongruities of daily life made her a Surrealist," writes Lee Miller's biographer, Carolyn Burke. Although she was never an official member of the group (according to Burke, she couldn't abide André Breton), her feeling for incongruity and unexpected juxtapositions, for dreamlike imagery and tears in consciousness, her ability to perceive instabilities in apparently ordinary scenes, and her ethical commitments to getting the picture against all odds make her one of the movement's great photographers.

Miller was surrounded by Surrealist men in both her personal and professional lives. Her mentor turned lover, Man Ray, introduced her to Surrealist art and artistic circles in late 1920s Paris; she starred in Jean Cocteau's *The Blood of a Poet* (1930); her second husband, Roland Penrose, was an established practitioner of Surrealism in

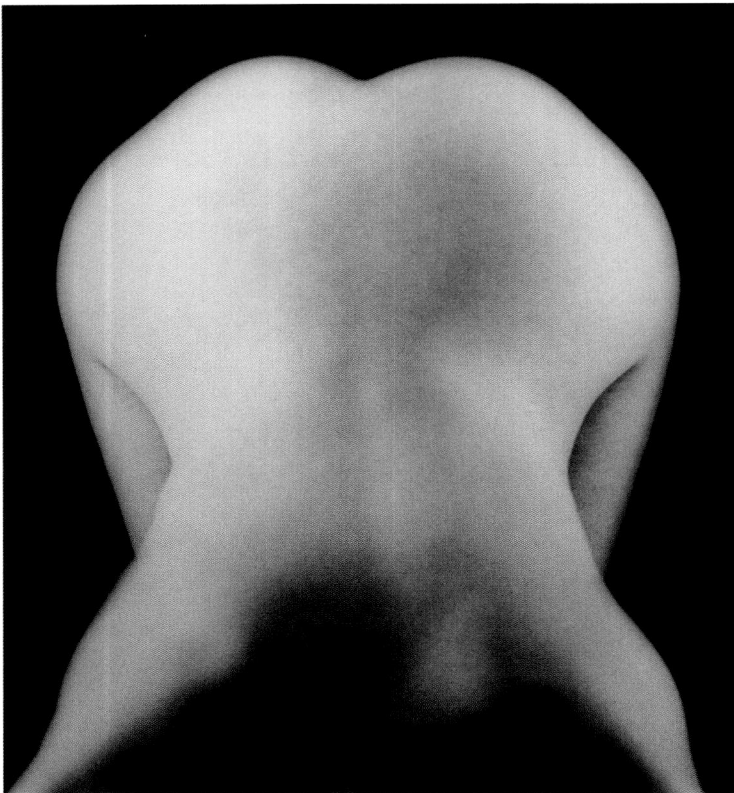

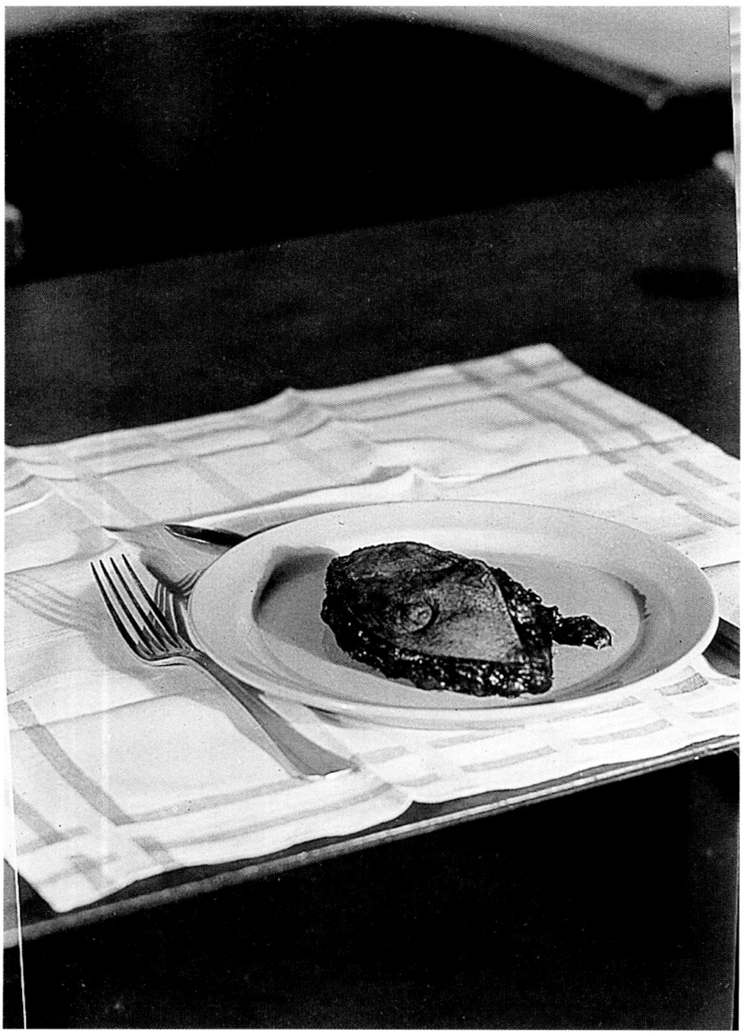

Britain and later a cofounder of the Institute of Contemporary Arts in London. But while these influences were important to her, Miller had her own decided view of the world. "I think she's a Surrealist from the beginning to the end," says Patricia Allmer, author of *Lee Miller: Photography, Surrealism, and Beyond* (2016).

In *The Lives of Lee Miller* (1985), recently rereleased in paperback, her son, Antony Penrose, depicts his mother as a woman who bolted from adventure to adventure, who "rode her own temperament through life as if she were clinging to the back of a runaway dragon." Born in Poughkeepsie, New York, in 1907, Miller got started with photography by having her picture taken hundreds of times—often nude—by her father, an amateur photographer with a darkroom tucked under the stairs of the family house. She continued modeling as a young woman in New York City, appearing on the cover of the March 1927 issue of *Vogue* within months of her meet-cute with Edward Steichen of Condé Nast (she stepped in front of a moving cab; he yanked her out of harm's way). She became one of his favorite models. In Steichen's viewfinder, Miller looks modern and eternal at the same time—Baudelaire's own definition of beauty. However, as Miller herself would later recall, "I looked like an angel, but I was a fiend inside."

The angel paid the bills, but the fiend wanted to hold the camera herself. In 1929, she got on a boat and tracked down the photographer Man Ray in Paris. "I'm your new student," she told him. He didn't take students, but he took her. For three years, they lived and worked together; Miller learned everything she could about making and developing pictures. He would sometimes pass assignments to her; as the story goes, Miller was at the Sorbonne medical school photographing something for Man Ray when she witnessed a mastectomy procedure. She took the severed breast to the offices of *Vogue* and photographed it on a dinner plate before she and the breast were thrown out.

Miller's Surrealism has to do with her ability to look "awry" at the world, says Allmer. For instance, there is the striking image of a woman's hand reaching for the doorknob as seen through the scratched shop window at Guerlain, which Miller calls *Untitled (Exploding Hand)* (ca. 1931). She captures otherwise imperceptible moments like this and, in spite of their ordinariness, finds great drama. There is an element of chance in this picture, but there is also an alertness to the potential readings of the work that is all her own.

By contrast, a studio image such as *Nude Bent Forward* (ca. 1930) clearly involved planning and forethought to set the camera and the lighting in just the right way so that when the model leaned over, naked, her torso would fill the frame, arms and neck cut off, the lower half of her body seeming to disappear into the shadows below. As Mary Ann Caws, author of *Surrealism* (2004), writes, the composition creates "the disquieting effect of making the body appear gradually to be dissolving."

The female body—so fetishized in Surrealist art—is almost unrecognizable in *Nude Bent Forward*. That we are looking at a body is clear; the grain of the skin has been beautifully, duskily rendered. But it is also contorted beyond recognition; there is something troubling in its visceral ambiguities.

In 1934, having left Man Ray and resettled in New York to start her own studio two years prior, Miller married the Egyptian businessman Aziz Eloui Bey, eventually moving with him to Cairo. The time she spent in Egypt was crucially important to her development as a photographer. In *Portrait of Space* (1937), her Surrealist gaze could see a whole world of suggestion in the torn and tattered mosquito net, the tent's window seeming to hang askew like an empty frame. The scholar Katharine Conley writes in *Surrealist Ghostliness* (2013) that the emptiness of this

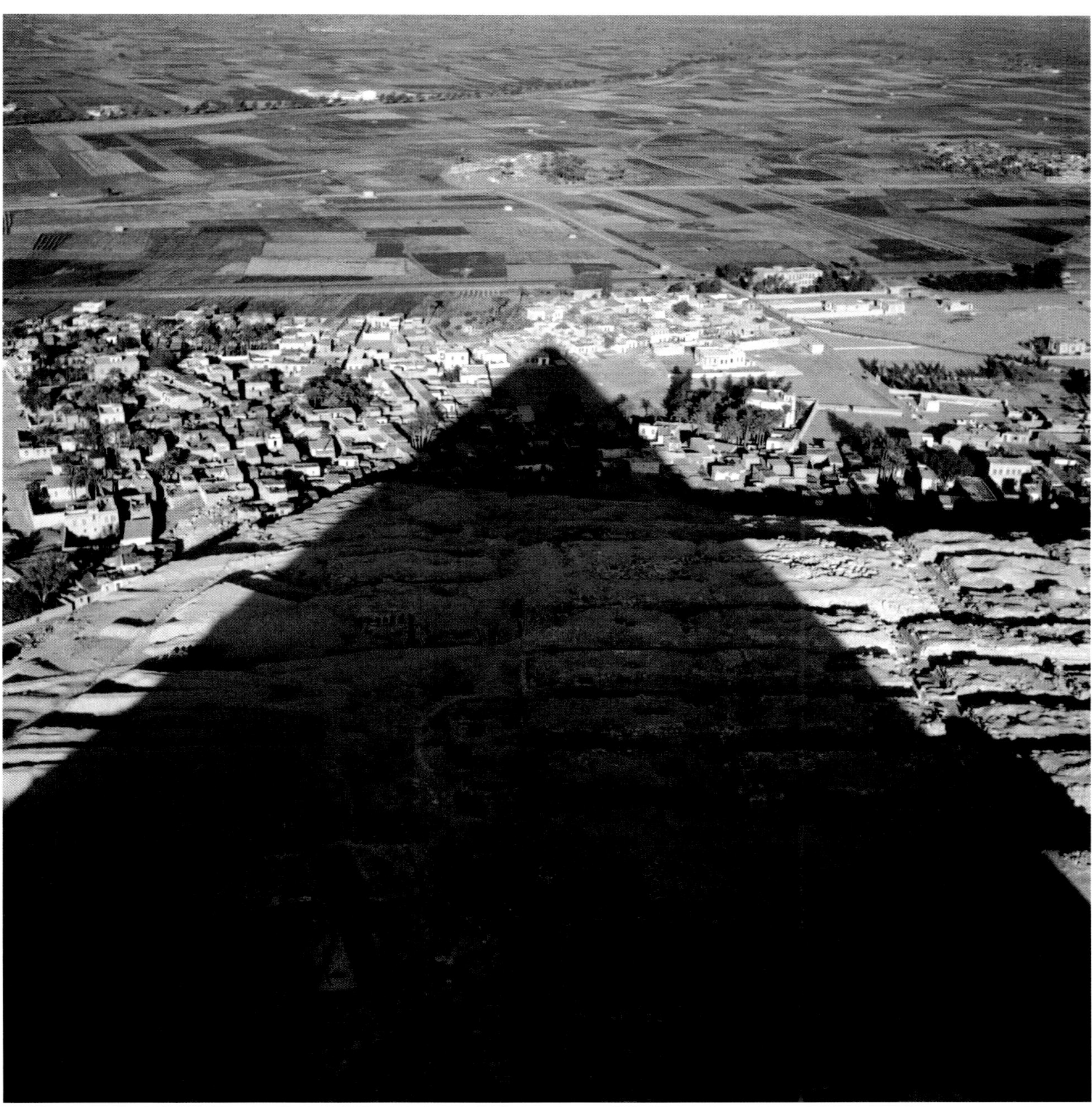

frame "resembles the 'unsilvered glass' of Breton and Soupault's *Magnetic Fields* that metaphorically divides a body's psychic unconscious from consciousness, separating outer from innermost realities."

Allmer points out that Miller is present in the form of a shadow in many works from this period—in a photograph of Deir el Soriani Monastery in Egypt about 1936; in one taken from the top of the Great Pyramid of Giza about 1937 (a shadow within a shadow); in the image of Eileen Agar looking pregnant with her camera at Brighton Pavilion in 1937. The shadow is a supremely Surrealist motif, "simply an effect," Allmer writes, "always in flux." Or, as the writer Pierre Mac Orlan put it in 1930, with reference to Eugène Atget's Paris scenes, "Photography makes use of light to study shadow. It is a solar art in the service of night." Solarization would also be one of Miller's great contributions to Surrealist photography—it was Miller and Man Ray who discovered what could happen if the lights were suddenly turned on during the development process: the tones reverse, and a ghostly outline forms. Man Ray would create a solarized portrait of Miller in profile, appearing like an electrified angel.

Allmer considers this interest in the shadow, and a willingness to include herself in the image, an important part of the ethical charge of Miller's work: "Perhaps, if you're a photographer, and you are there in these really traumatic situations, you are part of this story and not detached from it." Miller's involvement in world events was confirmed during World War II, a time when most of her Surrealist group (Breton and Man Ray among them) fled to the United States to escape the violence. (So much for Surrealism in the service of the revolution.) Miller, on the other hand, stuck it out in London, where she moved after Egypt to be with her second husband, Roland Penrose, surviving the Blitz and the constant threat of annihilation. She even put herself on the front lines of the U.S. invasion of Nazi-occupied Europe in 1944.

In Cocteau's *The Blood of a Poet*, a title card declares that the poet composes "a realistic documentary of unreal events." Miller's work in the war strikes me as a Surrealist corollary to that statement, a surreal documentary of real events. In wartime London, Miller photographed the destruction caused by the Blitz. Her eye was trained to see the uncanny qualities in the fragments of the city she encountered; she out-surrealed the Surrealists.

"She finds the battered typewriter or the mannequin standing in the street corner or the window blown in such a way that the glass makes a pattern. She's just constantly looking for the concretization of dreams," Antony Penrose tells me. "That's what she's finding." One such example is of a stone angel, fallen to the ground with her neck severed by a metal bar, a brick smashing her breast. Miller called it *Revenge on Culture* (1940). "Who is taking the revenge?" asks Caws, the author of *Surrealism*, when we speak. "She was taking her revenge on us for not knowing whose revenge it was or why . . . and which culture, of course. Everything about that particular image says to me that's why she's a Surrealist." Miller's wartime photographs would appear in a book called *Grim Glory: Pictures of Britain Under Fire* (1941), published so that U.S. audiences an ocean away from the conflict could appreciate the terrifying realities of life during the Blitz.

Although her accreditation did not permit her to report from combat zones, Miller found herself in Saint-Malo for the Allied offensive and, staying on with the infantry, was among the first people let into Dachau and Buchenwald after they were liberated. The image of Miller in Hitler's bathtub is well known (taken in collaboration with David E. Scherman), but the photographs that she made as the concentration camps were liberated are among the most haunting and disturbing documents of the war.

Suffering from alcoholism and probably post-traumatic stress disorder after her return home, Miller lost the desire to keep taking photographs. Production eventually slowed to such a point that her son didn't realize the "extent" of what she had made, the "depth and penetration" of her wartime work.

Miller, who in 1966 became Lady Penrose when Roland was knighted for his services to art, threw herself instead into cooking,

Miller could see a world of suggestion in the torn mosquito net, the tent's window seeming to hang askew like an empty frame.

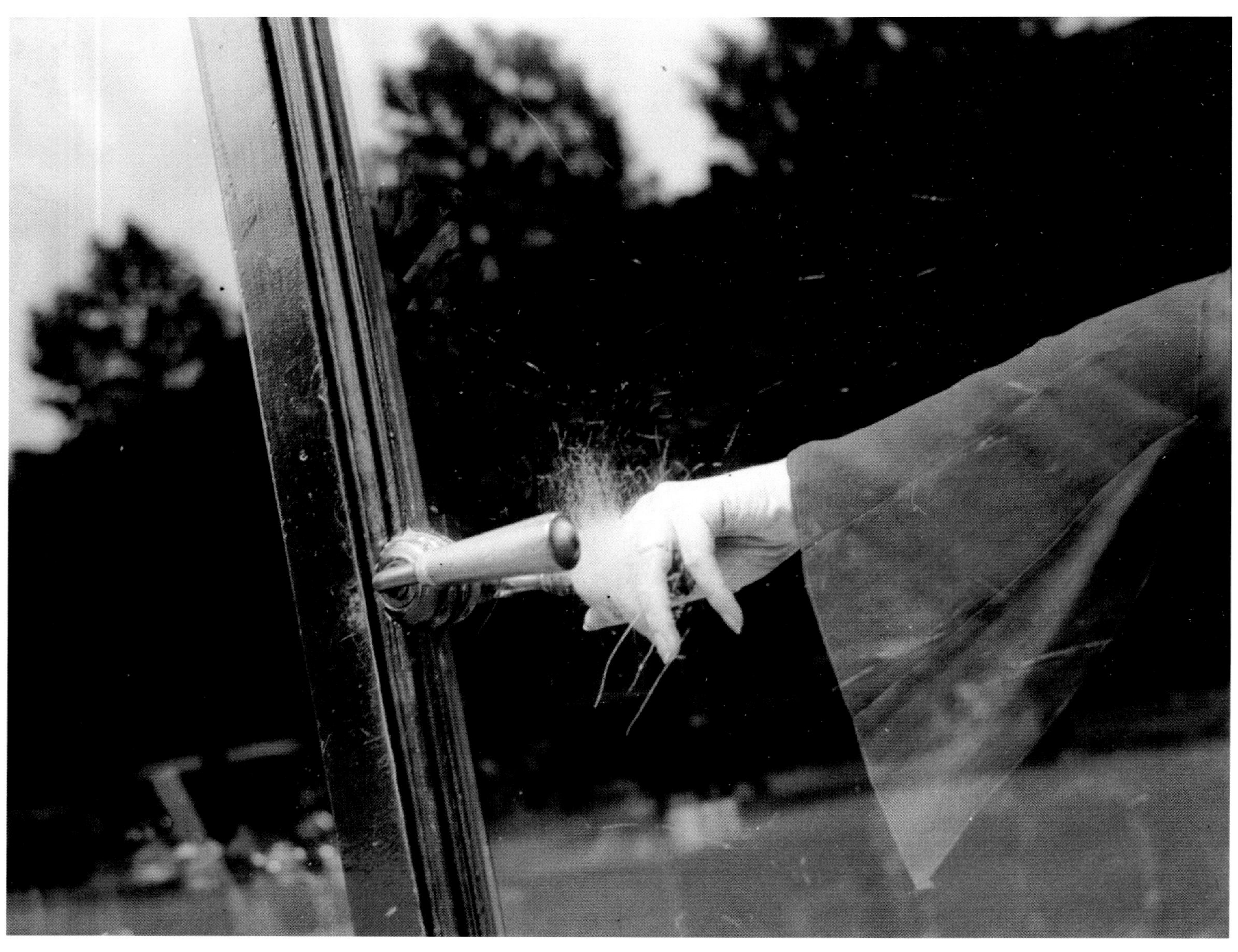

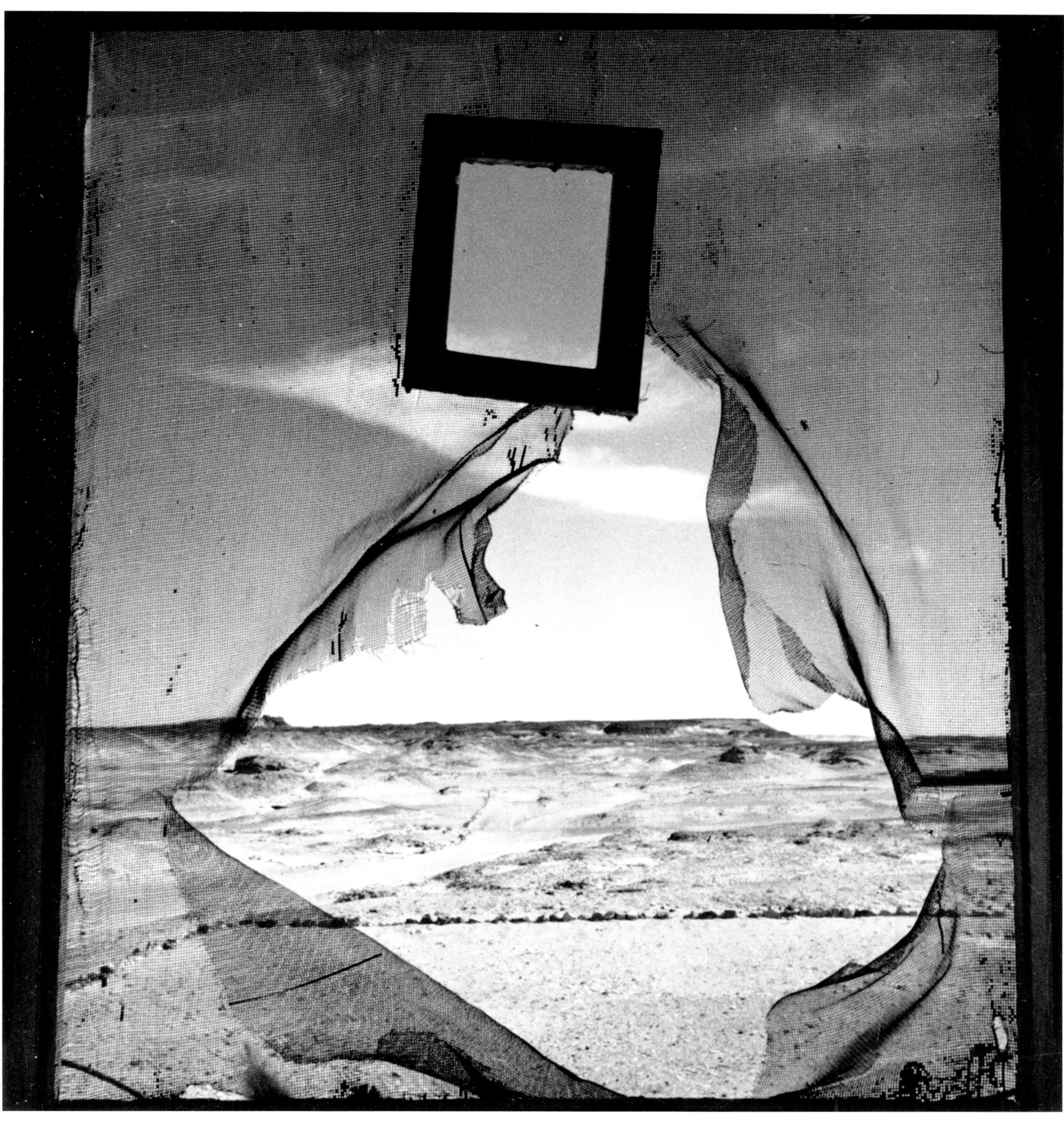

Lee Miller, *Portrait of Space*, Al Bulwayeb, near Siwa, Egypt, 1937
All photographs © Lee Miller Archives, England

training at Le Cordon Bleu London and taking great pride in whipping up the most original, surreal dishes she could: Her son remembers being served blue spaghetti and pink breasts made of cauliflower with cherry tomatoes for nipples. Her recipe for chicken was prepared with so many herbs it turned green. Miller's cooking is often underappreciated as an important continuation of her Surrealist work—it's domestic, it's fleeting, and it's not war photography, after all. But it was just as much about unsettling people's received ideas about how the world should be. A Surrealist from beginning to end.

Lauren Elkin is a writer based in London. She is the author of *Flâneuse: Women Walk the City* (2016) and *No. 91/92: Notes on a Parisian Commute* (2021).

Maja Daniels
On the Silence of Myth

Kristian Vistrup Madsen

Photography is notable both for its ability to objectively witness, and, paradoxically, for its access to the surreal. Something beyond our control can happen after the lens closes. It might be a light leak, movement recorded as blur, some shadow unaccounted for. History is similarly ambivalent, an uneasy conglomerate of fiction and testimony, which often employs photography in staking its claims. It is precisely in the overlap between these two murky territories that Maja Daniels, a Swedish photographer based in London and Gothenburg, begins her work.

To Daniels, the past is just as fictitious as the future. She leans into the all-too-human penchant for mythmaking and fantasy, our desire for saints and sorcerers and false closures. What becomes apparent is that history is a patchwork of stories and images, a condition that does not make it any less real. She looks for strangeness in what's already there: "I take that something that must be in the water, and I run with it," she told me recently.

One weird fish swimming upstream was Tenn Lars Persson, a mystic and photographer, whose early twentieth-century pictures of the Älvdalen region of Daniels's grandparents have found a place among her own. They appear first, in her book, *Elf Dalia* (2019), clearly juxtaposed in dialogue, but also in her work as it has developed since. The photographs increasingly form a kind of synthesis; it becomes more and more difficult, and, perhaps, irrelevant, to say which belong to whom. Another example is Gertrud Svensdotter, a twelve-year-old girl, also in Älvdalen, who was thought to have walked on water in 1668, an event that ignited the Swedish witch hunts. Can we see in Daniels's depictions of knobbly trees and people, shielding their eyes from the sun, some of the same magic and mystery that Persson portrayed a hundred years before? And in other little Älvdalen girls, a similar magnetic pull as Gertrud's?

Every one of Daniels's photographs is something of a mystery. Subjects often turn their backs to her lens, or appear without the sort of context that might give us an idea of their purpose or location. An animal in a forest or in a child's embrace; a collection of feathers held up against the light; a bonfire. About these individual images, we still have to ask what, who, where, why, but we can also expect the answers to refer, more or less, to the world as we know it. The greater mystery is in the space between them; how Daniels arranges her motifs to become part of a story.

Take the picture of a dragonfly on a tree stump, Persson's one of three women and a child seen from a distance in a pine forest, and that of a green-haired, dog-eared figure, facing away. Look at those pictures all together, spaces included, and ask what the logic of the assemblage is. You'd be hard pressed to answer. Yet in trying to make sense of these fragments of narrative, the possibility of a whole other constructed world, another time opens up. We get the recipe for mythmaking, but without losing the allure of the myth itself.

All photographs *Untitled,* **from the series** *On the Silence of Myth,* **2019–21**
Courtesy the artist

Page 94: Tenn Lars Persson, Älvdalen (1878–1938)
Courtesy Elfdalens Hembygdsförening (EHF)

Kristian Vistrup Madsen is a writer and art critic based in Berlin.

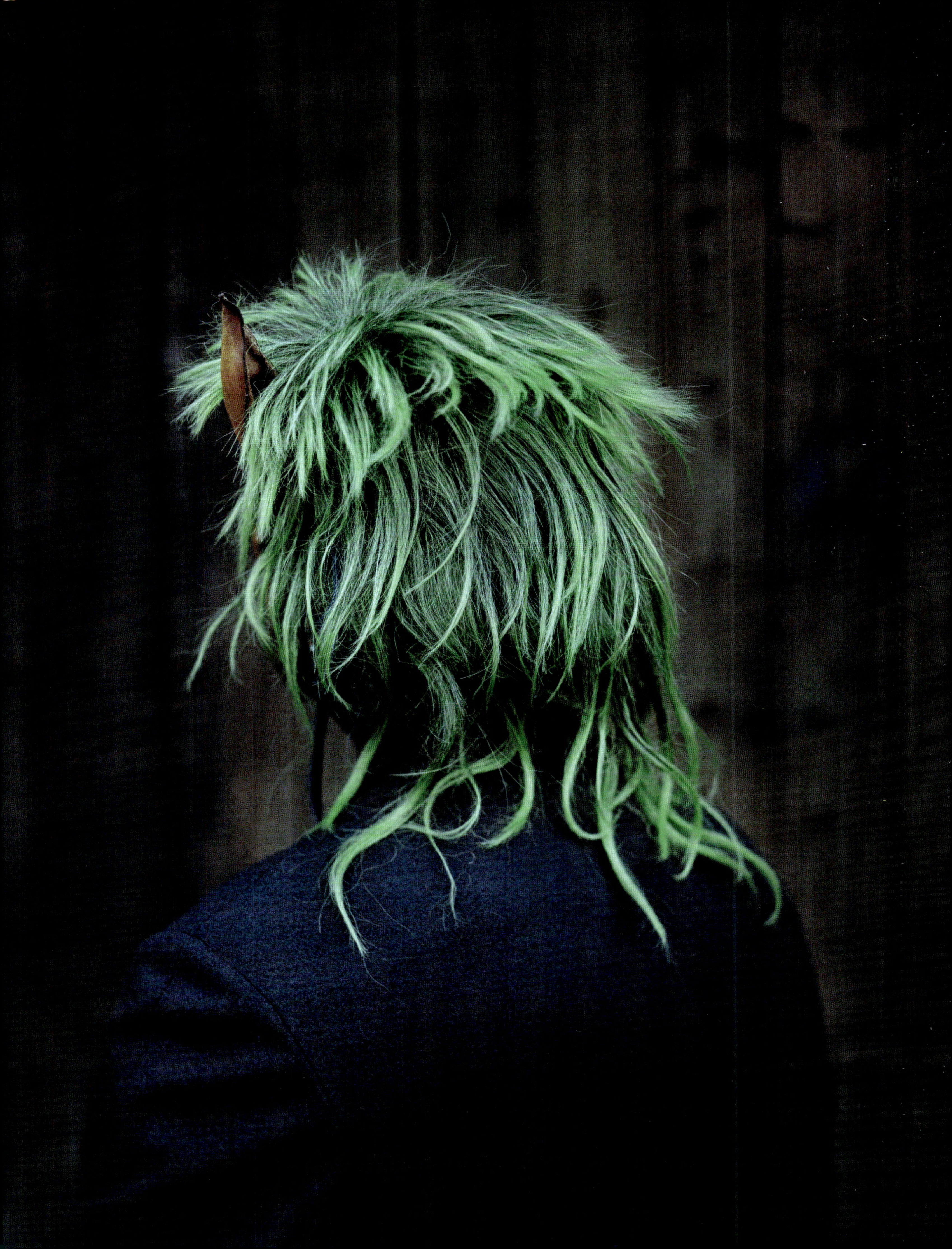

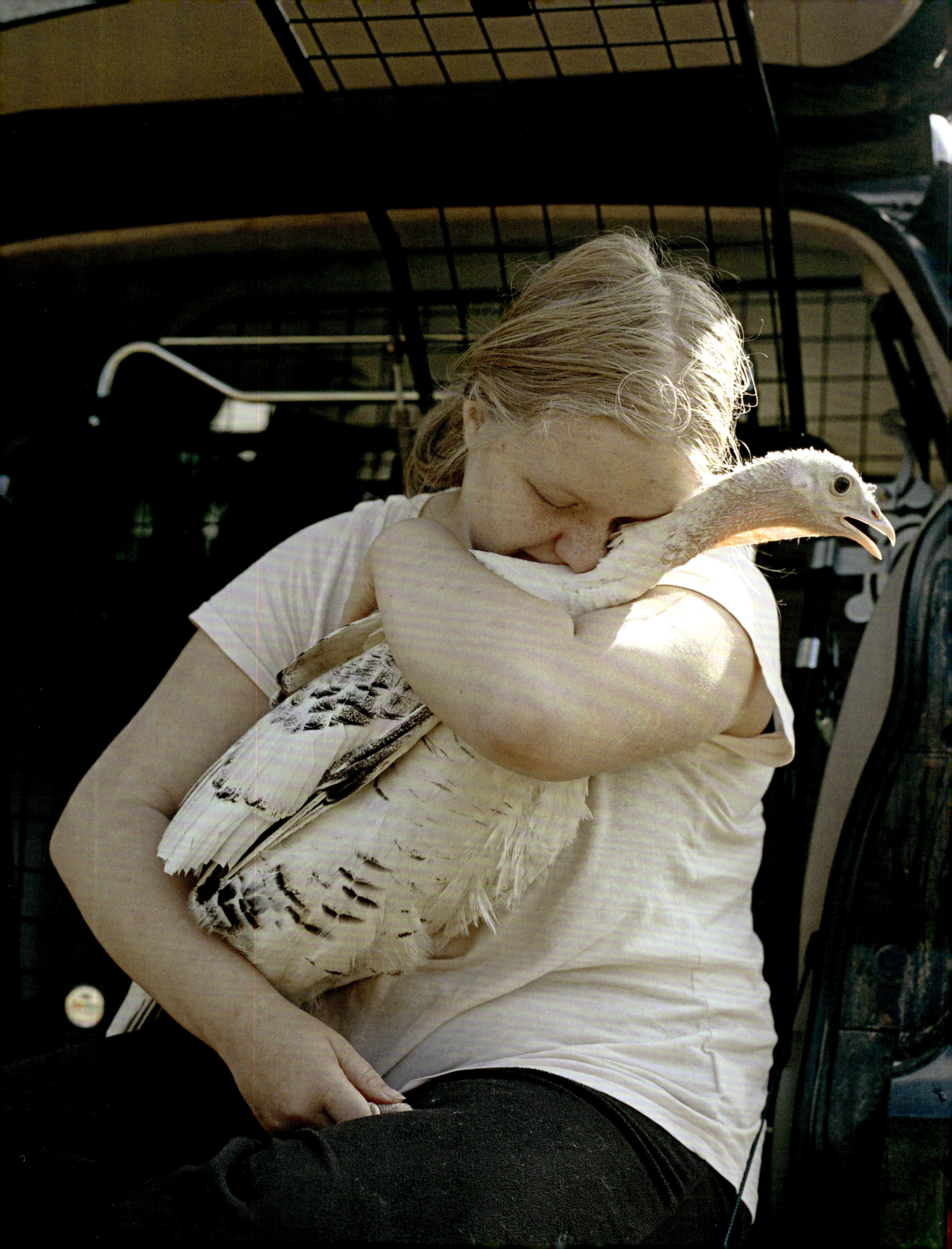

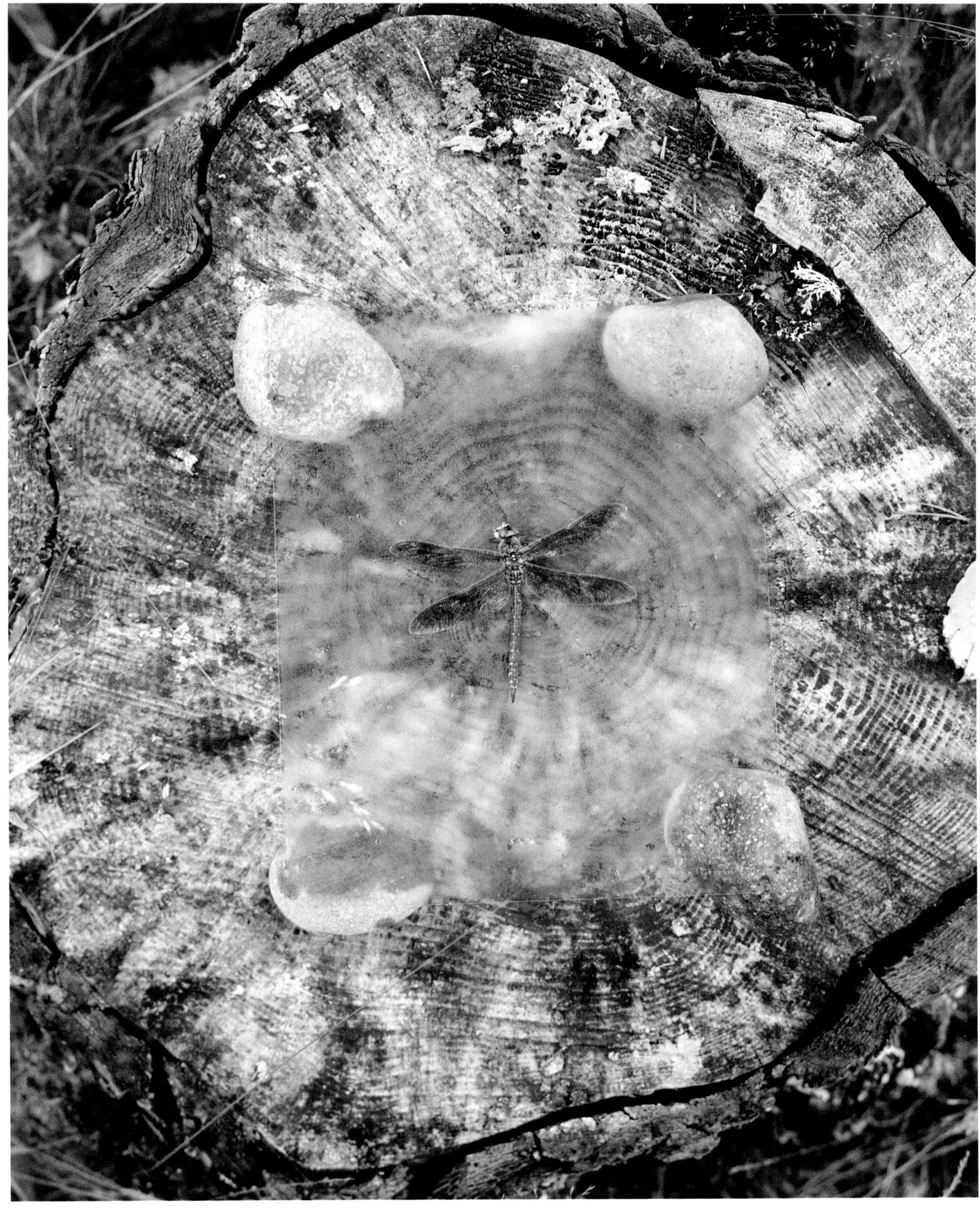

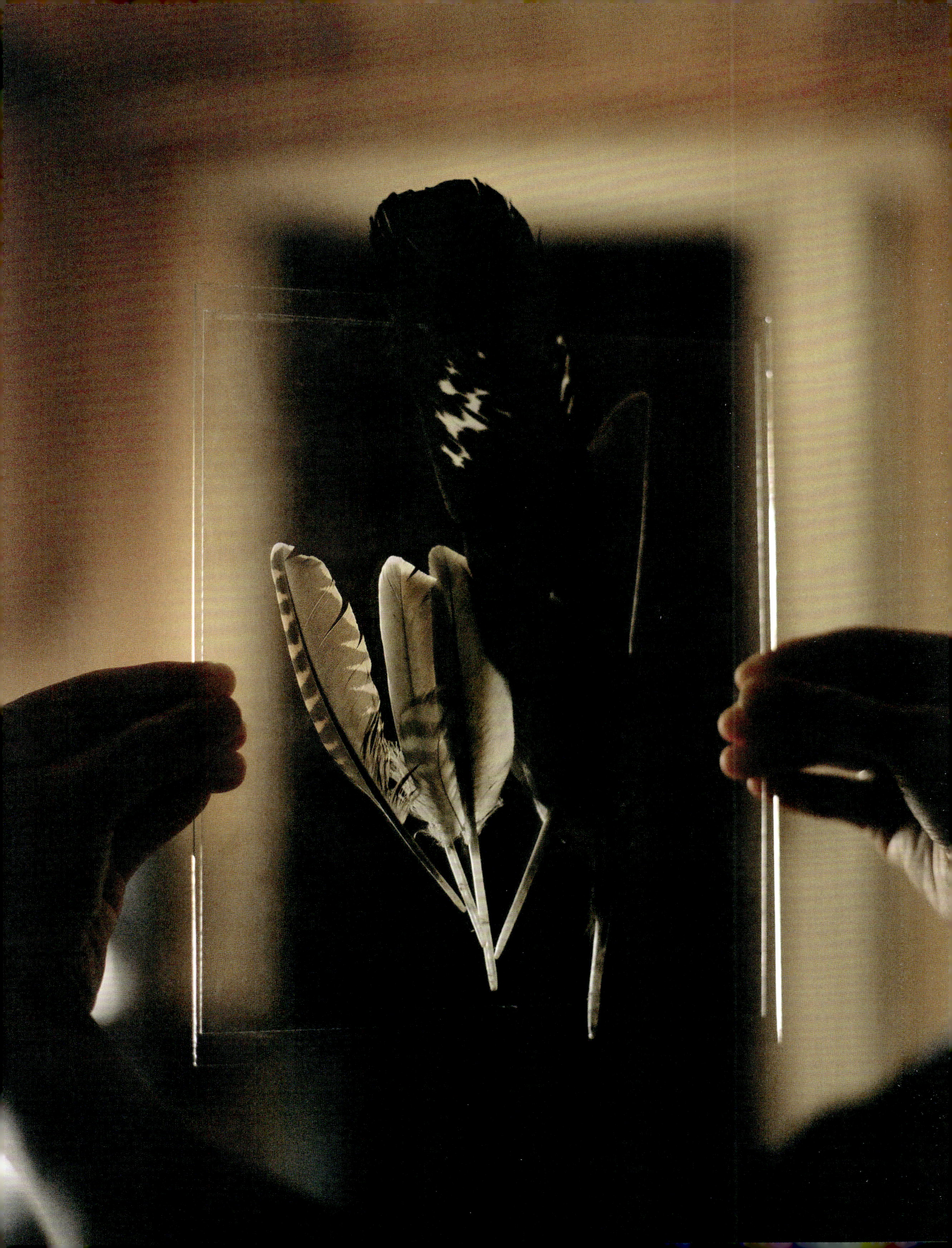

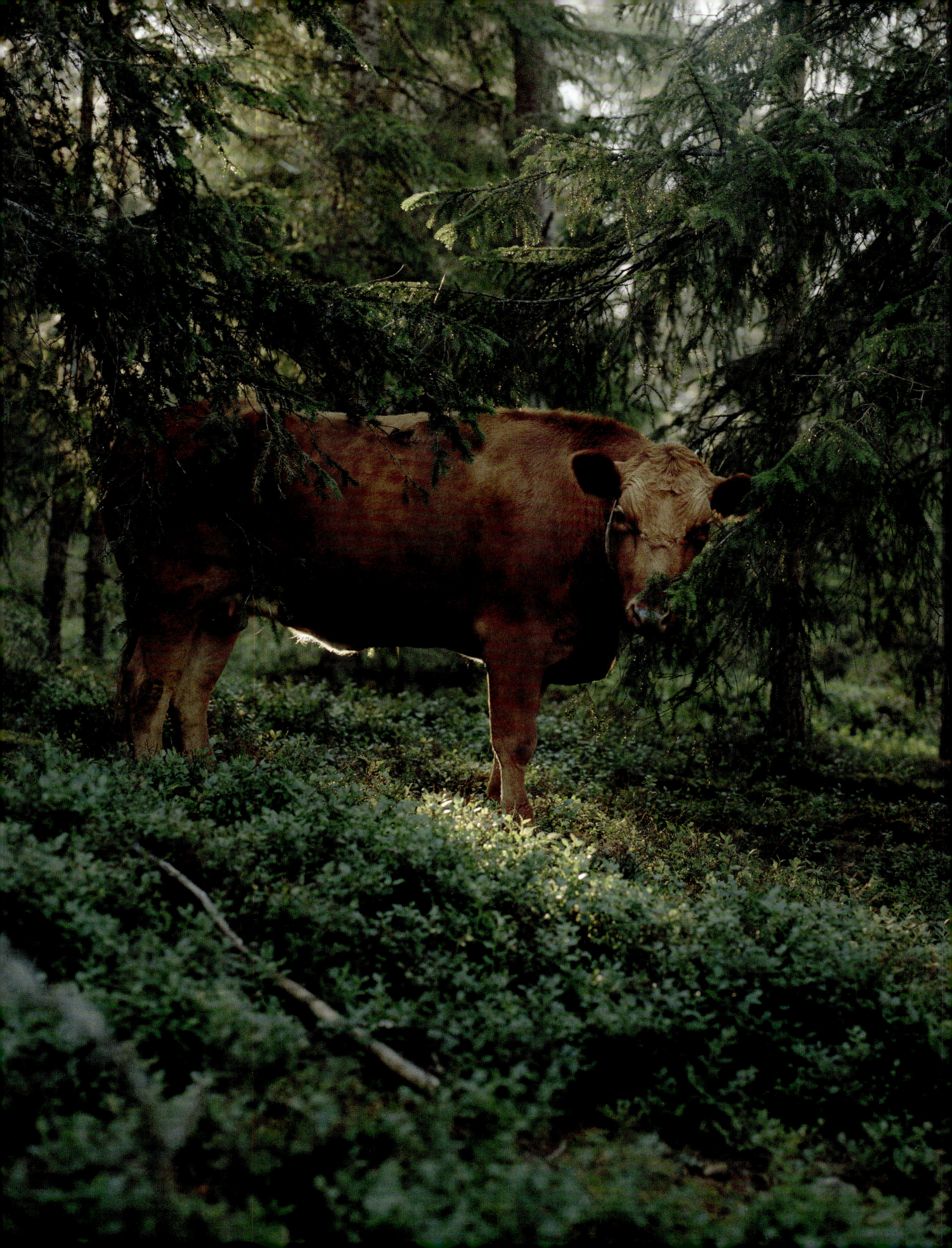

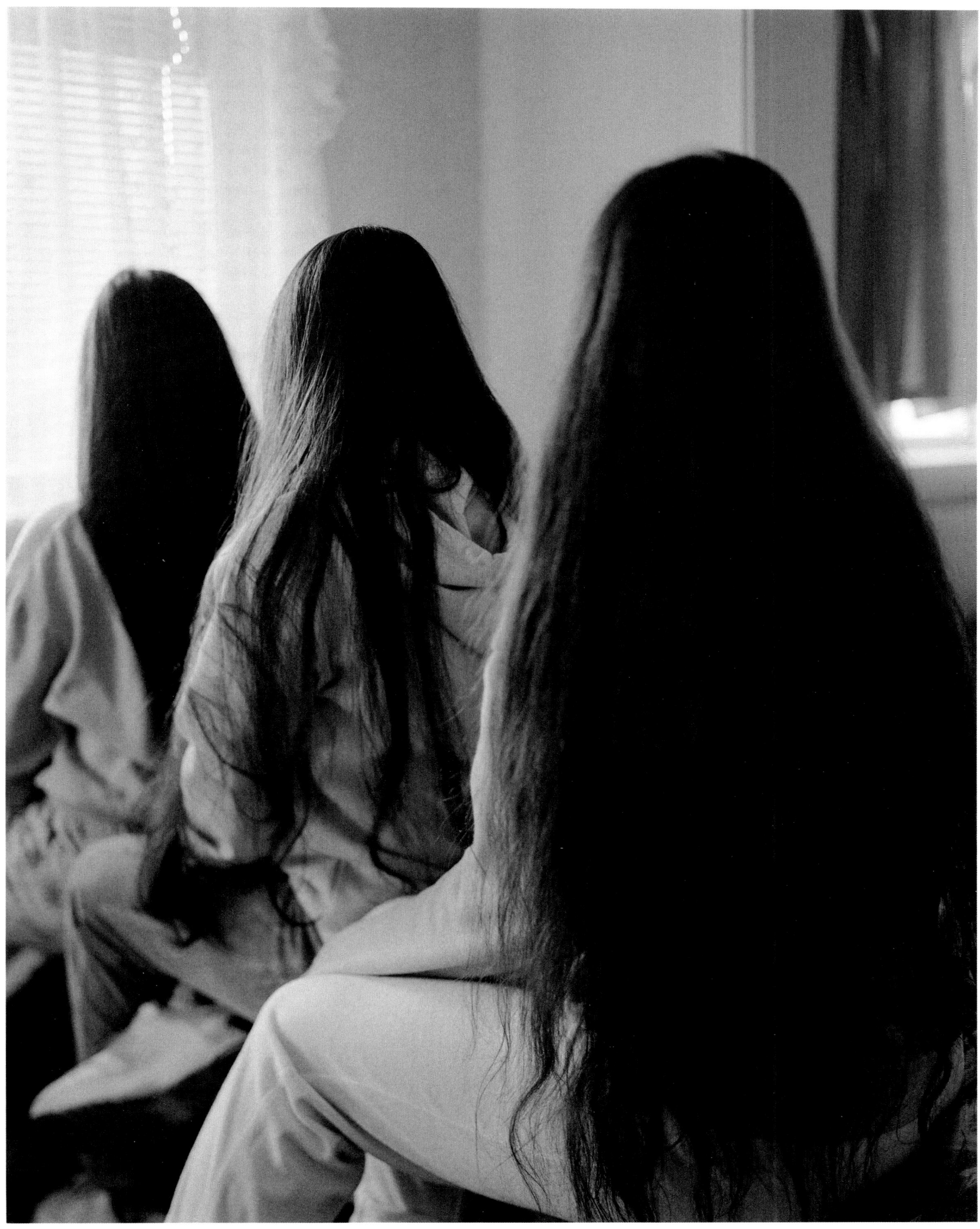

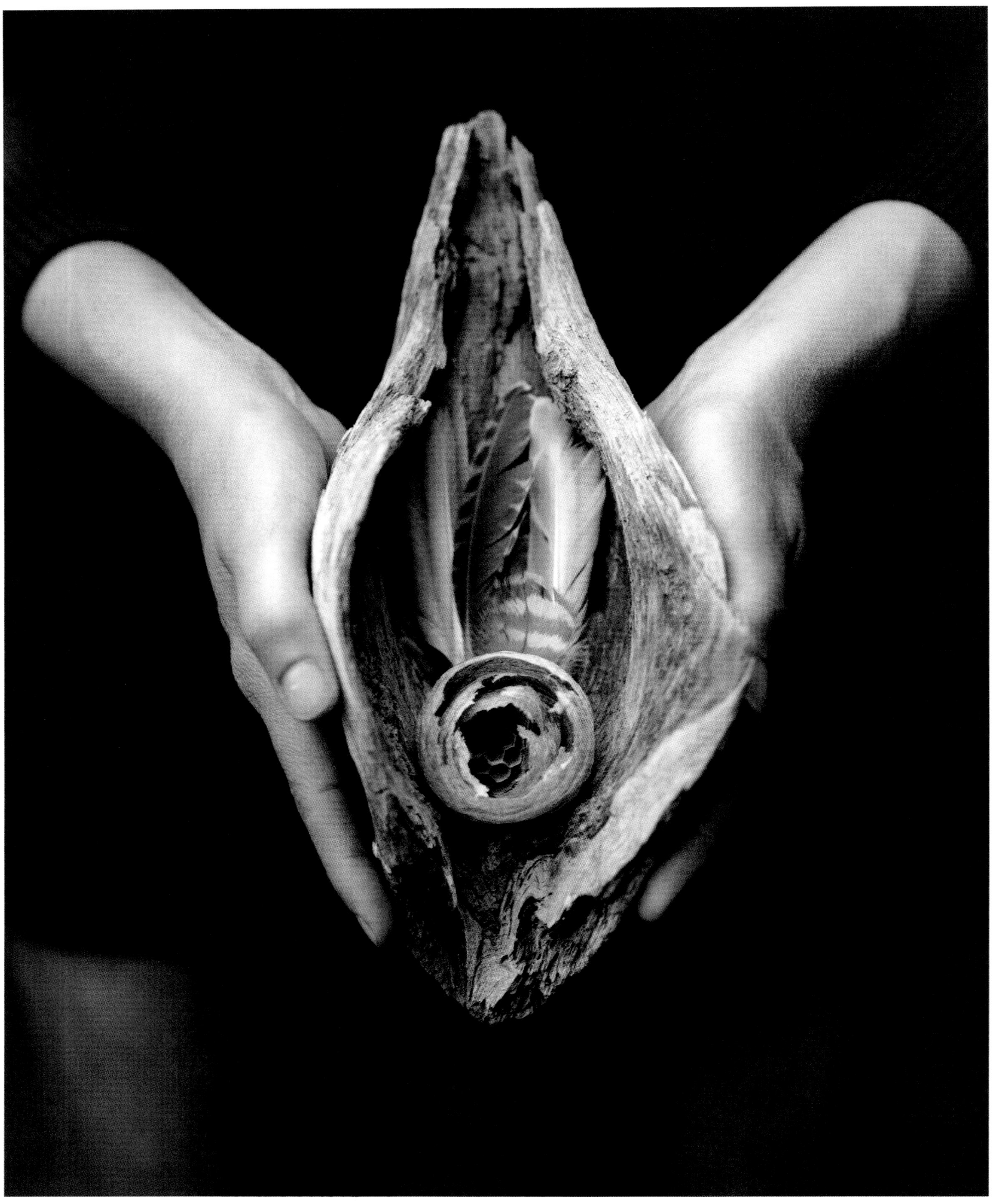

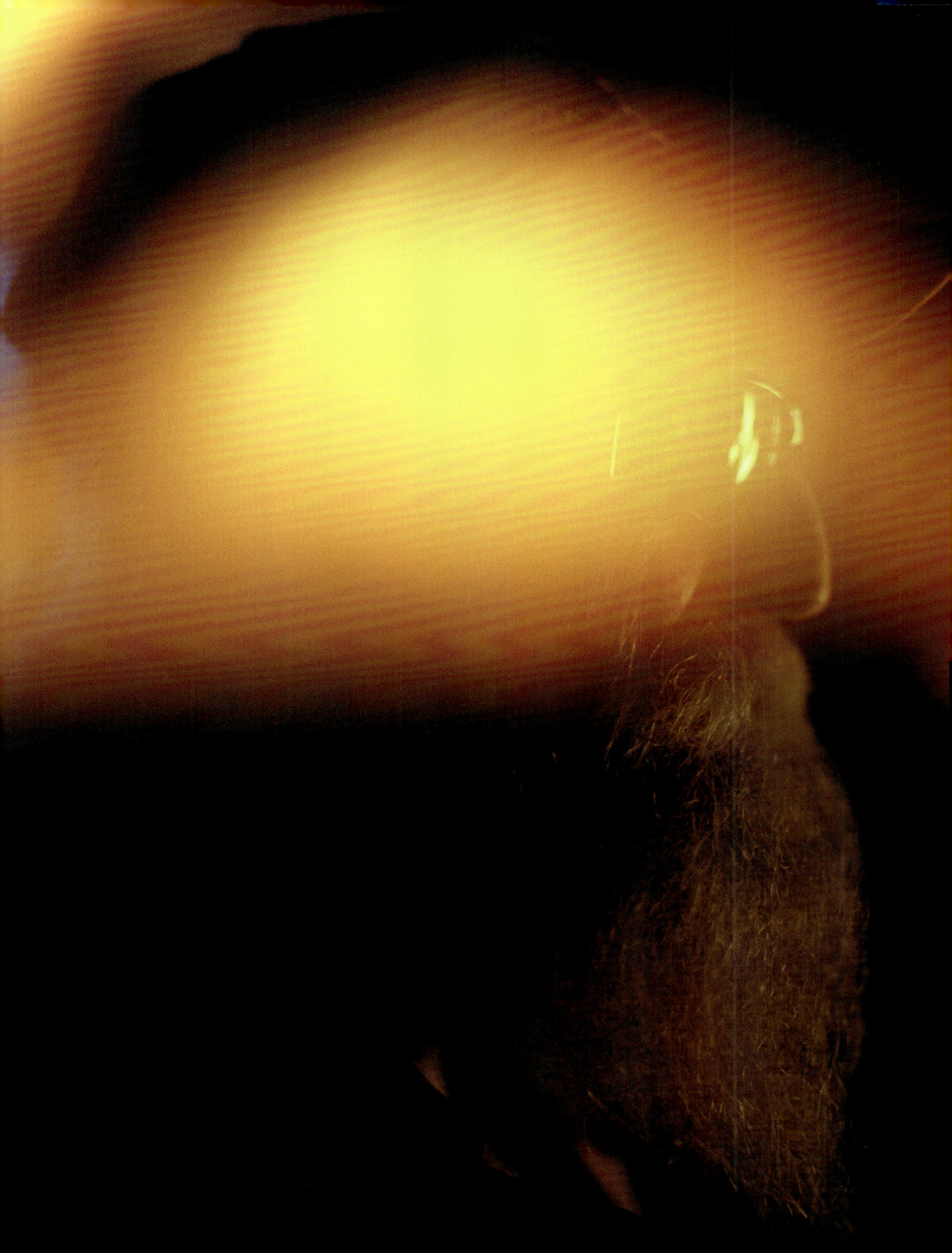

Vignetted, luminous monochromes of houses and yards tick by, as if seen from a train, or a moving car, each thick black frame like a window seal. Children in homemade costumes clamoring on front porches. Ghostly figures of boys suspended in midair. Solitary clapboard houses in bright, slanting sunshine with liquid-white exteriors. The sight of children collapsed in a yard exhausted after playing puts Nancy Rexroth in mind of photographs of the Battle of Gettysburg—"all those bodies strewn around," she told me recently. "It's also one of my pictures that I think of as deep Arbus."

They are photographs that feel at once timeless and long ago, strange and magic and familiar and reverberating: look closely, and they trigger images submerged somewhere in your own past, partly imagined, as slippery and vivid as dreams. Rexroth spent the early 1970s roaming rural towns in Ohio and elsewhere with a Diana camera, making the pictures that would compose *IOWA*, published in 1977, and one of the most extraordinary photobooks of its era and since. The title is an intentional misnomer. Only a handful of the photographs in *IOWA* were made in the state that shares its name. Growing up in Virginia, Rexroth's family made summer trips to see relatives in Iowa, and her photographs do not represent a literal place, but a feeling: the subconscious pull of memory. It's as if it has always been there, Rexroth once wrote, "morphing away on the dark side of things, sad and joyful, and filled with incredible longing."

The Diana camera was introduced to Rexroth by one of her MFA photography professors at Ohio State University, who had picked up Dianas for a dollar or two on a visit to New York's Chinatown. The Diana was plastic, prone to light leaks, and marketed as a toy. Rexroth took to it. Still new to Ohio, the twentysomething photographer carried the Diana down remote roads she'd never traveled, knocking on strangers' doors, asking to be let in. There was a "pulse" Rexroth felt in certain towns. She put herself in a state of mind she describes as a "daylight dream," using the settings of Ohio to stand in for the intense feeling she characterized as *IOWA*.

"You're a hunter, you get on your horse—your car—and you *pursue*," she tells me in one of our conversations. After we hang up, I think: Of course, Nancy Rexroth setting out with her little toy camera named after the Roman goddess of the hunt, in pursuit of Mnemosyne, the Greek goddess of memory, mother of the muses!

Once, in the 1970s, when Rexroth showed her pictures to the photographer Minor White, a founding editor of this magazine, and he asked her, "Why this camera? Why don't you just buy a Hasselblad and smear Vaseline on the lens?"

"The Diana is made for feelings," Rexroth wrote in *Aperture*'s "The Snapshot" issue in fall 1974. She might flick her hand over the shutter, to deliberately create blur. On one of the rare times when Rexroth returned to actual Iowa to photograph, she left her Diana cameras in the car, and they melted in the August sun, a plastic metaphor.

Rexroth's material is real life, but she pulls from it like a short-story writer, subtracting all that is inessential. "I don't work sculpturally, from the ground up," Rexroth says. "I omit, I edit, I compose." When making *IOWA*, she did not allow signs or cars to enter the picture.

In the same issue of *Aperture*, when Rexroth wrote that she sometimes made photographs with her eyes closed, she was telling a truth, just not the literal one. Rexroth tends to take numerous frames, moving in a dance, trying new compositions. It's the *people* in her pictures whose eyes are often closed or obscured. Think of the image of Rexroth's mother, blinking in delight as a sudden breeze lifts her hair skyward. Or Emmet Blackburn, a naive, retired widower whom Rexroth accompanied to visit his childhood home, which had been razed. Surely, here was a portrait of sorrow, that pulse of longing. But near the spot where his house had been, Emmet proceeded to dance a jig.

Nancy Rexroth
Her Own Private Iowa

Rebecca Bengal

Rebecca Bengal is a writer based in New York.

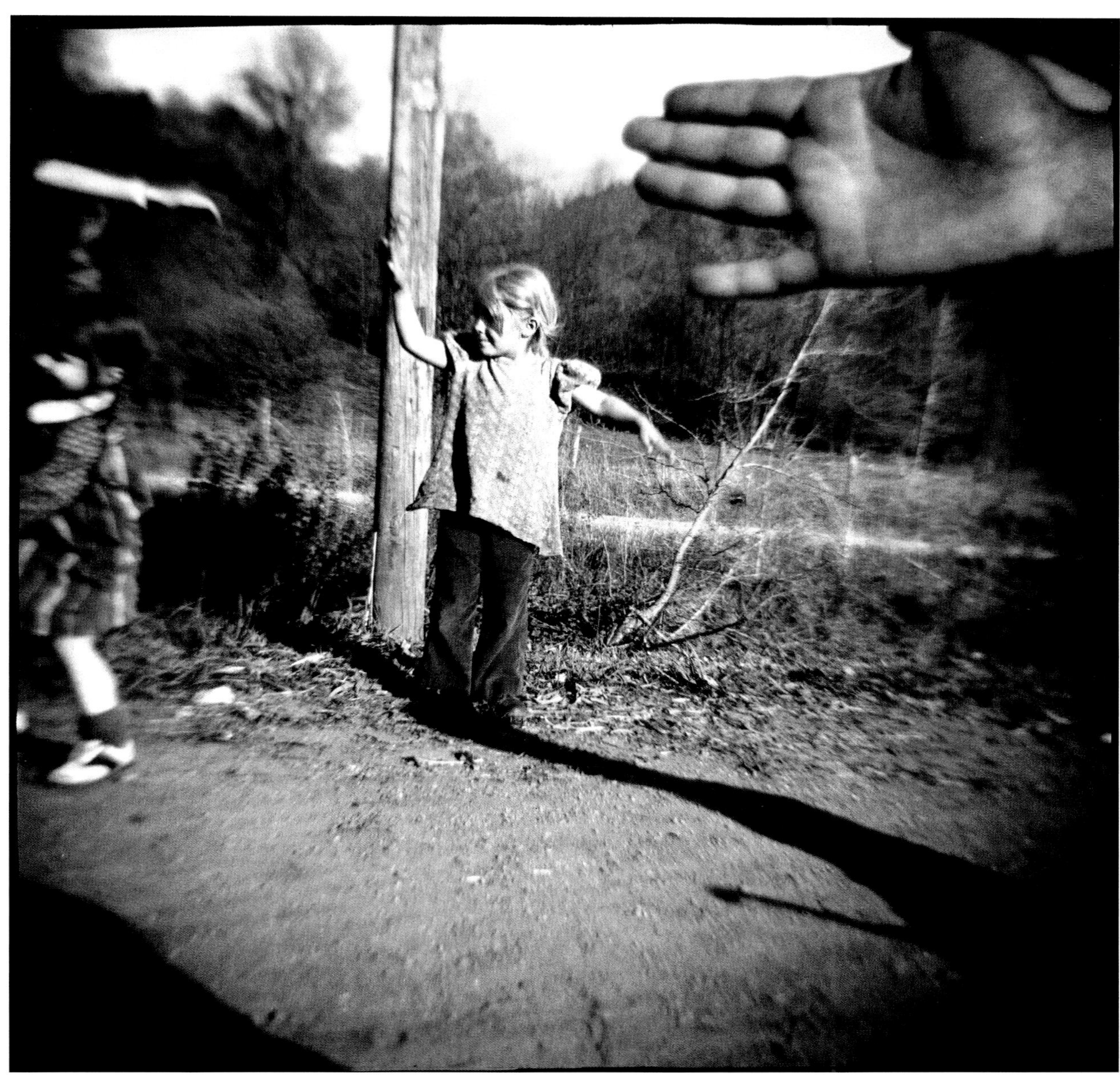

End of Day, Sugar Creek, Ohio, 1976

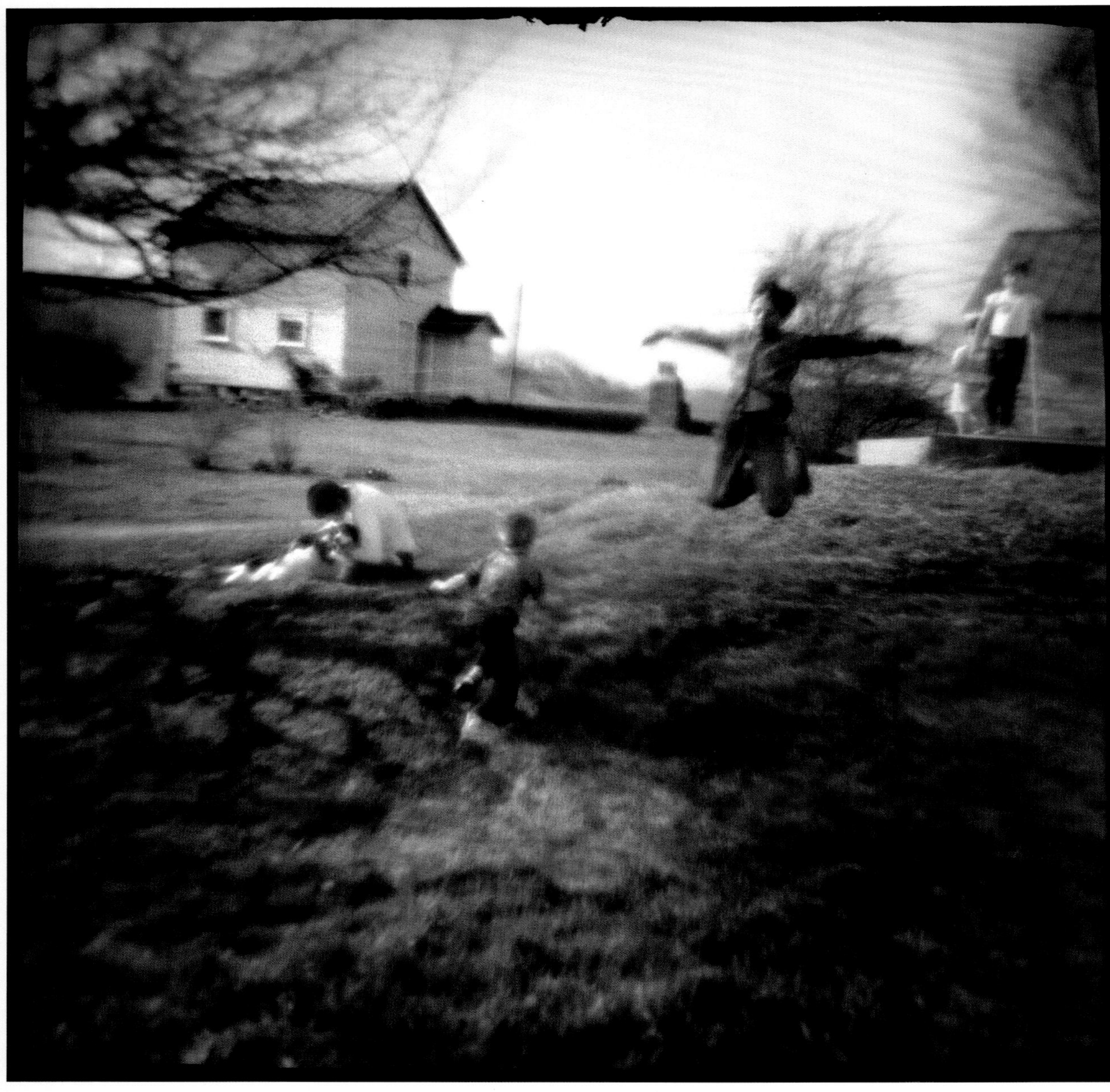

Boys Flying, Amesville,
Ohio, 1976

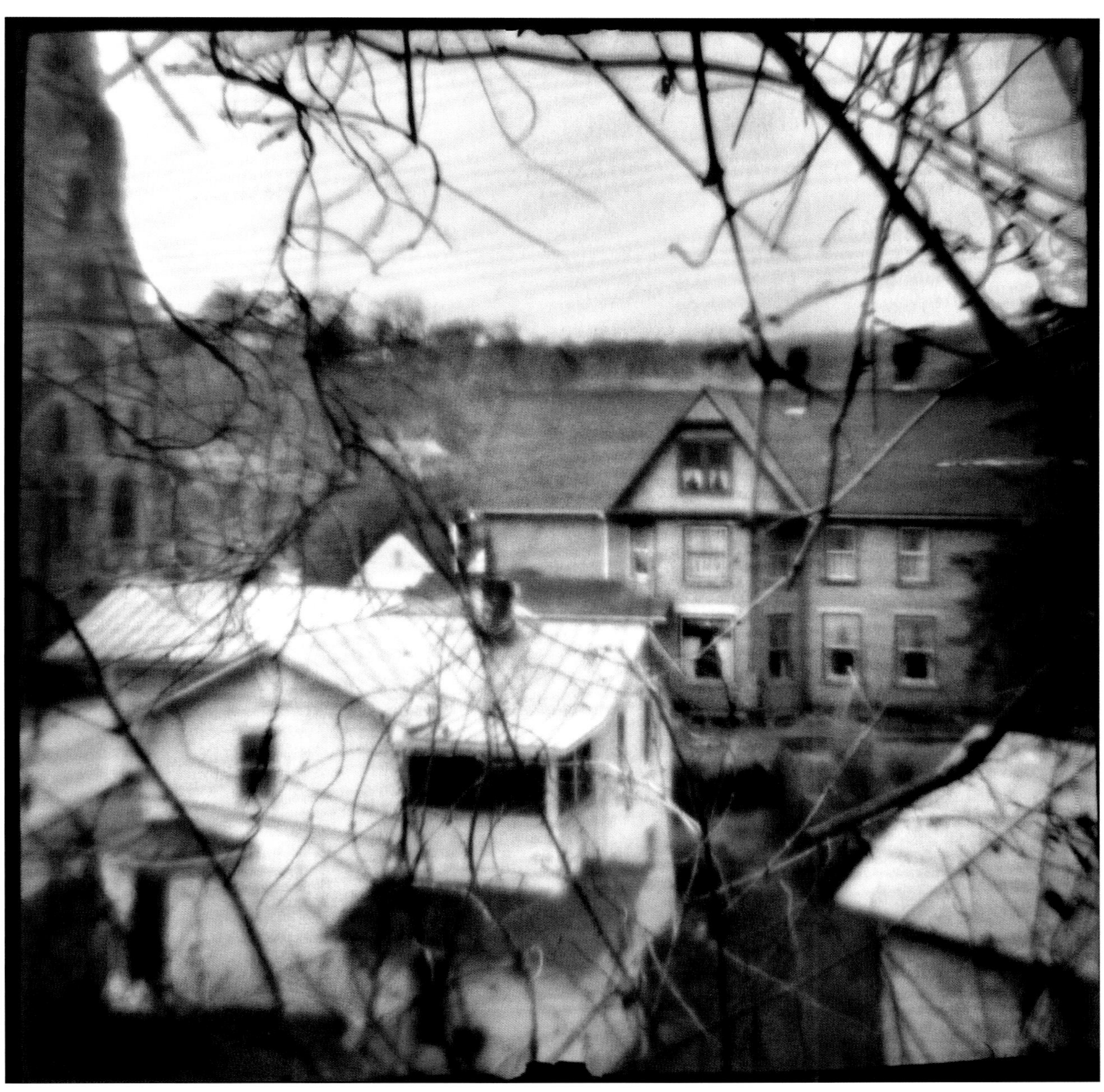

Complexity, Pomeroy, Ohio, 1976

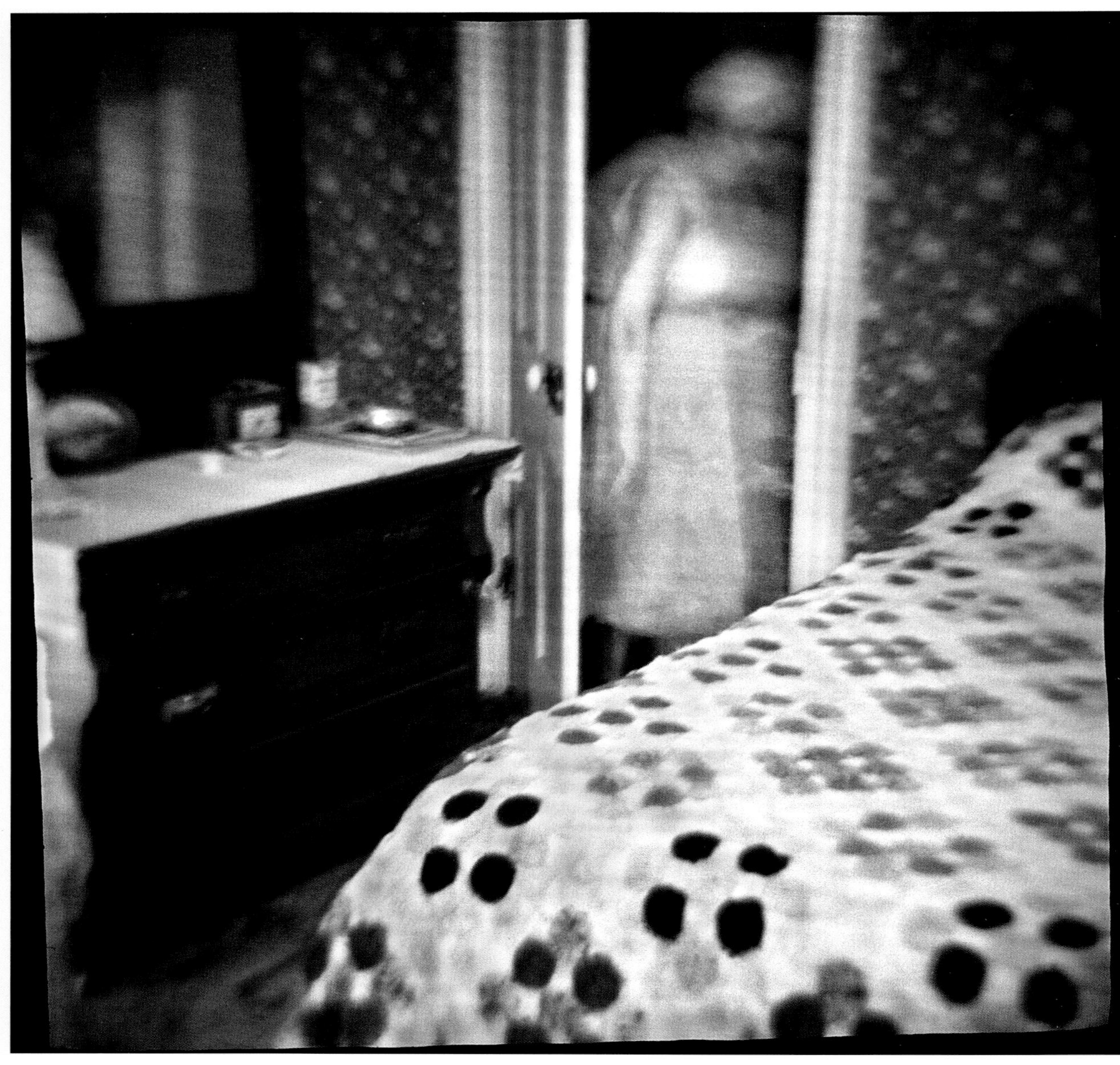

Clara in the Closet,
Carpenter, Ohio, 1973

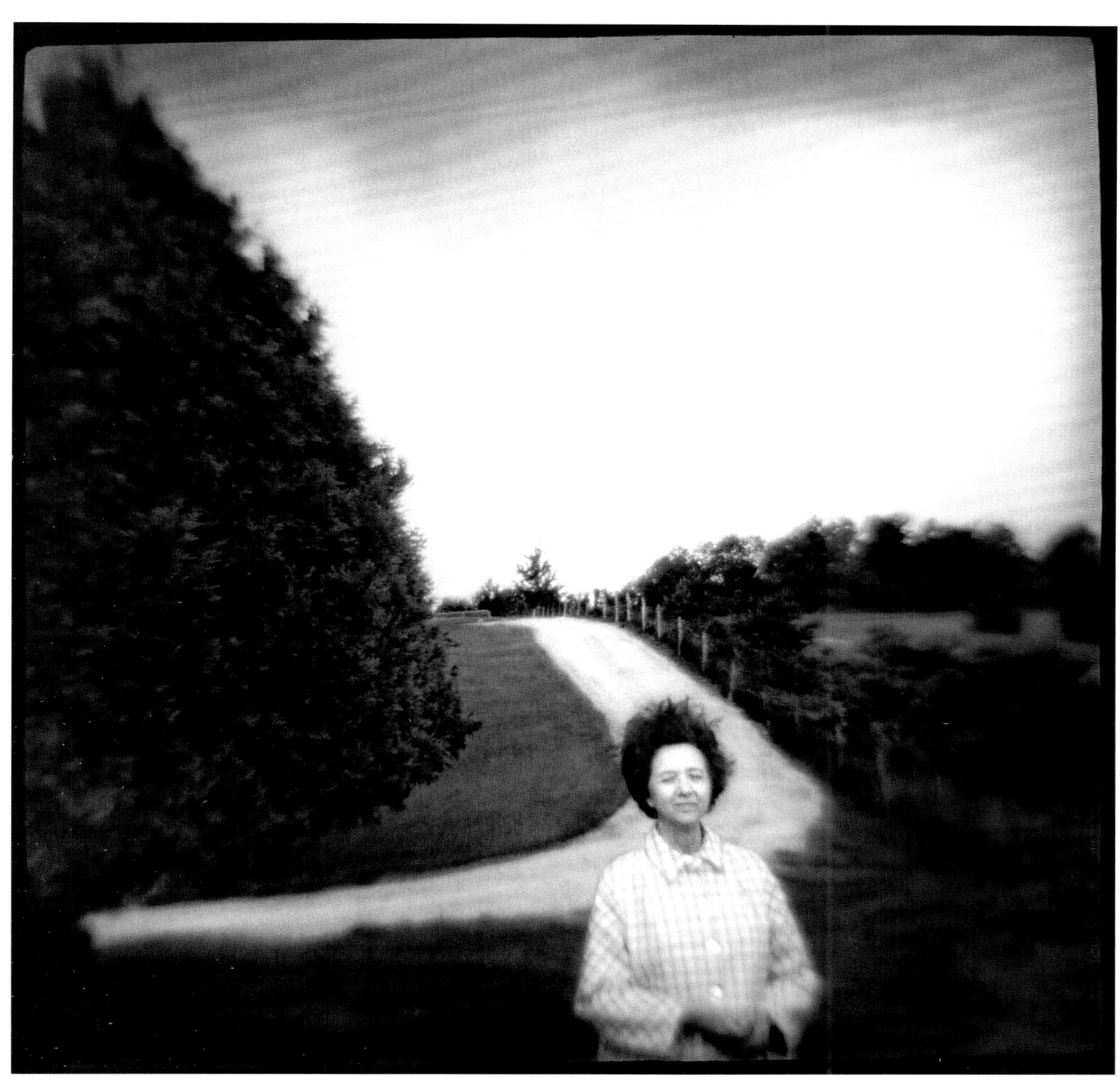

My Mother, Pennsville, Ohio, 1970
All photographs © The 1938 Rexroth Family Trust and courtesy the Cincinnati Art Museum

Elliott Jerome Brown Jr.
Where Cherries Blossom

Harry Tafoya

The photographer Elliott Jerome Brown Jr. makes imagery that is weird, obscure, ambiguous, and freaky, packed with impossible, hard-to-decipher elements that never betray any simple or obvious meaning. His titles are cryptic, often splitting the difference between punchy non sequiturs and deeply felt but emotionally abstract poetry—information that only gets more puzzling when you learn that Brown writes them in reference to *part* of the overall picture. His subjects, who are without exception Black men and women, are often out of frame, subtly distorted, or caught in the cross fire of competing optical illusions. In the rare instances when they face Brown's camera directly, their features are lit up with campfire-story menace or bolts of neon light, their expressions halfway between a belly laugh and a masklike grimace.

Inspired by Lorna Simpson, Carrie Mae Weems, and Deana Lawson, Brown's early work riffed on the idea of the domestic realm as a private theater of unguarded Black humanity, posing his friends and family in casual scenes heavy on themes of desire and intimacy. In subsequent years, Brown internalized his heroines' ambiguity (Simpson), drama (Weems), and boldness (Lawson), while veering away from literal living spaces into much odder kinds of interiority, ditching straightforward representation or easily nameable emotions in the process.

His recent work is more intuitive, informed by the contrived-casual body language on Instagram, notes and sketches on his iPhone, and the practicalities of photographing. Brown occasionally finds inspiration closer to home. Holes in the plastic lattice weave of his kitchen chair led to the unusual shot-from-below composition of *I want to impress leaves on paper with colors they could only know there, where cherries blossom in jacaranda blue* (2020). The portrait depicts two men embracing at a table. In the foreground, a hazy fist is either clutching or punching the viewer while what looks like a child's homework assignment and sixth-birthday candle are taped to the wall beside it. On closer observation, you realize that the "wall" is the underside of the table, the punch is actually holding them steady, and the embrace is both sweeter and stickier than at first appearance.

Brown's subjects' inner worlds are as elliptical and compelling as an M. C. Escher staircase, with an internal logic built up more from fiction than depiction. In breaking from the familiar, the artist has front-loaded his images with uncanny details that are striking and confounding: skin-crawling textures, poisonously bright colors. In the tradition of Hitchcock, much of the suspense found in Brown's photography comes from what he withholds from the frame. We seek the answers to the riddles: Why does he photograph from those angles? What are the reactions on his models' faces? Where in the flurry of impressions should we direct our focus?

In a 2020 interview with *W*, Brown explained, "Working with the margins at first grew out of a political positioning, recognizing that the margin is an important way to read the center. And what's held at the margin—there's a lot of power there . . . tucking things into the margins of the photograph allows me to indicate that there is something beyond the focus, or the purported focus." By keeping his viewer looking on from the furthest ends of the margins, Brown creates a vision of Black subjectivity that is infinitely definable, drawing the viewer's attention past more obvious emotional and political dimensions to the most fraught and unresolvable states of what it means to be human.

Opposite:
I want to impress leaves on paper with colors they could only know there, where cherries blossom in jacaranda blue. 2020

Harry Tafoya is an art critic based in New York.

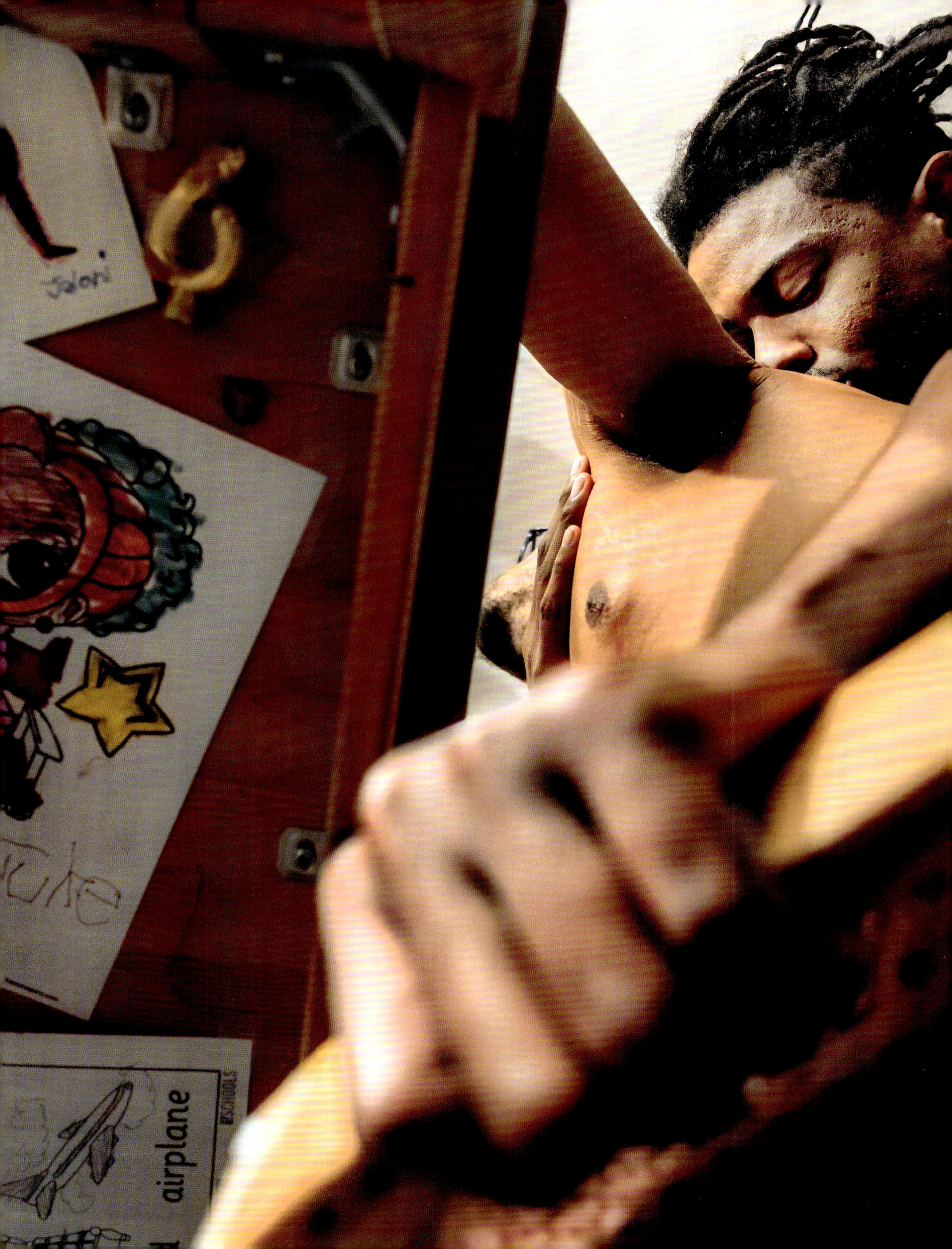
Jaloni
airplane
SCHOOLS

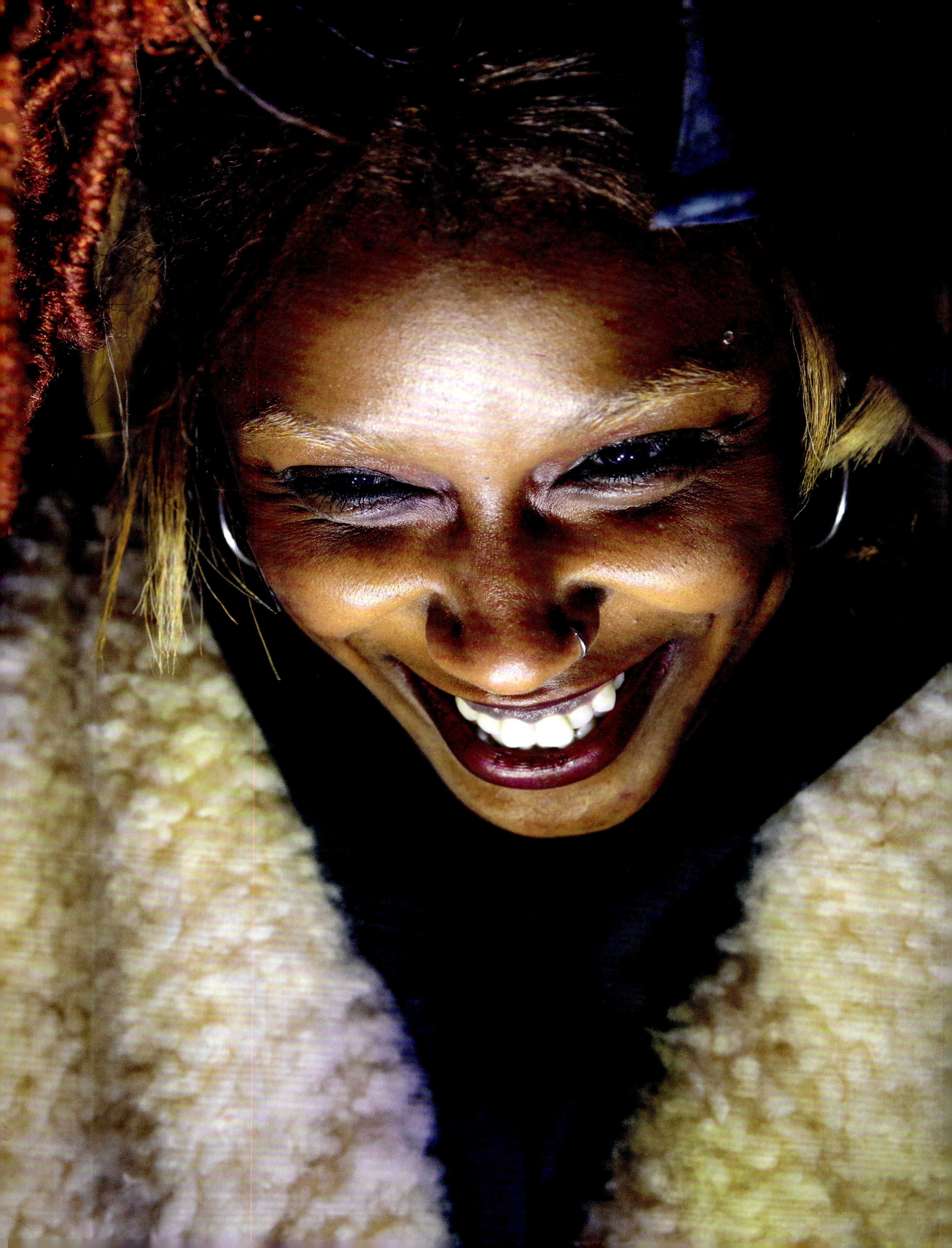

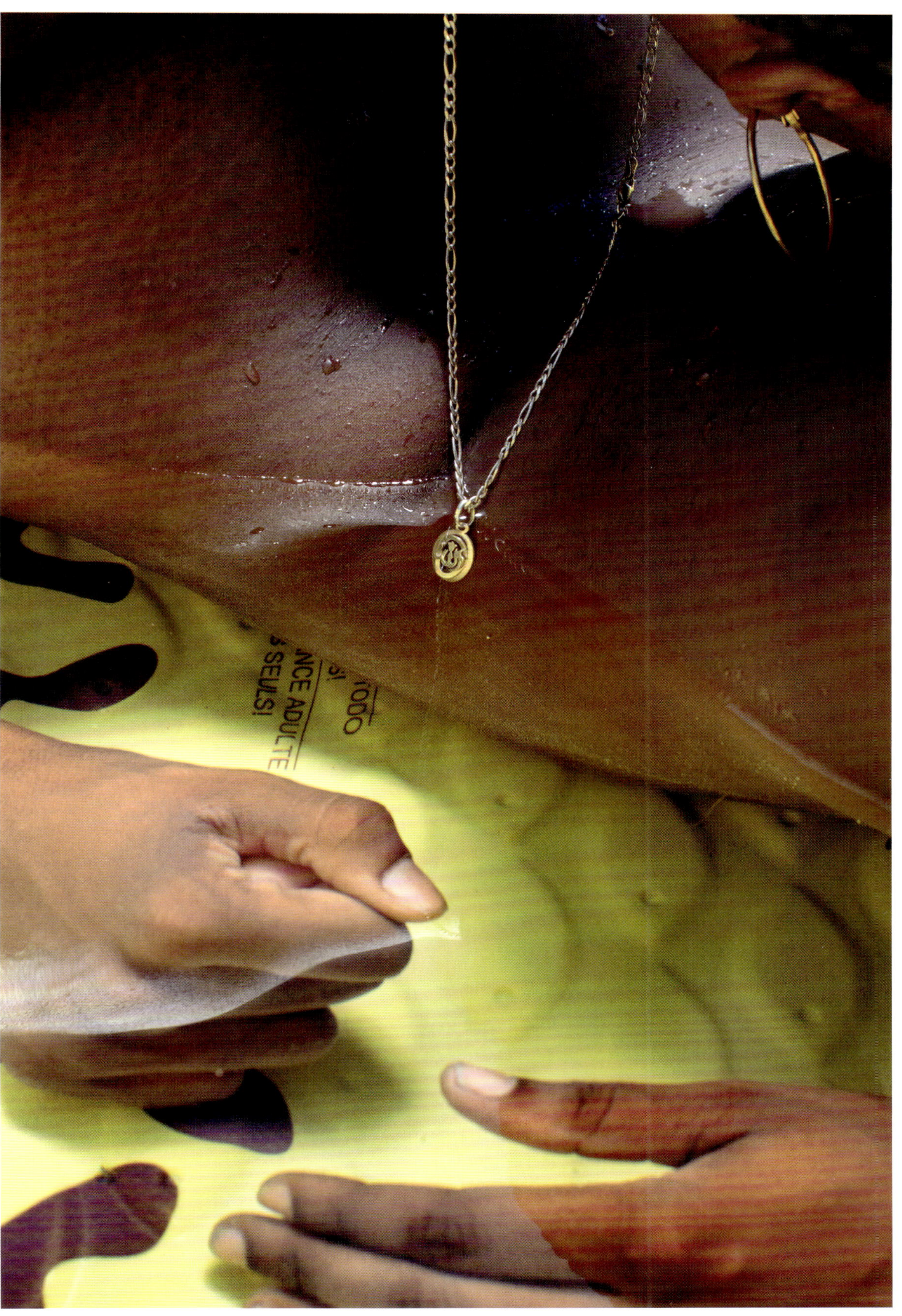

Opposite:
2021

This page:
A well commanded army tucked at the corners of his lips, 2019

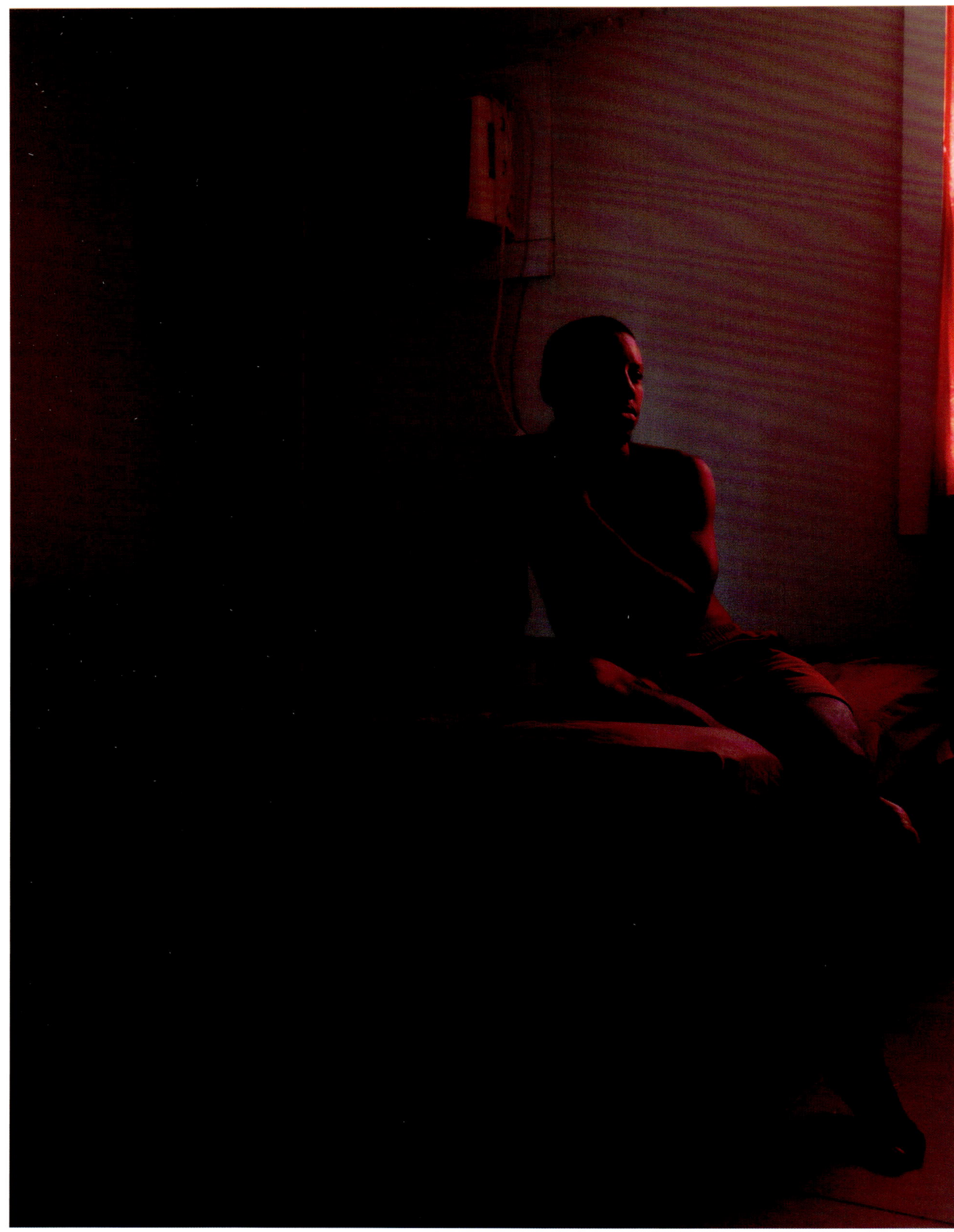

This page:
Slow want, 2020

Opposite:
Dish soap in the jacuzzi,
2020

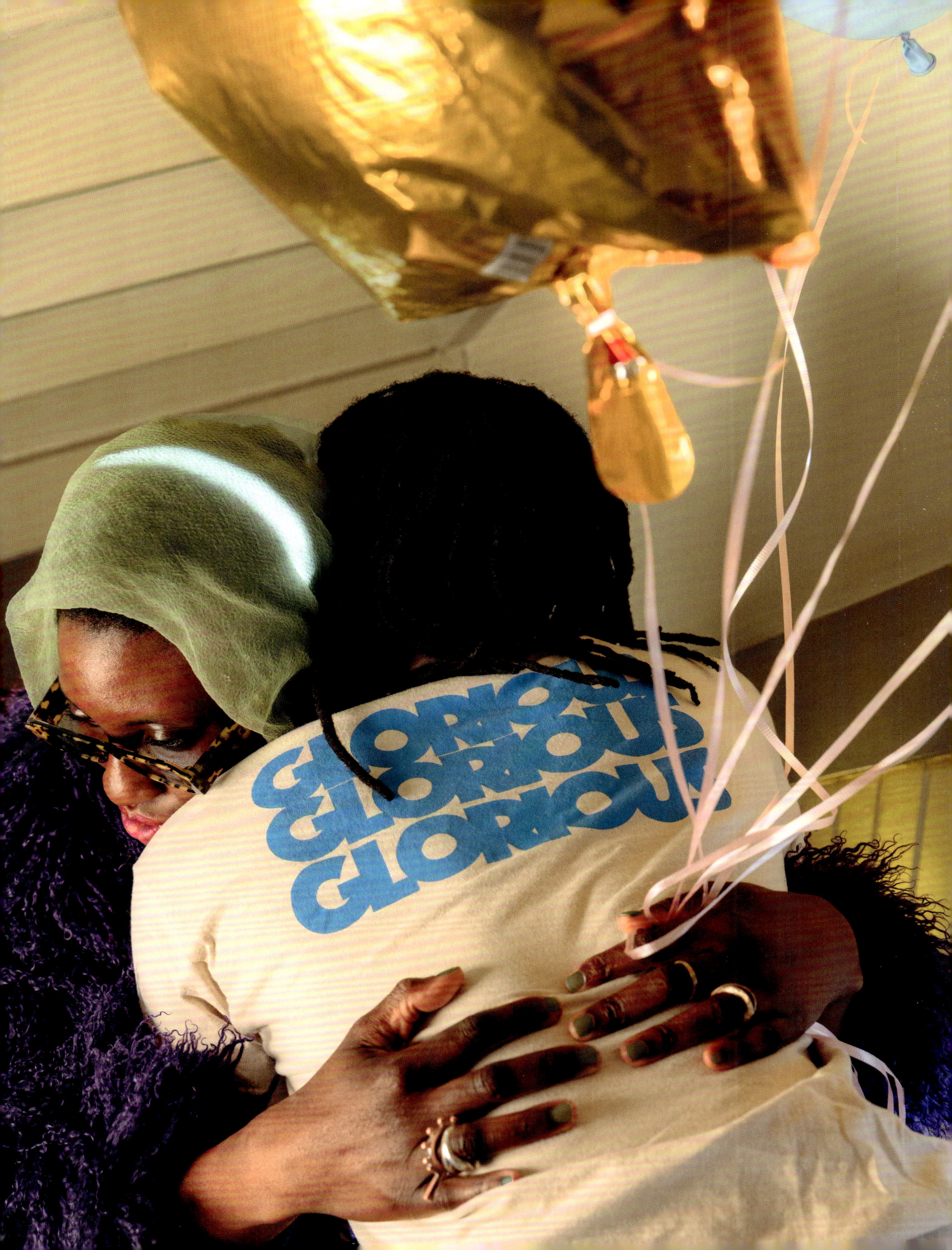

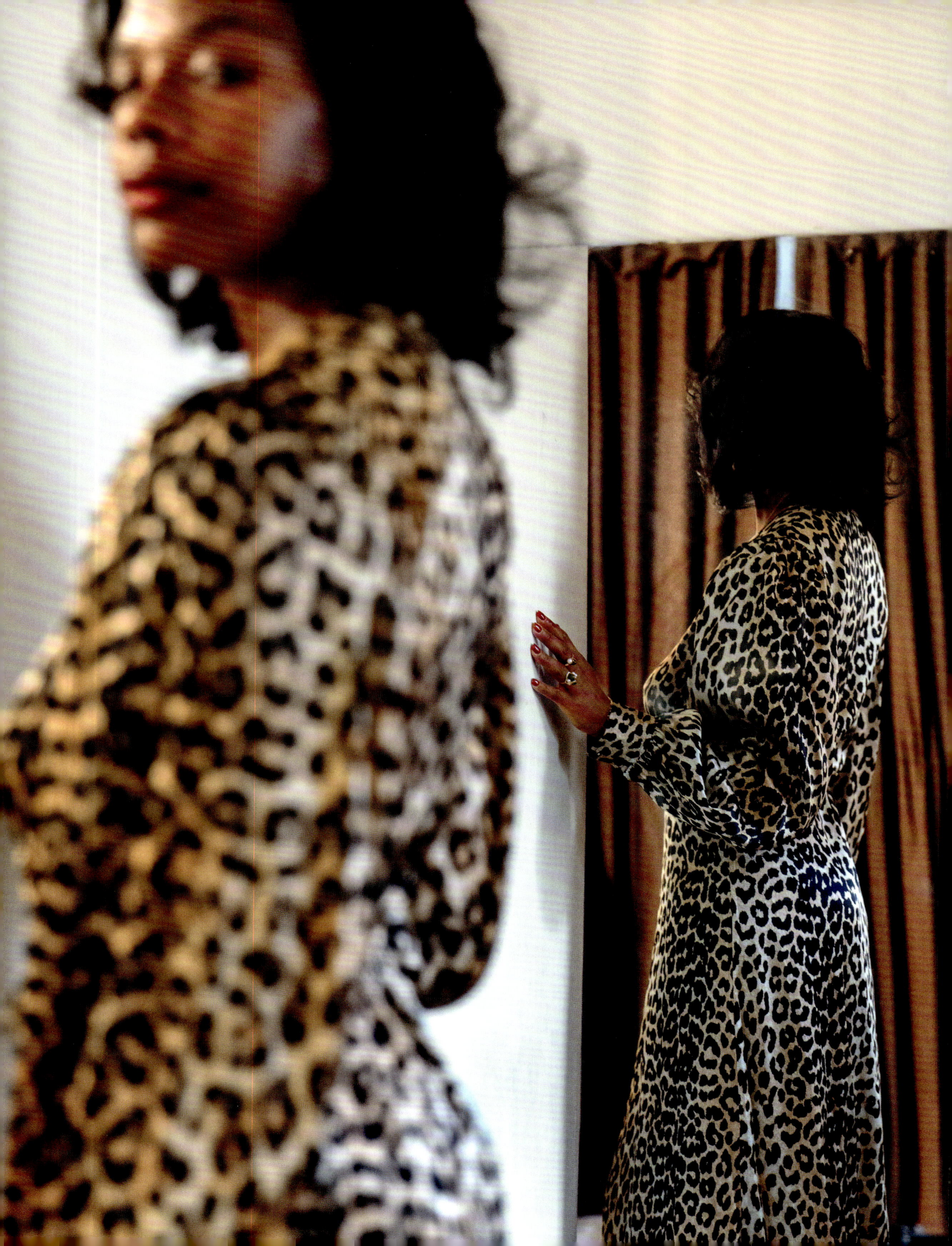

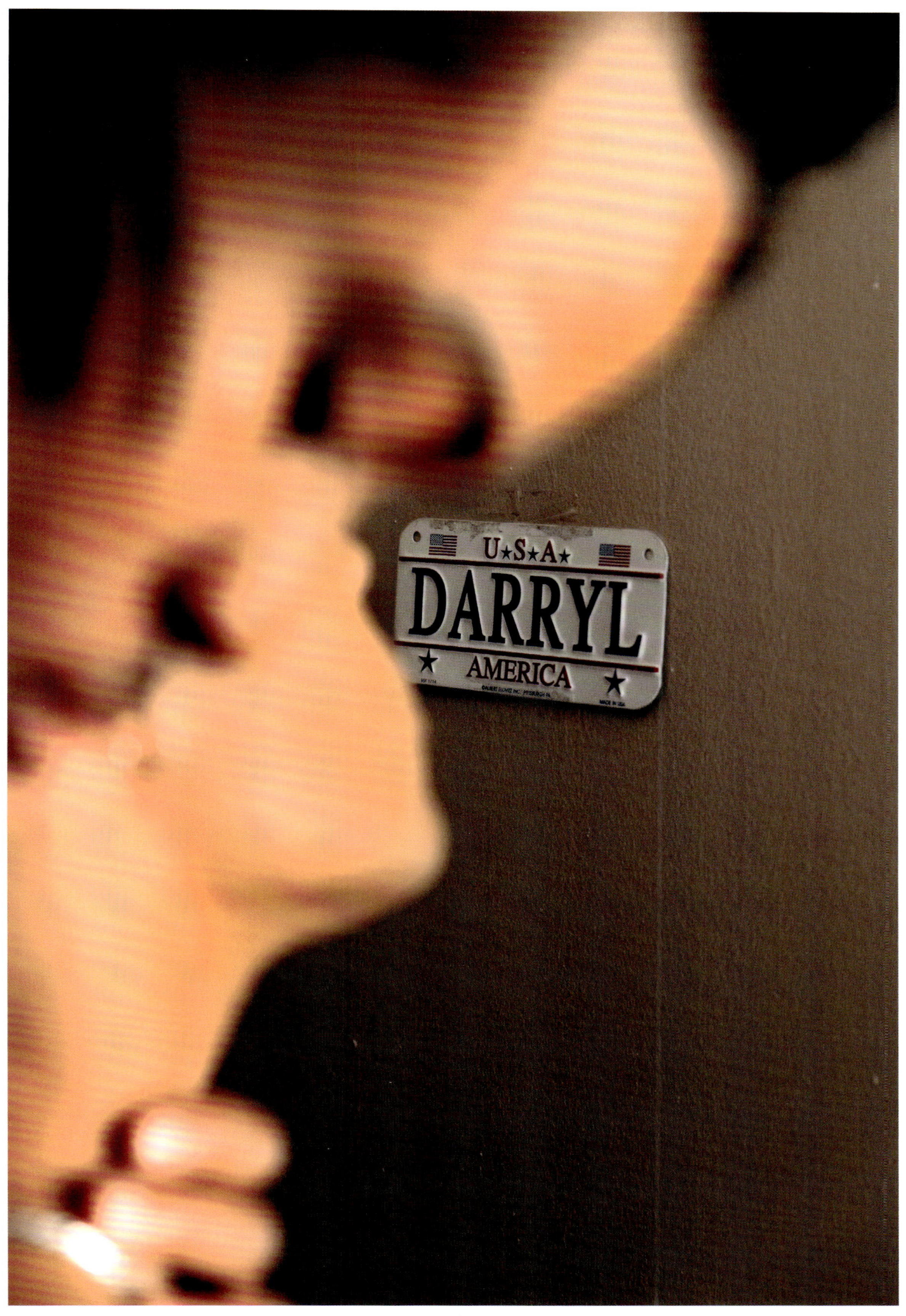

Opposite:
Fallen out of responsibility with myself, she was born into something that could receive her. **2020**

This page:
Slowly, surely (after Jill), **2020**
All photographs courtesy the artist and Nicelle Beauchene Gallery, New York

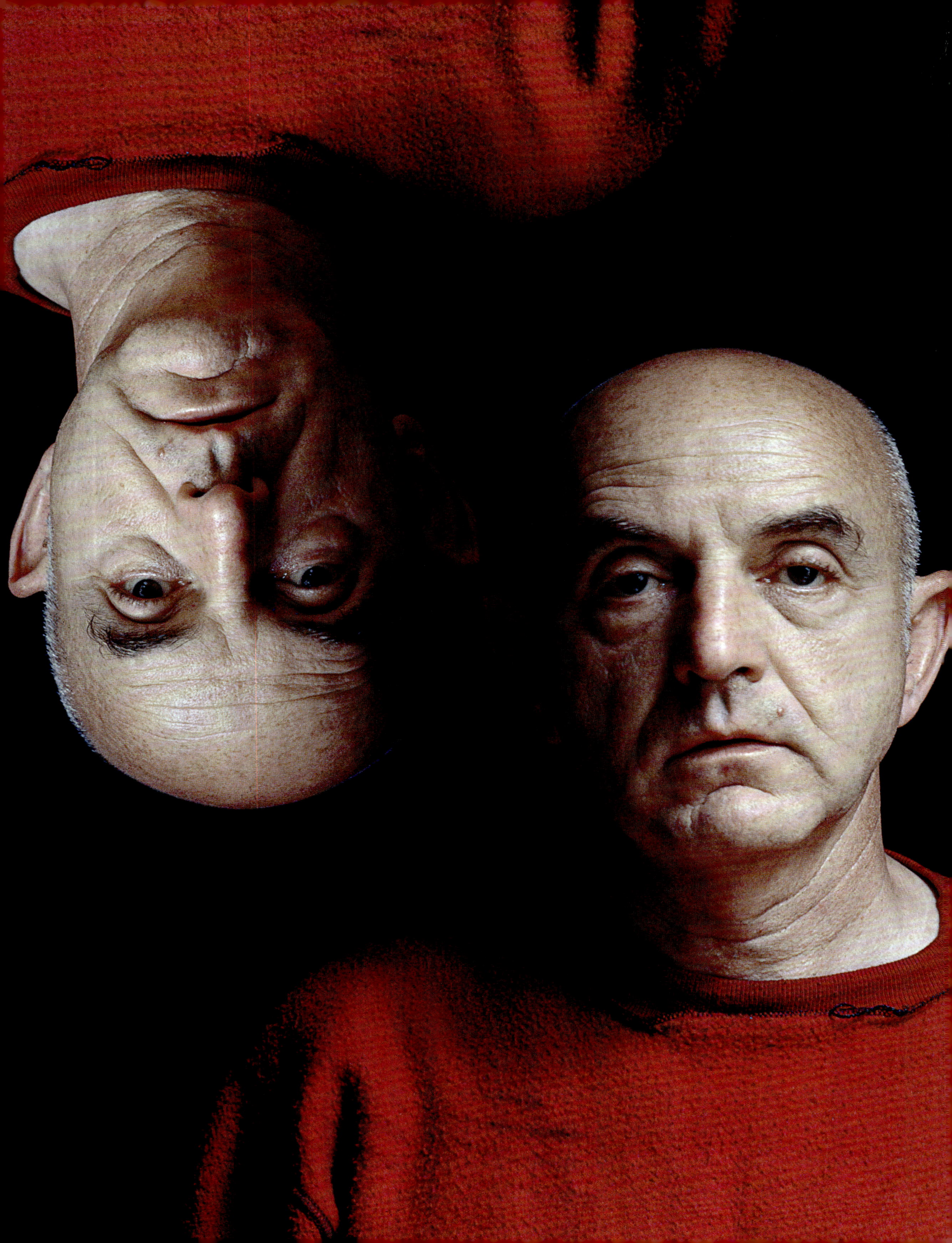

Duane Michals
The Human Condition

A Conversation with Jesse Dorris

Duane Michals doesn't mince words—about his photography, or anyone else's. And why should he? Born in 1932 in McKeesport, Pennsylvania, Michals had traveled the world by age thirty, from the truck stops of Texas to army service in Germany to the gray-gold landscape of Cold War Russia. By the mid-1960s, he found a home in downtown New York, a partner in the late architect Fred Gorrée, and the kind of success in commercial and editorial photography that allowed him to take risks in his own work: building sequences with the theatrical engagement of cinema, staging narratives about queer desires, and adding text in his unmistakable script. Michals risked sentimentality in pursuit of talking about "unphotographable things."

Last September, in the balm of late summer, Michals welcomed Jesse Dorris into the Gramercy Park apartment Michals shared for decades with Gorrée. Among framed photographs and stacks of books—Michals has published more than forty—they spoke about desire and fate. "I am moved by my work," Michals says. "The deep contentment of having written a really good sentence or having taken a really good picture, knowing that I've done it, is very sweet. It makes me melancholy . . . in a nice way."

Jesse Dorris: **What's the difference between luck and fate?**

Duane Michals: Fate is fate. You're predestined. This conversation was destined to happen. We're just fulfilling the destiny. I don't believe in that. I believe in accidents. I believe in spontaneous combustion. I believe that every second we're inventing a new universe. I believe in . . . [*Sings*] "I believe in magic . . . " I also have a song for every occasion.

JD: **I'm curious as to how you make the decision between staging a moment and willing something to happen, or setting up an occasion and just letting something magical happen, or going out and stumbling upon something.**

DM: Instinct. I trust my instinct more than I trust me. I'm completely unreliable. I wouldn't trust me if my life depended on it. I'm going to my hometown in McKeesport, making a movie this weekend. McKeesport has fallen on hard times. It's collapsed. Imploded. I used to go to the library all the time. I once took out a book nine times, and they wouldn't let me have it anymore. I never got over it.

JD: **What was the book?**

DM: It was called *Cities of America*. There were photographs of every major city. I wasn't interested in photography. I was interested in the cities. Fred and I had a house in the country for forty-four years, near Bennington, in the woods. I used to build model cities in the woods.

JD: **Did you ever strike up a more architectural practice with your photography?**

DM: Oh, no. Fred was an architect, and that was one of the reasons why I was enchanted by him—because I wanted to be an architect. He worked for Marcel Breuer for a long time, then he worked for Skidmore, Owings *&* Merrill, then he went on his own. But he was never ambitious. He was more of a homebody. I was always ambitious. Buddhists say . . . the Hindus say (excuse me, wrong sect) that in life you want just enough—not too much, not too little, just enough. I've had just enough ambition to not become Mapplethorpe, who, I felt, for somebody so "professionally gay," had very little insight on the subject. I had a long-term relationship with my Fred—and we were also gay. My whole life has been just enough.

> I'm telling you what the event was. It's not an observation. I've expanded the photograph from being a silent object.

JD: **How do you know it's just enough?**

DM: It suits me. I have wonderful instincts. I am not hip, I am not cool, but I am charming.

JD: **We're in this time where we are expected to make self-portraits of ourselves all the time . . .**

DM: That's why it's called "self-portrait."

JD: **Yes, exactly. For Instagram, for dating profiles, for professional reasons, we're always expected to be able to make these representations of ourselves. How do you take a self-portrait that is expressive of yourself?**

DM: I feel that you become the artist when you bring insight. It's one thing to photograph somebody, but it's another thing to bring insight, to annotate, to expand the moment of expression. Because, ultimately, portraiture is simply anatomy, and people like portraits mainly because they think they might look good. I once photographed a guy, and I heard he loved the picture. Then I heard he liked it because his nose looked small. No matter what the picture looked like, all he saw was a nose. Any picture of me where I look bald, I'm not thrilled.

JD: **Do you sleep well?**

DM: As Marilyn Monroe said so succinctly, I sleep with the radio on.

JD: **I do too.**

DM: Nothing in life prepares you for being old. Being old should be a reward, not a punishment. The only regret I will have when I die is that I will miss all the work I haven't done. But also, the other thing said about being old is that you must have more regrets. I have done everything—not everyone—but everything that I've always wanted to do.

JD: **You've done everything you've always wanted to do?**

DM: Yes. I've been everywhere, done everything . . . I won't travel anymore. I made about forty-one mini-movies. I have no ambitions for Hollywood. But if a studio called and said, "We have an extra three million dollars laying around. Would you like to play with it?" Of course, I would say yes. I always say, "I shoot first and ask questions later." I don't procrastinate.

JD: **How do you not procrastinate?**

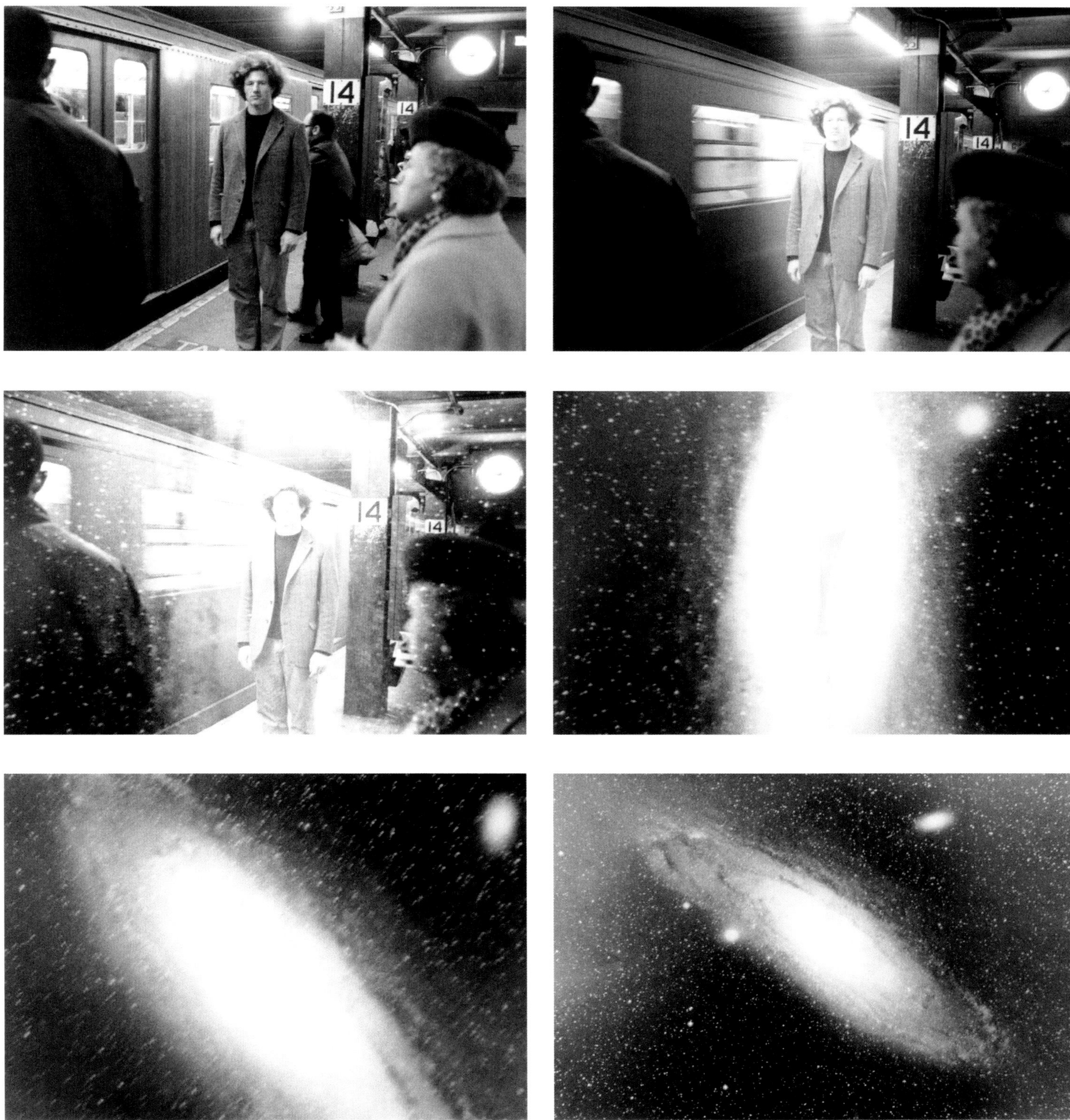

Page 114:
Upside Down Self-portrait,
1983

This page:
The Human Condition,
1969

DM: I have a huge curiosity. Everything is about curiosity. And if you have no curiosity, then go watch television and jack off, or jack off and then watch television.

JD: It depends on what you're watching.

DM: Exactly. Good. You're keeping up.

JD: It seems that curiosity is, maybe, what has propelled you to push the forms of your work.

DM: Oh, always. Another quote for you is: "You are either defined by the medium or you're redefining the medium." And I redefined photography. When I came on the scene, the definition of photography was "reportage, reportage, documentation." That was it. And portraiture. When I had an exhibition called *Sequences* at the Underground Gallery, Garry Winogrand came, and he said to me, "What is this? This isn't photography." I thought, Well, that's not *your* photography. But in those days, I didn't realize how it was considered a no-no. Completely. Then, when I began to write on photographs, I ran into a teacher from the School of Visual Arts, and he said, "What are you doing? The scuttlebutt at school is that your photographs are so bad you have to write under them to explain them." I said, "Tell them in five years they're all going to be writing on photographs." The thing is that it's so simple. Text has always gone with pictures. You pick up a *Daily News* and there is a picture of Donald Trump as he falls down a flight of steps off of Air Force One and breaks his hair. The caption tells you what you see. I was the news editor on our high-school paper. So I write with the photographs to tell you what you can't see. Photographs fail constantly.

JD: Do you think that some of the resistance to that was because you're asserting that photographs are failures?

DM: Yes.

JD: That there are things that photography can't do.

DM: Totally. I did *Empty New York* in the mid-1960s inspired by Atget, and then I did a shot of a bar on Third Avenue, and the title of the picture was *There Are Things Here Not Seen in This Photograph* (1977). The text says something like: "It was a very hot day. I come into the bar. I want a beer. I notice there's a cockroach going up the stool leg of the bar. On the jukebox somebody was singing 'Southern Nights.' Two drunks are arguing about Nixon in the corner. A bum was coming toward me to ask for money. It's time to leave."

JD: Why do you want viewers of the photographs to know all of those things?

DM: Because I am doing a story, and it's setting the stage. It's a total environment. I'm giving you the hum, the noise, the street sound. I'm telling you what the event was. It's not an observation. I'm sharing an event. I've expanded the photograph from being a silent object.

My other thing is: Don't tell me what I already know. Contradict me. I just did an article for the Queer Critique Group of Baxter Street and I ended it with: "Picture this. A room. A dark room.

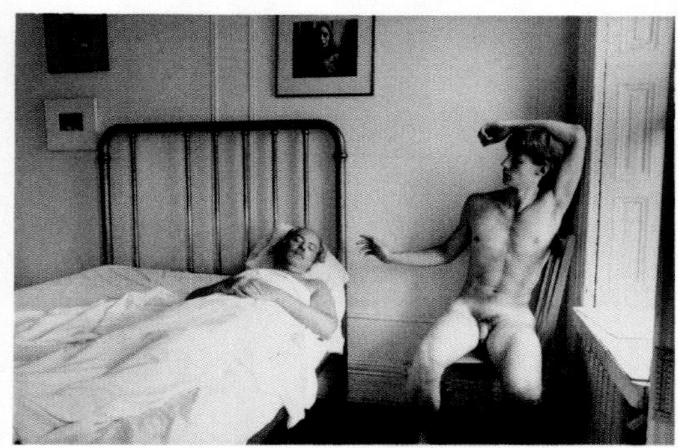

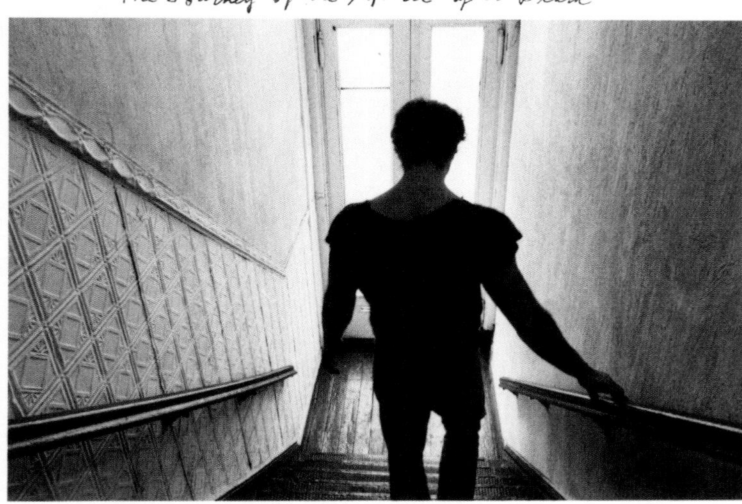

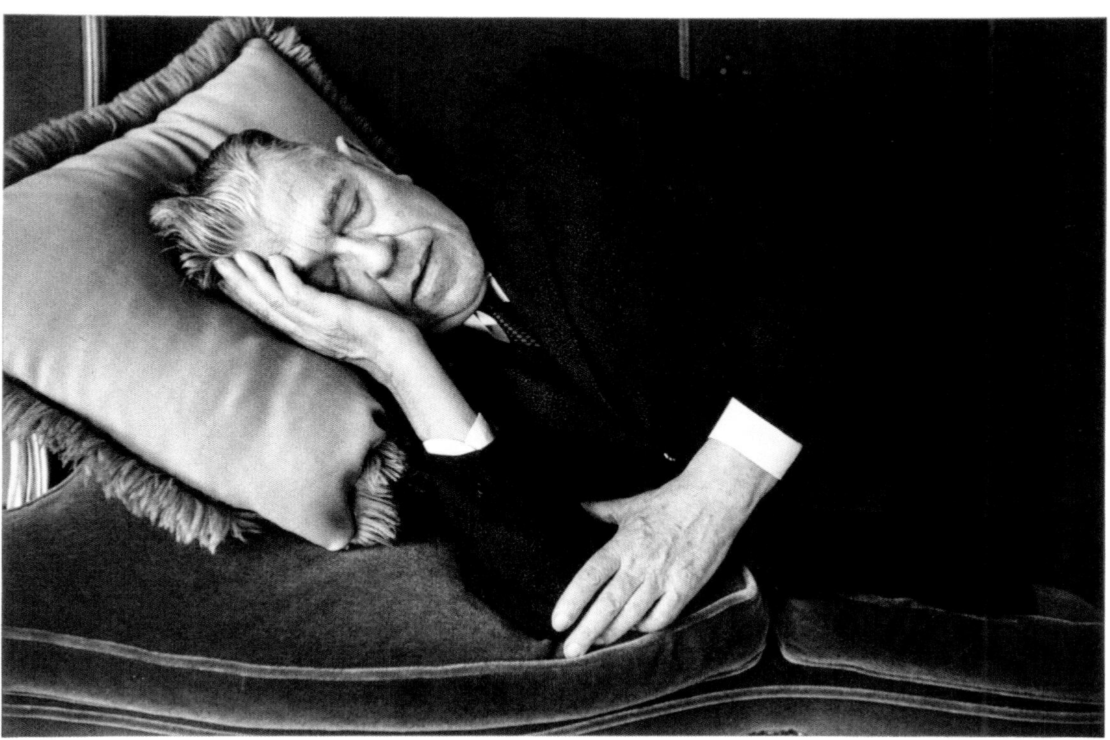

In the room are a table, chair, and a bed. Two naked men are standing there. Very, very close to each other. They're almost touching. And then what happens?" I love the premise. Because the photographer doesn't give me then what happened. The photographer shows me the two guys standing there.

JD: **Your work very much seems to be acknowledging and celebrating sex and sexuality.**

DM: Yes, absolutely.

JD: **But it's not about . . .**

DM: It's not about sexual acts.

JD: **Did you ever think you should take photographs of the acts? Did you ever want to make that a moment in your career?**

DM: No, not at all.

JD: **Why not?**

DM: Because it's been done so many times.

JD: **But you could have done it first.**

DM: No, I wouldn't have done it first. I love the theater. I like the drama. I did a book called *Homage to Cavafy* (1978). The first picture is about the father who has died. This happened to me. I was in Vienna. I came home. Fred took me to dinner Sunday night and he said, "Your father died." I was too late. So, it's a supposedly dead father in bed, and the son, nude, is sitting next to him in a chair, and the son has one hand in a fist and the other hand open—the fist, for me, is symbolic of the conflict between them, and the hand open is wanting to touch him and acknowledge him.

JD: **Why is the son nude?**

DM: It's a gay book. Right? You ask me why I'm not photographing dicks, then you say to me, "Why is the son nude?" There's another one of an empty room, because I see empty rooms as a theater set.

If you put too much information, it distracts. So a guy is in an empty room— a beautiful guy. He's pulling his shirt off. The caption says, in effect, "He did not realize it, but at the very moment that he had pulled it off, he had reached his peak, and after that moment he would begin to decline." We don't even know it, but there's always that moment when we have fulfilled our physical expectations. I did another picture, in that same book. It's a room, again. A window. A big fat guy; a bald guy holding up a picture of himself as a young man. And there's a cat on the ledge. And the caption says: "When he was a young man, it was impossible that he might grow old. Now that he's old, he cannot remember ever having been young." That was perfect. But tell me one other fucking gay photographer who ever talked about old age.

JD: **Tell me where you fit into the gay spectrum.**

DM: My mother got knocked up in 1931. She had to marry my dad. She didn't like

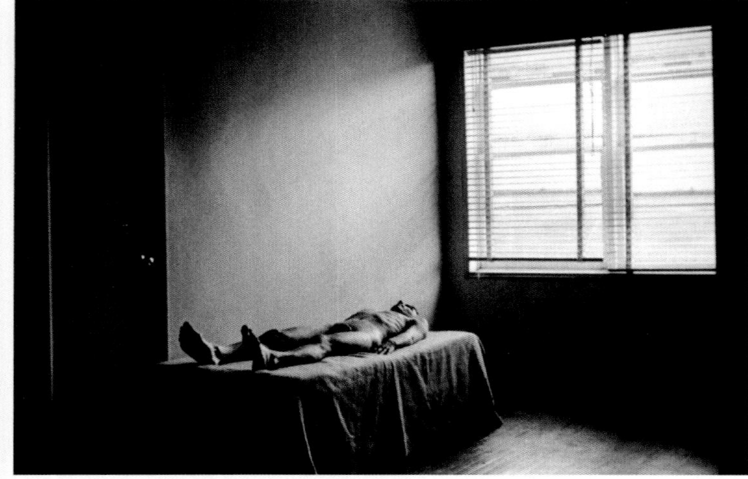
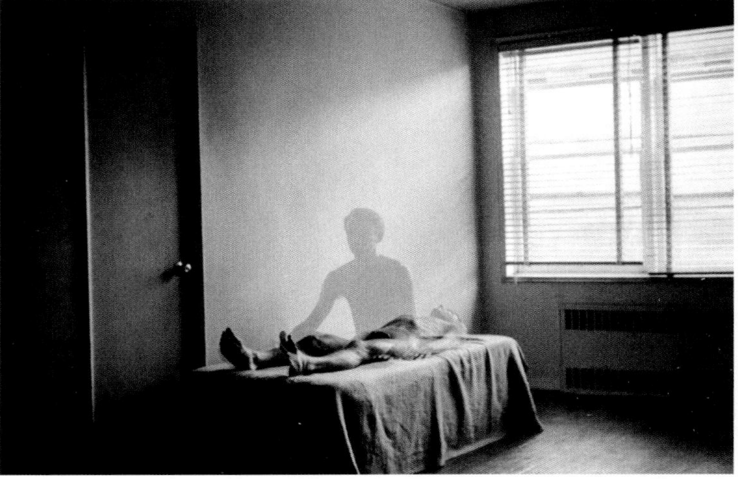
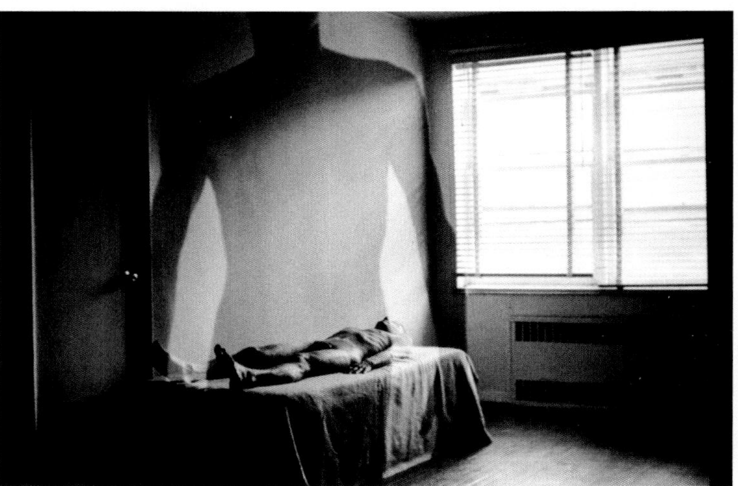
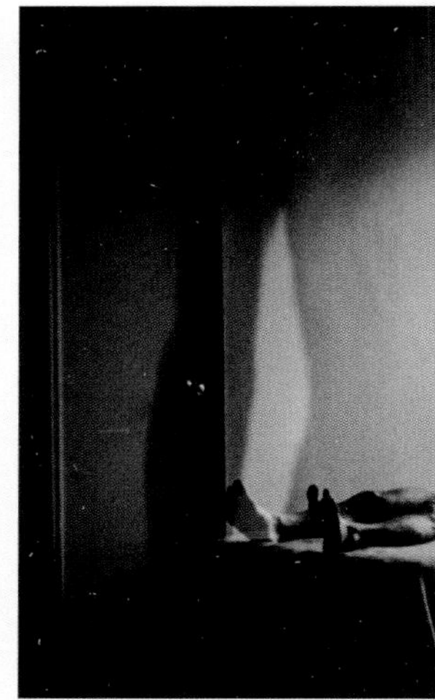

The Spirit Leaves the Body,
1968

Dreaming is magical. We die every night. We don't exist when we're in dreamland.

him, but they were Catholics. So my father was a no-show. He was there, but he wasn't there. When I was in high school there was Stuart Middleman, and Stuart Middleman was a sissy. He carried his books like this, and he hung out with the girls. You didn't want to be Stuart. But there was no "gay." I didn't even know what that was. That's all I knew. And I knew there were queers, but I wasn't quite sure what that was. I was always interested in an older man who would show an interest in me. I would have killed to have an older man put his arm around my shoulder and say, "Gee, Duane, that's good. Did you write that? That's amazing. Keep doing it." Nothing ugly. Fred was the first. Fred was a year older than I was, but I never found that older male affection. I was never interested in going to bars. I was never interested in pretending I'm a woman, dressing up in drag. Nothing like that. I think it's legitimate, but not for me.

JD: **I'm interested that you weren't, because of your interest in theater and the Grand Guignol and all of that.**

DM: I was interested in writing. I was interested in the drama. I wasn't interested in the costumes. There's a big difference.

JD: **I want to talk to you about the use of sleeping in your photography, in *The Fallen Angel* (1968) and *The Bogeyman* (1973). You were saying you want to show things that can't be seen.**

DM: Yes.

JD: **And sleep, in a way, is where you can't explain what you see. You're vanished.**

DM: We spend one third of our lives sleeping. A very early book I did in the 1980s was called *Sleep and Dream* (1984). Dreaming is magical. We die every night. We don't exist when we're in dreamland. When

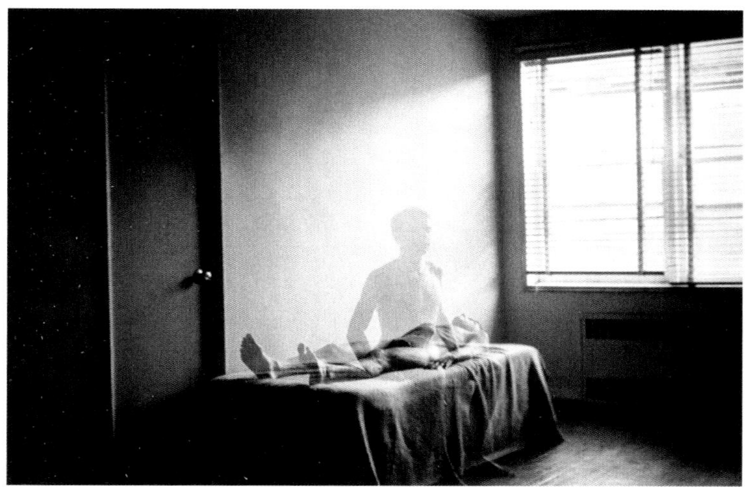
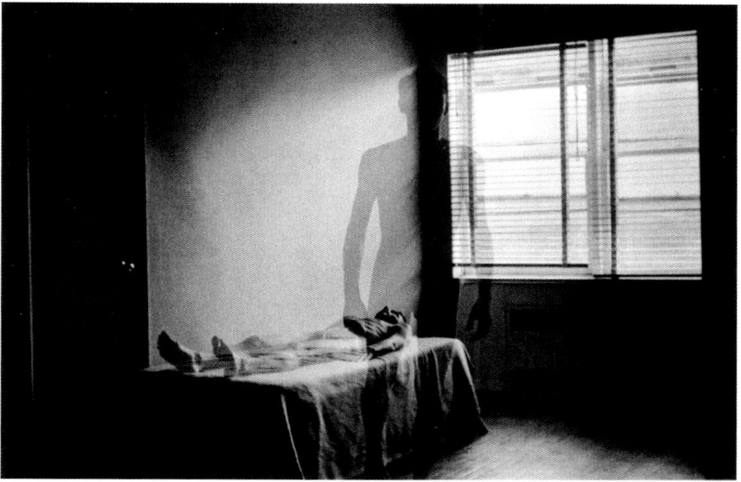
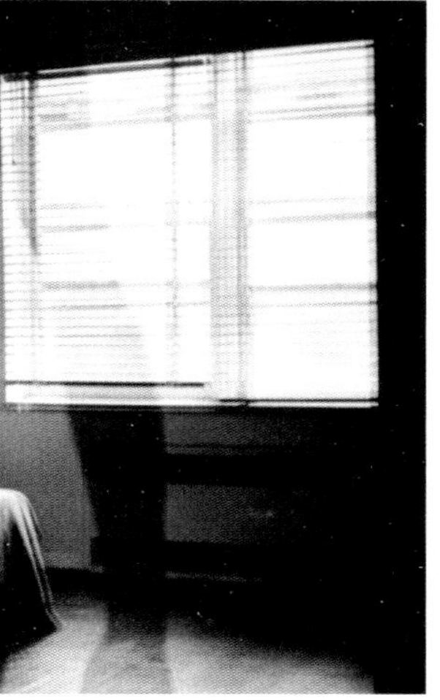
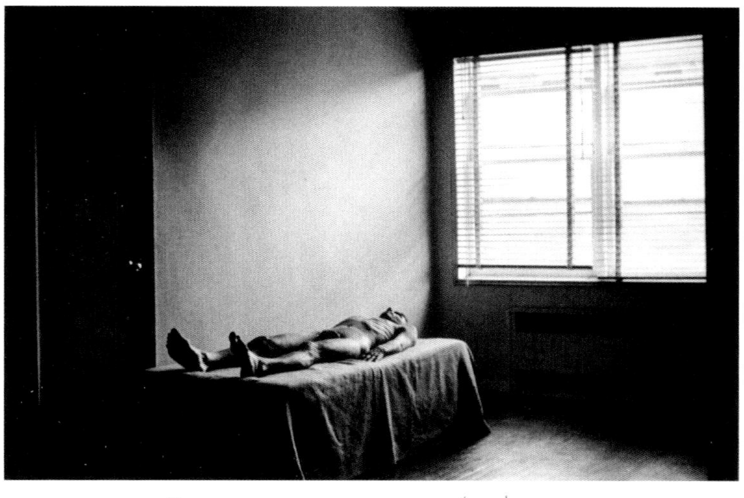

you're in dreamland, the most amazing things happen. When I visited Magritte, every day we would have lunch, and *Bonanza* would be playing on television dubbed in French, and he would take a nap—and I photographed him asleep on the sofa. He always wore a suit.

JD: Did he know you were photographing him while he was napping?

DM: Oh, no. He just gave me run of the house, which was amazing. I thought: I wonder what kind of dreams could Magritte have? What kind of dreams did Shakespeare have? Some people have more interesting dreams than they have lives while awake.

JD: Have you had lucid dreams?

DM: Only once . . . or twice . . . and I never got over it. I was walking down the street and on the corner was Al Seymour. I knew Al was dead. In the dream, I thought to myself, There's Al Seymour, but he's dead. I woke up and said, Wait a minute, I'm in a dream. So then, in the dream scenario, I was supposed to cross the street, but I wanted to go this way. I wanted to take over the dream. But I couldn't do it.

JD: But that's sort of photography, right? Taking over the dream? Directing.

DM: Not directing, but curiosity more than photography. But then I wondered: What if I wander down that street, and, if I couldn't find my way back to that same corner, I would never wake up?

JD: Do you think that would have been true?

DM: I can't say I can't wait to die, but I'm curious about it. I've done so many things about death. In the first sequence book I did in 1969, *Death Comes to the Old Lady*, the spirit leaves the body. And I did one where the guy in the subway becomes a star. The second book I did was called *The Journey of the Spirit After Death* (1971), based on *The Tibetan Book of the Dead*.

JD: Did you ever worry that you're sort of tempting . . . I know you don't believe in fate. But sort of tempting fate by manifesting these moments?

DM: No.

JD: It never bothered you?

DM: No, I don't believe in that at all. Because we make up life, and life is one moment. If you believe in some sort of predestination, then why bother? I think we're masters of our own fate, and if we're not brave enough to seize the moment, then that's what you get.

JD: What was it about sleep that caught you so intensely that you made a book?

DM: Oh, because I think the dreamworld is a legitimate world. Do the math. If we live for, say, sixty years, and one third of sixty would be twenty, then we sleep twenty years of our lives. And that's not worth the curiosity?

JD: Do you believe in what they call "dream logic," that there's a language . . .

DM: Yeah, the theater of the dream?

JD: Yeah, that we don't understand.

DM: I do. I think it has its own reality. It has its own rules. It's a whole other planet.

JD: How do you get the people in your photographs to do what you want them to do?

DM: I say, "Sit there."

JD: And do they?

DM: Yes.

JD: Because you're charming?

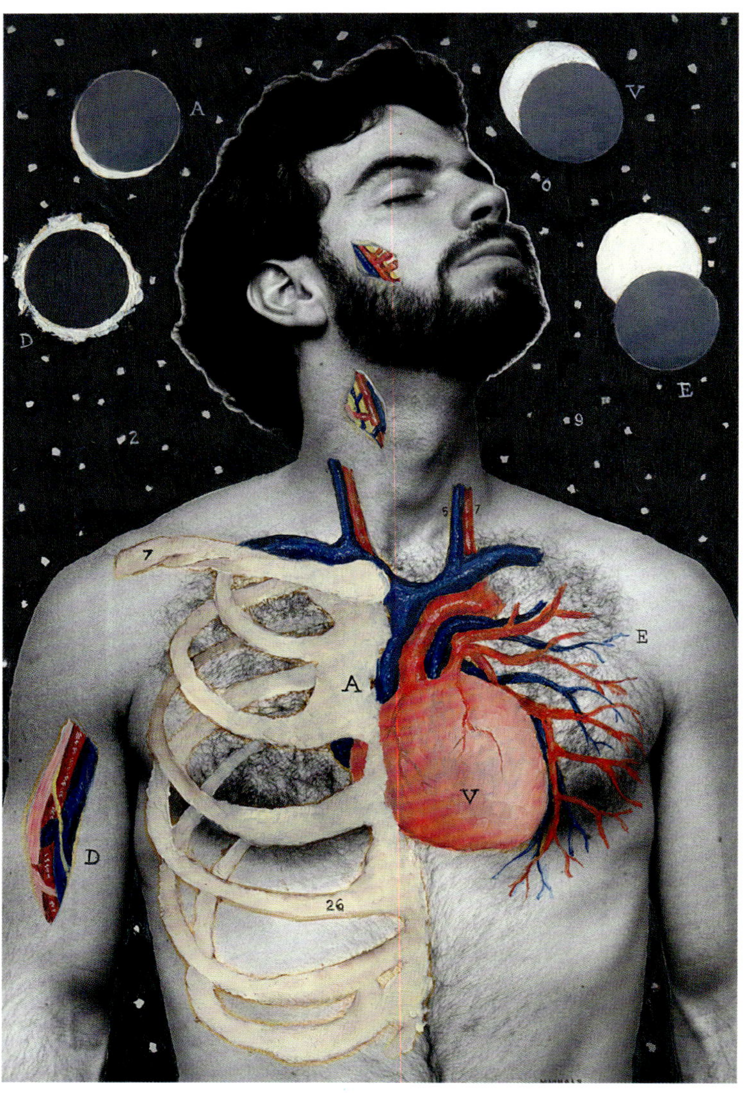

DM: No. First of all, the people in your photographs do not know what you want. I have to tell them. I hate those people who just walk around, and they snap. No. You take charge. Like, again, Garry Winogrand was a snapshooter. He shot, like, five thousand rolls of film he never even looked at. He liked to take pictures, and all the pictures he took were accidents.

JD: But what's the difference between an accident and chance?

DM: It's the same thing. An accident is chance. Chance is an accident.

JD: Do you have thousands of rolls of film?

DM: No. For myself, I shoot very, very little. Elaine May made her movie *Ishtar* (1987), and they took a break, and the cameraman said to her, "While you're taking lunch, do you want me to keep the cameras going?" She said, "Yeah, something might happen." Shakespeare didn't wait for something to happen. Real artists take charge. They make it happen—with latitude. I make things happen. When I go to McKeesport, I might expect something to happen I'm not counting on, and I will use it. But I come with a frame of reference.

JD: You have to set it up first.

DM: Yes. So I set up the premise, and then, my challenge to the young photographer is: Now, tell me what happened.

JD: What if they don't know?

DM: Then fuck them. I don't care what they do. Figure it out. That's their job. Their problem is, they don't know. They do not know that knowing is an option. Nobody teaches you that it's an option.

JD: That's really true.

DM: My great thing was, I never went to photography school. I'd have to unlearn everything.

JD: I'm thinking now of you beginning to write on your photographs, and I'm wondering how your handwriting looked to you.

DM: Oh, I don't pay attention. It looks as it is. And don't forget: I was a graphic designer, so I have a sense of the appropriateness of things.

JD: Did your handwriting change as you did it over the years?

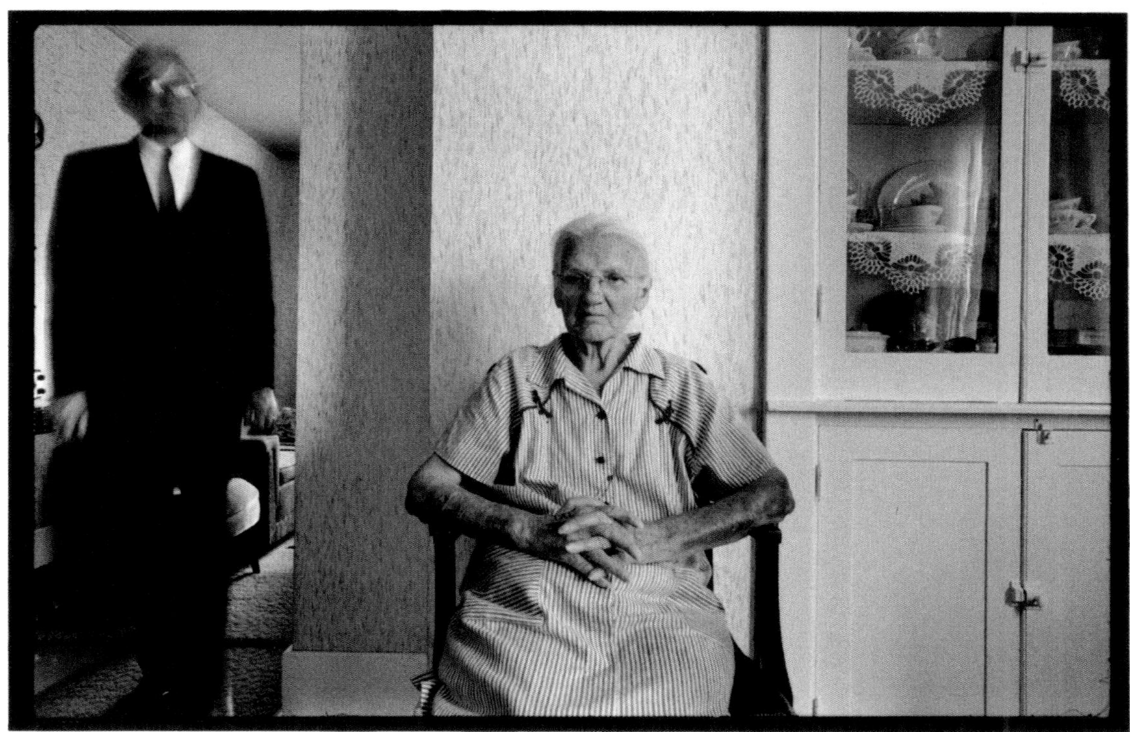

DM: Essentially, no. But now I try to write better. It always gets described that my handwriting is "chicken scrawl."

JD: **So why didn't you make your scripts beautiful?**

DM: Because it's not about beauty. It's about intelligence.

JD: **Which brings us to your use of double exposures. How does that go wrong?**

DM: Oh, because you could be lousy. I discovered double exposures when I went to Russia with my thirteen-dollar borrowed Argus—because it double exposed gratuitously. Then I began to look at these double exposures, and I said, "That's good. That's interesting." So I began to control it. Like that picture I did called *The Illuminated Man* (1968). That just didn't happen. I had that in my head. I was meditating. I knew that when you went up to Park between 34th and 42nd, there's a tunnel, and cabs go down it, and I would see these spotlights coming in. So I took my friend Ted Titolo— he's in all my early pictures, he's also in *Chance Meeting* (1970)—I put him in the tunnel on a Sunday, when there was very little traffic, and I stationed him so the sun

would hit his face. Then I exposed for the tunnel, which means his face would be way overexposed and blur out on purpose. The spirit leaves the body. It's totally controlled.

JD: **It's a transcendence that's totally controlled?**

DM: Yes. It freed me to another level of expression. Everything I've done has been to free me from the shackles of photography.

JD: **It frees you how?**

DM: The bottom line is expression. It's not technique. Technique is at the service of expression. People get hung up on technique and have nothing to express. I didn't start out wanting to be a photographer. I came to New York because I loved books and magazines, and I wanted to get a job as a designer. Henry Wolf was the great art director those days, and there was an opening at *Harper's Bazaar*. So I made two magazines for my portfolio. I made one based on *Du*, my favorite Swiss magazine, where they do a whole issue on a single subject. And I invented a magazine called *Contact*. It was contact with life, contact with theater, contact with art, contact with

poetry. I did a whole issue on Russia, using my own photographs. When I showed it to Henry, he said, "Who took the pictures?" I said, "I did." He said, "Oh, you should be a photographer." He wouldn't hire me. But when he went to *Show* a year later to be the art director, he hired me for the first issue. Then I went to see Lou Silverstein, the legendary art director of the *New York Times*. He wouldn't hire me as a designer. But, eventually, he gave me a variety of things to shoot for the *Times*, including the annual report.

JD: **Did your partner Fred's Alzheimer's affect the way you think about language?**

DM: Not at all. I do think about how I think but never while I'm thinking. I don't pay attention to it. I'm completely on automatic. I don't think about the act of writing. The best time for me to have ideas is when I wake up. Seven to nine is when my mind is just throwing things at me.

JD: **Is that because of sleep? Everything's been stored up?**

DM: I don't ask. And I don't tell.

JD: **Did you photograph Fred at the end?**

DM: No. Are you kidding?

JD: **People make work out of all kinds of things.**

DM: Avedon made photographs of his father when he was dying and published them a year later. But there are times you don't take a picture. I would never photograph Fred while he was dying. Oh my God. The last thing I would do. How could that part of your brain kick in when the great love of your life is dying? We had fifty-seven years together and I'm going to start: "Fred, would you hold that pose? Open your mouth more, please. No, keep the eyes shut. No gurgling noise. I'm trying to take a picture." Nonsense.

JD: **I think for some people that is how they process their lives.**

DM: I can't. [*Sings*] "Some people can thrive and bloom / living life in the living room." Best Stephen Sondheim song ever. "Some people can be content / playing bingo and paying rent. That's peachy for some people." All my friends in McKeesport were living—are still living—lives in the living room. I burned the living room down.

JD: **You were never typical.**

DM: Fred and I were never typical gay people of our generation. When we bought a house, we lived in the country. We didn't go to Fire Island. We didn't go to the Hamptons. We didn't do any of that. We bought a farmhouse with lots of land. We're big gardeners. That's one of the things we had in common. What works is, the more you have in common with somebody, the better it is for the relationship. Opposites don't attract. It's about the more you share. Fred was the great love of my life. And all relationships evolve. Nobody lives happily ever after. We avoided all the pitfalls.

JD: **How?**

DM: Well, very easily—because we had other issues in our lives. We weren't dick focused. Of course, we were dick focused. But when I wasn't around, I didn't have to worry that Fred was hanging out in a bar.

JD: **Were you monogamous?**

DM: No. But eventually, we evolved. I think because we shared so much . . .

JD: **And you not photographing him? Do you think that might have helped?**

DM: It was never an issue. We kept our lives separate. I learned early on that we didn't work that way. Have I out-talked you? I'll show you pictures. This is Fred and myself in happier days. That's Fred, that's me.

JD: **Oh, you're so handsome.**

DM: This is the last time Fred was in the country. There's our garden. Then this is Fred when he had Alzheimer's. That's Fred and me here. This is Fred at the end. Sit down. I wrote something very nice about him. I wrote a poem. It said: "Dear Friend, / If you should die before me, / I would build you a pyramid, / And each stone would be a memory / Of a moment we had shared. / And I would remember you. // And when you awaken / From your dream of death / Should you chance to find / This pyramid in your travels, / Remember me, / And how I once loved you long ago." It always breaks my heart.

JD: **Duane, that's so beautiful. Did you publish that somewhere?**

DM: It's from when I sent out Fred's death notice.

JD: **It's just gorgeous.**

DM: Here, you can have a copy.

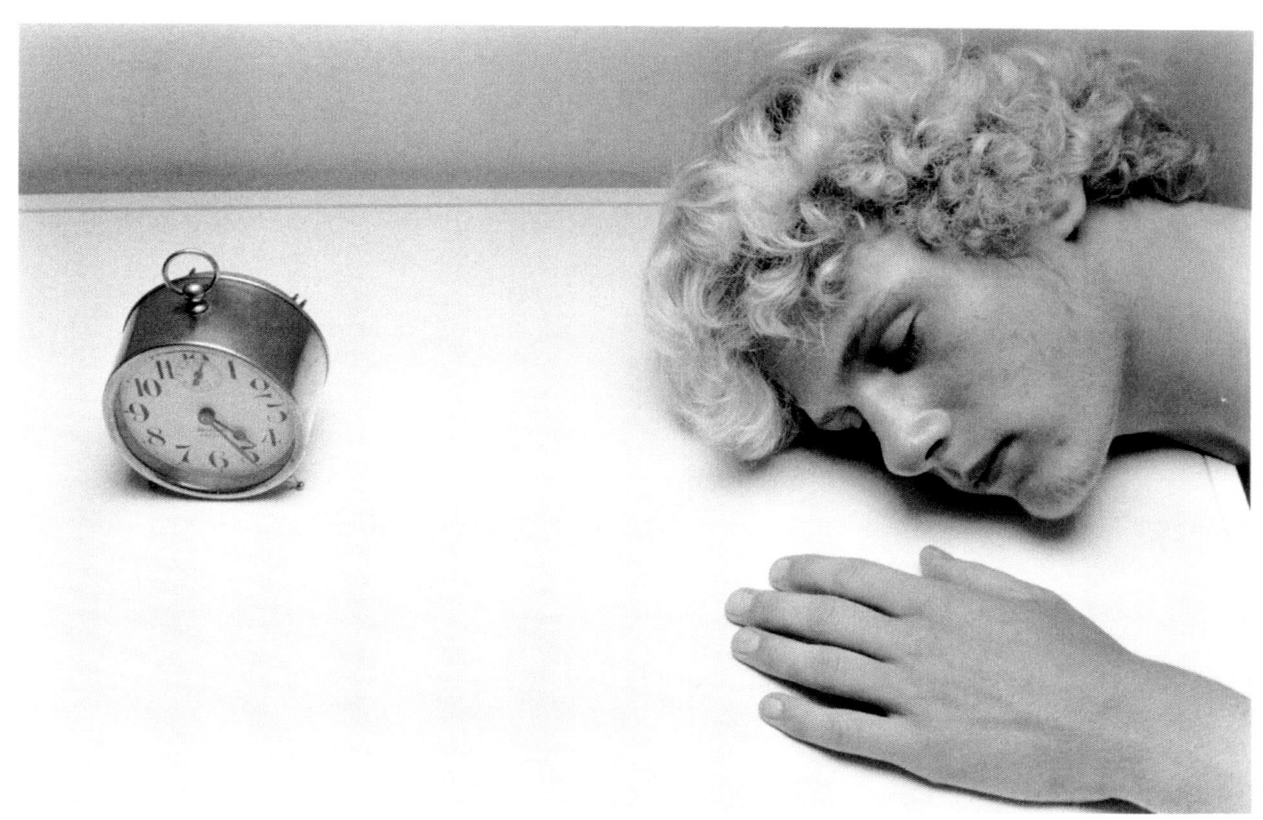

Ah Dreams, 1984
All photographs © the artist
and courtesy DC Moore
Gallery, New York

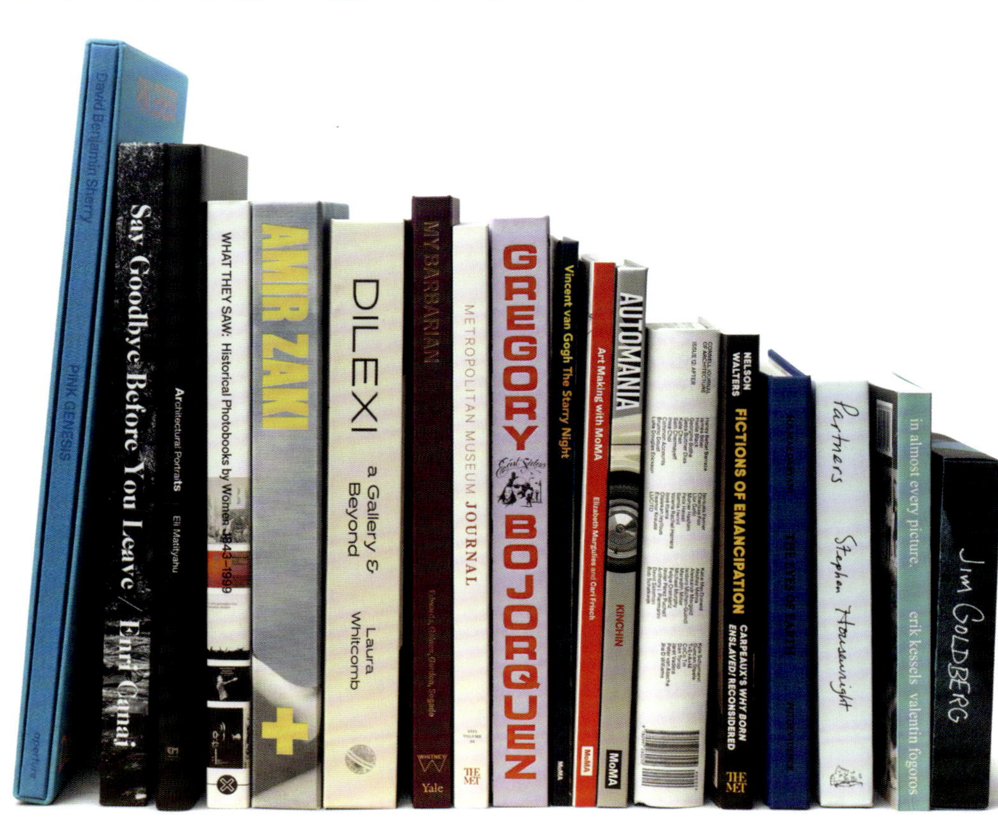

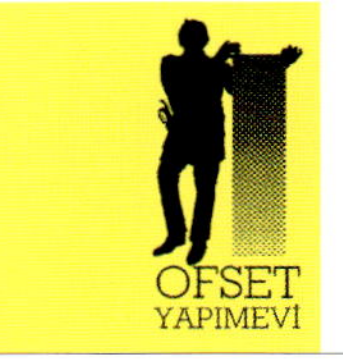

aperture Archive

Every issue since 1952. All online.
aperture.org/archive

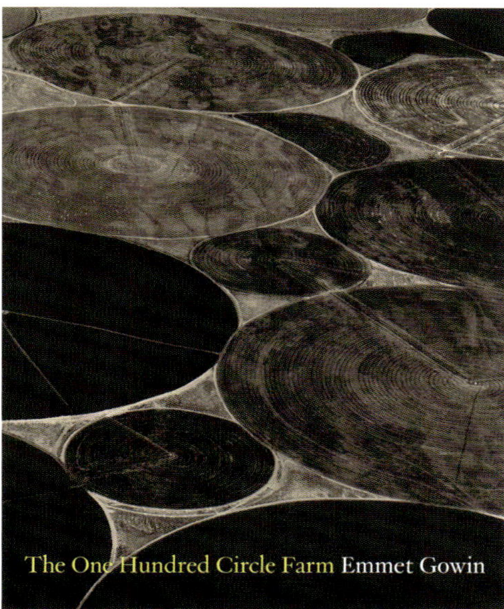

The One Hundred Circle Farm

Emmet Gowin

Afterword by Lucas Bessire

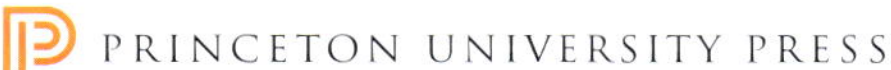

A powerful photographic study of the impact of irrigation systems on the landscape of the United States

PRINCETON UNIVERSITY PRESS

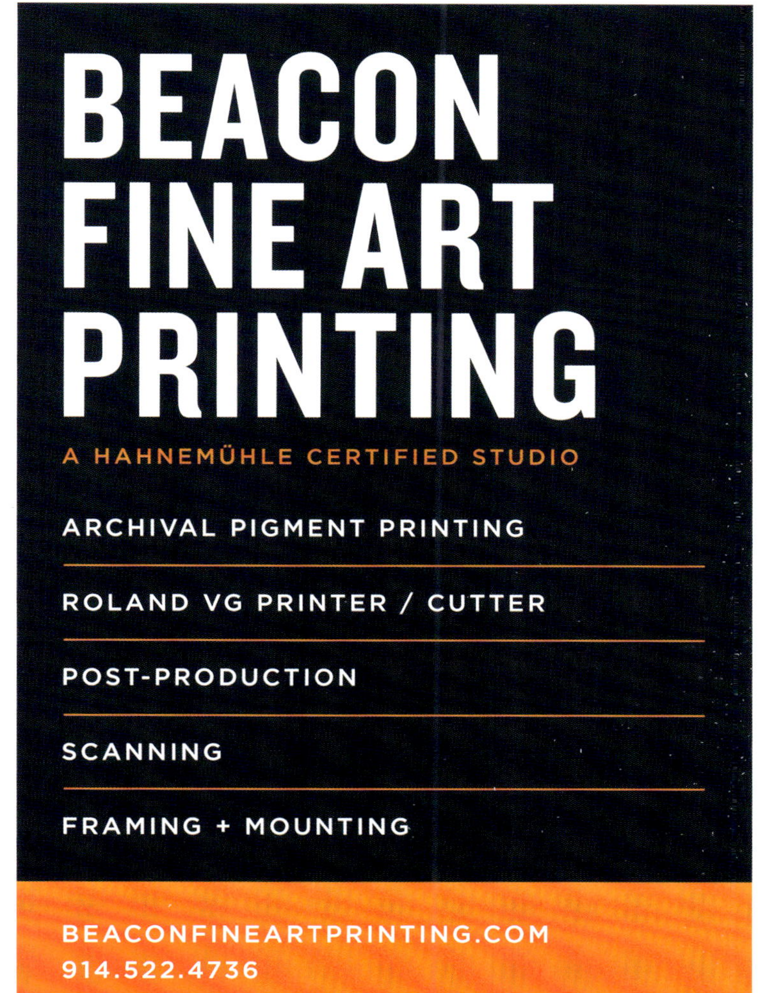

www.mica.edu/aperture

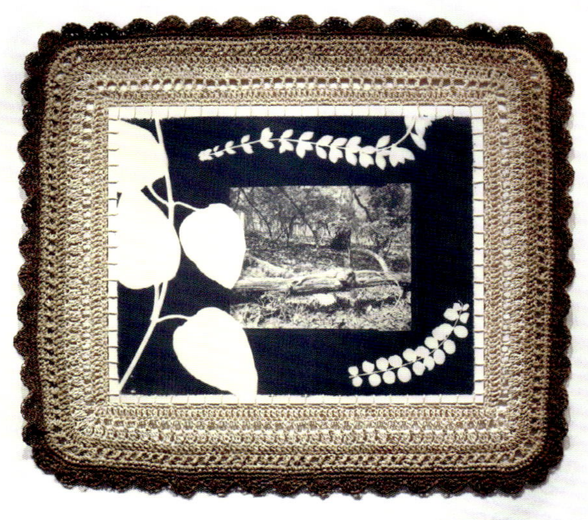

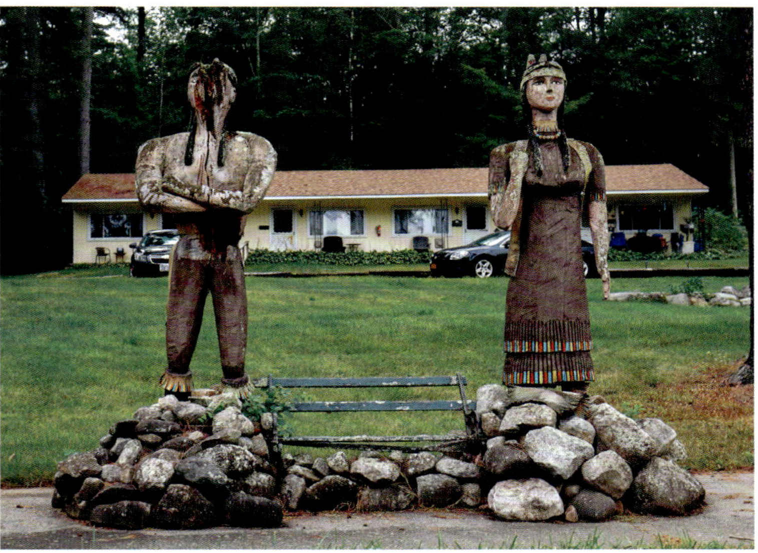

M|C|A
PHOTOGRAPHY

Congratulations to our December 2021 graduates

left: Jessie Hansen, *Entry 1* from *A Diary of a Sunbeam*, 2021

right: Tanya Kovacevic, *Native Family*, 2021

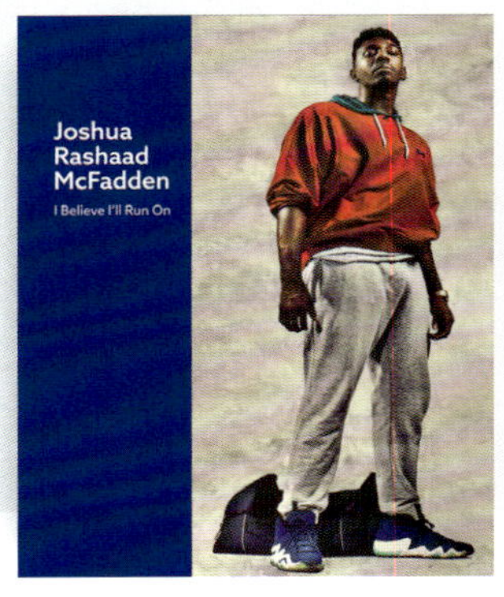

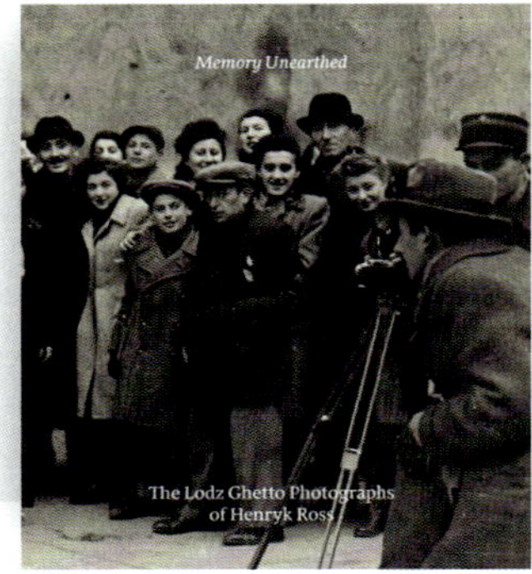

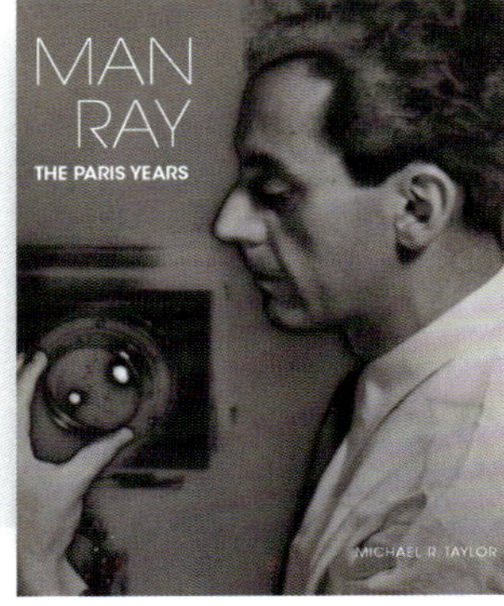

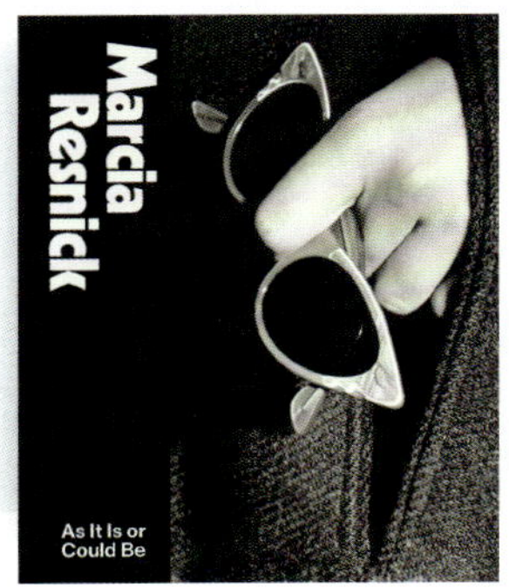

**Joshua Rashaad McFadden:
I Believe I'll Run On**
With an essay by LaCharles Ward
and a conversation between
Joshua Rashaad McFadden
and Lyle Ashton Harris

Published in association with the
George Eastman Museum

**Memory Unearthed:
The Lódz Ghetto Photographs
of Henryk Ross**
Edited by Maia-Mari Sutnik

Distributed for the Art Gallery of Ontario

**Man Ray:
The Paris Years**
Michael R. Taylor

Distributed for the Virginia Museum
of Fine Arts

**Marcia Resnick:
As It Is or Could Be**
Frank H. Goodyear III, Lisa
Hostetler, and Casey Riley

Published in association with the Bowdoin
College Museum of Art, George Eastman
Museum, and Minneapolis Institute of Art

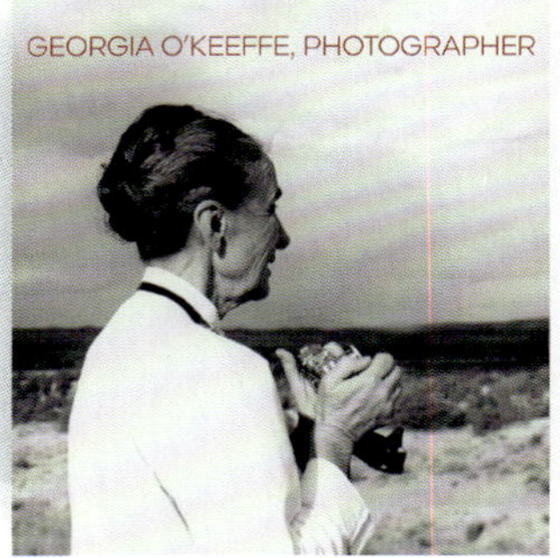

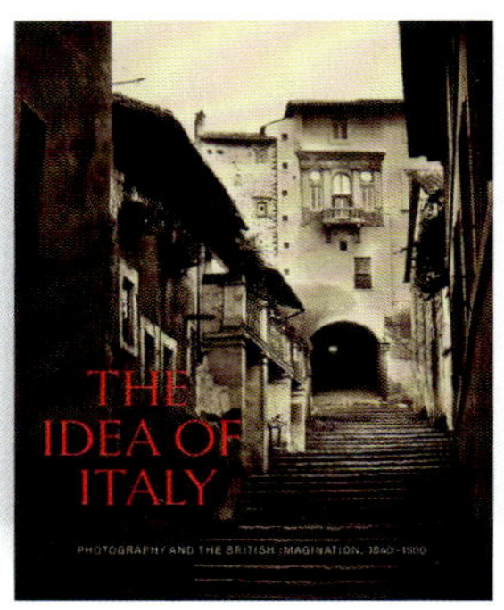

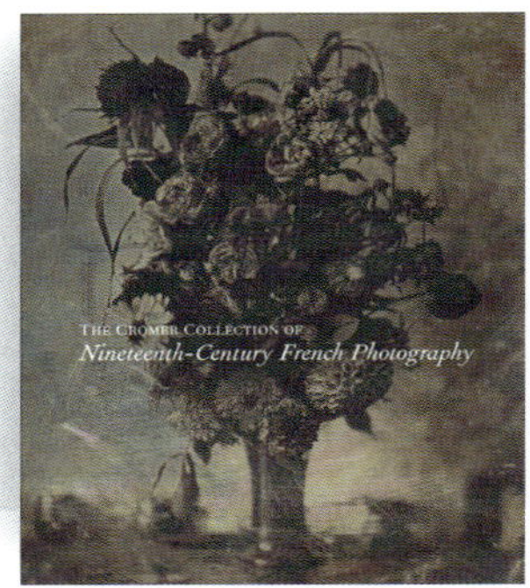

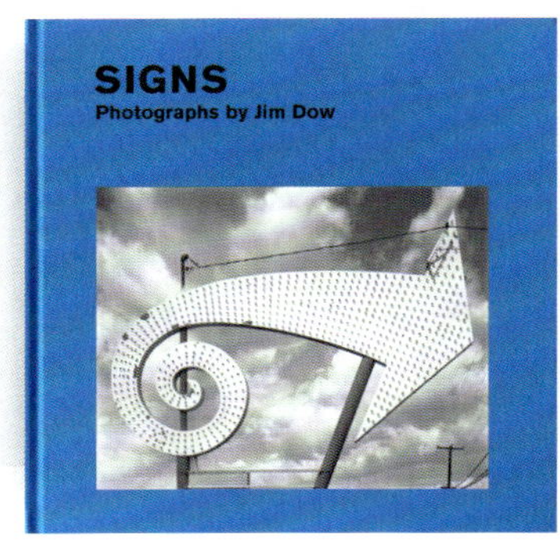

Georgia O'Keeffe, Photographer
Lisa Volpe

Published in association with the Museum of
Fine Arts, Houston

**The Idea of Italy:
Photography and the British
Imagination, 1840–1900**
Edited by Maria Antonella
Pelizzari and Scott Wilcox

Distributed for the Yale Center for British Art

**The Cromer Collection of
Nineteenth-Century French
Photography**
With contributions by Sylvie
Aubenas, Eleonore Challine, Ellen
Handy, Jacob W. Lewis, Anne de
Mondenard, and Heather A. Shannon

Published in association with the
George Eastman Museum

**Signs:
Photographs by Jim Dow**
With essays by Jim Dow and
April M. Watson

Distributed for the Nelson-Atkins
Museum of Art

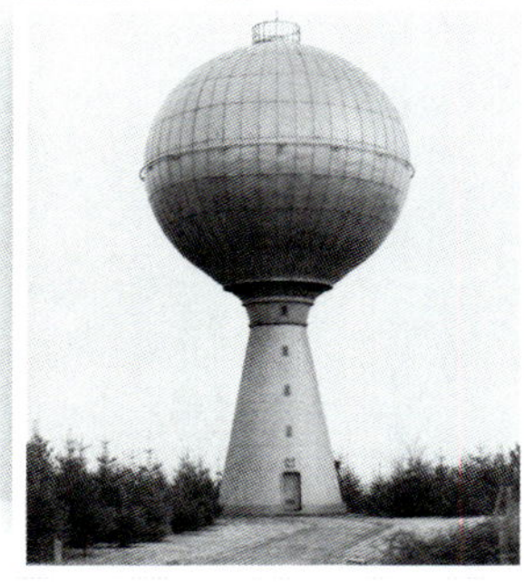

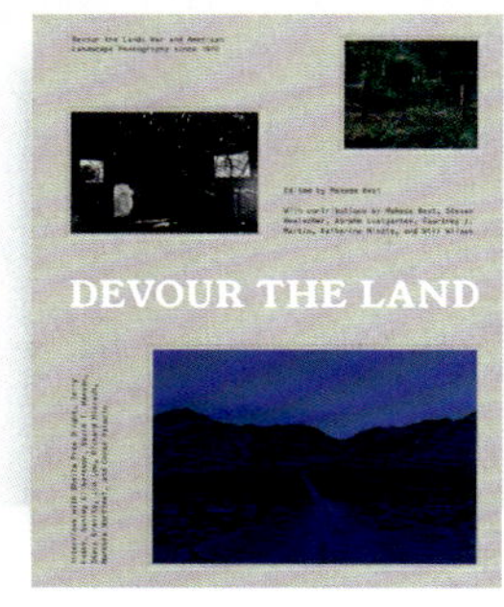

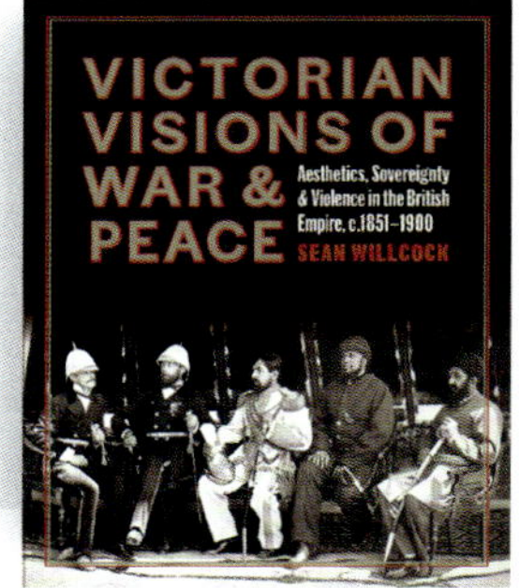

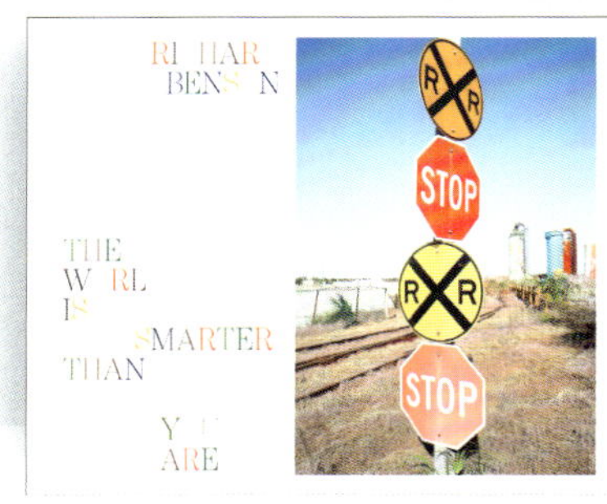

Bernd & Hilla Becher
Jeff L. Rosenheim; With essays by
Gabriele Conrath-Scholl, Virginia
Heckert, Lucy Sante, and an
interview with Max Becher

Published by The Metropolitan Museum of Art/
Distributed by Yale University Press

**Devour the Land:
War and American Landscape
Photography since 1970**
Edited by Makeda Best

Distributed for the Harvard Art Museums

**Victorian Visions of War & Peace:
Aesthetics, Sovereignty, and
Violence in the British Empire**
Sean Willcock

Distributed for the Paul Mellon Centre for
Studies in British Art

**Richard Benson:
The World Is Smarter Than You Are**
Peter Barberie

Published in association with the Philadelphia
Museum of Art

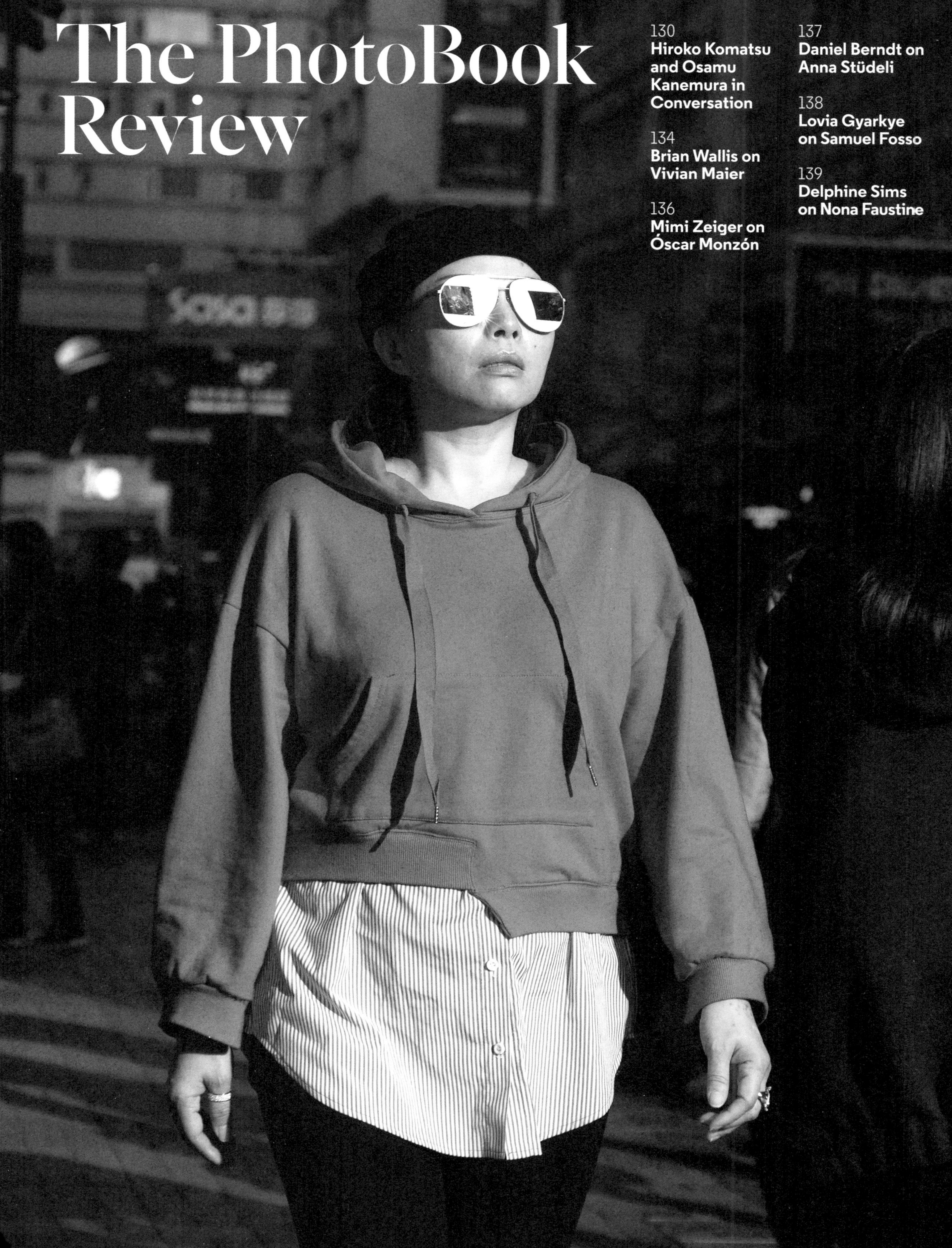

The PhotoBook Review

Sincerity Department

In October 2021, Hiroko Komatsu and Osamu Kanemura held a parallel set of exhibitions at the newly reopened gallery space of dieFirma, New York—Komatsu's *Sincerity Department Loyal Division* and Kanemura's *Looper Syndicate*. In Komatsu's installation, upstairs, visitors were welcomed by a subtle and moving smell, a combination of photographic paper and printing chemicals, that enveloped them as they walked through photographs, and on photographs, in a multisensorial experience. Amidst the prints, Komatsu also presented a selection of her new artist books. Downstairs, in Kanemura's exhibition, visitors encountered a monumental collage made of twenty thousand color photographs, mainly of the artist's hometown, Tokyo, and a few of New York, complemented by a (loud) film on a loop as well as a myriad of books on pedestals that all were invited to browse. Pauline Vermare recently spoke with Komatsu and Kanemura about these experimental installations.

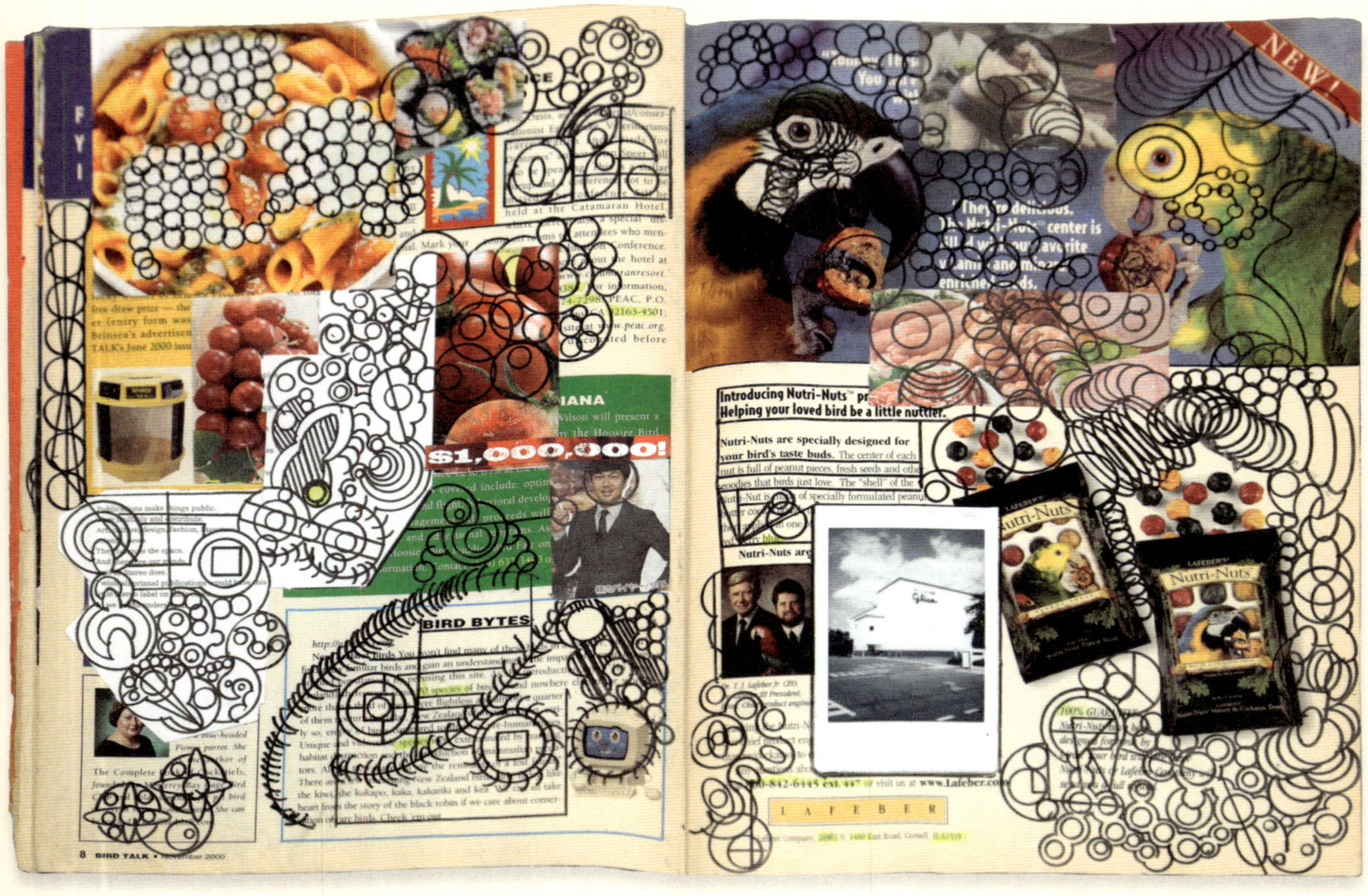

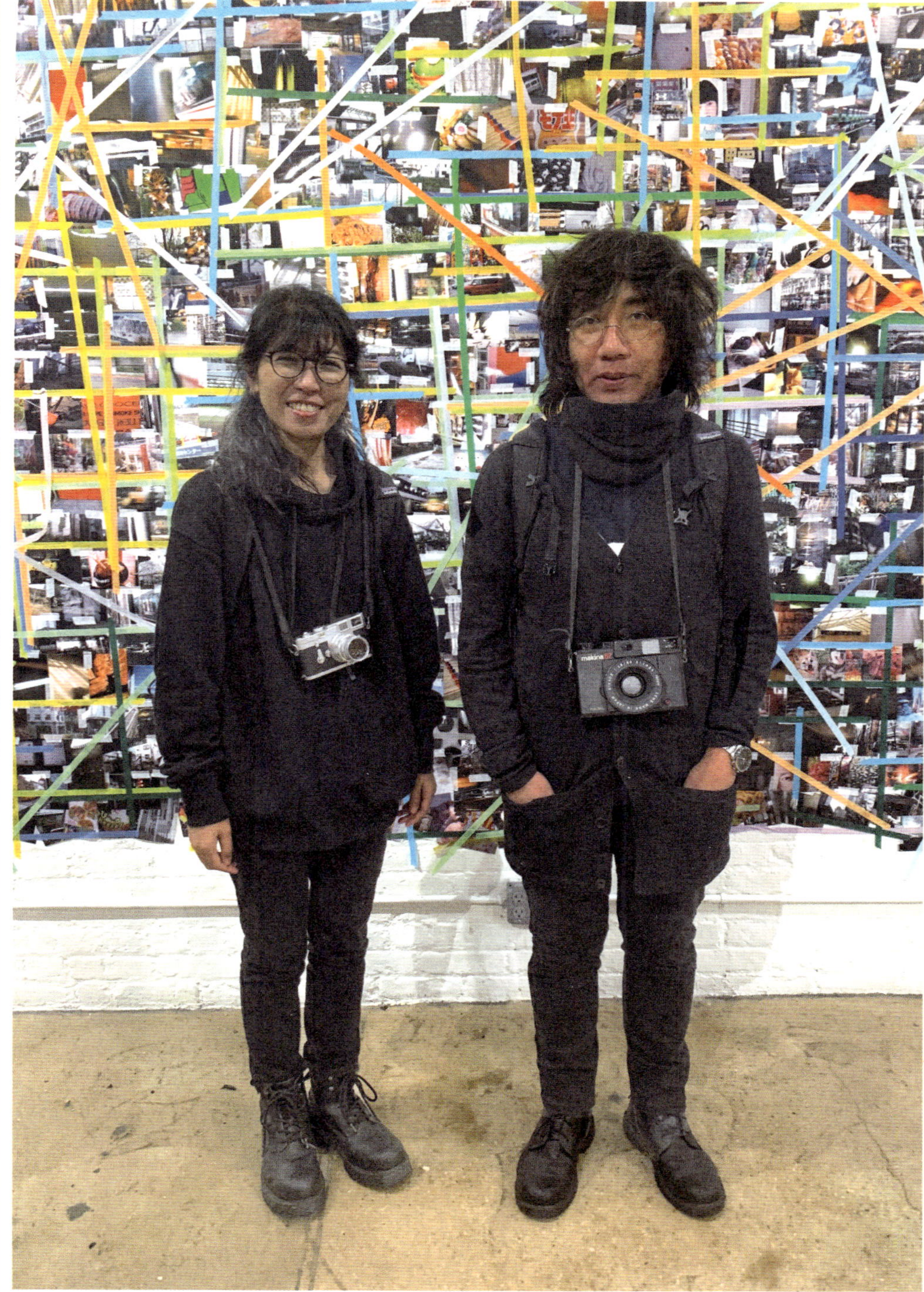

Pauline Vermare: What struck me first as I visited both of your installations is their incredible physicality: the utter joy of being surrounded by unframed prints and handmade books, of being in such direct contact with your art in an intimate and nonprecious way. It seems like a visceral reaction to our world, a desire to *re-materialize*, which feels so good in the midst of this COVID crisis. How did this work come to life?

Osamu Kanemura: While many people have been staying home for the past year, I've been out taking photographs of Tokyo using the Ricoh GR. I've been thinking that a digital camera should be completely different from a film camera and wondering how I could exhibit digital photography that is more than an imitation of film photography. That's why I decided to present a large number of photographs, not in a conventional way where enlarged, framed photographs are exhibited in a white-cube gallery but as an installation and as handmade books.

Hiroko Komatsu: Same as Osamu, I was busy going outside to take pictures. Actually, I found it very easy to do so because there were few people outside amid the pandemic. In Tokyo, there had been a building rush linked to the Olympic Games, but much of the construction had been halted as part of lockdown. I enjoyed taking photographs of those empty construction sites, which gave me an impression of shiny ruins. When people look at those pictures, they can't tell whether the scenery shows the process of building or of demolishing something. Those who work in these sites are so-called blue workers, and I believe those sites are where you can see the people who make up the lower part of our society and our infrastructure most clearly. As a photographer, I think it is very important to visit such places to take pictures.

PV: Osamu, would you tell us about your other camera of choice, the Plaubel Makina? In your excellent 2019 book, *Beta Exercise: The Theory and Practice of Osamu Kanemura*, a collection of your interviews and writings, you explain: "The Plaubel Makina, which creates an element of unintentional noise, taught me the importance of unintended effects. . . . This adds street snap-like motion to static, urban landscape photos." Why did you choose that camera?

OK: Well, Daido Moriyama was already photographing Tokyo with a 35mm camera, and I didn't want to do the same thing as

Opposite:
Spread from Osamu
Kanemura, *Bird Study*
(Artist book, 2021)

This page:
Hiroko Komatsu and
Osamu Kanemura, 2021

him. So I decided to use a camera with better image quality, which was a 6-by-7 camera. I chose Plaubel Makina because it was lighter, which is an important factor for someone like me who shoots all day long. One of the features of the camera is that its viewfinder coverage is 80 percent. With such a wide coverage, when I try to take a picture of something, the object in the foreground enters the picture. Now, I consciously include things in the foreground in my photographs, but I used to think such a photograph would be a failure. Eventually, I realized that it would be more interesting if things I hadn't imagined or things I had thought of as obstacles were in the images. This kind of "noise" in photography should be appreciated, I thought.

PV: Both of you have incorporated the creation of objects into your recent practice, which we are surrounded with tonight as they feature prominently in the exhibition. I'd love for you both, maybe starting with Hiroko, to talk about those incredible objects—they're something more than books, really. *Black Book #1* (2021) actually is a bottle, filled with little cut-out pieces of paper that are the words from Greta Thunberg's book *No One Is Too Small to Make a Difference*. Another one is filled with Theodore Kaczynski's *Industrial Society and Its Future: The Unabomber Manifesto*. Hiroko, can you tell us about those books, those objects, and how you started making them?

HK: In making my first artist book, *Book #1* (2016), I wasn't interested in selecting photographs from the approximately one thousand photographs to be shown in my exhibition and arranging them. Nor did I want to make a catalog from the photographs. I felt such a book would not represent what I was doing. I've been photographing my exhibition sites with the same camera I use in making the work outside. One time, I put those photographs of my installation side by side with the ones I took outside, and there was something consistent about them, and that inspired me to put them together for *Book #1*. Digital technology is also an important tool for me, and I digitally scan images made with an 8mm camera. The idea behind my artist book *Black Book #1* is that text and photographs are very similar. A single photograph is not enough to make sense. A single word doesn't make sense by itself, either. And when you put together multiple photographs or words, a meaning emerges. Also, when you take a picture, you frame a part of reality, and then you move the image to another place, such as an exhibition venue or bookstore. I thought the process was very similar to cutting out texts from a book and putting them in an object—in this installation, a bottle.

PV: **In your case, and in Osamu's work with books as well as with photographs, there's this idea of accumulation. Osamu, you have recently been making two kinds of books: the ones that are collages of images and elements that you cut out and assemble in colorful, unique albums and those made from existing books that you intervene on, by drawing in them, cutting them. When did you start this process?**

OK: Before, I had a strong idea of what a photobook should be like. The reason I'm interested in handmade books is because it's very interesting to see the preconceived notions of books that I've been trapped in until now breaking down. I couldn't treat photobooks violently because I was thinking about distribution and preservation. But once I got rid of those things, many ideas came to me. For example, I cut or fold the pages of a book with a cutter or use tape that will not be well preserved. I made my first artist book two years ago. I was beginning to feel uncomfortable about my black-and-white photographs because they were like tableaux. It was also then that I visited New York and bookdummypress (bdp). I was shocked to see the handmade books of Victor Sira, the director of bdp. I thought, This is more like a drawing. I also found it very interesting that he didn't aim to complete his works but presented them

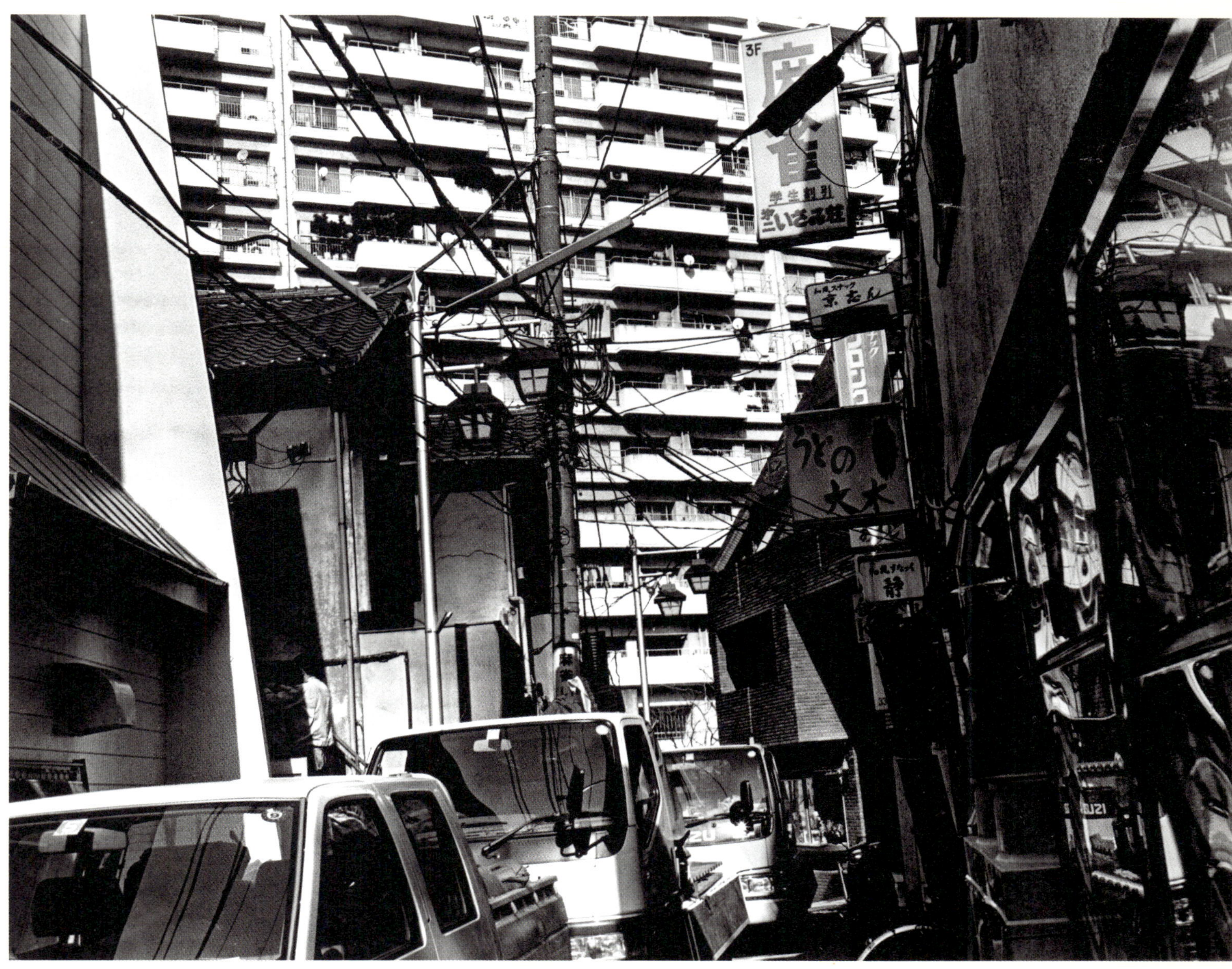

Osamu Kanemura, *All the needles on are red*, 1998, from *Spider's Strategy* (Osiris, 2001) All photographs courtesy dieFirma, New York

A single photograph is not enough to make sense. A single word doesn't make sense by itself, either.

unfinished. I decided to do what he was doing, with collage as a start.

In making collages, I use such materials as digital photographs and clippings from magazines and newspapers. I also realized that I could do things with digital photography that are difficult to do with film photography: taking photographs of my life, of what I see on a daily basis, and displaying my politics. I'm *Zainichi*—a Korean living in Japan—and because of my origins, I've encountered situations that have forced me to feel uncomfortable with the Japanese system since I was a child. In Japan, for example, you can see ads of racist magazines in major national newspapers. They say, "*Zainichi* Koreans should leave Japan." This is also my daily life, and I'm clipping those words, too, in my collages. I like to make something out of something that exists, rather than creating something from scratch.

When I make my artist books, I use other people's photographs, texts, and printed matters, and by doing so, I try to deconstruct the meaning and context of others' materials and create another context. In this respect, photography is the same. It's about framing the part of reality that exists in front of us. You may have noticed that I have repeatedly drawn circles in my artist books, using a special ruler. In other words, I drew the shape of an object with a tool, which made me realize that what I do with a camera is photograph the shape of an object. My every action serves to expand my concept of photography.

Pauline Vermare is an independent photography curator based in New York. Interview translation by Yuri Mano.

Reviews

The still unfolding saga of Vivian Maier, the Chicago street photographer whose extraordinary archive was discovered at an unclaimed storage auction, is predicated on mystery. When the contents of the five lockers containing Maier's earthly possessions were first breached in 2007, then dispersed to various pickers, literally nothing was known about the woman who filled them. The eight tons of artifacts she left in storage included over 140,000 photographic images, most unprocessed or unprinted, and comprised the sum total of Maier's strange and fascinating vision of the world. But it was a full two years before the principal buyer, twenty-six-year-old real estate agent John Maloof, identified Maier and realized that, unbeknownst to him, she had been living nearby and had just died at the age of eighty-three.

Granted full access by Maloof to the mountain of detritus left behind by the secretive Maier, the biographer Ann Marks, a former Dow Jones executive, aims in her new book ***Vivian Maier Developed: The Untold Story of the Photographer Nanny*** (**Atria Books, 2021; 368 pages, $40**) to solve the mysteries of this once-lost life. And a fascinating life it is, quite apart from Maier's remarkable photography. Born in New York in 1926, Maier was the product of a shattered marriage, cast in the shadow, according to Marks, of her mother's out-of-wedlock birth in rural France. Shuttled back to France in 1932, Maier lived from age six to twelve among relatives in their alpine village, before returning to New York. Then, in 1950, after the death of her grandmother, twenty-four-year-old Maier returned to France to claim an inheritance, a move that seems to have established her independence and given her confidence. While there, she began photographing the landscape and farmworkers in earnest, hoping, she said, to make postcards.

Back in the United States, Maier sought employment as a live-in childcare worker, a career she followed nonstop for forty-five years, from 1951 to 1996, briefly in New York and California, then mainly in Chicago. Wholly distinct from Maier's quirky and prodigious photographic output, Marks's biography is a rare and detailed chronicle of a professional governess (or, as Marks says, a "nanny"). After stable employment with one family for eleven years, Maier tended to the children of the TV star Phil Donahue. During this time, she pursued her photography ambitiously, capturing urban street subjects with wit and clever style, seeking out movie stars at premieres or boldly approaching

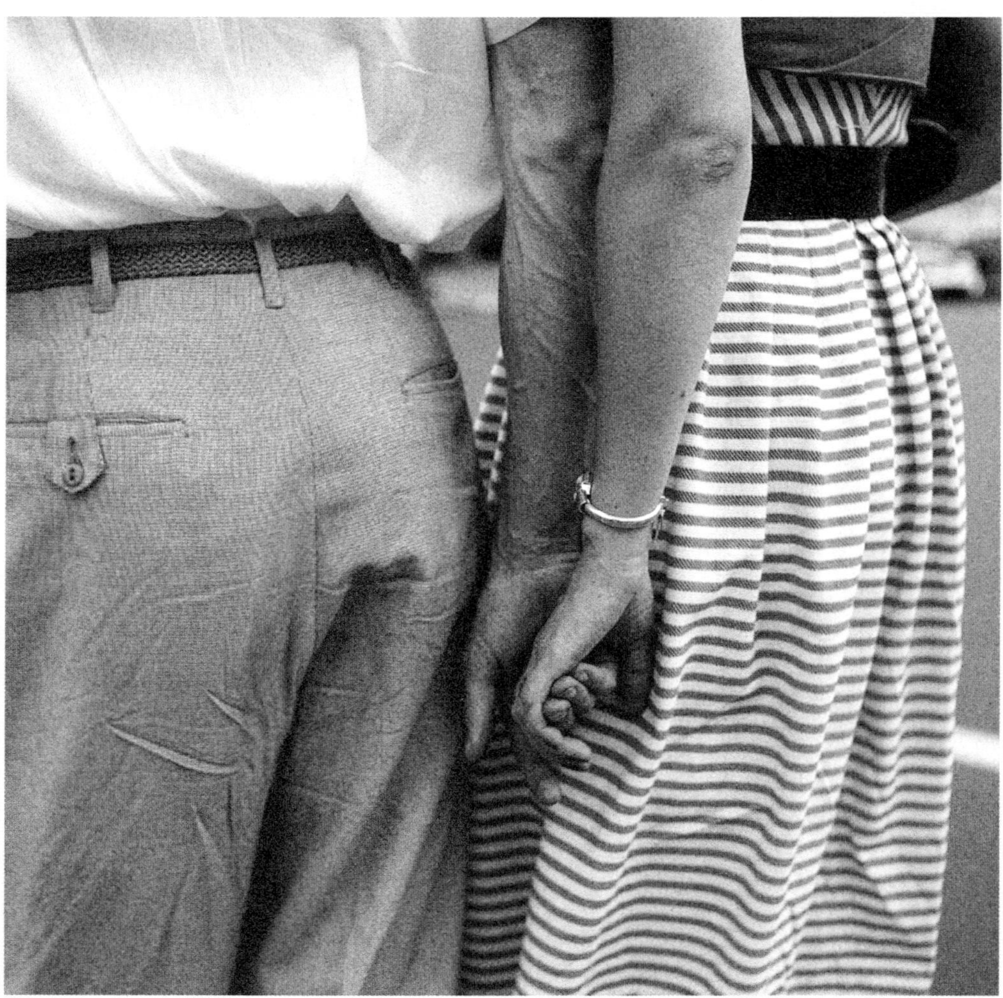

Vivian Maier, *Beach lovers,*
New Jersey, 1953
© Estate of Vivian Maier

campaigning politicians. Though Maier was largely self-taught, she was by no means naive or timid. She attended exhibitions at the Museum of Modern Art and owned dozens of photography books. Despite her industriousness, Maier never exhibited or sold her prints, and she rarely showed them to others; she had no public life, nor did she seek one. Apparently, taking photographs was, for her, an end in itself. When Maier's odd habits and circumspection about her past life raised questions from her employers and young charges, she called herself "a spy," "a mystery woman."

Many of the mysteries of Maier's life were already fathomed by the artist and researcher Pamela Bannos in her scholarly biography of 2017, *Vivian Maier: A Photographer's Life and Afterlife*, so it is not as if her story was completely untold. But given access to the Maloof Collection photographs and documentary material (which Bannos was denied) and an inordinate passion for genealogical detective work, Marks adds considerable detail and color to what is known about Maier's ascetic life. Marks succeeds best in ferreting out new biographical information about Maier's complex family and her previously unidentified photographic subjects. She clarifies the tormented life of Maier's estranged brother Carl, who was diagnosed as schizophrenic. And she identifies portraits of Carola Hemes and Geneva McKenzie, two New York women photographers who may have influenced Maier.

While Marks is a diligent and inventive detective, when she deviates from facts, her interpretations are often clumsy and problematic. She overreaches when, with little evidence, she paints Maier as a civil rights advocate and a protofeminist, or later when she blithely argues that Maier's life as an independent working woman (the title of the French-language edition calls her *une femme libre*, a "free woman") should be seen as a modern-day inspiration. This is a curiously sentimental conclusion for Marks, since her principal goal seems to be to judge Maier's eccentricities and late-life decline—as evidenced by her newspaper hoarding—as aberrant and owed principally to a genetic strain of mental illness traced through her family. Marks even calls in a team of psychoanalysts to retroactively diagnose Maier's traits and judge them against normative behavior. I was reminded of the critic Rose Lichter-Marck's *New Yorker* review of Maloof's 2013 film *Finding Vivian Maier*, in which she wrote, "Stories of difficult women can be unflattering even when they are told in praise. The unconventional choices of women are explained in the language of

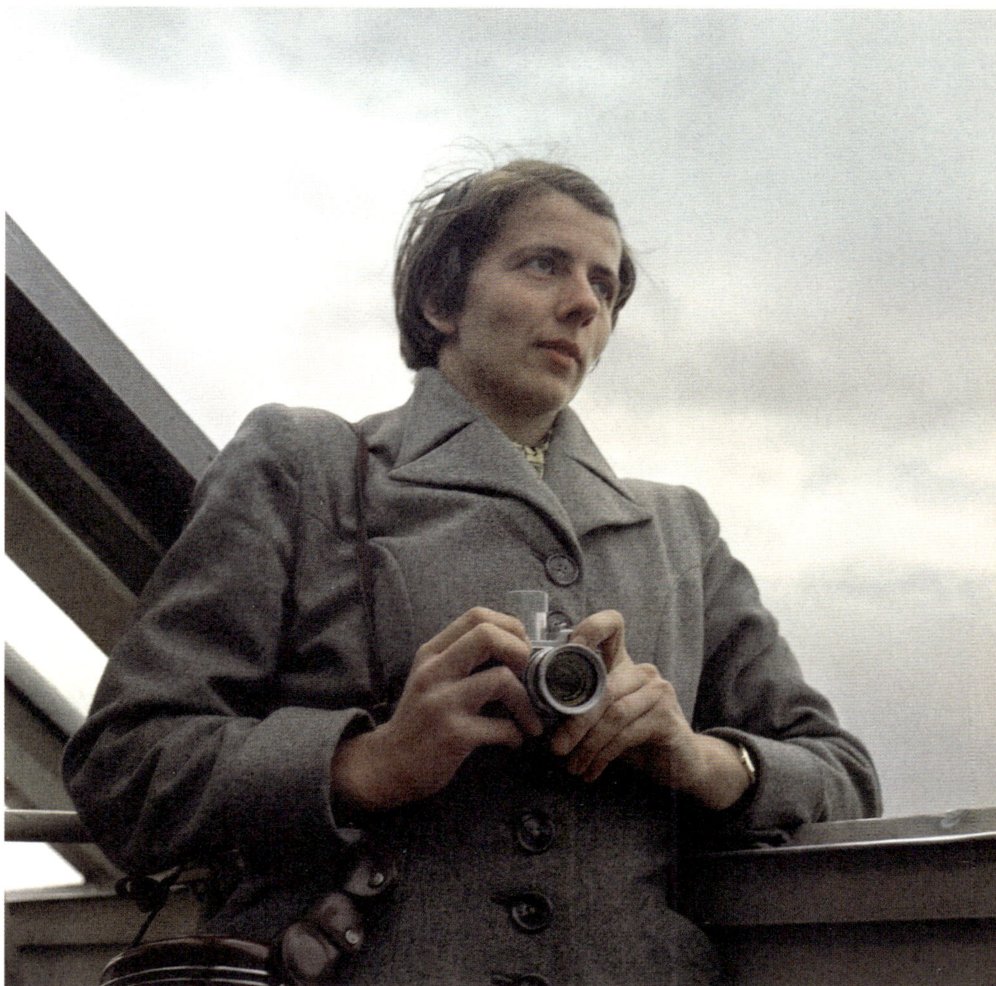

Vivian Maier, *Self-Portrait,* 1958
© Estate of Vivian Maier and courtesy Maloof Collection and Howard Greenberg Gallery, New York

mental illness, trauma, or sexual repression, as symptoms of pathology rather than as an active response to structural challenges or mere preference."

Marks sees endless photographs and accumulations as evidence of pathology, where others may see them as a radical creative preference. Like Andy Warhol, another notorious hoarder, Maier seems to have had a deliberate plan and an alternative methodology for her collecting. Her rapacious assemblings included, according to Marks, dozens of binders of carefully curated newspaper clippings, banal home movies of street scenes, uninteresting landscape views, endless reel-to-reel interviews, copious documentations of graffiti, unassuming family photographs, obsessive celebrity snapshots, and various other personal collections. Against the formalistic demands of the emerging art photography, of which she was clearly aware, and alongside her own vaunted street photography, Maier appears to have been diligently constructing a weirder photographic archive of everyday life in mid-century America. Without privileging the artist's intentions over those of any interested viewer, I would simply note that amid the myriad facts and details assembled by Marks, other, better versions of Vivian Maier remain to be told. —**Brian Wallis**

Marks sees endless photographs and accumulations as evidence of pathology, where others may see them as a radical creative preference.

Óscar Monzón

In 1956, Alison and Peter Smithson, then enfants terribles on the British architecture scene, penned a treatise for *Ark* magazine celebrating the popular art of advertising and effectively collapsing distinctions between lowly and venerated forms of cultural production: "For us it would be the objects on the beaches, the piece of paper blowing about the street, the throw-away object and the pop-package. For today we collect ads."

That last line, effectively also the title of their essay, resonates with an optimism absent from our moment, one saturated in capitalist spectacle, where every surface from street to screen comes with a sales pitch. The Smithsons' treatise is credited with introducing the phrase "Pop art" into the world. In the decades since, there have been endless debates on the highs and lows of advertising as art and the benefits, or cautions, of urban life steeped in media.

Guy Debord, Marshall McLuhan, and Rem Koolhaas, among many others, have all weighed in. The Spanish photographer Óscar Monzón enters this discourse not with words but with images.

His book ***ORDER*** (**RVB, 2021; 120 pages, \$57**), in fact, includes no text (not even page numbers) minus the enigmatic title. If Pop art entreated that we appreciate the beauty in the ubiquitous aesthetic of advertising, Monzón offers global cities full of pathos. A slim, tabloid-sized paperback, *ORDER* is a floppy and slightly unwieldy object. The opening series of black-and-white photographs, each sprawled across a double-page spread, share similar compositions and subjects: individual pedestrians, centered in the frame, walk down the street of a bustling city. An office worker clutches a mobile phone. A man trots with a backpack. A modelesque woman swings a shopping bag. Their eyes are downturned, seemingly shut—sleepwalkers of the metropolis. In later pages, closed eyes are replaced by dark sunglasses.

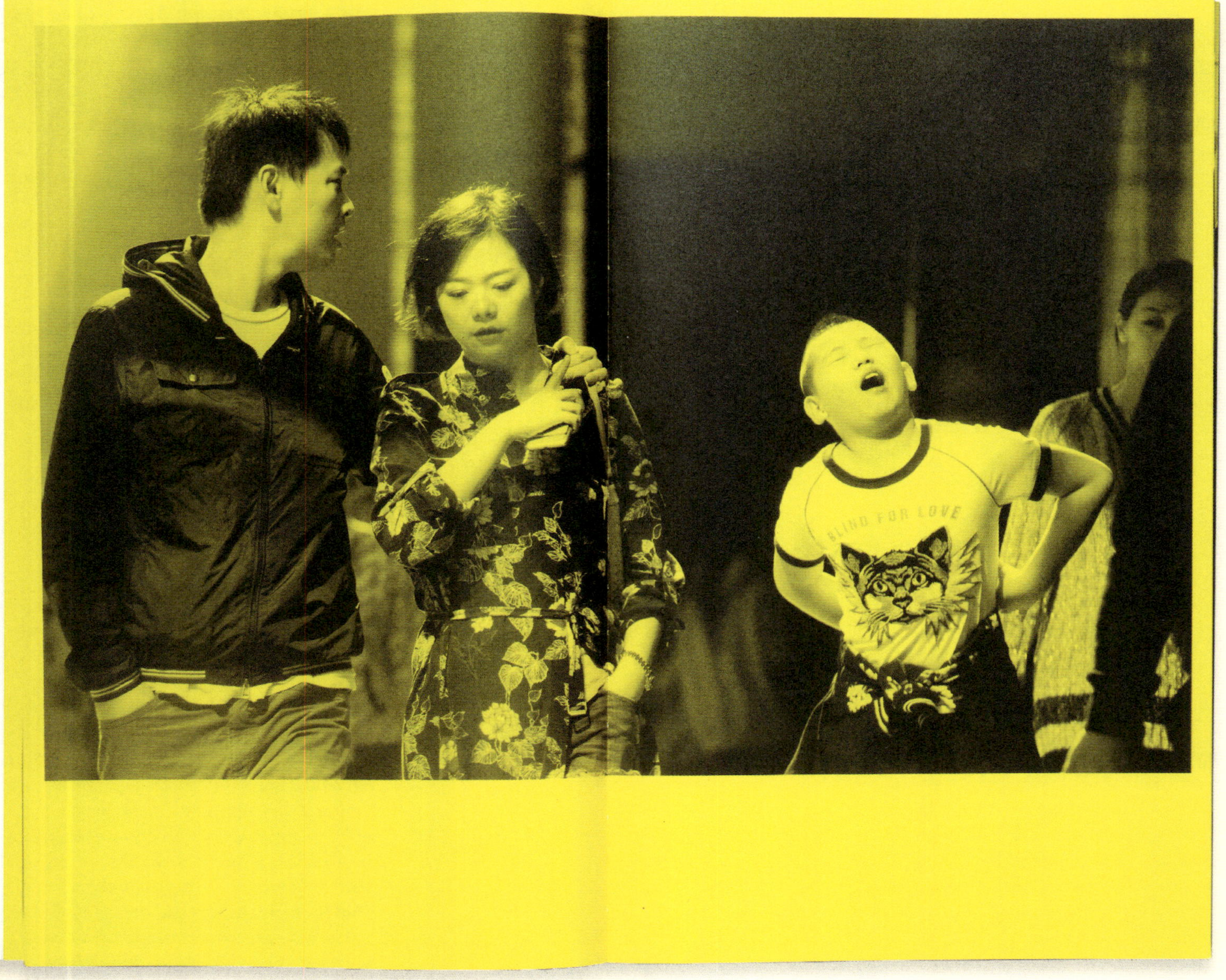

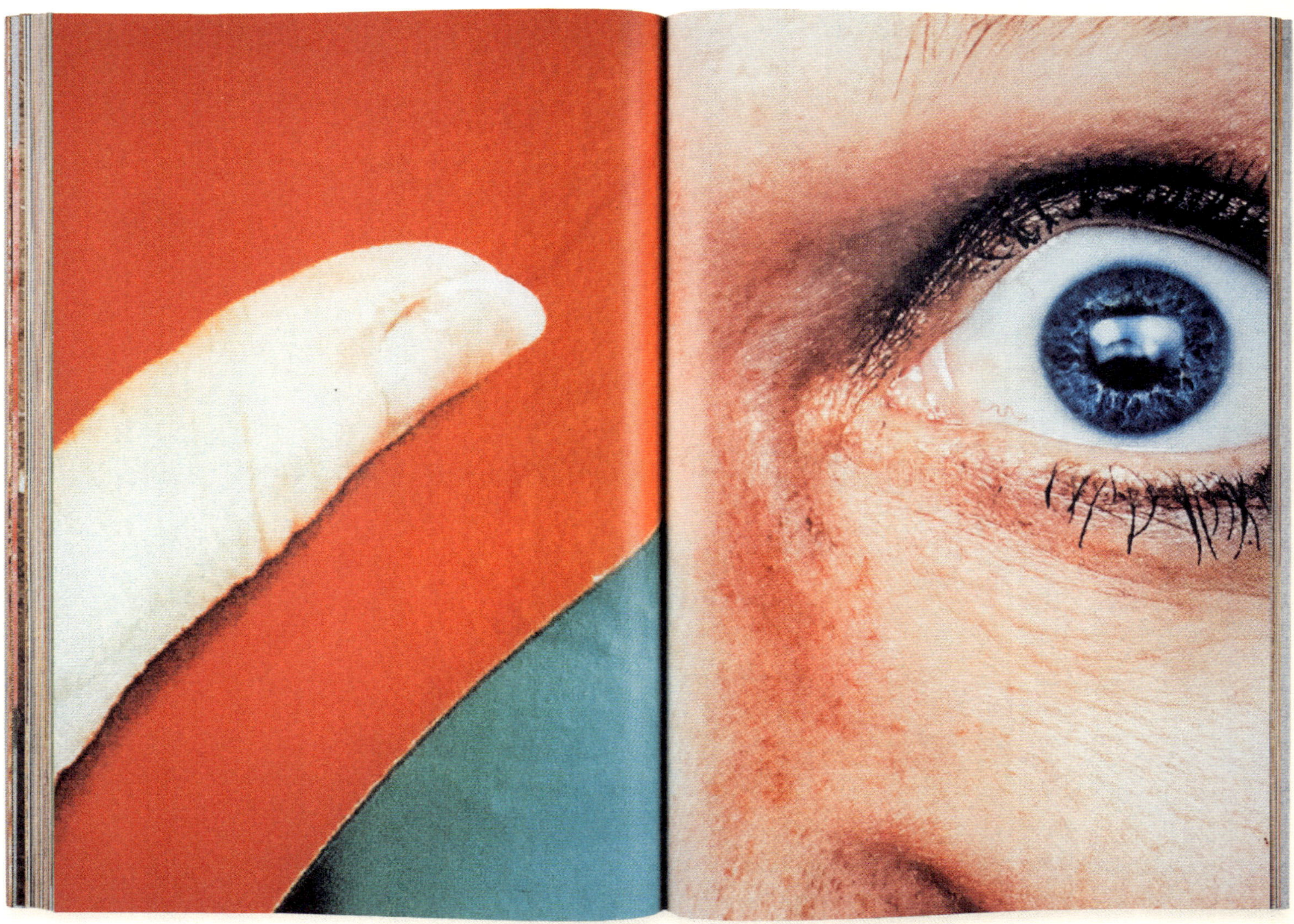

Only advertisements direct their gaze to the camera. One image, printed on a black page, shows an ominous, single eye staring out from a watery gutter, as if the veil of reality has been pulled back and corporate gods are peeking through. In the single, full-bleed color photograph that punctuates the book, a lurid, idol-sized face is reflected in the windshield of a taxi, obscuring its driver. The photographs in *ORDER* were taken between 2014 and 2019 in New York, Tokyo, Hong Kong, Berlin, Rome, and Madrid. This is the smooth space of globalized, capitalized urbanism. Place, defined by retail storefronts and marketing campaigns, is anyplace.

ORDER concludes with a series of black-and-white duotones presented on bright, canary-yellow pages, where subjects, no longer blind recipients, broadcast their own messages via their clothing's mantralike slogans—STAY REAL. BLIND FOR LOVE. OBEY. One image in this section stands out: A protester is being carried away by two men and a police officer. In her hands is what we might assume to be a protest sign, turned backward, its words obscured. Unlike the subjects on previous pages who docilely move through cities, blind and acquiescing to the media swirling around them, she alone presents a point of resistance. But then is quickly absorbed back into the crowd.
—**Mimi Zeiger**

Anna Stüdeli

Anna Stüdeli's work exudes an uneasy tension. Concerned with our basic instincts and how they come into play within social interaction, she evokes the repulsive in the attractive and vice versa in order to explore the ambiguity of our impulses and motivations in relation to our surroundings.

Born in Switzerland and living between Zurich and Hamburg, Stüdeli produces mainly sculptures and installations out of plaster, latex, horsehair, and other materials. ***PRIMAL* (Edition Patrick Frey, 2021; 156 pages, $50)**, her first photobook, is the result of the artist's ongoing reflection on commercial photography and how it generates demand by seducing and teasing consumers. Stüdeli has assembled an archive of more than 1,200 close-ups she took of billboard ads and advertising posters. In 2017, she used some of these images in her video installation *Appetite*; *PRIMAL* contains a selection of over 120 of them.

The book presents the close-ups as full bleeds, mostly in pairs on opposite pages, or sometimes individually as full spreads. Stripped of any context and the semiotics that are the prerequisites for advertisement, Stüdeli's often unsettling close-ups are devoid of their original message. Through zooming and radical cropping, Stüdeli dissects and negates the perfectionistic visual language of ad campaigns, which often promote unrealistic body types or sexualize basic commodities. Her photographs draw attention to bizarre, comical, and grotesque details that are at odds with the whitewashed and glossy aesthetic of most advertising. As Urs Stahel writes in his accompanying essay, Stüdeli "operates at the frontiers of obscenity, with disgust, at the switch point between decent and indecent."

This perspective is further amplified through Stüdeli's peculiar juxtapositions: an image of reptile skin is paired with that of wrinkled human skin; a sausage end depicted next to what seems to be the fragment of a woman's leg is followed by a full spread of a cow's udder. Stüdeli focuses on wrinkles, liver spots, scars. Recurring motifs such as open mouths, tongues, ears, eyes, hands, and fingers become allegories for our senses and the way we relate to the world—consumed with desire to consume. Some of the details Stüdeli captured appear completely abstract. Some highlight the qualities of the original: halftone dots, seams, creases, and scratches.

Stüdeli puts an emphasis on the latency of images and the fact that they might convey something not necessarily intended. With *PRIMAL*, the artist picks up on the Situationists' satirical critique of consumer culture and mass media. Stüdeli's approach is similar to that of the so-called rephotographers and appropriation artists such as Richard Prince, Gretchen Bender, Sherrie Levine, and Vikky Alexander, who began in the late 1970s and early '80s to copy, isolate, enlarge, and juxtapose (fragments of) existing photographs in order to question concepts of authorship as well as the dynamics of media dissemination and the alienating effects of capitalism.

Stüdeli, however, seems more interested in the potential of the image to reveal an elementary truth. She shows that even the idealized and polished contains, and is driven by, something more basic, raw, and primal.
—**Daniel Berndt**

Samuel Fosso

Before Samuel Fosso—an artist of remarkable talent and wit—achieved international fame, he operated a commercial studio in Bangui, the capital of the Central African Republic. Studio Photo Nationale, which Fosso opened in 1975 at just thirteen years old, subsidized the artist's experiments in self-portraiture. During the day, he tended to his clients, slyly capturing their sensibilities against a spare backdrop. At night, he turned the camera to himself and transformed his studio into what the Nigerian curator Okwui Enwezor termed "a theater of fantasy." Possibility drives Fosso's practice; his images taunt fixed notions of identity.

Studio Photo Nationale (**Sébastien Girard/MEP, 2021; 76 pages, €120**), a book of Fosso's commercial studio portraits from the 1980s, reveals the artist applying his philosophy of self-invention beyond himself. These images are not just a paean to Fosso's archive, which was almost destroyed in 2014 after a break-in at his studio in Bangui, they also gesture toward a level of sensitivity that marks his later work. Fosso, it seems, always possessed an enduring belief in African people's abilities to shape-shift.

Published on the occasion of his retrospective touring in Europe, the delicate volume is housed in a slipcase with a black-

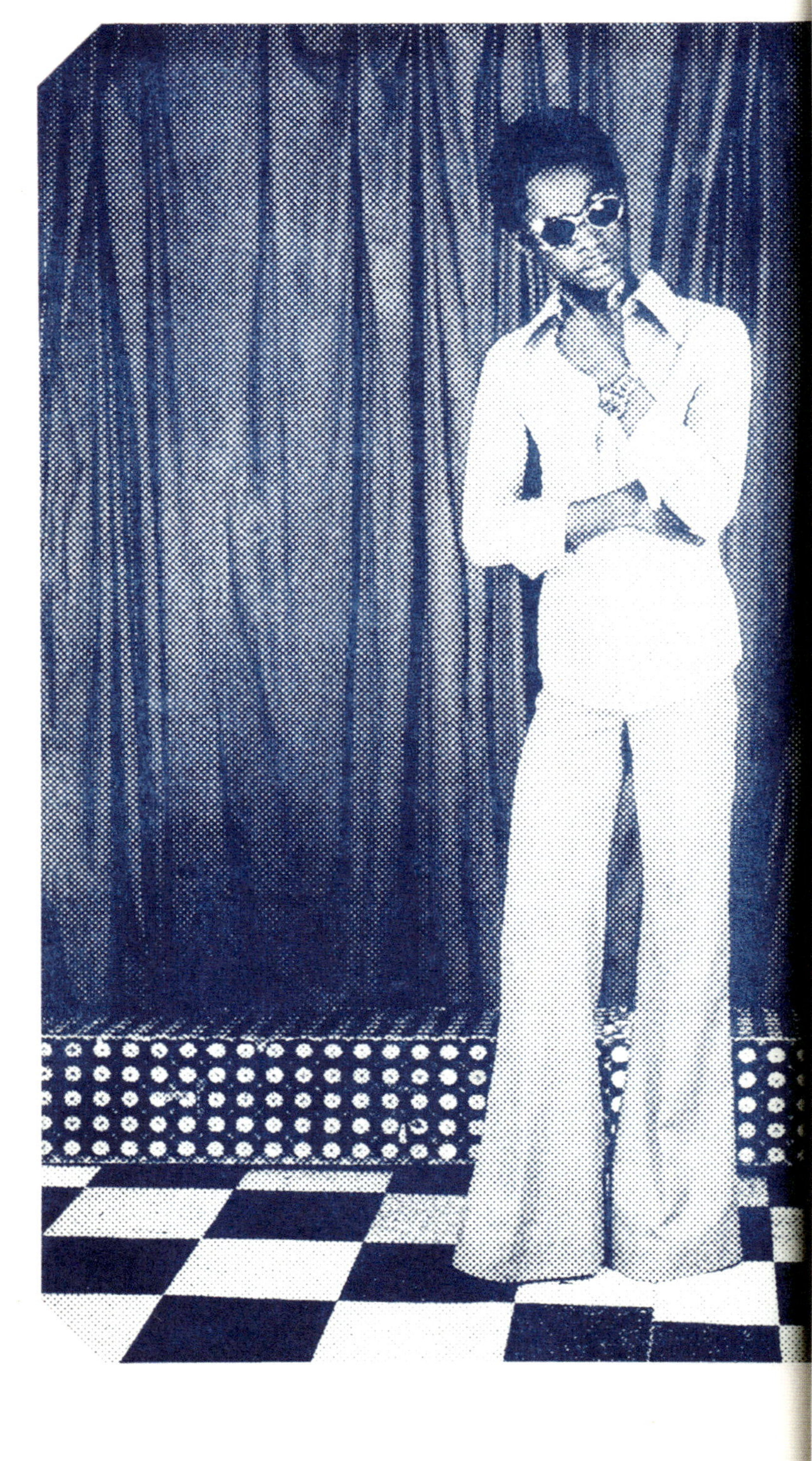

Cover and interior of Samuel Fosso, *Studio Photo Nationale* (Sébastien Girard/MEP, 2021)

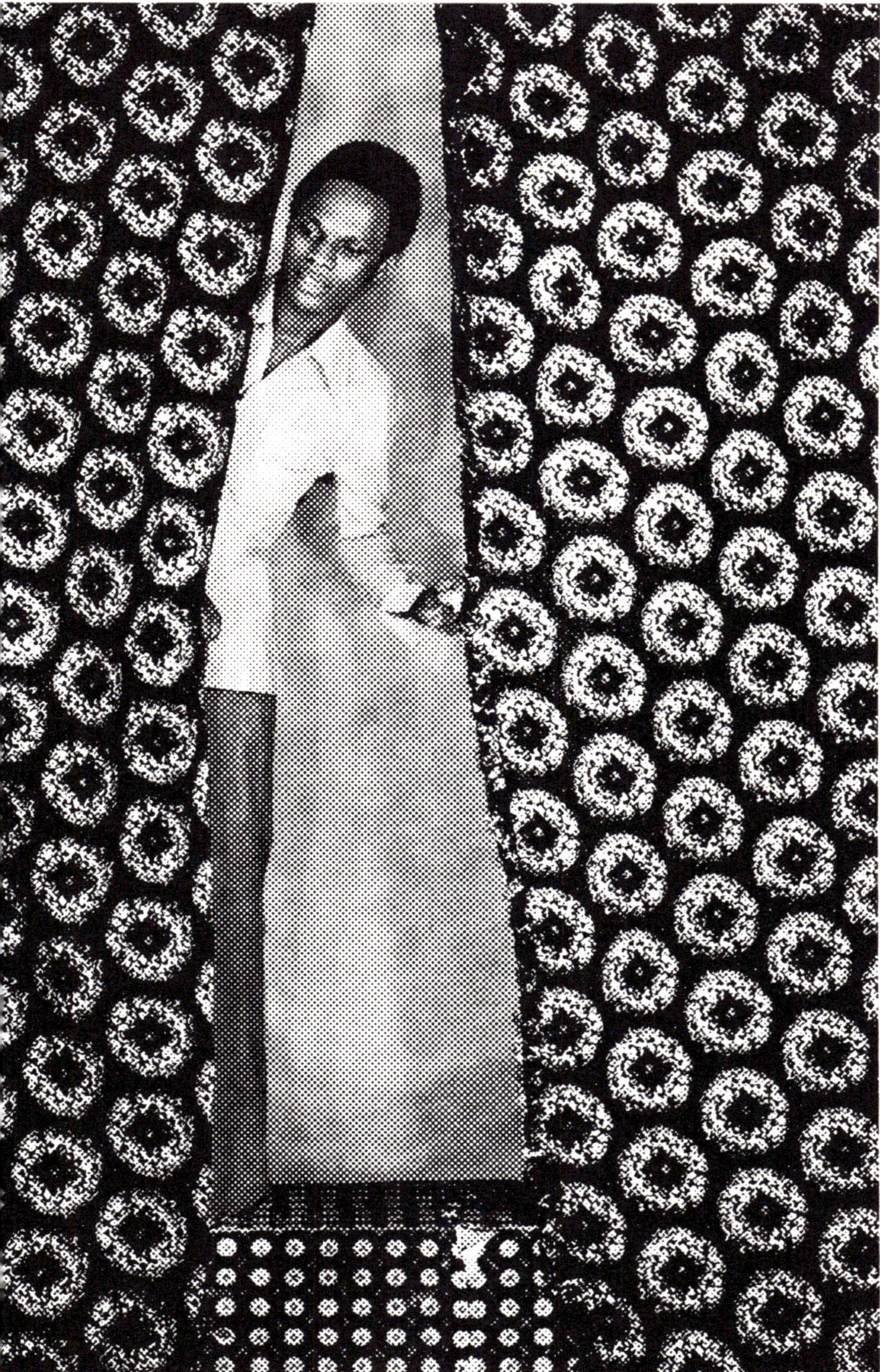

and-white photograph of Fosso. His youthful face peeks out from behind a curtain emblazoned with a loud pattern. Beneath the photograph, his name and that of his studio appear in an unfussy black font. The artist makes cameos throughout the risograph-printed book: on the cover, posing in sunglasses; on the first page, beaming from behind the studio's front desk; and later, staring stoically into the distance. But he is not the center of attention—not exactly.

Studio Photo Nationale is a quiet experience. There are no words to be found within its Japanese-style folded and spiral-bound pages. The black-and-white images sit perfectly centered, accompanied only by a blue page number. The portraits of Fosso's clients must, therefore, speak for themselves. And *speak* they do. They are slick, playful, mesmerizing, and humorous. Couples share effortless affection. Groups pose with feverish verve. Everyone is well-dressed. This is a photo-album of history's coolest family.

Visual affinities abound within the pages of *Studio Photo Nationale*: pairs of girls, women, youthful boys, et cetera. Take the two men on page twenty-four, one cradles a radio while the other sits cross-legged, staring seriously into the camera. Or the women on page thirty-eight, posing defiantly behind a fence. Studio props also reappear. The patterns coalesce, and you begin to see the tradition from which Fosso's studio portraits follow. I'm thinking, most obviously, of the portraitists Malick Sidibé and Seydou Keïta, whose photographs captured the vibrant lifestyles of Malians in the decades preceding Fosso's studio opening. Perhaps, then, the greatest gift of this archival project is preservation—not just of Fosso's older work but of his community's spirit.
—**Lovia Gyarkye**

Nona Faustine

The New York–based photographer Nona Faustine bares her clenched white teeth, gritting hard as she lunges forward, attempting the impossible task of toppling a set of classical architectural columns. Her white heel is firmly planted and directed toward the pillar, the object of its potential metaphor: foundational white patriarchy. Appearing on the rough cloth cover of Faustine's first monograph, **White Shoes (MACK, 2021; 72 pages, $60)**, the drama of her action is a somber invitation to step into another reality and join Faustine in the labor of surfacing history, marking its trace, and upholding those who have been made unknown.

White Shoes is the title for Faustine's series of self-portraits—oftentimes nude—

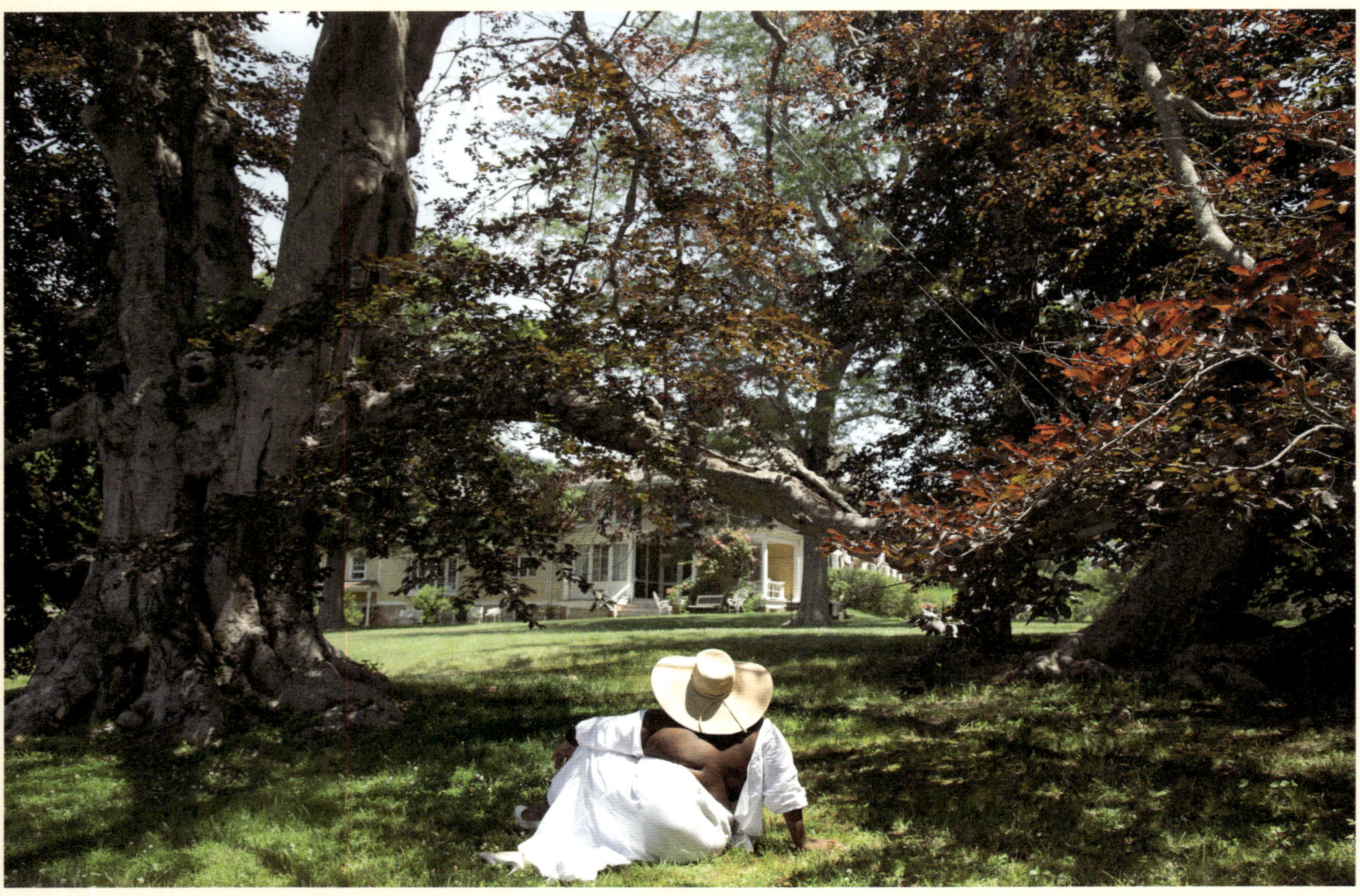

in which she contorts herself into various poses across the New York landscape. The white heels act as a transporting talisman, allowing Faustine to commune with Black ancestors she has recovered through extensive research and those that are beyond the archive. Each image envisions her connection to geographies and the past: Faustine's stunning brown figure marks sites where histories of enslavement once occurred but have subsequently been effaced.

The book features writings by Faustine, Jessica Lanay, Seph Rodney, and Pamela Sneed, along with an interview with the artist. Rodney, for example, outlines how Faustine's nude self-possession asserts new ways of knowing the world. Her powerful and vulnerable self-portraits are in dialogue with earlier generations of radical body-performance art by Eleanor Antin, Eiko Otake, Adrian Piper, and Ana Mendieta as well as the photographs of Laura Aguilar, Carrie Mae Weems, Renée Cox, and Carla Williams.

When Faustine mobilizes the hypervisibility of her large, dark-skinned figure, she confronts a visual culture steeped with colorism and fat phobia. Such a body has been involuntarily ungendered, violently stereotyped, discriminated against, discarded, and censored. The physicality of this book, with its exquisite color reproductions, directly counters the elision of Faustine's flesh—the spectrum of brown hues in her folds, rolls, nipples, dimples, and buttocks—from our cultural and institutional lives.

An incisive, poetic title, printed in light gray, informs each image like a reverberating echo: *Of My Body I Will Make Monuments in Your Honor*. The hum of Faustine's writing and photographs deeply affects the viewer and offers an experience of time outside of linear chronologies. Lanay's essay in part uses the grammatical concepts of the theorist Tina Campt to read Faustine's photographs as a fantastical future that hasn't yet happened but must, a future that will collectively counteract the erasure of Black life.

White Shoes unveils a kind of love letter to New York, extending the lineage of photobooks that use the city as a recurring character and backdrop. Faustine's commitment to her home, her multigenerational Black matriarchal family, and the people who live and once lived in the city manifests here as a Black feminist text that expertly intertwines love, care, and research, with a scathing critique. Faustine is a conjurer who helps the past haunt us, insisting it cannot be erased.
—**Delphine Sims**

Spotlight

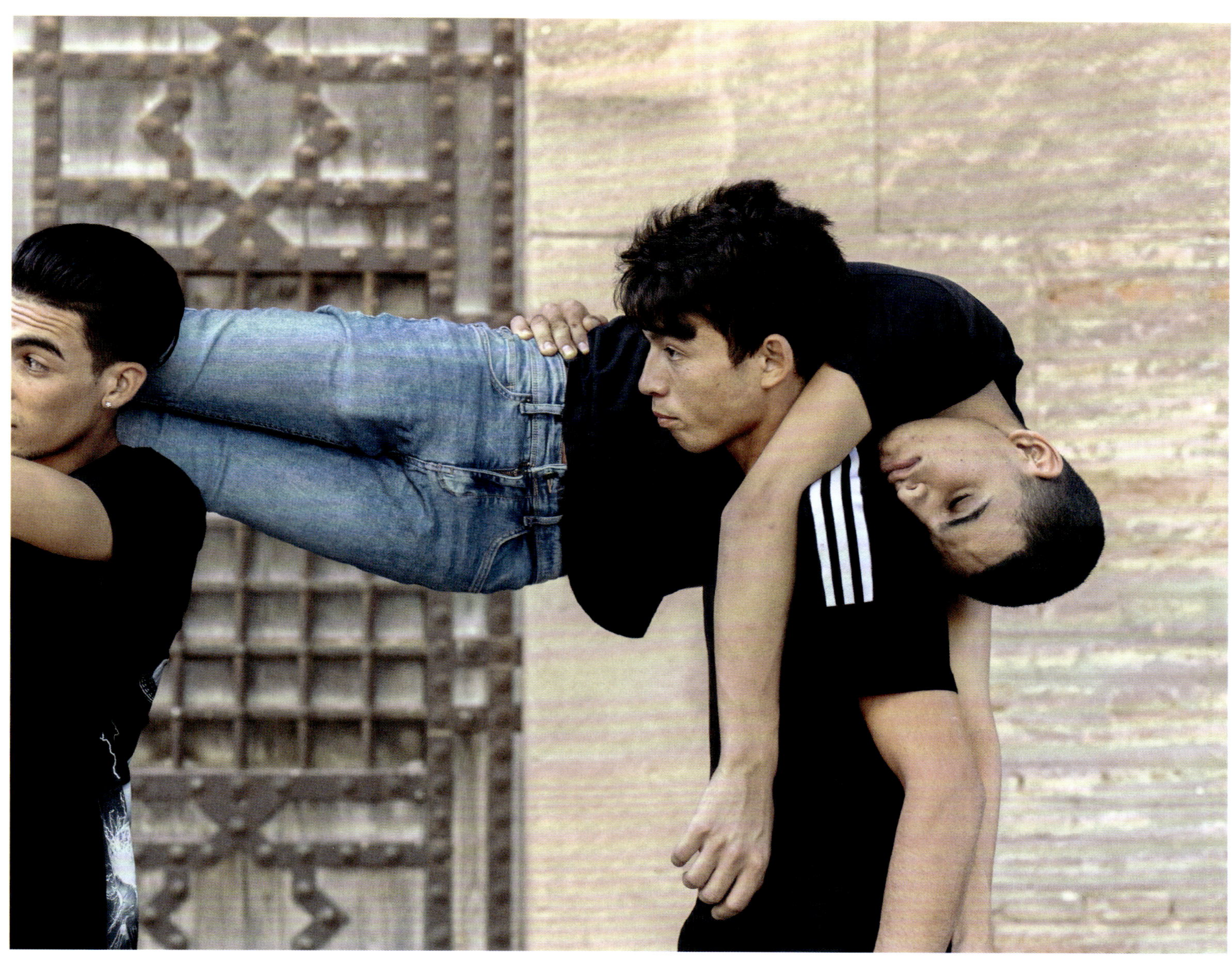

In his recent series, Felipe Romero Beltrán collaborates with young immigrant men navigating legal limbo in Spain.
Kaelen Wilson-Goldie

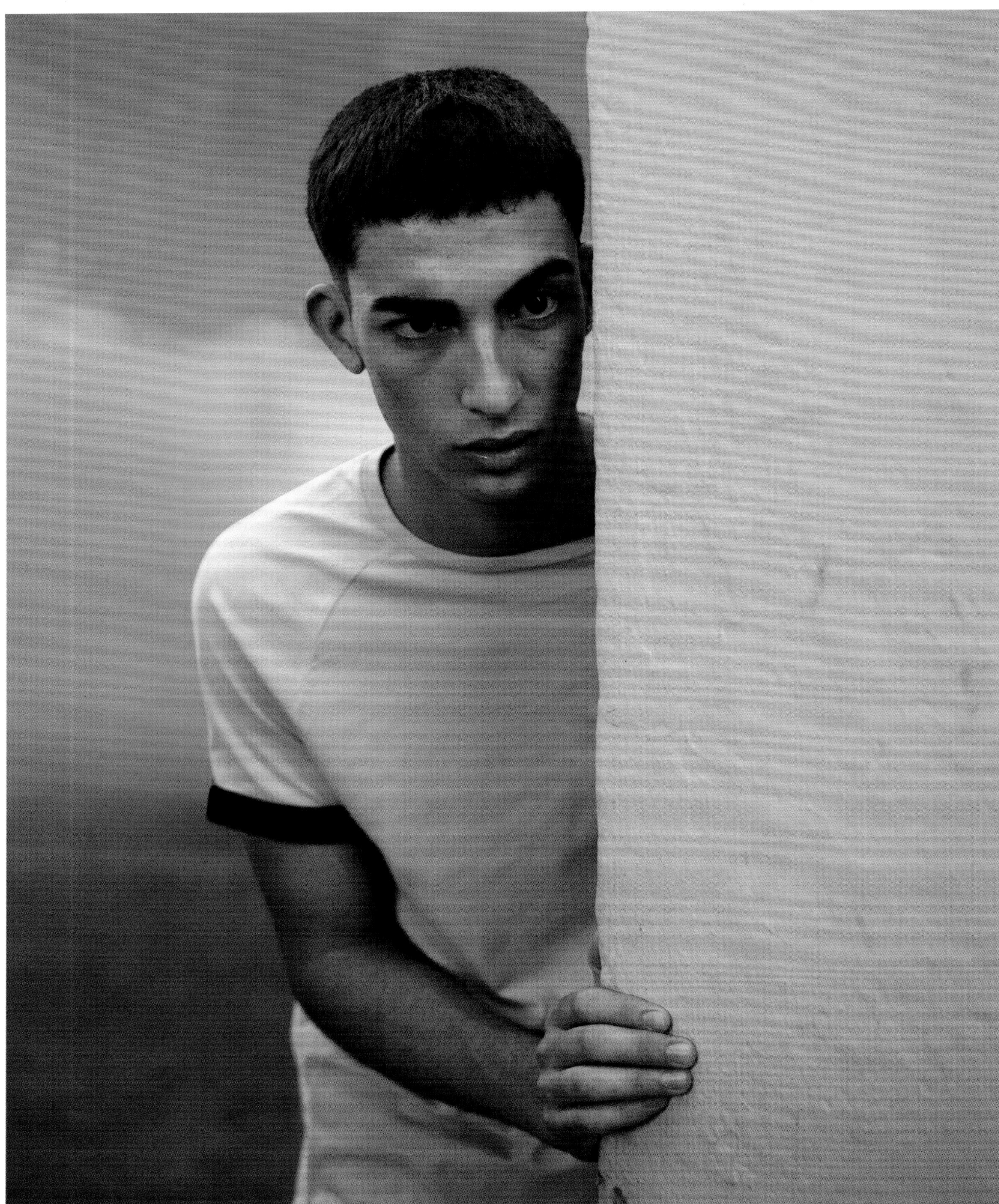

Previous page:
Bilal's body is carried by
his friends after a fainting
episode

This page:
Youssef's escape route

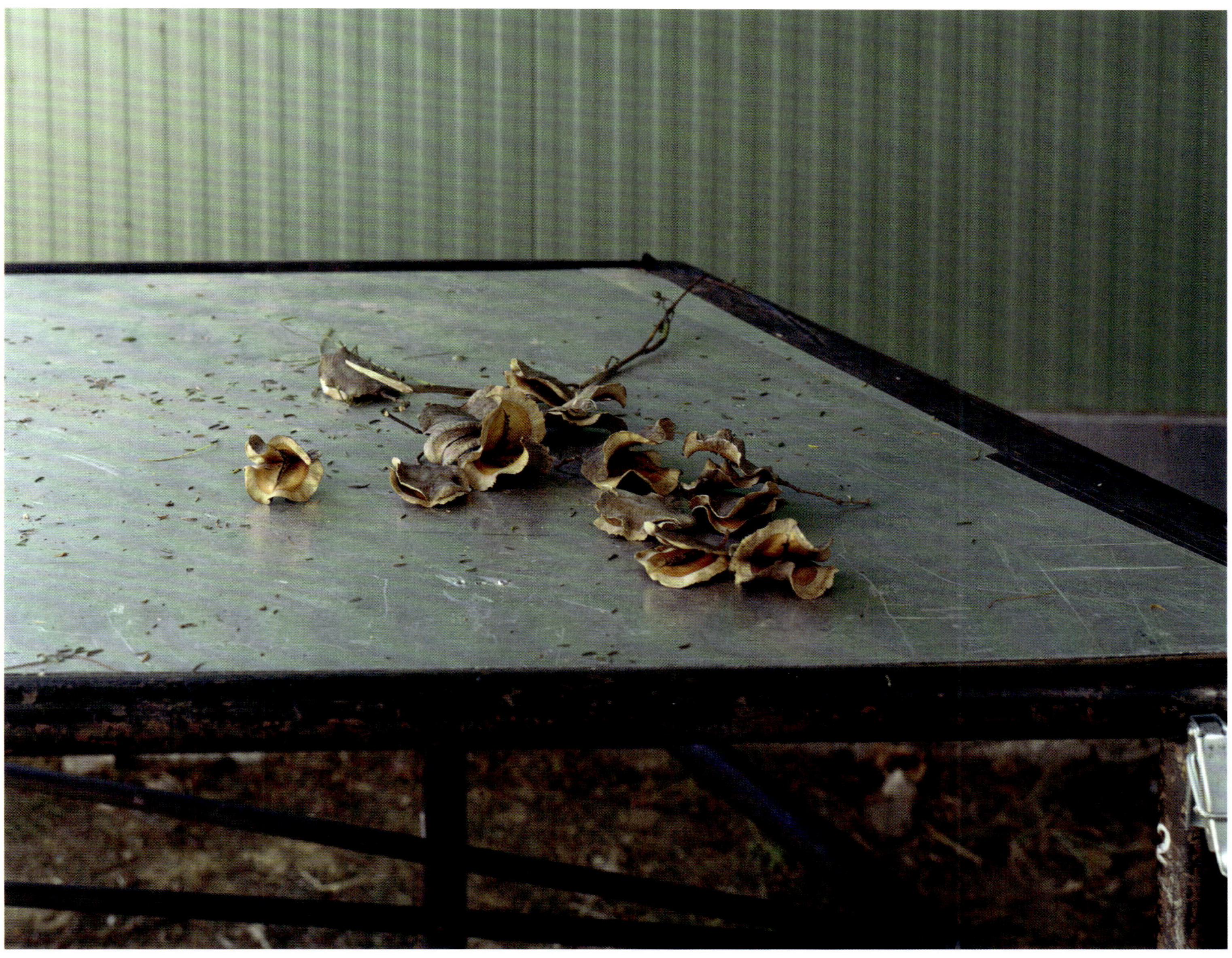

Found objects at a refuge center

The southern Spanish city of Seville offers an utterly excessive amalgamation of Moorish architecture, Gothic iconography, and enough religious fervor to put a saint (or a saint's name) on nearly every corner. In the photographs of Felipe Romero Beltrán, those details of historical layers and visual textures appear muted and subdued, distilled down to the corner of a bright yellow wall, an old column swallowed by concrete, or the mere glimpse of intricate woodwork on a heavy door. For a few years now, Romero Beltrán has been working on a series of images and related videos, titled *Dialect* (2020–ongoing), delving into the routines, memories, and experiences of a small group of young immigrants who crossed into Spain from Morocco as minors and are living in a refuge center, awaiting the normalization of their legal status.

The photographs include ruminative still lifes (blackened tomatoes, dried leaves on a table) and architectural curios (a painted-over pattern of bricks, resonant place names like Abu Yacub) as well as lively portraits of the young men (Youssef Elhafidi, Hamza Gharnili, and Bilal Siasse, among others) who appear, by turns, bored, exuberant, and reflective of their circumstances. The videos, more didactic in nature, document the palpable struggle that Romero Beltrán's subjects endure when they try to read aloud from the first few pages of Spain's immigration law, the prose leaden and opaque in any language. The remarkable sensitivity with which Romero Beltrán captures the lives of these young men—enmeshed as they are in the structures of the refuge center, the city of Seville, and the wider politicization of illegal migration to Spain—may have something to do with his own path, often precarious, from South America to Europe via a major detour to the Middle East.

It's not that you can adequately compare the Colombian civil war to the Palestinian-Israeli conflict and say that one is more dangerous than the other. It's just that if you grew up accustomed to the forms of violence exchanged between, say, far-right paramilitaries and the left-wing

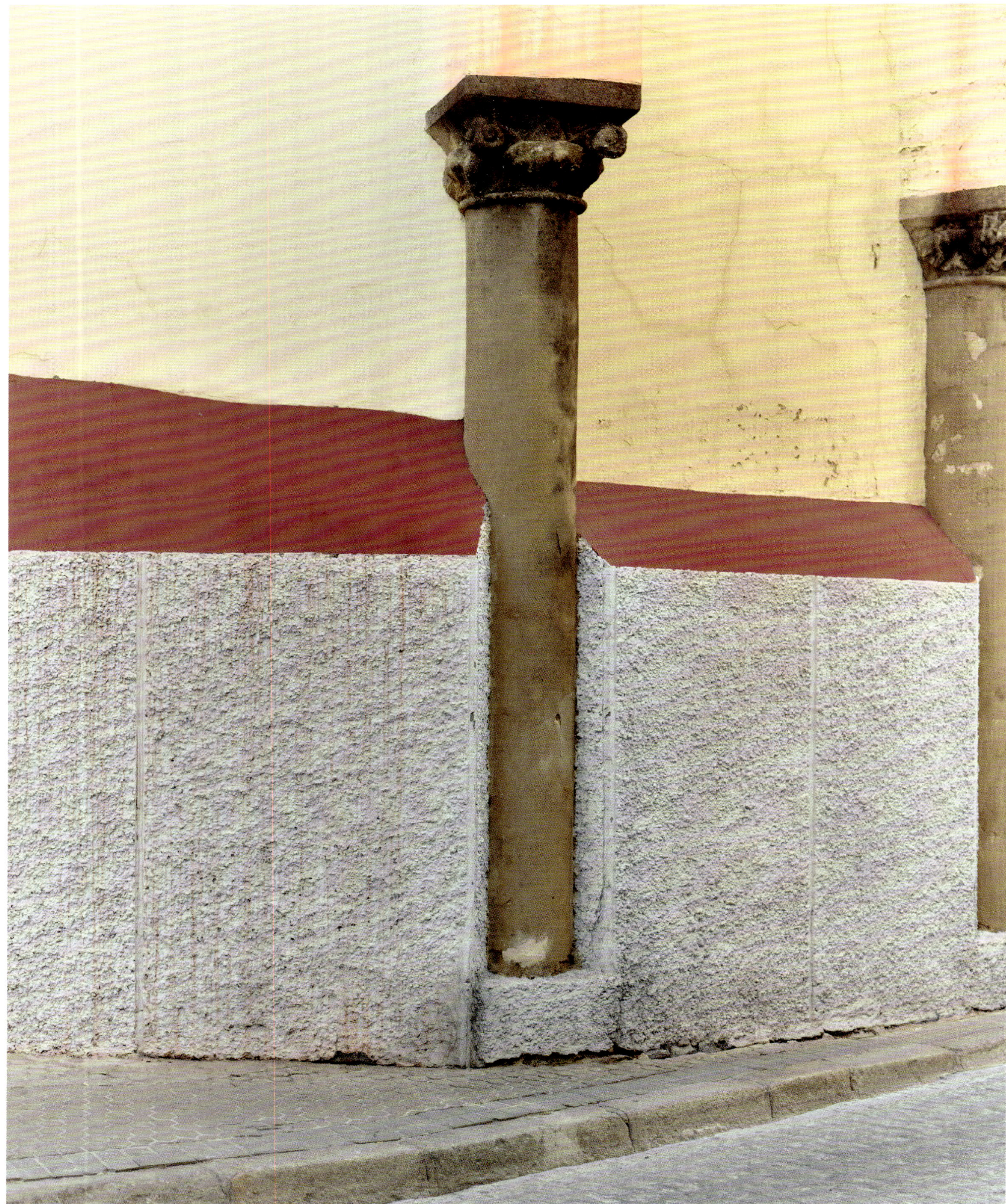

This page:
Path to the refuge center

Opposite:
Hamza arrives

militant group FARC, then you might not necessarily experience fear or even trepidation as an initial response to the idea of studying at a storied art school in Jerusalem. That's how it was for Romero Beltrán, who was born and raised in Bogotá, arrived at the Bezalel Academy of Arts and Design in 2014, and spent a year and half there taking quizzical black-and-white pictures of blocked streets and barricaded houses in the middle of a territorial (and existential) struggle whose contours shifted without warning on a nearly daily basis.

West Bank (2014), the project that Romero Beltrán embarked on during his time at Bezalel, detailing the brutality and absurdity of imposing borderlines in labyrinthine urban environments, may not have been the work that catapulted him to international attention, but it did mark a crucial turning point. After Jerusalem, Romero Beltrán's formidable training in classical documentary photography—which began at the Motivarte School of Photography, in Buenos Aires,

The sensitivity with which he captures the lives of these young men may have something to do with his own path from South America to Europe.

a crucible of Argentinean photojournalism, and continues in Madrid, where he is currently writing a dissertation on the documentary tradition—expanded outward to embrace elements of performance and conceptual art. *Dialect*, with its insistence on complexity, theatrics, and mystery, has less in common with photojournalistic projects on asylum and illegal migration into Europe than it does with critical and philosophical inquiries such as Yto Barrada's *A Life Full of Holes: The Strait Project* (1998–2004), Hassan Khan's video installation *Jewel* (2010), and Bouchra Khalili's *The Mapping Journey Project* (2008–11), all of which predate the current refugee crisis by several years.

Romero Beltrán first met the subjects of *Dialect* during a theater workshop, part of a project on inclusion, organized by the mother of his then girlfriend, now fiancée. His soon-to-be mother-in-law invited Romero Beltrán to speak with the group about his own experience as a migrant in Spain. Learning he was a photographer, some of the participants

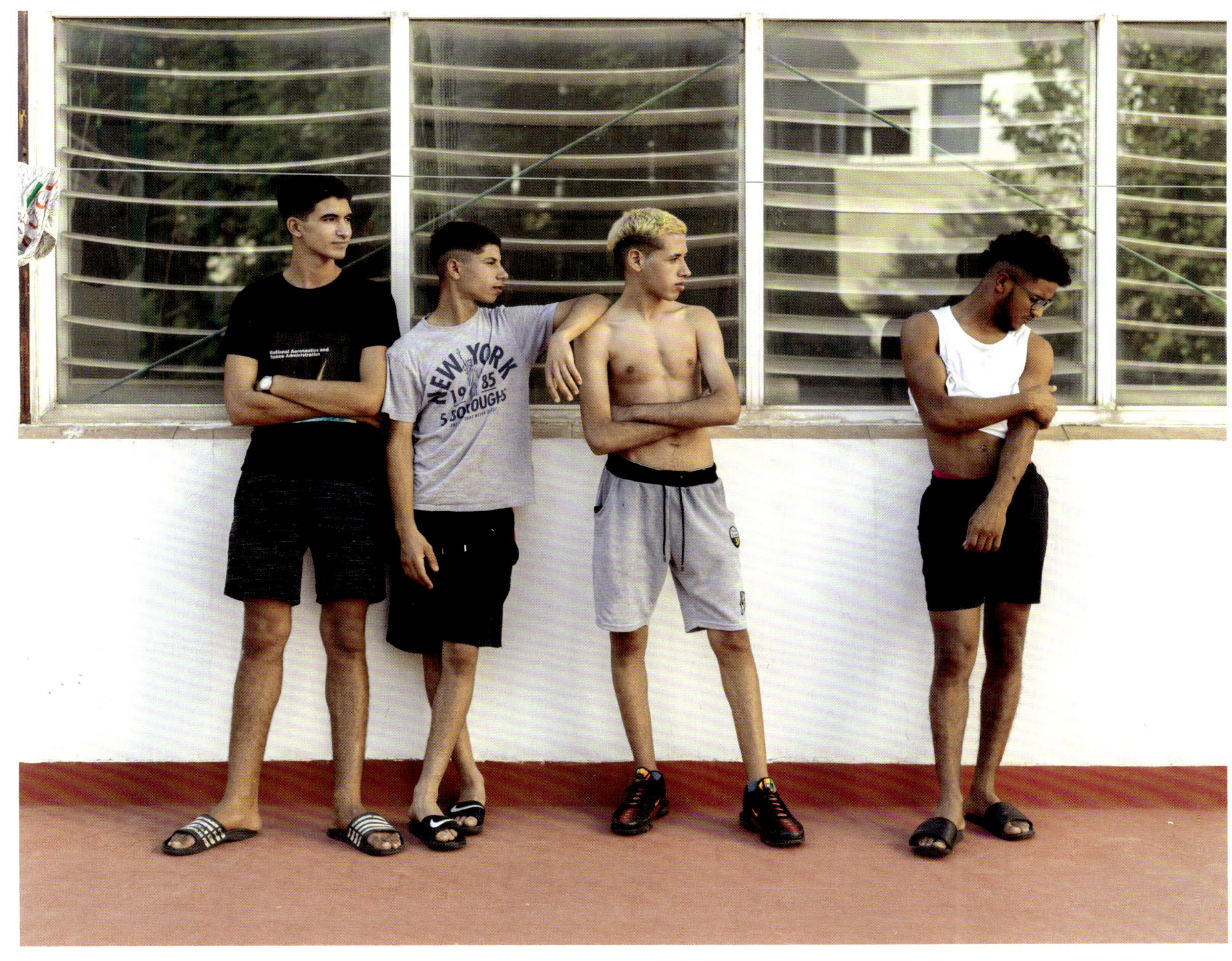

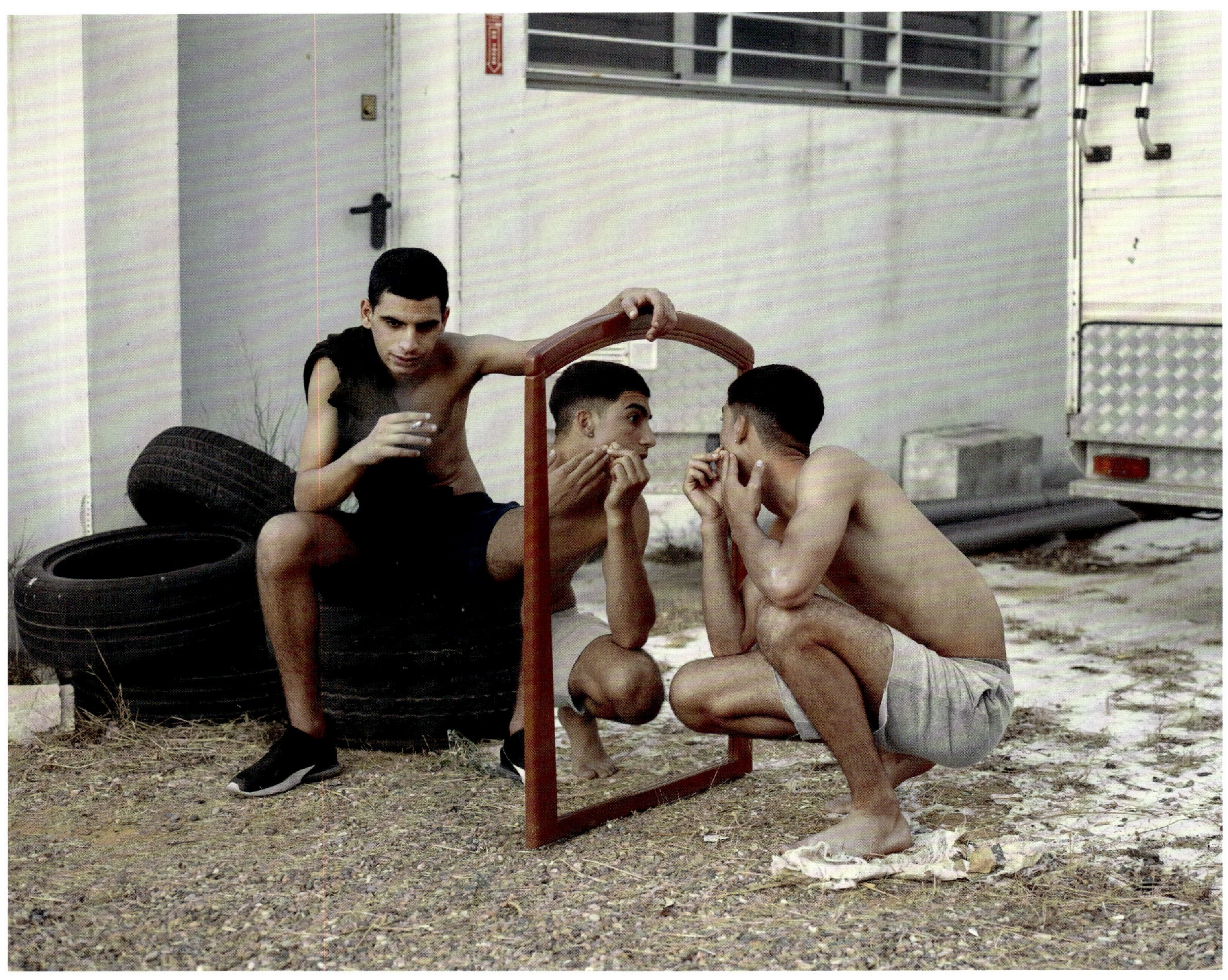

asked him to take a few pictures that they could use on social media and send home to their families. The boys were all teenagers at the time. Romero Beltrán's collaboration with them evolved into an artwork as they entered adulthood.

Rather than presenting types, tropes, or tragic cases, Romero Beltrán's images introduce viewers to the humorous quirks and wondrous specificities of Youssef, Hamza, Bilal, and other young men, named and almost knowable characters who, moreover, have a say in how the work is made and shown. Romero Beltrán always photographs with a digital camera and shares his pictures with his subjects. If they don't like them, he trashes them. The ethics of how they work together are dynamic and sometimes complicated. But in a world flooded with depictions of atrocity, they are sound.

Romero Beltrán's series has grown beyond documentary to include staged pictures not only of images that the young men didn't like and decided to repeat, but also of their past experiences, their dreams. One of the most striking photographs in the series shows the body of Bilal draped over the shoulders of two friends reenacting a moment when Bilal fainted during his journey from Tangier to Seville. *Dialect* has given its subjects a chance to relive some of the more difficult moments in their young lives, and, in doing so, in remaking the droop of a young man's hips, the fall of his arm, the sight of his worried brow smoothing out, transform those moments into gestures of real beauty, of tension being poetically undone by novel forms of collective support.

Kaelen Wilson-Goldie is a regular contributor to *Aperture* and *Artforum*.

Felipe Romero Beltrán is the winner of the 2022 Aperture Portfolio Prize. His solo exhibition of *Dialect* will be on view at Baxter St at the Camera Club of New York in summer 2022.

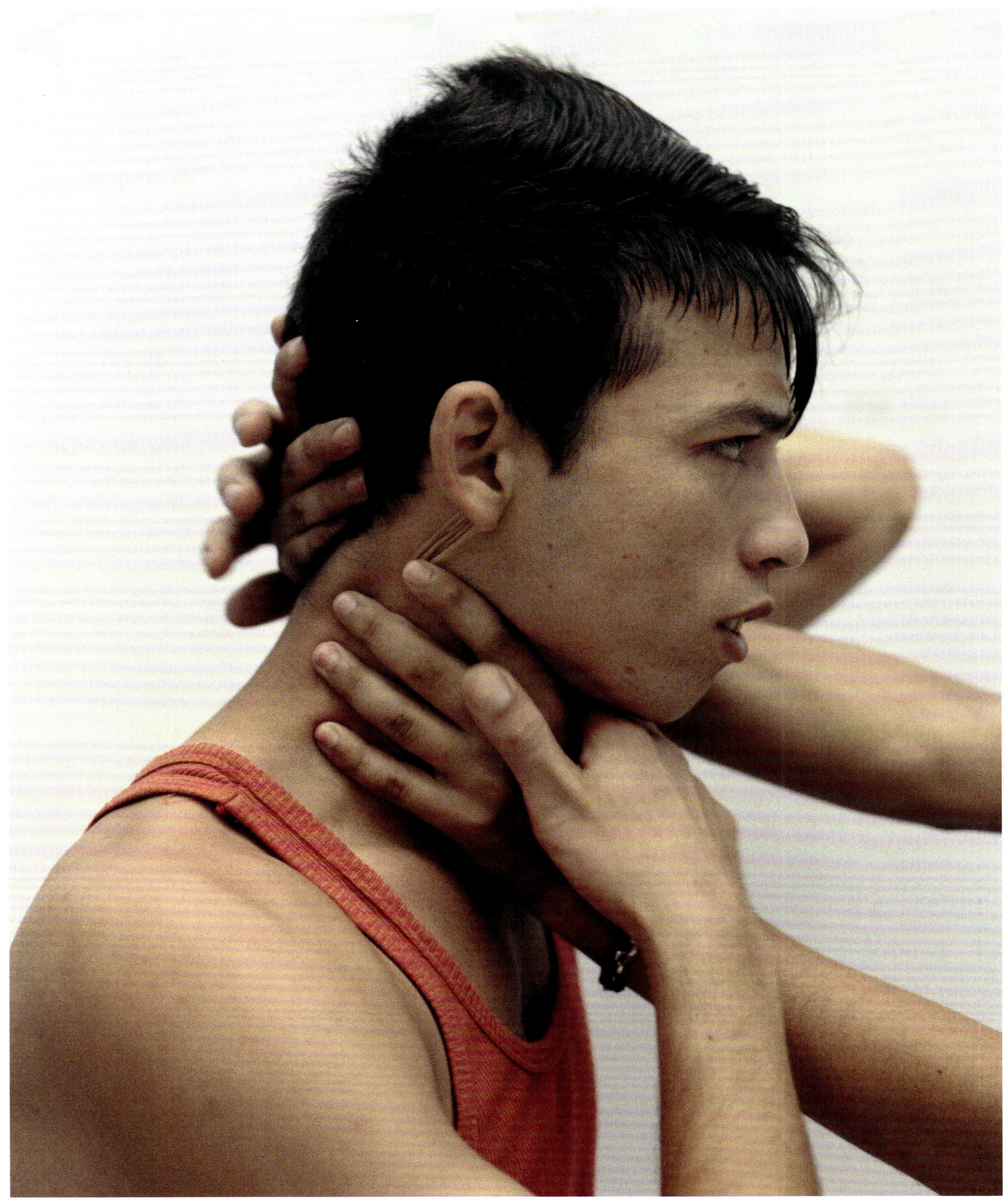

Fight between Hamza and Aziz. **All photographs from the series** *Dialect* **Seville, 2020–22**
Courtesy the artist

Endnote
Jim Jarmusch

During the pandemic, with productions canceled or stalled, the acclaimed filmmaker Jim Jarmusch edited down hundreds of the photo-based collages he's been making over the years and assembled them into a book, *Some Collages* (2021)—discovering along the way that the principles of collage, an intuitive, spontaneous form, are at the heart of all he does.

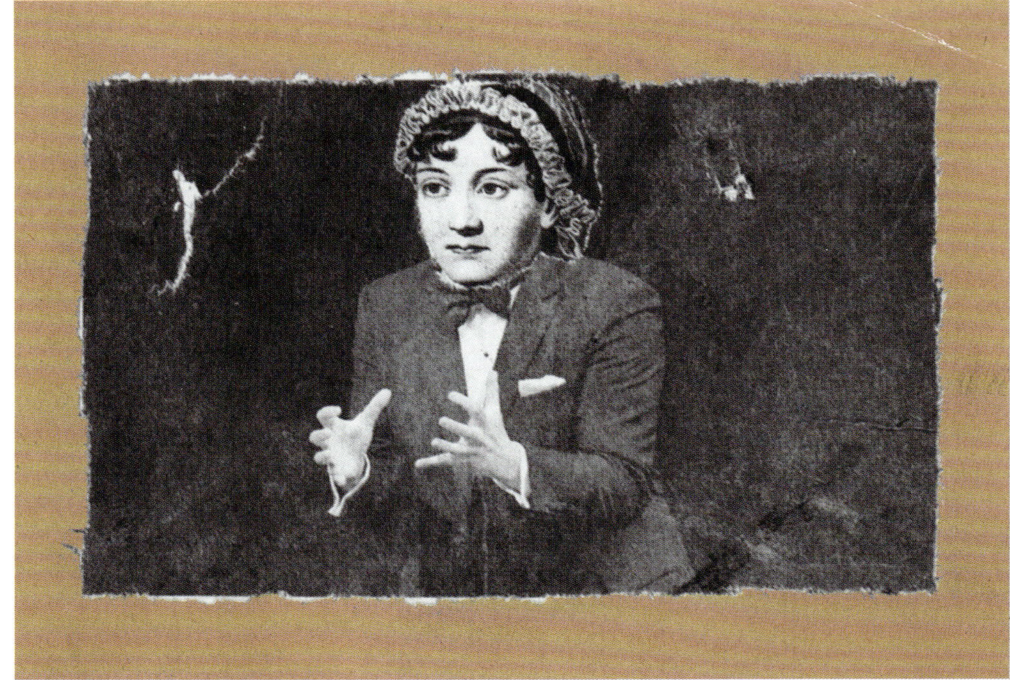

Page from Jim Jarmusch, *Some Collages* (Anthology Editions, 2021)

When did you begin making these collages?
I might have made some many years ago. But I didn't start focusing on this reductive style of appropriation until the last ten years, probably.

Why a book of them now?
I mostly kept the collages to myself. I gave them to friends or mailed some in letters. I can carry my whole little kit around in basically a briefcase. I started making them in hotel rooms, or in places where I was waiting for other things to happen. Then during the pandemic, when moving forward with film projects became difficult, I was encouraged to look into publishing the collages. There were more than five hundred. I'm still making them.

What is in your collage kit?
I use specific tools. Ballpoint pens that have run out of ink are my cutting tool. I like rough edges and only use newsprint. I don't like glossy magazine paper. The fragility of newsprint—I love it visually and as a texture. I can carry around my kit filled with backgrounds, envelopes with heads, rulers, tweezers, some glue. They are kind of therapeutic, because I like going into another world and not really thinking about what I'm doing.

For example, if I make one that seems too pointed in its intention, I get rid of it. I like those that are abstract or dreamlike.

Do you have a big archive of ephemera from which you source?
In my studio, I have a huge flat file with twelve drawers. I love this piece of metal furniture. It has several drawers full of newspapers. The other day, I was getting some Chinese newspapers in Chinatown. So, I have a lot of newspapers and a lot of paper for my backgrounds.

I'm a little obsessive about ephemera, not in a collector way, because I'm not organized, but as a gatherer. I have film posters—some of the big French metro ones—I have ticket stubs, backstage passes, odd business cards from people like Allen Ginsberg and Jack Smith, art-opening invitations, a piece of stationery from my favorite hotel, the El Minzah in Tangier. I have all of John Waters's Christmas cards from twenty years—but those aren't for my collages.

Is there a connection between collage making and filmmaking?
Certainly. Collage is a guide to how I create anything, but I wasn't really aware of that until recently. The procedure for my collage making, and the restriction and oblique strategies that I use, is also found in the writing and the editing of my films, as well as in my music. I always start with collecting elements from which I will make the script. And then when I'm shooting, I am photographing things from which I will create the film in the cutting room. Collages are just a reduction of my approach.

I do the same with music. I will start with recording a track and then begin adding or developing it, or giving it to other musicians. That is closely tied to my collages. As far as photographic stuff, I always take my own location photographs, or refer to existing photographs for reference or inspiration for the design of a film, especially for the production designer and for the cinematographer. It's a very important part of finding our visual way.

The theme for this issue is "Sleepwalking." How are you sleeping these days?
I sleep well but wake up with a kind of anxiety that is related to climate collapse and the nearly complete lack of action or response by those who have the real power to have an effect. This is really bothering me deep inside.